The Vintage
Book of the Devil

Francis Spufford was born in 1964. He is the recipient of a Somerset Maugham Award and was voted the *Sunday Times* Young Writer of the Year in 1997. He is the author of *I May Be Some Time: Ice and the English Imagination*, which won the 1997 Writers' Guild Prize for Non-Fiction. He has also edited *The Chatto Book of Cabbages and Kings: Lists in Literature* and co-edited *Cultural Babbage: Technology, Time and Invention*. He reviews regularly for the *Guardian* and lives in Cambridge with his wife and daughter.

THE VINTAGE
BOOK OF THE DEVIL

WITH AN INTRODUCTION BY
Himself

EDITED BY
Francis Spufford

VINTAGE

Published by Vintage 1997

2 4 6 8 10 9 7 5 3 1

Selection and introduction
copyright © Francis Spufford 1992

First published in Great Britain as
The Chatto Book of the Devil by
Chatto & Windus Ltd, 1992

Vintage
Random House, 20 Vauxhall Bridge Road,
London SW1V 2SA

Random House Australia (Pty) Limited
20 Alfred Street, Milsons Point, Sydney
New South Wales 2061, Australia

Random House New Zealand Limited
18 Poland Road, Glenfield,
Auckland 10, New Zealand

Random House South Africa (Pty) Limited
Endulini, 5A Jubilee Road, Parktown 2193,
South Africa

Random House UK Limited Reg. No. 954009

A CIP catalogue record for this book
is available from the British Library

ISBN 0 09 974461 9

Papers used by Random House UK Ltd are natural,
recyclable products made from wood grown in sustain-
able forests. The manufacturing processes conform to the
environmental regulations of the country of origin

Printed and bound in Great Britain by
Cox & Wyman, Reading, Berkshire

Contents

Pardon me for making a speech for the devil.

DANIEL DEFOE

Introduction

Are you sitting comfortably, humanity? Then I'll begin. I had hoped that, now the greater part of you no longer believe in me, I would have a modicum of leisure *pour cultiver mon jardin* (forgive me if I plagiarise: it is the natural style of a creature as compound as myself, made piecemeal of borrowed terrors) but the flood of speaking engagements shows no signs of slackening. Your interest in me has somehow failed to wane alongside your credulity, which might be flattering if so many of the invitations were not so ... restricting. A proud and damnèd spirit can hardly be expected to jump at the chance of making little girls vomit on camera, or to feel anything more than boredom surveying another cinema-full of drunken adolescents, each waiting to release their little spew of adrenalin when shown exactly what they are expecting. Here and there, it is true, evangelical Christians seem to call on me for a larger performance; but though in crude outline it may resemble my old and cosmic roles, they have so little grasp of history or theology that the finer points entirely pass them by. They have far more in common than they would like to admit with those repulsively spotty filmgoers, who have at least the frankness to admit that they want to be frightened.

'I must admit', wrote Sidney Smith, 'that I should like to roast a Quaker.' *I* must admit that I should like to roast a fundamentalist or two, and had I my previous resources, I should certainly contrive a night-sweat for the most importunate of them: one of those agreeable crises of faith with which the hotter kind of protestant used to torment themselves, tossing and turning, convinced their sins had destined them to spend time in my still hotter company. Ah, how their daytime rectitude turned over on itself when darkness fell! How seriously they pondered their errors and omissions, making of tiny blots a darkness quite substantial enough for me to take up residence! Let no-one say the devil has forgotten how to have fun. Great days, great days. Alas, these latterday zealots hardly have the stamina for really damaging self-accusation. Anything subtle I might say is drowned by amateur guitar music. My purpose as far as they are concerned is to simplify the world, not to complicate it (poor things, they find it bewildering enough already). They apply me like a patent medicine marked 'For External Use Only. Do Not Swallow' and send me off to hover significantly over the heads of talkative bishops, secular humanists, and the staff of the Natural History Museum: all innocent enough people in their way. No doubt – it is a phenomenon I have often observed – they prefer the predictable fright of seeing me roam about seeking whom I may devour to the rather more troubling truth that most of you are totally indifferent to their little dramas. No doubt; but does that excuse their constant efforts to 'cast me out' of new converts, with all the concomitant writhing that entails, *toute cette comédie*, or their insulting incuriosity about my movements over the last 2,000 years?

To hear them, you would think that I had never worn laurels for Milton, or represented the French Revolution for Victor Hugo, or been set down by that nice man George Herbert as 'our sinnes in perspective' – a sensible judgement, which, if you had all taken more notice, might have sent me into restful retirement some time ago. You would think that I . . . but all in good time, my dears. In short, you would think that nothing had changed since I made my lightning dash into the lake of Galilee, disguised as several tons of ambulant pork, at the behest of that miracle-working rabbi who had such a success with the epileptics. (And *he*, I might add, left no clear instructions about me. Sometimes I seemed to be Tiberius Caesar, sometimes your own malevolence. Sometimes, yes, the Prince of Darkness with this world in thrall. That's the price of talking in parables. Do you know what he meant for sure? I thought not. My memory tells me I spent much of the time waiting – for he did not mention me very often – like an overhead projector ordered from an educational supply company and left to grow dusty in a school cupboard, because the teacher does not often need it. You will forgive me if I do not mention *him* much, in return. It causes me some distress to think of him, though whether that is because something about him truly gives me reason to be frightened, or whether I am only faking it for my own amusement, and your greater confusion, is something you will have to decide for yourselves, as you have always had to. Do I give offence? Oh, I hope so.)

But I see the rest of you, those who never went to see *The Exorcist*, and have never 'showered in the blood of the lamb' (as Gore Vidal puts it) beginning to grow smug, which will not do at all, when I have worked so hard on your behalf, demonising your political enemies, lending my horns at your direction to Jews and Moslems and Protestants and Catholics and Freemasons and Liberals and Communists and Capitalists and Blacks and Whites and Nazis and Atheists and Mormons, and, in general, whomsoever you wished for your own squalid purposes to fail to recognise as human for long enough to stamp upon. Afterwards, I seem to remember, you inserted my name in the newspapers in order to stop thinking about what you had done, you used me as an alibi. 'Some evils', you said, 'go beyond our comprehension. Who could do such a thing as [insert the name of your most recent atrocity]? It is enough to make you believe in the devil.'

How convenient, how very convenient. Let me tell you, as an old hand in the massacre game, as one who well remembers Hugh of Lincoln – that charming if nonexistent child you claimed the Jews had turned into matzo balls, just before you relieved them of their homes, lives and property – let me say that you have been using me as a cover story for centuries, and *it is wearing thin*. Not that I care about your numerous victims, of course. Doubtless if the time had been right, and I had sprung to mind, they would have done it to you. As Goethe had me say to Faust, there is nothing worse than a devil who grows sentimental; and, along with your tendency to have me get you off the gory hook you have hung yourselves on, there is nothing I deplore more than your perverse pleasure in having me preach. I have been drafted into the strangest pulpits. No: my present complaint about you, you odious race of vermin, is that you *go on doing it*, even now; you persist to a remarkable degree in the mental habits you acquired in previous generations, though you no longer understand the roles you designed for me then. Tricked out in the miserable remnants of belief, you send me off to provide an explanation you then dismiss, for this, or that, or the other occurrence.

This is what I mean by your invitations being restrictive. Lately, it has been child abuse. Here my usual appetite for bad taste fails me. Perhaps there were real 'Satanic rituals', perhaps there were none, perhaps the adults only winked their way through their rites in order to build an atmosphere: it does not greatly matter, except to the children involved. What does matter is that the Satanic aspect of the thing, whether or not it was only imagined, made immediate sense to you, because you remain besotted by the idea of opposites. You like a thing to have an opposite. You used to think that God was *up* on high and I was deep *down* below; you gave God *light* and me *dark*; you made him *white* and me pitchy *black* (except in Ethiopia where, as Diderot enjoyed pointing out in the *Encyclopédie*, God was a normal healthy black and I was horribly blanched). That was very far from the whole story, but it seems to be the bit you remember. You treat me as a backwards God, as the master of everything upside-down and inside-out, despite being quite unable to decide whether you want the frontwards God himself any more. I am counter-nature, the defiler, the reverse of the page, the other side of the coin of normality. It is a denuded role, a scrap, a travesty, an incoherence: apparently you like it all the same. Opposites have magical power. So your idea of the normal, happy family has a verso to it, a dreadful possibility that you hold at arms' length, and when it turns out that in some council-house living-room innocence has been turned on its head, in I come 'naturally', either in the minds of the perpetrators themselves, or just in yours, looking on in horror. From what you remember of me, I am the perfect symbol for the wrong that has been done. The ritual trimmings that the abusers may have used are right in line with the phoney tradition of the Black Mass, which fascinates you with its suggestion that there is a whole timelessly evil anti-religion lurking somewhere nearby, although it was only improvised by some naughty French courtiers at the end of the seventeenth century. And 'improvised' is the right word. All that stuff about head-down crucifixes has had to be thrown together anew every time you wanted to indulge your taste for opposites. Quite what you think the 'opposite' of a sacrament would be, I do not know. But it made the same sort of sense that this supposed ritual in the present should substitute, for a consecrated communion wafer (which many of you no longer find very familiar), the bodies of children, which are probably your strongest token of innocence.

I respectfully submit that this will go on happening, and I will continue to be trotted out on this ludicrous and painful errand, so long as you continue to allow opposites to command your imaginations; so long as you do, the powerless and the pitiless and the confused among you will go on taking to themselves the thrilling power of exactly inverting your values. It is not good for you, and, more importantly, it is demeaning for me. One meets the most unpleasant people. Hey-ho. You may not realise that I was once the Accuser of Humanity before the Tribunal of Eternity. Spare a thought for a malign old concept, past his prime? On consideration, perhaps not. But to think that I am the opposite of God! I am about as much the opposite of God as eggs are bacon's opposite, or toast the opposite of marmalade ... Admittedly, you have some excuse for your sloppiness. The idea that I am the essence of evil is at the very root of me. The single serious question that I make you ask is, can evil be real? Can it be a thing in itself, or is it only the absence of good? I am the answer you have been coming up with for a very long time. I am the name for the appalling possibility that evil might have an existence as subtle and as powerful as good, unflawed by the madness of the psychopath, transcending the daylight explanations for how an ordinary German baker or locksmith could become a guardian of the barbed wire. I am the evil you suspect might flourish for itself alone, eager and unillusioned in the pursuit of cruelty.

'The recognition of other people as such, is love' wrote Simone Weil, my chickadees; and while most ordinary wickednesses can be ascribed to lack of recognition, you do wonder – don't you? – if there might be a force that recognises you as you are, with all the twists of your contorted little hearts, and still cares for you not one bit; a wise evil that can see you whole, and finds it fun to blight you anyway; a power that finds your virtues merely comic, and will eat you up.

Ah, I feel immortal longings in me as I speak these lines. The echo of an ancestral hunger stirs in me again. A race as plump as you deserves a predator. (You find me a little over the top, perhaps? I remind you of a hokey vampire movie? Of course I do. Where did you imagine that that toothy simulacrum received his urbane manners, his wordy pose of superiority, except from me?) I am afraid, though, that this lovely dream of supernatural power was one you could never make up your minds to give to me, however often you toyed with it. Your more impressive religious thinkers ruled it out altogether. It was your constant fear, but it never described the things you actually let me do. A modicum of success as a tempter was all I was allowed: you will note, please, that even then I could do nothing without your consent.

The fact the dream has lingered on so long, you may attribute to the well-worn grooves your speculations run in, not to the creeds most of you have abandoned. More precisely, in the present century, you have to thank the way your philosophy and psychoanalysis *abstract* the pros and cons of good and evil when they deal with them. Religious good and evil, lifted out of the stories and theologies that set them in exact relation to one another, took on a mythic weightlessness, and were manipulated thus so dextrously that you might be forgiven for concluding they are indeed opposing faces of a single metaphor. (Forgiven, but not by me. I leave forgiving to those who do it well. It is not my *métier*.) Freud and Jung admired my diabolic plumage, but forgot the dying bird. Both men, equally fascinated, were too excited by the new things that they found to say, to pay that much attention to my older functions. The first, acute about your wish to keep your good and evil split apart, decided that the 'evil' impulses in the human soul were that part of the first undifferentiated knot of desires that conscious controls banished into unconsciousness when infancy ended. Thereafter the bad acted as hidden counterpart to the good that could be acknowledged, and had its badness confirmed by being suppressed. The second gentleman, Herr Doktor Jung, called me 'the shadow' – that ancient metaphor – and thought I was that element of the psyche, not always a destructive part, that haunted and sought to invert conscious designs. Both, in their different ways, paid tribute to the imaginative integrity with which light and dark divide the universe between them. They were investigating, though, only the substructure of belief in me, and not my elaborate development from it.

Charcoal half the world if you like, and chalk up the other half as brightly as you can, and I am still not God's opposite, for that implies an equivalence between us that has never been conceded, except by theorists and commentators far separated from the experience of belief. It might have been reasonable to credit a duo of gods. I could – cheerfully – have taken charge of dearth and leukaemia, rainstorms and catastrophes, calves born with two heads and other entertaining genetic variations. It would have left the field free for God to be the deity of pleasant things alone. You could have praised him for the sunshine in your insipid ceremonies, happily curtailing his responsibilities as the price of keeping him stainless. But no: in Christianity, in Judaism and in Islam this sizeable promotion forever eluded me. I never had the powers given my cousin Ahriman, who in the Zoroastrian scheme slugs it out until the end of time with shining Ormuzd. Only in heresies and other strange off-shoots (soon withered) of the Big Three do I appear as a fully fledged god of air and darkness. (Oh, and I must mention my little Yezidis, *toujours fidèles* – a Mesopotamian sect much harassed by their neighbours. They worship me under the emblem of the Peacock, the first of all the beasts of the earth for pride, considering that the wise creator resigned the earth to me, and that I will remember my friends when I am reinstated in heaven. Thank-you, Yezidis: I am touched. Your hopes are misplaced, and your numbers do not inspire much confidence, but I dare say a sulphurous tear might trickle down my hollow cheek if I were given to emotional display.)

Having invented me, you proved reluctant to give me any scope. I am the dualistic fringe of monotheism. I represent a tempting possibility, never wholly indulged in a system which insisted on one god, one creator, one sovereign of heaven. You only half-detached me from the maker of all things, and instead of empire, I inherited an array of minor tasks that would not challenge the central tenets of your creeds. Was I given any adequate explanation for this spiritual shilly-shallying? Some justification for the make-work I was given after I emerged from the place where concepts are born, the cave of making where I had slumbered with my friends the Platonic cube and the perfect triangle since the dawn of time? None – none that satisfies the cold demands of reason, as the sceptics of the Enlightenment found out when they investigated. Slyboots Bayle (Pierre to you) wrote an enormous entry on the two-godded Manichaeans in his dictionary of philosophy, and half his labour went to hint that the Manichaeans' *logic* was impeccable. There is no doubt about it: the belief that good and evil thrash it out on equal terms is far more watertight than what the orthodox believed. It even answers better to your experience of living. Air crashes are explained without throwing up theological para-doxes. The Lisbon earthquake would not have bothered any eighteenth-century believer if they could have blamed it squarely on my doings.

All one can say is that the orthodox could not sign their names to this neat picture of the world without losing something they considered far more valuable, that is, the promise of religion. Reason ain't in it, only hope, my dears. With me given equal time, God could not be the universal Dad you like to have. He could not be the centre, the moveless mover, the 'infinitely gentle, infinitely suffering thing', with no limits to his love. He could not roost in every heart, or draw all that he has made back to himself, by your consent. If he were not in aircrashes, and earthquakes too, he could hardly be there very much to hold your hand when they happened. He has to take responsibility. He has to be the whole of things – the whole of health and of disease, the whole of pleasure and of boredom too. He can't be fighting his corner against a powerful and co-equal me if he's to be the right recipient of the Psalms (ah yes, but I have Baudelaire, nonetheless). He must have known you in your mother's womb, and fashioned all your inward parts, as the psalmist put it; or made you rear up from a blood-clot, as the Qur'an prefers to say. Of course if he is all-good and all-powerful, the paradoxes start at once. If he is the onlie begetter of what is, if he braided your DNA into its dandy double helix and pressed your genes for you, why do you have cancer, some of you? And hydrocephaly? What are gangrene, wasps and HIV doing in his world, the world that's his uniquely, without so much as a smidgeon of my handiwork?

Your answers are brave ones, if predictable. You used to go a bundle on the notion that the world had slumped from what God first intended, because you had been bad. Another line suggests each individual who gets visited by one of God's less friendly possibilities must somehow deserve it deep down, if one could spot the sin in question. Another still proposes that the dreadful things that happen *are* God's love, which operates by very different rules from yours. John Stuart Mill replied to that robustly; he said he wouldn't admire any quality in God that he would not admire in one of his friends. A whole clutch of answers put the Judaean rabbi I mentioned earlier at the core of the problem: *I* think to make God powerless as well as powerful, meek on top of magnificent, only restates the question. (But who listens to me? My vested interests are obvious.) Or, finally, you say that the definition of 'almighty' is that there's no evil out of which good cannot be brought.

One thing is clear. Your worship of one god begins and ends in mystery. You could have me and God engaged in immortal fisticuffs. Instead (excuse me while I lick my lips) you have the Problem of Pain without which your good god would have no value to you, but which still shakes his image perpetually in your minds, fills it with unresolved tension, so that cracks are constantly appearing in your convictions about him – crannies which I call hell and home. I made my first appearance in your tradition in about the second century BC, a time when repeated invasions and national humiliations provided an overplus of pain to the inhabitants of Palestine. There was too much of it, repeated too often, and lasting too long, for them to be able to accept it came from God, as previous tribulations had done. This time there appeared to be no deliverance from Pharaoh in prospect, nor any just proportion between the suffering and any sin they might have collectively committed. So they set up me with a measure of malevolent autonomy, and laid their trials at my door. This was my true genesis, by the way: they manufactured me from stray allusions in the scriptures, which never had spelled devil until then. Till then the serpent in Eden was only a snake, and the famous passage in Isaiah about the bright and morning star referred to the King of Babylon, not to me. I never flourished in my angel infancy, or fell downwards to darkness on extended wings, before they decided I did in retrospect. Before then the person who bears my name in the Book of Job had been a servant of the Lord, of sorts, status undetermined; perhaps an overzealous executioner in the department of divine retribution, not unlike the Angel of Death, whose singleminded pursuit of his duty required restraint by all the other qualities that figured in the universal godhead. Satan, the early name for me, meant 'obstacle' or 'hindrance' in Hebrew. The angel Jacob wrestled with was a 'satan' in that sense, for his own good, and even when I had grown to be a personage the rabbi still used the word in the old way, for a friend of his: 'Get thee behind me, satan'.

My usual genealogies are false. There's nothing immemorial about me, I'm afraid. Still, a portion of diabolic luck was to be mine. Although Judaism soon discovered I offered no solution to the perennial Problem – for if I caused pain it had to be admitted that God caused me to be: what goes around comes around – and rapidly demoted me again to metaphor, a feeble force of human wickedness, the new religion started by the rabbi took me up, ah yes, my friends, caressed and fondled me, gave me my horns, and installed me in all the temples that they hated. The Christians could have said the pagan gods were fictions. Some did; most chose otherwise. They fought (they said) against principalities and powers, not against mortal enemies. And so Apollo and Dionysus were taken to be my pseudonyms, and the worshippers of the Roman pantheon ceased to be merely deluded. As a legion of my followers they had to be wrestled out of darkness into light. There was no middle ground, just saved and damned.

I grew by leaps and bounds. Wherever faith was hindered, they supposed I was in operation, trying desert monks with visions and fighting hard for every solitary soul. And then the Fathers of the Early Church, the Augustines and Origens, Tertullians and Irenaeuses, tended to be educated types, much too educated to quit wholesale the science and astronomy they'd learned at school. They christianised it. Welcome, crystal spheres. Welcome, hordes of demons; for the 'daimons', who had been familiar spirits thronging in the lower air and helping the likes of Socrates out with ideas, all turned into me as well, or at least into my followers, kicked out of heaven with me and reduced to spreading vapours on the earth.

The Fathers scripted, too, a history of the world that featured me at several points. I'd fallen; then I'd taken spiritual possession of the globe when your first parents bit the apple; then I'd had all that I'd usurped taken back from me by the rabbi, leaving only those deserving to be damned; now, restless but restrained by God's enormous fingers, I roamed about, nibbling here and there at the resolve of Christians to see if I could break my chains, but otherwise bound to my work. I collaborated reluctantly with the Lord to run the universe. He had the power, the majesty, the benevolence, the choirs of stars praising his name in Latin. I had the furnaces in the basement. I ran a hygienic soul-disposal service, privatised in theory (all questions about it were referred from God to me) yet sustained by policy decisions taken elsewhere. Most of the shares in my operation were held by God through nominees. Or let me show you from another angle. At the great trials of souls, I stood up for the prosecution, wigged in visible darkness and gowned in brimstone. You cowered in the dock. My briefs were researched to the point of absurdity – I could question you on everything from bad behaviour in the nursery at the age of two to your evasions on your deathbed when the priest came by. But in the end the focus was the judge. I did his bidding willy-nilly. When you were guilty, you would say 'He frowned'. When you were adjudged innocent, usually because of mitigating factors he supplied, you said he smiled. His wrath and mercy ran the court.

Now, I do not regret those days, my palmy salad days. I was, after all, at my biggest and my best. I was allowed some bold forensic argument, some juicy victories (though you, you cheapskates, tended to believe that when I roasted even my most legitimate of prizes, with bastings of venality, the juice escaped me, and I tasted only ashes). I'd had my entrée into your religion, I was a spiritual fact of life. It would take centuries to winkle me out again. But, as you notice, the same old pattern had asserted itself. You had installed me as an intermediate figure between you and God, to dramatise whatever wasn't safe and Christian, and to take the pressure off the Lord by sopping up some fraction of the evil in the world. And yet, since I was no earthly use in shouldering his burden of responsibility, you couldn't find that much for me to do. My presence in your pictures of the world ran deep, not wide. Take an example. My repertoire was always small, even including the parts I took that had no base at all in scripture. I'd fallen; I'd tempted Eve; I'd run the errands in the trying of Job; I'd dallied with the rabbi in the wilderness. So much for holy writ. You'd added in the following: I tempted souls; I helped to judge them.

Later, there were witches and *l'affaire de Faust* in all their numerous varieties, for you grew keen on pacts with me, signed in heart's blood, when change and Reformation multiplied the people you were fearful of, and wanted to see safely demonised. These roles, I grant you, spanned the whole of time, from God's first *fiat* to the final trump. (Indeed, they seem quite generous when you consider my sole office in the whole Qur'an consists of undermining Eden.) But look how few they are, compared to all the massed events that filled both Testaments. And see how slender in their scope they are, compared to teachings that encompassed your whole lives, with moral truths for every moral situation. There was no need to mention me when you discussed the way, the truth, the life, and so on. And although my disjoined appearances could be ingeniously linked together to give me a consistent rationale – a note in the *dramatis personae* of the great drama of time – when I was off the stage, you never missed me. When sacred stories were turned into actual plays, by butchers in Chester and shepherd-boys in Oberammagau, I'd pop up at the start, I'd fart to get a laugh when the rabbi harrowed hell, and otherwise I'd stay out of the serious stuff. The actor who played me could whip off his devil mask behind the scenes and double up as Noah, Mary, Judas, Pontius P et al., before he needed to get back to me again. *Sic transit gloria diaboli*.

Of course, my unimportance was entirely orthodox. What was true of mumming butchers was true as well of Doctors of the Church. Each fat conspectus of the Christian doctrine mentioned me – for they were sure without a doubt that I *existed* – but, once more, the fact of me was carefully dammed up in little sections rather near the front, in case I should spill out and trickle into doctrines where I had no business. Aquinas (whom I read before the joke about the mineral water made sense in any European tongue) was typical. He devoted tens of pages to me among the thousands of his *Summa Theologica*. And why was this? Because, beneath the skies made by the all-good, all-commanding God, evil could have no real being. Evil was just a lack, like holes in cheese. Evil could make nothing happen, they agreed, and salved the reputation of their precious God with arguments that shrunk me to a fly, lost in a flood of ointment. Even a book devoted to my fall, *De Casu Diaboli* by St Anselm, took as its real subject how God's handiwork could ever fall away from grace. Anselm took me as the type of all that fall, not as a mover or a shaker of events. I remember he concluded that no blame attached to God if an archangel plummeted, any more than you, assuming you are sensible, would blame the waves that smashed you on a rock if you went boating in a boat without a rudder. What laid me low was trying to bear the waves of light that rolled from God without the rudder (that is, faithful humbleness) I had been freely offered. The technical expression for this view is *privatio boni*: it means that evil is an emptiness where good was supposed to be. I'm sure you see this pretty form of words cannot exactly solve the great Conundrum that accompanies faith in a God who's good *and* powerful. The Doctors of religion knew this very well, but stitched me up too tight to help in the debate; it went on, vigorously, elsewhere. So, theologically redundant, I was passed into the hands of folklore.

My names multiplied: Old Nick, Old Scratch, Old Almost Anything in almost every language. In Germany, the reek of asafoetida made them bring me in. It's *teufelsdröckh*, or 'devil's dung', in the vernacular. I built bridges, ditches, dykes and causeways; none too bright, I usually accepted mangy dogs who crossed my bridges first as my reward for building them. I found some seasonal employment marking haddock with my pitchy fingers, two swart black prints each, just abaft the shoulders. Besides all which, no veteran trouper turns down work in pantos. When I wasn't being frightening in my serious roles, I was available for pratfalls, slapstick, sudden drops down open manhole covers. I'm sure that those who saw me in these parts cried out 'Behind you!' as I crept up on the hero. St Dunstan took me by the nose with redhot tongs and threw me over Sussex into Kent, where I stained the waters red in Tunbridge Wells by bathing my abused protuberance. It isn't really surprising. What you people fear, you like to laugh at. To me, however, the biggest joke was that you kept employing me at all, long after you had found I was no aid at all in your most pressing spiritual task – forgiving God for making such a mess of things. Such, I suppose, is the inevitable fate of gods of darkness sneaked into monotheism. Whenever you thought hard, I soon stopped making sense. The subtler thinkers took me as a proof that *evil* is absurd, a matter of pretensions, pride and wind.

It grew more popular, in the end, to remove me from religion altogether, than to cope with the absurdities of my story. You had to have it one way, or the other, as atheists grew fond of pointing out. If I was real and earnest, God was faulty to the same extent. If God was total, mighty, all-embracing, how could I have come to be at all? A rebel against omnipotence? It makes me laugh, at any rate. Perversely, nonetheless (but what single one of your thoughts about me fails to be perverse?) this aspect of impossibility contained my future: it was the seed from which your recent devils sprang. Once faith in my existence began to fade, I started on a new life as a character, and not by any means one that was always unsympathetic either. You granted me a measure of pathos.

Without quite stopping fearing me, you grew to feel for me as well. Poor devil! Put upon, evicted, spurned, et cetera: my story could bear this construction, and did increasingly, as you grew more and more inclined to treat it *as* a story.

The process was gradual. It began while I was still a serious proposition. One theologian of the Middle Ages had surmised that I had fallen, not through being bad, but just by wanting to be good by my own unaided efforts, unpropped-up by God. Isn't that human? Don't you recognise yourselves a little? Of course, your sympathy is an accident (and I don't want it). Yet it came of forgetting for a moment that, at the dawn of time, when there were only God and angels, I'd've had nothing to be good *about* on my ownsome. Obeying God made up the sum of goodness. You were taken in because, if God is thought of seriously, there is no story at all. Despite which, the story went on being told, most famously in *Paradise Lost*. Milton was not on my side, it should be said: Blake was probably wrong to place him in 'the devil's party, without knowing it', and C. S. Lewis was probably right to say that he intended me to be an obvious monster. He generated sympathy for me by being an efficient narrator. To tell the story of the fall, he had to anthropomorphise it, and my impossible rebellion took on life, the more so as I was the only person in the story whose motives and limitations are recognisable. The infiniteness of his God could be asserted, but not demonstrated; so while the wrongness of my defiance was never in doubt, there still remained a space for it to happen in. Milton's beliefs, passionately held, proved less communicative than the events of the narration. Instead of squeezing the story flat, which his beliefs would certainly have done if he had brought a theological seriousness to bear, they furnished it only with a storylike geography – in which, as ever, up = light = good, down = darkness = evil. As always, too, the traditional determinism was in force. Desiring anything independently of God made the thing that I desired come automatically to be wicked. My resistance to his monopoly of good made me the devil; there was nothing else for me to become. In Milton's lines, though, you saw me in the throes of my inevitable change. Existing in my little pocket of impossible possibility, you – Milton's readers – watched me imagine that I had a field of choice like yours, in which one could decide what to do next: and thus my planned catastrophe looked like a rather sympathetic failure. I wanted to be other than a quiet archangel. It was my ill fortune that the sole spare role, in an imagined cosmos where every role besides commingled in the godhead, was as Adversary. By falling then, I gained the sort of self you have, although my progress toward selfhood amounted, *ipso facto*, to a descent into sin and lies. People who took me for the hero were not misreading Milton's cosmology; they were responding to the odd, mixed architecture of the poem, noticing something the scheme of it implied. It remains perfectly true that he intended no kind thoughts to accrue to me. The self I gained, in his eyes, was a spiritual error, a product of my separateness from God and good and light and harmony.

Now, you expect me to go on from here like this – to say that after Milton's century humanity lost patience very fast with absolute monarchs of all kinds, including the celestial sort; and that, newly endowed with steam-trains, freedom of the press, and gas, you took me up as quite a liberal thing to be – the first and protean tyrant-slayer, Garibaldi with bat-wings, my wickedness a jovial form of charm. And this, I suppose is true. There certainly were editions of myself along these lines, running concurrently with older goaty ones – and folklore dribbled on, my lack of brain in it ever more pronounced, till I could be outwitted by the tuppenny protagonists of penny dreadfuls – but the sympathy I'm thinking of, post-Milton, was a darker thing, and comes as close to tickling my fancy as any product can of your predictable imaginations.

Some writers took me as an image for human selfhood badly founded, doomed (as Milton had it) for the flames, because its anger could make nothing happen, and it refused to let the anger go, from spite. Why, this is hell, nor am I out of it, *you* said for once. For some reason, you find this species of the self heroic – at least since the Romantics set the fashion for a youthful exit. It just cries *no*, however evidently pointless the refusal. Byron re-wrote part of Milton's plot; his *Cain* gives me fine lines, if you like braggadocio, and he made me sound quite like a liberal aristocrat with sideburns, circa 1820. He had me say (of God) 'I will not call his evil good!' But damnation was still my destination. I ended badly, as before. My cry was pointless – which was, indeed, the point. All the clubfooted lord asserted was the honour, the magnificence, of standing for an instant separate from the sole sources of health, whether these were defined as God or liberty or human love, not giving a damn (quite literally) for the consequences, before the certain drop from the untenable height of refusal to the depths of what is actually the case. In short, cutting off your nose to spite your face. Instead of theological impossibility, those who used me in this recherché role substituted the impossibility of bucking time, and nature. They made me an opponent, not to God as such, but to the compromise of being at all. The 'nay' I said for them (I was the universe's first naysayer ever) was drowned at once, exactly as expected, by the music of the spheres.

For once, I liked the work. It stretched me to incarnate a despair begotten on impossibility. It almost compensated for the dreary stuff you've forced on me in these, my years of decline, when history had led me to expect you'd let me slip into oblivion, instead of acting out the dregs of your demands. My dears, it almost made me like you. *Not quite*, I'll add hastily. However much you may now think you like me, however flexible I seem to you to be as a mode of expression, you should know the feeling isn't mutual. Wherever I touch closely on your minds, misery is never far away. Somewhere, this very moment, a madman makes me his excuse for acting. Somewhere, not far from you, a child is being beaten. You would be best advised, ladies and gentlemen, to stay away from me. I am not safe; I am, even penned in this dimming circle of stage fire, no friend of yours.

LUCIFER

Editor's Note

Traditionally, books on this subject open with a warning, cunningly worded, to the effect that the author knows far more than he (usually *he*) is telling. He has evidence of potent Satanic activity taking place *right now*, in a suburb near you, the reader – and he advises you in the strongest terms not to indulge your curiosity any more than you have already done by shelling out for the book in your hand. When these warnings are not straightforward teasers, little ploys to get the reader's attention, they signal a strange self-conceit on the author's part. He, he would have you know, is a seasoned traveller in the infernal regions of human behaviour; or, perhaps, a warrior himself in the spiritual battle against the dark, with secrets to protect. The fact that this kind of thing is hysterical gobbledegook does not prevent it sending a tremor of uncertainty through anybody who encounters it, for the world is demonstrably strange and dangerous, though it hardly needs malign Powers with a capital P to make it so. I want, then, to make the opposite declaration. I know absolutely nothing about Satanism or the occult. I made no attempt to research either subject, and I would be grateful if nobody wrote to me now offering enlightenment or Awful Truths. Despite the somewhat free range of my sulphurous colleague's remarks in the foregoing, this is a *literary* anthology. It only tries to put together some of the ways the devil has been written about, from the sensational to the dead-serious, with a very wide ground in between occupied by all those writers who simply rummaged the devil out of the box of imagining, and gave him lines to say. I have not organised it chronologically, or the multiple strands of the devil's career would be hopelessly entangled; I hope they are not too entangled now. The different sections gather up his different aspects. For the most part the pieces run in rough chronological order *inside* the sections, except when they had to go next to each other to make a point.

I have drawn shamelessly on Jeffrey Burton Russell's four books *Satan*, *Lucifer*, *The Devil* and *Mephistopheles*, a sane and endlessly learned history of what the devil has meant in Christianity, Islam and Judaism. I am grateful, too, to all the people who have talked to me about the devil, especially those who surprised me into taking him seriously as a source of anguish and misery, however little I agree with their views. The introduction requires no apologies, I think, but I would be sorry if they mistook the display of spleen in it for the whole of my opinions. I must also thank: the British Library and Cambridge University Library for supplying me with all the books I consulted; *The Times* for letting me reuse phrases and sentences from an article there in spring 1991; Jonathan Burnham for saving me from a diet of perpetual lentils by organising a timely cheque; Allegra Huston for putting me onto Hawthorne, Melville, and more; Jenny Uglow (lecteur, semblable, soeur) for commenting liberally on the draft of the introduction; and most of all Ian Hunt, no less than an archangel ruin'd, who has seen the floor disappear under a tide of paper more times than he can count, and the kitchen fill up with rancid crockery more times than he can bear. This book is for him: he has the eyebrows for it.

As I was walking among the fires of hell, delighted with the enjoyments of Genius, which to Angels look like torments and insanity, I collected some of their Proverbs; thinking that as the sayings used in a nation mark its character, so the Proverbs of Hell show the nature of Infernal wisdom better than any description of buildings or garments.

WILLIAM BLAKE

One

PLEASED TO MEET YOU

Luther, taking up a caterpillar, said: 'Tis an emblem
of the devil in its crawling walk, and bears his
colours in its changing hue.'
Luther's Table-Talk

Aujourd'hui, grâce au progrès, Satan est un être très
supportable qui n'exhale aucune odeur sulfureuse, qui
cause agréablement et se présente convenablement
en société.
Auguste Gruson, 1845

Jesus Meets a Good Old Hermit

At length an aged Syre farre off he sawe
Come slowely footing, euerie step he guest
One of his feete he from the graue did drawe,
Three legges he had, the woodden was the best,
And all the waie he went, he euer blest
   With benedicities, and prayers store,
   But the bad ground was blessed ne'r the more,
And all his head with snowe of Age was waxen hore.

A good old Hermit he might seeme to be,
That for deuotion had the world forsaken,
And now was trauailing some Saint to see,
Since to his beads he had himselfe betaken,
Whear all his former sinnes he might awaken,
   And them might wash away with dropping brine,
   And almes, and fasts, and churches discipline,
And dead, might rest his bones vnder the holy shrine.

But when he neerer came, he lowted lowe
With prone obeysance, and with curt'sie kinde,
That at his feete his head he seemd to throwe;
What needs him now another Saint to finde?
Affections are the sailes, and faith the wind,
   That to this Saint a thousand soules conueigh
   Each hour: O happy Pilgrims thither strey!
What caren they for beasts, or for the wearie way?

Soone the old Palmer his deuotions sung,
Like pleasing anthems, moduled in time,
For well that aged Syre could tip his tongue
With golden foyle of eloquence, and lime,
And licke his rugged speech with phrases prime.
   Ay me, quoth he, how many yeares haue beene,
   Since these old eyes the Sunne of heau'n haue seene!
Certes the Sonne of heau'n they now behold I weene.

Ah, mote my humble cell so blessed be
As heau'n to welcome in his lowely roofe,

And be the Temple for thy deitie!
Loe how my cottage worships thee aloofe,
That vnder ground hath hid his head, in proofe
　It doth adore thee with the seeling lowe,
　Here honie, milke, and chesnuts wild doe growe,
The boughs a bed of leaues vpon thee shall bestowe.

But oh, he said, and therewith sigh't full deepe,
The heau'ns, alas, too enuious are growne,
Because our fields thy presence from them keepe;
For stones doe growe, where corne was lately sowne:
(So stooping downe, he gather'd vp a stone)
　But thou with corne canst make this stone to eare.
　What needen we the angrie heau'ns to feare?
Let them enuie vs still, so we enjoy thee here.

Thus on they wandred, but those holy weeds
A monstrous Serpent, and no man did couer.
So vnder greenest hearbs the Adder feeds:
And round about that stinking corps did houer
The dismall Prince of gloomie night, and ouer
　His euer-damned head the Shadowes err'd
　Of thousand peccant ghosts, vnseene, vnheard,
And all the Tyrant feares, and all the Tyrant fear'd.

He was the Sonne of blackest Acheron,
Whear many frozen soules doe chattring lie,
And rul'd the burning waues of Phlegethon,
Whear many more in flaming sulphur frie,
At once compel'd to liue and forc't to die,
　Whear nothing can be heard for the loud crie
　Of oh, and ah, and out alas that I
Or once againe might liue, or once at length might die.

Giles Fletcher the younger, 'Christs Victorie on Earth', 1610

St Thomas Meets a Very Large Snake in India

And the apostle inquired of him, saying: Tell me of what seed and of
what race thou art.
　And he said unto him: I am a reptile of the reptile nature and noxious

son of the noxious *father*: of him that hurt and smote the four brethren which stood upright: I am son to him that sitteth on a throne over all the earth, that receiveth back his own from them that borrow: I am son to him that girdeth about the sphere: and I am kin to him that is outside the ocean, whose tail is set in his own mouth: I am he that entered through the barrier into paradise and spake with Eve the things which my father bade me speak unto her: I am he that kindled and inflamed Cain to kill his own brother, and on mine account did thorns and thistles grow up in the earth: I am he that cast down the angels from above and bound them in lusts after women, that children born of earth might come of them and I might work my will in them: I am he that hardened Pharaoh's heart that he should slay the children of Israel and enslave them with the yoke of cruelty: I am he that caused the multitude to err in the wilderness when they made the calf: I am he that inflamed Herod and enkindled Caiaphas unto false accusation of a lie before Pilate; for this was fitting to me: I am he that stirred up Judas and bribed him to deliver up the Christ: I am he that inhabiteth and holdeth the deep of hell; but the Son of God hath wronged me, against my will, and taken them that were his own from me: I am kin to him that is to come from the east, unto whom also power is given to do what he will upon the earth.

The Acts of Thomas in *The Apocryphal New Testament*,
ed. M. R. James, 1924

St Benedict Meets a Doctor

Vpon a certaine tyme as he was goinge to the oratory of *S. Iohne*, which is in the topp of the mountaine: the olde enemy of mankinde vpon a mule like a phisition, met him caryinge in his hand an horne and a morter. And when he demanded whether he was goinge. To your monkes (quoth he) to giue them a drench.

The Dialogues of S. Gregorie the Great, trans. into English by 'PW', 1608

The Youngest Daughter Meets a Wooing Knight

There was a knicht riding frae the east,
    Sing the Cather banks, the bonnie brume
Wha had been wooing at monie a place.
    And ye may beguile a young thing sune

[22]

He came unto a widow's door,
And speird whare her three dochters were.

The auldest ane's to a washing gane,
The second's to a baking gane.

The youngest ane's to a wedding gane,
And it will be nicht or she be hame.

He sat him doun upon a stane,
Till thir three lasses came tripping hame.

The auldest ane's to the bed making,
And the second ane's to the sheet spreading.

The youngest ane was bauld and bricht,
And she was to lye with this unco knicht.

'Gin ye will answer me questions ten,
The morn ye sall be made my ain.

'O what is heigher nor the tree?
And what is deeper nor the sea?

'Or what is heavier nor the lead?
And what is better nor the breid?

'O what is whiter nor the milk?
Or what is safter nor the silk?

'Or what is sharper nor a thorn?
Or what is louder nor a horn?

'Or what is greener nor the grass?
Or what is waur nor a woman was?'

'O heaven is higher nor the tree,
And hell is deeper nor the sea.

'O sin is heavier nor the lead,
The blessing's better nor the bread.

'The snaw is whiter nor the milk,
And the down is safter nor the silk.

'Hunger is sharper nor a thorn,
And shame is louder nor a horn.

'The pies are greener nor the grass,
And Clootie's waur nor a woman was.'

As sune as she the fiend did name,
He flew awa in a blazing flame.

The English and Scottish Popular Ballads, ed. F. J. Child, 1882

Some Swedes Meet an Antecessor in a High-Crowned Hat

We of the Province *of* Elfdale, *do confess, that we used to go to a* Gravel-Pit, *which lays hard by a* Cross-way, *and there we put on a* Vest *over our heads, and then danced round, and after this ran to the* Cross-way, *and called the* Devil *thrice, first with a* still Voice: *the second time* somewhat louder: *and the third time* very loud, *with these words,* Antecessor come and carry us to Blockula. *Whereupon immediately he used to appear, but in different* Habits: *but for the most part, we saw him in a* Gray-Coat, *and red and blew Stockings. He had a* red beard, *a* high crowned Hat, *with* Linnen *of diverse colours, wrapt about it, and long* Garters *upon his* Stockings. *It is very remarkable, that the* Devil *never appears to the* Witches, *with a* Sword *at his side.*

George Sinclair, *Satans Invisible World Discovered*, 1685

A Scots Calvinist Meets a Pious Youth

As I thus wended my way, I beheld a young man of a mysterious appearance coming towards me. I tried to shun him, being bent on my own contemplations; but he cast himself in my way, so that I could not well avoid him; and more than that, I felt a sort of invisible power that drew me towards him, something like the force of enchantment, which I could not resist. As we approached each other, our eyes met, and I can never describe the strange sensations that thrilled through my whole frame at that impressive moment; a moment to me fraught with the most tremendous consequences; the beginning of a series of adventures which has puzzled myself, and will puzzle the world when I am no more in it. That time will now soon arrive, sooner than any one can devise who knows not the tumult of my thoughts, and the labour of my spirit; and when it hath come and passed over, – when my flesh and my bones are decayed, and my soul has passed to its everlasting home, then shall the sons of men ponder on the events of my life; wonder and tremble, and tremble and wonder how such things should be.

That stranger youth and I approached each other in silence, and slowly, with our eyes fixed on each other's eyes. We approached till not more than a yard intervened between us, and then stood still and gazed, measuring each other from head to foot. What was my astonishment, on perceiving that he was the same being as myself! The clothes were the same to the smallest item. The form was the same; the apparent age; the colour of the hair; the eyes; and, as far as recollection could serve me from viewing my own features in a glass, the features too were the very same. I conceived at first, that I saw a vision, and that my guardian angel had appeared to me at this important era of my life; but this singular being read my thoughts in my looks, anticipating the very words that I was going to utter.

'You think I am your brother,' said he; 'or that I am your second self. I am indeed your brother, not according to the flesh, but in my belief of the same truths, and my assurance in the same mode of redemption, than which, I hold nothing so great or so glorious on earth.'

'Then you are an associate well adapted to my present state,' said I. 'For this time is a time of great rejoicing in spirit to me. I am on my way to return thanks to the Most High for my redemption from the bonds of sin and misery. If you will join with me heart and hand in youthful thanksgiving, then shall we two go and worship together; but if not, go your way, and I shall go mine.'

'Ah, you little know with how much pleasure I will accompany you, and join with you in your elevated devotions,' said he fervently. 'Your state is a state to be envied indeed; but I have been advised of it, and am come to be a humble disciple of yours; to be initiated into the true way of salvation by conversing with you, and perhaps by being assisted by your prayers.'

My spiritual pride being greatly elevated by this address, I began to assume the preceptor, and questioned this extraordinary youth with regard to his religious principles, telling him plainly, if he was one who expected acceptance with God at all, on account of good works, that I would hold no communion with him. He renounced these at once, with the greatest vehemence, and declared his acquiescence in my faith. I asked if he believed in the eternal and irrevocable decrees of God, regarding the salvation and condemnation of all mankind? He answered that he did so: aye, what would signify all things else that he believed, if he did not believe in that? We then went on to commune about all our points of belief; and in every thing that I suggested, he acquiesced, and, as I thought that day, often carried them to extremes, so that I had a secret dread he was advancing blasphemies. Yet he had such a way with him, and paid such a deference to all my opinions, that I was quite captivated, and, at the same time, I stood in a sort of awe of him, which I could not account for, and several times was seized with an involuntary inclination to escape from his presence, by making a sudden retreat. But he seemed constantly to anticipate my thoughts, and was sure to divert my purpose by some turn in the conversation that particularly interested me. He took care to dwell much on the theme of the impossibility of those ever falling away, who were once accepted and received into covenant with God, for he seemed to know, that in that confidence, and that trust, my whole hopes were centred.

We moved about from one place to another, until the day was wholly spent. My mind had all the while been kept in a state of agitation resembling the motion of a whirlpool, and when we came to separate, I then discovered that the purpose for which I had sought the fields had been neglected, and that I had been diverted from the worship of God, by attending to the quibbles and dogmas of this singular and unaccountable being, who seemed to have more knowledge and information than all the persons I had ever known put together.

We parted with expressions of mutual regret, and when I left him I felt a deliverance, but at the same time a certain consciousness that I was not thus to get free of him, but that he was like to be an acquaintance that was to stick to me for good or for evil. I was astonished at his acuteness and knowledge about every thing; but as for his likeness to me, that was quite unaccountable. He was the same person in every respect, but yet he was not always so; for I observed several times, when we were speaking of certain divines and their tenets, that his face assumed something of the appearance of theirs; and it struck me, that by setting his features to the mould of other people's, he entered at once into their conceptions and feelings. I had been greatly flattered, and greatly interested by his conversation; whether I had been the better for it or the worse, I could not tell.

The next day was with me a day of holy exultation. It was begun by my reverend father laying his hands upon my head and blessing me, and then dedicating me to the Lord in the most awful and impressive manner. It was in no common way that he exercised this profound rite, for it was done with all the zeal and enthusiasm of a devotee to the true cause, and a champion on the side he had espoused. He used these remarkable words, which I have still treasured up in my heart: – 'I give him unto Thee only, to Thee wholly, and to Thee for ever. I dedicate him unto Thee, soul, body, and spirit. Not as the wicked of this world, or the hirelings of a church profanely called by Thy name, do I dedicate this Thy servant to Thee: Not in words and form, learned by rote, and dictated by the limbs of Antichrist, but, Lord, I give him into Thy hand, as a captain putteth a sword into the hand of his sovereign, wherewith to lay waste his enemies. May he be a two-edged weapon in Thy hand, and a spear coming out of Thy mouth, to destroy, and overcome, and pass over; and may the enemies of Thy church fall down before him, and be as dung to fat the land!'

From that moment, I conceived it decreed, not that I should be a minister of the gospel, but a champion of it, to cut off the enemies of the Lord from the face of the earth; and I rejoiced in the commission, finding it more congenial to my nature to be cutting sinners off with the sword, than to be haranguing them from the pulpit, striving to produce an effect, which God, by his act of absolute predestination, had for ever rendered impracticable. The more I pondered on these things, the more I saw of the folly and inconsistency of ministers, in spending their lives, striving and remonstrating with sinners, in order to induce them to do that which they had it not in their power to do. Seeing that God had from all eternity decided the fate of every individual that was to be born of woman, how vain it was in man to endeavour to save those whom their Maker had, by an unchangeable decree, doomed to destruction. I could not disbelieve the doctrine which the best of men had taught me, and toward which he made the whole of the Scriptures to bear, and yet it made the economy of the Christian world appear to me as an absolute contradiction. How much more wise would it be, thought I, to begin and cut sinners off with the sword! for till that is effected, the saints can never inherit the earth in peace. Should I be honoured as an instrument to begin this great work of purification, I should rejoice in it. But then, where had I the means, or under what direction was I to begin? There was one thing clear, I was now the Lord's, and it behoved me to bestir myself in his service. O that I had an host at my command, then would I be as a devouring fire among the workers of iniquity!

Full of these great ideas, I hurried through the city, and sought again the private path through the field and wood of Finnieston, in which my reverend preceptor had the privilege of walking for study, and to which he had a key that was always at my command. Near one of the stiles, I perceived a young man sitting in a devout posture, reading on a Bible. He rose, lifted his hat, and made an obeisance to me, which I returned and walked on. I had not well crossed the stile, till it struck me I knew the face of the youth, and that he was some intimate acquaintance, to whom I ought to have spoken. I walked on, and returned, and walked on again, trying to recollect who he was; but for my life I could not. There was, however, a fascination in his look and manner, that drew me back toward him in spite of myself, and I resolved to go to him, if it were merely to speak and see who he was.

I came up to him and addressed him, but he was so intent on his book, that, though I spoke, he lifted not his eyes. I looked on the book also, and still it seemed a Bible, having columns, chapters, and verses; but it was in a language of which I was wholly ignorant, and all intersected with red lines, and verses. A sensation resembling a stroke of electricity came over me, on first casting my eyes on that mysterious book, and I stood motionless. He looked up, smiled, closed his book, and put it in his bosom. 'You seem strangely affected, dear sir, by looking on my book,' said he mildly.

'In the name of God, what book is that?' said I: 'Is it a Bible?'

'It is *my* Bible, sir,' said he; 'but I will cease reading it, for I am glad to see you. Pray, is not this a day of holy festivity with you?'

I stared in his face, but made no answer, for my senses were bewildered.

'Do you not know me?' said he. 'You appear to be somehow at a loss. Had not you and I some sweet communion and fellowship yesterday?'

'I beg your pardon, sir,' said I. 'But surely if you are the young gentleman with whom I spent the hours yesterday, you have the cameleon art of changing your appearance; I never could have recognized you.'

'My countenance changes with my studies and sensations,' said he. 'It is a natural peculiarity in me, over which I have not full control. If I contemplate a man's features seriously, mine own gradually assume the very same appearance and character. And what is more, by contemplating a face minutely, I not only attain the same likeness, but, with the likeness, I attain the very same ideas as well as the same mode of arranging them, so that, you see, by looking at a person attentively, I by degrees assume his likeness, and by assuming his likeness I attain to the possession of his most secret thoughts. This, I say, is a peculiarity in my nature, a gift of the God that made me; but whether or not given me for a blessing, he knows himself, and so do I. At all events, I have this privilege, – I can never be mistaken of a character in whom I am interested.'

'It is a rare qualification,' replied I, 'and I would give worlds to possess it. Then, it appears, that it is needless to dissemble with you, since you can at any time extract our most secret thoughts from our bosoms. You already know my natural character?'

'Yes,' said he, 'and it is that which attaches me to you. By assuming your likeness yesterday, I became acquainted with your character, and was no less astonished at the profundity and range of your thoughts, than at the heroic magnanimity with which these were combined. And now, in addition to these, you are dedicated to the great work of the Lord; for which reasons I have resolved to attach myself as closely to you as possible, and to render you all the service of which my poor abilities are capable.'

I inquired the next day what his name was; as I said I was often at a loss for it, when talking with him. He replied, that there was no occasion for any one friend ever naming another, when their society was held in private, as ours was; for his part he had never once named me since we first met, and never intended to do so, unless by my own request. 'But if you cannot converse without naming me, you may call me Gil for the present,' added he; 'and if I think proper to take another name at any future period, it shall be with your approbation.'

'Gil!' said I; 'Have you no name but Gil? Or which of your names is it? Your Christian or surname?'

'O, you must have a surname too, must you!' replied he. 'Very well, you may call me Gil-Martin. It is not my *Christian* name; but it *is* a name which may serve your turn.'

'This is very strange!' said I. 'Are you ashamed of your parents, that you refuse to give your real name?'

'I have no parents save one, whom I do not acknowledge,' said he proudly; 'therefore, pray drop that subject, for it is a disagreeable one. I am a being of a very peculiar temper, for though I have servants and subjects more than I can number, yet, to gratify a certain whim, I have left them, and retired to this city, and for all the society it contains, you see I have attached myself only to you. This is a secret, and I tell it you only in friendship, therefore pray let it remain one, and say not another word about the matter.'

I assented, and said no more concerning it; for it instantly struck me that this was no other than the Czar Peter of Russia, having heard that he had been travelling through Europe in disguise, and I cannot say that I had not thenceforward great and mighty hopes of high preferment, as a defender and avenger of the oppressed Christian Church, under the influence of this great potentate. He had hinted as much already, as that it was more honourable, and of more avail to put down the wicked with the sword, than try to reform them, and I thought myself quite justified in supposing that he intended me for some great employment, that he had thus selected me for his companion out of all the rest in Scotland, and even pretended to learn the great truths of religion from my mouth.

From that time I felt disposed to yield to such a great prince's suggestions without hesitation.

James Hogg, *Private Memoirs and Confessions of a Justified Sinner*, 1824

Father Olavida Meets a Wedding Guest

'The company were dispersed through various alleys of the garden; the bridegroom and bride wandered through one where the delicious perfume of the orange tree mingled itself with that of the myrtles in blow. On their return to the hall, both of them asked, Had the company heard the exquisite sounds that floated through the garden just before they quitted it? No one had heard them. They expressed their surprise. The Englishman had never quitted the hall; it was said he smiled with a most particular and extraordinary expression as the remark was made. His silence had been noticed before, but it was ascribed to his ignorance of the Spanish language, an ignorance that Spaniards are not anxious either to expose or remove by speaking to a stranger. The subject of the music was not again reverted to till the guests were seated at supper, when Donna Ines and her young husband, exchanging a smile of delighted surprise, exclaimed they heard the same delicious sounds floating round them. The guests listened, but no one else could hear it; – every one felt there was something extraordinary in this. Hush! was uttered by every voice almost at the same moment. A dead silence followed, – you would think, from their intent looks, that they listened with their very eyes. This deep silence, contrasted with the splendour of the feast, and the light effused from torches held by the domestics, produced a singular effect, – it seemed for some moments like an assembly of the dead. The silence was interrupted, though the cause of wonder had not ceased, by the entrance of Father Olavida, the Confessor of Donna Isabella, who had been called away previous to the feast, to administer extreme unction to a dying man in the neighbourhood. He was a priest of uncommon sanctity, beloved in the family, and respected in the neighbourhood, where he had displayed uncommon taste and talents for exorcism; – in fact, this was the good Father's *forte*, and he piqued himself on it accordingly. The devil never fell into worse hands than Father Olavida's, for when he was so contumacious as to resist Latin, and even the first verses of the Gospel of St John in Greek, which the good Father never had recourse to but in cases of extreme stubbornness and difficulty, – then he always applied to the Inquisition; and if the devils were ever so obstinate before, they were always seen to fly out of the possessed, just as, in the midst of their cries, (no doubt of blasphemy), they were tied to the stake. Some held out even till the flames surrounded them; but even the most stubborn must have been dislodged when the operation was over, for the devil himself could no longer tenant a crisp and glutinous lump of cinders. Thus Father Olavida's fame spread far and wide, and the Cardoza family had made uncommon interest to procure him for a Confessor, and happily succeeded. The ceremony he had just been performing, had cast a shade over the good Father's countenance, but it dispersed as he mingled among the guests, and was introduced to them. Room was soon made for him, and he happened accidentally to be seated opposite the Englishman. As the wine was presented to him, Father Olavida, (who, as I observed, was a man of singular sanctity), prepared to utter a short internal prayer. He hesitated, – trembled, – desisted; and, putting down the wine, wiped the drops from his forehead with the sleeve of his habit. Donna Isabella gave a sign to a domestic, and other wine of a higher quality was offered to him. His lips moved, as if in the effort to pronounce a benediction on it and the company, but the effort again failed; and the change in his countenance was so extraordinary, that it was perceived by all the guests. He felt the sensation that his extraordinary appearance excited, and attempted to remove it by again endeavouring to lift the cup to his lips. So strong was the anxiety with which the company watched him, that the only sound heard in that spacious and crowded hall, was the rustling of his habit, as he attempted to lift the cup to his lips once more – in vain. The guests sat in astonished silence. Father Olavida alone remained standing; but at that moment the Englishman rose, and appeared determined to fix Olavida's regards by a gaze like that of fascination. Olavida rocked, reeled, grasped the arm of a page, and at last, closing his eyes for a moment, as if to escape the horrible fascination of that unearthly glare, (the Englishman's eyes were observed by all the guests, from the moment of his entrance, to effuse a most fearful and preternatural lustre), exclaimed, 'Who is among us? – Who? – I cannot utter a blessing while he is here. I cannot feel one. Where he treads, the earth is parched! – Where he breathes, the air is fire! – Where he feeds, the food is poison! – Where he turns, his glance is lightning! – *Who is among us? – Who?*' repeated the priest in the agony of adjuration, while his cowl fallen back, his few thin hairs around the scalp instinct and alive with terrible emotion, his outspread arms protruded from the sleeves of his habit, and extended towards the awful stranger, suggested the idea of an inspired being in the dreadful rapture of prophetic denunciation. He stood – still stood, and the Englishman stood calmly opposite to him. There was an agitated irregularity in the attitudes of those around them, which contrasted strongly the fixed and stern postures of those two, who remained gazing silently at each other. 'Who knows him?' exclaimed Olavida, starting apparently from a trance; 'who knows him? who brought him here?'

The guests severally disclaimed all knowledge of the Englishman, and each asked the other in whispers, 'who *had* brought him there?' Father Olavida then pointed his arm to each of the company, and asked each individually, 'Do you know him?' 'No! no! no!' was uttered with vehement emphasis by every individual. 'But I know him,' said Olavida, 'by these cold drops!' and he wiped them off; – 'by these convulsed joints!' and he attempted to sign the cross, but could not. He raised his voice, and evidently speaking with increased difficulty, – 'By this bread and wine, which the faithful receive as the body and blood of Christ, but which *his* presence converts into matter as viperous as the suicide foam of the dying Judas, – by all these – I know him, and command him to be gone! – He is – he is –' and he bent forwards as he spoke, and gazed on the Englishman with an expression which the mixture of rage, hatred, and fear, rendered terrible. All the guests rose at these words, – the whole company now presented two singular groupes, that of the amazed guests all collected together, and repeating, 'Who, what is he?' and that of the Englishman, who stood unmoved, and Olavida, who dropped dead in the attitude of pointing to him.

Charles Robert Maturin, *Melmoth the Wanderer*, 1820

Tom Walker Meets a Woodcutter

It was late in the dusk of evening when Tom Walker reached the old fort, and he paused there for a while to rest himself. Any one but he would have felt unwilling to linger in this lonely melancholy place, for the common people had a bad opinion of it from the stories handed down from the time of the Indian wars; when it was asserted that the savages held incantations here and made sacrifices to the evil spirit. Tom Walker, however, was not a man to be troubled with any fears of the kind.

He reposed himself for some time on the trunk of a fallen hemlock, listening to the boding cry of the tree toad, and delving with his walking staff into a mound of black mould at his feet. As he turned up the soil unconsciously, his staff struck against something hard. He raked it out of the vegetable mould, and lo! a cloven skull with an Indian tomahawk buried deep in it, lay before him. The rust on the weapon showed the time that had elapsed since this death blow had been given. It was a dreary memento of the fierce struggle that had taken place in this last foothold of the Indian warriors.

'Humph!' said Tom Walker, as he gave the skull a kick to shake the dirt from it.

'Let that skull alone!' said a gruff voice.

Tom lifted up his eyes and beheld a great black man, seated directly opposite him on the stump of a tree. He was exceedingly surprised, having neither seen nor heard any one approach, and he was still more perplexed on observing, as well as the gathering gloom would permit, that the stranger was neither negro nor Indian. It is true, he was dressed in a rude, half Indian garb, and had a red belt or sash swathed round his body, but his face was neither black nor copper colour, but swarthy and dingy and begrimed with soot, as if he had been accustomed to toil among fires and forges. He had a shock of coarse black hair, that stood out from his head in all directions; and bore an axe on his shoulder.

He scowled for a moment at Tom with a pair of great red eyes.

'What are you doing on my grounds?' said the black man, with a hoarse growling voice.

'Your grounds?' said Tom, with a sneer; 'no more your grounds than mine: they belong to Deacon Peabody.'

'Deacon Peabody be d—d,' said the stranger, 'as I flatter myself he will be, if he does not look more to his own sins and less to those of his neighbours. Look yonder, and see how Deacon Peabody is faring.'

Tom looked in the direction that the stranger pointed, and beheld one of the great trees, fair and flourishing without, but rotten at the core, and saw that it had been nearly hewn through, so that the first high wind was likely to blow it down. On the bark of the tree was scored the name of Deacon Peabody, an eminent man, who had waxed wealthy by driving shrewd bargains with the Indians. He now looked round and found most of the tall trees marked with the name of some great man of the colony, and all more or less scored by the axe. The one on which he had been seated, and which had evidently just been hewn down, bore the name of Crowninshield; and he recollected a mighty rich man of that name, who made a vulgar display of wealth, which it was whispered he had acquired by buccaneering.

'He's just ready for burning!' said the black man, with a growl of triumph. 'You see I am likely to have a good stock of firewood for winter.'

'But what right have you,' said Tom, 'to cut down Deacon Peabody's timber?'

'The right of prior claim,' said the other. 'This woodland belonged to me long before one of your white faced race put foot upon the soil.'

'And pray, who are you, if I may be so bold?' said Tom.

'Oh, I go by various names. I am the Wild Huntsman in some countries; the Black Miner in others. In this neighbourhood I am known by the name of the Black Woodsman. I am he to whom the red men consecrated this spot, and in honour of whom they now and then roasted a white man by way of sweet smelling sacrifice. Since the red men have been exterminated by you white savages, I amuse myself by presiding at the persecutions of quakers and anabaptists; I am the great patron and prompter of slave dealers, and the grand master of the Salem witches.'

'The upshot of all which is, that, if I mistake not,' said Tom, sturdily, 'you are he commonly called Old Scratch.'

'The same at your service!' replied the black man, with a half civil nod.

Such was the opening of this interview, according to the old story, though it has almost too familiar an air to be credited. One would think that to meet with such a singular personage in this wild lonely place, would have shaken any man's nerves: but Tom was a hard minded fellow, not easily daunted, and he had lived so long with a termagant wife, that he did not even fear the devil.

'The Devil and Tom Walker' in *Tales of a Traveller*
by Washington Irving, 1824

The Philosophical Chef Bon-Bon Meets a Clergyman Wearing Sunglasses

He had been thus occupied for some minutes, when 'I am in no hurry, Monsieur Bon-Bon,' suddenly whispered a whining voice in the apartment.

'The devil!' ejaculated our hero, starting to his feet, overturning the table at his side, and staring around him in astonishment.

'Very true,' calmly replied the voice.

'Very true! – what is very true? – how came you here?' vociferated the metaphysician, as his eye fell upon something which lay stretched at full length upon the bed.

'I was saying,' said the intruder, without attending to the interrogatories, 'I was saying that I am not at all pushed for time – that the business upon which I took the liberty of calling is of no pressing importance – in short that I can very well wait until you have finished your Exposition.'

'My Exposition! – there now! – how do *you* know? – how came *you* to understand that I was writing an exposition? – good God!'

'Hush!' replied the figure, in a shrill under tone: and, arising quickly from the bed, he made a single step towards our hero, while an iron lamp that depended overhead swung convulsively back from his approach.

The philosopher's amazement did not prevent a narrow scrutiny of the

[34]

stranger's dress and appearance. The outlines of a figure, exceedingly lean, but much above the common height, were rendered minutely distinct by means of a faded suit of black cloth which fitted tight to the skin, but was otherwise cut very much in the style of a century ago. These garments had evidently been intended for a much shorter person than their present owner. His ankles and wrists were left naked for several inches. In his shoes, however, a pair of very brilliant buckles gave the lie to the extreme poverty implied by the other portions of his dress. His head was bare, and entirely bald, with the exception of the hinder part, from which depended a *queue* of considerable length. A pair of green spectacles, with side glasses, protected his eyes from the influence of the light, and at the same time prevented our hero from ascertaining either their color or their conformation. About the entire person there was no evidence of a shirt; but a white cravat, of filthy appearance, was tied with extreme precision around the throat, and the ends, hanging down formally side by side, gave (although I dare say unintentionally) the idea of an ecclesiastic. Indeed, many other points both in his appearance and demeanour might have very well sustained a conception of that nature. Over his left ear, he carried, after the fashion of a modern clerk, an instrument resembling the *stylus* of the ancients. In a breast-pocket of his coat appeared conspicuously a small black volume fastened with clasps of steel. This book, whether accidentally or not, was so turned outwardly from the person as to discover the words '*Rituel Catholique*' in white letters upon the back. His entire physiognomy was interestingly saturnine – even cadaverously pale. The forehead was lofty, and deeply furrowed with the ridges of contemplation. The corners of the mouth were drawn down into an expression of the most submissive humility. There was also a clasping of the hands, as he stepped towards our hero – a deep sigh – and altogether a look of such utter sanctity as could not have failed to be unequivocally prepossessing. Every shadow of anger faded from the countenance of the metaphysician, as, having completed a satisfactory survey of his visitor's person, he shook him cordially by the hand, and conducted him to a seat.

There would however be a radical error in attributing this instantaneous transition of feeling in the philosopher, to any one of those causes which might naturally be supposed to have an influence. Indeed Pierre Bon-Bon, from what I have been able to understand of his disposition, was of all men the least likely to be imposed upon by any speciousness of exterior deportment. It was impossible that so accurate an observer of men and things should have failed to discover, upon the moment, the real character of the personage who had thus intruded upon his hospitality. To say no more, the conformation of his visitor's feet was sufficiently remarkable –

he maintained lightly upon his head an inordinately tall hat – there was a tremulous swelling about the hinder part of his breeches – and the vibration of his coat tail was a palpable fact. Judge then with what feelings of satisfaction our hero found himself thrown thus at once into the society of a person for whom he had at all times entertained the most unqualified respect. He was, however, too much of the diplomatist to let escape him any intimation of his suspicions in regard to the true state of affairs. It was not his cue to appear at all conscious of the high honor he thus unexpectedly enjoyed, but by leading his guest into conversation, to elicit some important ethical ideas, which might, in obtaining a place in his contemplated publication, enlighten the human race, and at the same time immortalize himself – ideas which, I should have added, his visitor's great age, and well known proficiency in the science of morals, might very well have enabled him to afford.

Actuated by these enlightened views, our hero bade the gentleman sit down, while he himself took occasion to throw some faggots upon the fire, and place upon the now re-established table some bottles of *Mousseux*. Having quickly completed these operations, he drew his chair *vis-à-vis* to his companion's and waited until the latter should open the conversation. But plans even the most skillfully matured are often thwarted in the outset of their application, and the *restaurateur* found himself *nonplussed* by the very first words of his visitor's speech.

'I see you know me, Bon-Bon,' said he: 'ha! ha! ha! – he! he! he! – hi! hi! hi! – ho! ho! ho! – hu! hu! hu!' – and the devil, dropping at once the sanctity of his demeanour, opened to its fullest extent a mouth from ear to ear, so as to display a set of jagged and fan-like teeth, and throwing back his head, laughed long, loudly, wickedly, and uproariously, while the black dog, crouching down upon his haunches, joined lustily in the chorus, and the tabby cat, flying off at a tangent, stood up on end and shrieked in the farthest corner of the apartment.

Not so the philosopher; he was too much a man of the world either to laugh like the dog, or by shrieks to betray the indecorous trepidation of the cat. It must be confessed, he felt a little astonishment to see the white letters which formed the words '*Rituel Catholique*' on the book in his guest's pocket, momently changing both their color and their import, and in a few seconds, in place of the original title, the words *Regître des Condamnés* blaze forth in characters of red. This startling circumstance, when Bon-Bon replied to his visitor's remark, imparted to his manner an air of embarrassment which probably might not otherwise have been observed.

'Why, sir,' said the philosopher, 'why, sir, to speak sincerely – I believe you are – upon my word – the d—dest – that is to say I think – I imagine – I *have* some faint – some *very* faint idea – of the remarkable honor –'

'Oh! – ah! – yes! – very well!' interrupted his Majesty; 'say no more – I see how it is.' And hereupon, taking off his green spectacles, he wiped the glasses carefully with the sleeve of his coat, and deposited them in his pocket.

If Bon-Bon had been astonished at the incident of the book, his amazement was now much increased by the spectacle which here presented itself to view. In raising his eyes, with a strong feeling of curiosity to ascertain the color of his guest's, he found them by no means black, as he had anticipated – nor gray, as might have been imagined – nor yet hazel nor blue – nor indeed yellow nor red – nor purple – nor white – nor green – nor any other color in the heavens above, or in the earth beneath, or in the waters under the earth. In short Pierre Bon-Bon not only saw plainly that his Majesty had no eyes whatsoever, but could discover no indications of their having existed at any previous period; for the space where eyes should naturally have been, was, I am constrained to say, simply a dead level of flesh.

Edgar Allan Poe, 'Bon-Bon', 1835

Heine Meets a Contemporary

I call'd the devil, and he came,
And a thrill of astonishment through me ran.
He is not ugly, he is not lame,
But a perfectly charming agreeable man.
A man whose prime is not yet gone by,
With worldly knowledge and breeding high.
As a good diplomatist he's of weight,
And argues soundly on church and state.
He is somewhat pale, but then, you know,
He has work'd at Sanskrit and Hegel so.
His favourite poet is still Fouqué;
But the critical science he means to lay
Aside, and his studious zeal to smother
In favour of Hecate, his dear grandmother.
My legal learning with praise he noted,
He, too, to the law had his time devoted.
He said that my friendship in his eyes
Was a boon he could not too deeply prize;
Then asks if we have not met before,
At the house of the Spanish Ambassador?

Whereon, when I look at him, it appears
He is a man that I've known for years.

Heinrich Heine, *Book of Songs/Buch der Lieder*, 1827;
trans. John E. Wallis, 1856

A Coonskinned Cynic Meets a Cosmopolitan

'Hands off!' cried the bachelor, involuntarily covering dejection with moroseness.

'Hands off? that sort of label won't do in our Fair. Whoever in our Fair has fine feelings loves to feel the nap of fine cloth, especially when a fine fellow wears it.'

'And who of my fine-fellow species may you be? From the Brazils, ain't you? Toucan fowl. Fine feathers on foul meat.'

This ungentle mention of the toucan was not improbably suggested by the parti-hued, and rather plumagy aspect of the stranger, no bigot it would seem, but a liberalist, in dress, and whose wardrobe, almost anywhere than on the liberal Mississippi, used to all sorts of fantastic informalities, might, even to observers less critical than the bachelor, have looked, if anything, a little out of the common; but not more so perhaps, than, considering the bear and raccoon costume, the bachelor's own appearance. In short, the stranger sported a vesture barred with various hues, that of the cochineal predominating, in style participating of a Highland plaid, Emir's robe, and French blouse; from its plaited sort of front peeped glimpses of a flowered regatta-shirt, while, for the rest, white trowsers of ample duck flowed over maroon-colored slippers, and a jaunty smoking-cap of regal purple crowned him off at top; king of traveled good-fellows, evidently. Grotesque as all was, nothing looked stiff or unused; all showed signs of easy service, the least wonted thing setting like a wonted glove. That genial hand, which had just been laid on the ungenial shoulder, was now carelessly thrust down before him, sailor-fashion, into a sort of Indian belt, confining the redundant vesture; the other held, by its long bright cherry-stem, a Nuremburgh pipe in blast, its great porcelain bowl painted in miniature with linked crests and arms of interlinked nations – a florid show. As by subtle saturations of its mellowing essence the tobacco had ripened the bowl, so it looked as if something similar of the interior spirit came rosily out on the cheek. But rosy pipe-bowl, or rosy countenance, all was lost on that unrosy man, the bachelor, who, waiting a moment till the commotion, caused by the boat's renewed progress, had a little abated, thus continued:

'Hark ye,' jeeringly eying the cap and belt, 'did you ever see Signor Marzetti in the African pantomime?'

'No; – good performer?'

'Excellent; plays the intelligent ape till he seems it. With such naturalness can a being endowed with an immortal spirit enter into that of a monkey. But where's your tail? In the pantomime, Marzetti, no hypocrite in his mockery, prides himself on that.'

The stranger, now at rest, sideways and genially, on one hip, his right leg cavalierly crossed before the other, the toe of his vertical slipper pointed easily down on the deck, whiffed out a long, leisurely sort of indifferent and charitable puff, betokening him more or less of the mature man of the world, a character which, like its opposite, the sincere Christian's, is not always swift to take offense; and then, drawing near, still smoking, again laid his hand, this time with mild impressiveness, on the ursine shoulder, and not unamiably said: 'That in your address there is a sufficiency of the *fortiter in re* few unbiased observers will question; but that this is duly attempered with the *suaviter in modo* may admit, I think, of an honest doubt. My dear fellow,' beaming his eyes full upon him, 'what injury have I done you, that you should receive my greeting with a curtailed civility?'

'Off hands;' once more shaking the friendly member from him. 'Who in the name of the great chimpanzee, in whose likeness, you, Marzetti, and the other chatterers are made, who in thunder are you?'

'A cosmopolitan, a catholic man; who, being such, ties himself to no narrow tailor or teacher, but federates, in heart as in costume, something of the various gallantries of men under various suns. Oh, one roams not over the gallant globe in vain. Bred by it, is a fraternal and fusing feeling. No man is a stranger. You accost anybody. Warm and confiding, you wait not for measured advances. And though, indeed, mine, in this instance, have met with no very hilarious encouragement, yet the principle of a true citizen of the world is still to return good for ill. – My dear fellow, tell me how I can serve you.'

'By dispatching yourself, Mr Popinjay-of-the-world, into the heart of the Lunar Mountains. You are another of them. Out of my sight!'

'Is the sight of humanity so very disagreeable to you then? Ah, I may be foolish, but for my part, in all its aspects, I love it. Served up à la Pole, or à la Moor, à la Ladrone, or à la Yankee, that good dish, man, still delights me; or rather is man a wine I never weary of comparing and sipping; wherefore am I a pledged cosmopolitan, a sort of London-Dock-Vault connoisseur, going about from Teheran to Natchitoches, a taster of races; in all his vintages, smacking my lips over this racy creature, man, continually. But as there are teetotal palates which have a distaste even for Amontillado, so I suppose there may be teetotal souls which relish not even the very best brands of humanity. Excuse me, but it just occurs to me that you, my dear fellow, possibly lead a solitary life.' . . .

'But put a case. Can you deny – I dare you to deny – that the man leading a solitary life is peculiarly exposed to the sorriest misconceptions touching strangers?'

'Yes, I *do* deny it,' again, in his impulsiveness, snapping at the controversial bait, 'and I will confute you there in a trice. Look, you –'

'Now, now, now, my dear fellow,' thrusting out both vertical palms for double shields, 'you crowd me too hard. You don't give one a chance. Say what you will, to shun a social proposition like mine, to shun society in any way, evinces a churlish nature – cold, loveless; as, to embrace it, shows one warm and friendly, in fact, sunshiny.'

Here the other, all agog again, in his perverse way, launched forth into the unkindest references to deaf old worldlings keeping in the deafening world; and gouty gluttons limping to their gouty gormandizings; and corseted coquets clasping their corseted cavaliers in the waltz, all for disinterested society's sake; and thousands, bankrupt through lavishness, ruining themselves out of pure love of the sweet company of man – no envies, rivalries, or other unhandsome motive to it.

'Ah, now,' deprecating with his pipe, 'irony is so unjust; never could abide irony; something Satanic about irony. God defend me from Irony, and Satire, his bosom friend.'

Herman Melville, *The Confidence-Man*, 1857

Onuphrius Meets a Dandy

Tout à coup son œil s'alluma, il avait vu quelque chose d'extraordinaire: un jeune homme qui venait d'entrer; il pouvait avoir vingt-cinq ans, un frac noir, le pantalon pareil, un gilet de velours rouge taillé en pourpoint, des gants blancs, un binocle d'or, des cheveux en brosse, une barbe rousse à la Saint-Mégrin, il n'y avait là rien d'étrange, plusieurs merveilleux avaient le même costume; ses traits étaient parfaitement réguliers, son profit fin et correct eût fait envie à plus d'une petite-maîtresse, mais il y avait tant d'ironie dans cette bouche pâle et mince, dont les coins fuyaient perpétuellement sous l'ombre de leurs moustaches fauves, tant de méchanceté dans cette prunelle qui flamboyait à travers la glace du lorgnon comme l'œil d'un vampire, qu'il était impossible de ne pas le distinguer entre mille.

Il se déganta. Lord Byron ou Bonaparte se fussent honorés de sa petite main aux doigts ronds et effilés, si frêle, si blanche, si transparente, qu'on eût craint de la briser en la serrant; il portait un gros anneau à l'index, le chaton était le fatal rubis; il brillait d'un éclat si vif, qu'il vous forçait à baisser les yeux.

Un frisson courut dans les cheveux d'Onuphrius.

La lumière des candélabres devint blafarde et verte; les yeux des femmes et les diamants s'éteignirent; le rubis radieux étincelait seul au milieu du salon obscurci comme un soleil dans la brume.

L'enivrement de la fête, la folie du bal étaient au plus haut degré; personne, Onuphrius excepté, ne fit attention à cette circonstance; ce singulier personnage se glissait comme une ombre entre les groupes, disant un mot à celui-ci, donnant une poignée de main à celui-là, saluant les femmes avec un air de respect dérisoire et de galanterie exagérée qui faisait rougir les unes et mordre les lèvres aux autres; on eût dit que son regard de lynx et de loup-cervier plongeait au profond de leur cœur; un satanique dédain perçait dans ses moindres mouvements, un imperceptible clignement d'œil, un pli du front, l'ondulation des sourcils, la proéminence que conservait toujours sa lèvre inférieure, même dans son détestable demi-sourire, tout trahissait en lui, malgré la politesse de ses manières et l'humilité de ses discours, des pensées d'orgueil qu'il aurait voulu réprimer.

Théophile Gautier, 'Onuphrius' in *Contes Fantastiques*, 1832

An Evening Party Hears a Naturalistic Comment on the Comtesse de Stasseville

'Now, looking at her' – the narrator turned to Doctor Beylasset, who stood leaning one elbow on a Buhl cabinet, and whose fine bald brow reflected back the light of a candelabra the servants had lighted a moment before above his head – 'looking at the Comtesse de Stasseville from the sound commonplace *physiological* point of view – as you doctors do, an example our moralists might follow with advantage – you could not help seeing quite plainly that, in this impressionable nature, everything was bound to strike home, to penetrate inwards, like the line of faded rose traced by the strongly retracted lips, like the stiff, unquivering nostrils, that narrowed under excitement instead of dilating, like the eyes, so deeply sunk within their orbits that they seemed sometimes to be retreating backwards into the brain altogether. In spite of her apparent delicacy of constitution and a physical weakness whose effects could be traced through her whole being like the gradual spreading of a crack in a substance splitting from excess of dryness, she bore the most unmistakable signs of a strong will, the Volta battery within us which is the centre of our nerves. Everything about her testified to this more strikingly than in any other living being I have ever seen. This flux and reflux of slumbering will-power, of *potential* energy (forgive the pedantry of the expression), was manifested even in her hands, aristocratic and princely in their whiteness, the opalescent smoothness of the nails, and their general elegance, but which, in their extreme leanness, the complication of swollen veins that marked them with a thousand corded blue lines, and above all, the nervous, furtive way they had of grasping things, resembled those harpy claws which classic poetry, with its exuberance of fantastic imagery, attributes to certain fabulous monsters with women's faces and bosoms. When, after darting out one of her sayings, one of her shafts of sarcasm, as keen and glittering as the poisoned arrows of the savages, she passed her viperish tongue over her sibilant lips, you felt instinctively that in a supreme emergency, some fatal moment of destiny, the woman, at once so frail and so strong, would be quite capable of adopting the Negro's resource of resolutely swallowing that lambent tongue. To look at her was to be convinced she was, among womankind, an example of those organisms to be found in every domain of nature which, by predilection or instinct, look to the bottom rather than to the surface of things; one of those beings predestined for occult associations, plunging into the depths of life as bold swimmers dive deep, and swim beneath the surface, or as miners breathe the air of subterranean vaults. Such creatures love mystery for its own sake, and out of the very profundity of their nature, create it around them, loving and pursuing it even to the extent of downright deception – for, after all, what is deception but a doubling of mystery, a further darkening of the curtains of secrecy, a weaving about them of wilful darkness? It may well be such natures love deception for deception's sake, as others love art for art's sake, or as the Poles love battle.' Here the Doctor gravely nodded his head in sign of agreement. 'You think so! well! so do I. I am convinced there are souls whose happiness consists in imposture. These find a hateful, but intoxicating, bliss in the very notion of falsehood and deceit, in the thought that *they alone know their true selves*, and they are playing off a Comedy of Errors upon society, reimbursing themselves for the expense of representation with all the fine contempt they feel for their poor dupes.'

'But what you're saying now is simply atrocious!' suddenly exclaimed the Baronne de Mascranny, interrupting, in the tone of one whose belief in her fellow-creatures is scandalized.

Every woman in his audience (and very possibly some amateurs of secret pleasures were amongst the number) had experienced a certain thrill at the speaker's last words. I knew it by the Comtesse de Damnaglio's naked back, which at the minute was in such close proximity to my eyes. The particular sort of nervous thrill I mean is familiar to everybody by experience. It is sometimes poetically called *the Angel of Death going by*. Was it this time perhaps the Spirit of Truth going by? . . .

'Why, yes!' returned the narrator, 'atrocious enough, no doubt! Only, is it true? People who *wear their hearts on their sleeve*, as people say, can form no notion of the furtive joys of systematic hypocrisy, the solitary gratifications of such as live and breathe without difficulty under the confinement of a mask. But, if you come to think of it, it is easy to understand how the satisfactions they enjoy have actually all the deep intensity of hell's fiery delights. For what *is* hell but a heaven reversed, below instead of above? The two words *devilish* and *divine*, when applied to extremes of enjoyment, express one and the same idea, *viz.*, sensations that overpass the bounds of nature and reach the supernatural. Was Madame de Stasseville one of these strange souls? I would rather not say either yes or no! All I propose to do is to give her story to the best of my ability. No one really knows the rights of it, and my only object is to throw what light I may on the mysterious tale by a naturalistic study of her personality, such as Cuvier bestowed on the subjects of his science. This and nothing more.'

Jules Amadée Barbey d'Aurevilly, 'Beneath the Cards of a Game of Whist', 1850; in *Les Diaboliques*, trans. Ernest Boyd, 1926

Lucy Snowe Sees 'Vashti' Act in Brussels

The theatre was full – crammed to its roof: royal and noble were there: palace and hotel had emptied their inmates into those tiers so thronged and so hushed. Deeply did I feel myself privileged in having a place before that stage; I longed to see a being of whose powers I had heard reports which made me conceive peculiar anticipations. I wondered if she would justify her renown: with strange curiosity, with feelings severe and austere, yet of riveted interest, I waited. She was a study of such nature as had not encountered my eyes yet: a great and new planet she was: but in what shape? I waited her rising.

She rose at nine that December night; above the horizon I saw her come. She could shine yet with pale grandeur and steady might; but that star verged already on its judgement day. Seen near – it was a chaos – hollow, half consumed: an orb perished or perishing – half lava, half glow.

I had heard this woman termed 'plain,' and I expected bony harshness and grimness – something large, angular, sallow. What I saw was the shadow of a royal Vashti: a queen, fair as the day once, turned pale now like twilight, and wasted like wax in a flame.

For a while – a long while – I thought it was only a woman, though an unique woman, who moved in might and grace before this multitude. By-and-by I recognised my mistake. Behold! I found upon her something neither of woman nor of man: in each of her eyes sat a devil. These evil forces bore her through the tragedy, kept up her feeble strength – for she was but a frail creature; and as the action rose and the stir deepened, how wildly they shook her with their passions of the pit! They wrote HELL on her straight, haughty brow. They tuned her voice to the note of torment. They writhed her regal face to a demoniac mask. Hate, and Murder, and Madness incarnate she stood.

It was a marvellous sight: a mighty revelation.

It was a spectacle low, horrible, immoral.

Swordsmen thrust through, and dying in their blood on the arena sand; bulls goring horses disembowelled, made a meeker vision for the public – a milder condiment for a people's palate – than Vashti torn by seven devils: devils which cried sore and rent the tenement they haunted, but still refused to be exorcised.

Suffering had struck that stage empress; and she stood before her audience neither yielding to, nor enduring, nor in finite measure, resenting it: she stood locked in struggle, rigid in resistance. She stood, not dressed, but draped in pale antique folds, long and regular like sculpture. A background and entourage and flooring of deepest crimson threw her out, white like alabaster – like silver: rather, be it said, like Death.

. . . I have said that she does not *resent* her grief. No; the weakness of that word would make it a lie. To her, what hurts becomes immediately embodied: she looks on it as a thing that can be attacked, worried down, torn in shreds. Scarcely a substance herself, she grapples to conflict with abstractions. Before calamity she is a tigress; she rends her woes, shivers them in compulsed abhorrence. Pain, for her, has no result in good; tears water no harvest of wisdom: on sickness, on death itself, she looks with the eye of a rebel. Wicked perhaps, she is, but also she is strong; and her strength has conquered Beauty, has overcome Grace, and bound both at her side, captives peerlessly fair, and docile as fair. Even in the uttermost frenzy of energy is each maenad movement royally, imperially, incedingly upborne. Her hair, flying loose in revel or war, is still an angel's hair, and glorious under a halo. Fallen, insurgent, banished, she remembers the heaven where she rebelled. Heaven's light, following her exile, pierces its confines, and discloses their forlorn remoteness.

Charlotte Brontë, *Villette*, 1850

The Village Boys Meet an Angel

At last I made bold to ask him to tell us who he was.

'An angel,' he said, quite simply, and set another bird free and clapped his hands and made it fly away.

A kind of awe fell upon us when we heard him say that, and we were afraid again; but he said we need not be troubled, there was no occasion for us to be afraid of an angel, and he liked us, anyway. He went on chatting as simply and unaffectedly as ever; and while he talked he made a crowd of little men and women the size of your finger, and they went diligently to work and cleared and leveled off a space a couple of yards square in the grass and began to build a cunning little castle in it, the women mixing the mortar and carrying it up the scaffoldings in pails on their heads, just as our work-women have always done, and the men laying the courses of masonry – five hundred of these toy people swarming briskly about and working diligently and wiping the sweat off their faces as natural as life. In the absorbing interest of watching those five hundred little people make the castle grow step by step and course by course, and take shape and symmetry, that feeling and awe soon passed away and we were quite comfortable and at home again. We asked if we might make some people, and he said yes, and told Seppi to make some cannon for the walls, and told Nikolaus to make some halberdiers, with breastplates and greaves and helmets, and I was to make some cavalry, with horses, and in allotting these tasks he called us by our names, but did not say how he knew them. Then Seppi asked him what his own name was, and he said, tranquilly, 'Satan,' and held out a chip and caught a little woman on it who was falling from the scaffolding and put her back where she belonged, and said, 'She is an idiot to step backward like that and not notice what she is about.'

It caught us suddenly, that name did, and our work dropped out of our hands and broke to pieces – a cannon, a halberdier, and a horse. Satan laughed, and asked what was the matter. I said, 'Nothing, only it seemed a strange name for an angel.' He asked why.

'Because it's – it's – well, it's his name, you know.'

'Yes – he is my uncle.'

He said it placidly, but it took our breath for a moment and made our

[45]

hearts beat. He did not seem to notice that, but mended our halberdiers and things with a touch, handing them to us finished, and said, 'Don't you remember? – he was an angel himself, once.'

'Yes – it's true,' said Seppi; 'I didn't think of that.'

'Before the Fall he was blameless.'

'Yes,' said Nikolaus, 'he was without sin.'

'It is a good family – ours,' said Satan; 'there is not a better. He is the only member of it that has ever sinned.'

I should not be able to make any one understand how exciting it all was. You know that kind of quiver that trembles around through you when you are seeing something so strange and enchanting and wonderful that it is just a fearful joy to be alive and look at it; and you know how you gaze, and your lips turn dry and your breath comes short, but you wouldn't be anywhere but there, not for the world. I was bursting to ask one question – I had it on my tongue's end and could hardly hold it back – but I was ashamed to ask it; it might be a rudeness. Satan set an ox down that he had been making, and smiled up at me and said:

'It wouldn't be a rudeness, and I should forgive it if it was. Have I seen him? Millions of times. From the time that I was a little child a thousand years old I was his second favorite among the nursery angels of our blood and lineage – to use a human phrase – yes, from that time until the Fall, eight thousand years, measured as you count time.'

'Eight – thousand!'

'Yes.' He turned to Seppi, and went on as if answering something that was in Seppi's mind: 'Why, naturally I look like a boy, for that is what I am. With us what you call time is a spacious thing; it takes a long stretch of it to grow an angel to full age.' There was a question in my mind, and he turned to me and answered it, 'I am sixteen thousand years old – counting as you count.' Then he turned to Nikòlaus and said: 'No, the Fall did not affect me nor the rest of the relationship. It was only he that I was named for who ate of the fruit of the tree and then beguiled the man and the woman with it. We others are still ignorant of sin; we are not able to commit it; we are without blemish, and shall abide in that estate always. We –' Two of the little workmen were quarreling, and in buzzing little bumblebee voices they were cursing and swearing at each other; now came blows and blood; then they locked themselves together in a life-and-death struggle. Satan reached out his hand and crushed the life out of them with his fingers, threw them away, wiped the red from his fingers on his handkerchief, and went on talking where he had left off: 'We cannot do wrong; neither have we any disposition to do it, for we do not know what it is.'

It seemed a strange speech, in the circumstances, but we barely noticed that, we were so shocked and grieved at the wanton murder he had committed – for murder it was, that was its true name, and it was without palliation or excuse, for the men had not wronged him in any way. It made us miserable, for we loved him, and had thought him so noble and so beautiful and gracious, and had honestly believed he was an angel; and to have him do this cruel thing – ah, it lowered him so, and we had had such pride in him. He went right on talking, just as if nothing had happened, telling about his travels, and the interesting things he had seen in the big worlds of our solar system and of other solar systems far away in the remotenesses of space, and about the customs of the immortals that inhabit them, somehow fascinating us, enchanting us, charming us in spite of the pitiful scene that was now under our eyes, for the wives of the little dead men had found the crushed and shapeless bodies and were crying over them, and sobbing and lamenting, and a priest was kneeling there with his hands crossed upon his breast, praying; and crowds and crowds of pitying friends were massed about them, reverently uncovered, with their bare heads bowed, and many with the tears running down – a scene which Satan paid no attention to until the small noise of the weeping and praying began to annoy him, then he reached out and took the heavy board seat out of our swing and brought it down and mashed all those people into the earth just as if they had been flies, and went on talking just the same.

Mark Twain, *The Mysterious Stranger*, (posthumously) 1916

Geoffrey Tempest, Snatched From his Grub Street Garret, Meets Prince Lucio de Rimânez

Outside, the prince's carriage waited, drawn by two spirited black horses caparisoned in silver; magnificent thoroughbreds, which pawed the ground and champed their bits impatient of delay, – at sight of his master the smart footman in attendance threw the door open, touching his hat respectfully. We stepped in, I preceding my companion at his expressed desire; and as I sank back among the easy cushions, I felt the complacent consciousness of luxury and power to such an extent that it seemed as if I had left my days of adversity already a long way behind me. Hunger and happiness disputed my sensations between them, and I was in that vague light-headed condition common to long fasting, in which nothing seems absolutely tangible or real. I knew I should not properly grasp the solid truth of my wonderful good luck till my physical needs were satisfied and I was, so to speak, once more in a naturally balanced bodily condition.

At present my brain was in a whirl, – my thoughts were all dim and disconnected, – and I appeared to myself to be in some whimsical dream from which I should wake up directly. The carriage rolled on rubber-tyred wheels and made no noise as it went, one could only hear the even rapid trot of the horses. By-and-by I saw in the semi-darkness my new friend's brilliant dark eyes fixed upon me with a curiously intent expression.

'Do you not feel the world already at your feet?' he queried half playfully, half ironically – 'Like a football, waiting to be kicked? It is such an absurd world, you know – so easily moved. Wise men in all ages have done their best to make it less ridiculous, – with no result, inasmuch as it continues to prefer folly to wisdom. A football, or let us say a shuttle-cock among worlds, ready to be tossed up anyhow and anywhere, provided the battledore be of gold!'

'You speak a trifle bitterly, prince' – I said – 'But no doubt you have had a wide experience among men?'

'I have,' he returned with emphasis – 'My kingdom is a vast one.'

'You are a ruling power then?' I exclaimed with some astonishment – 'Yours is not a title of honour only?'

'Oh, as your rules of aristocracy go, it *is* a mere title of honour' – he replied quickly – 'When I say that my kingdom is a vast one, I mean that I rule wherever men obey the influence of wealth. From this point of view, am I wrong in calling my kingdom vast? – is it not almost boundless?'

'I perceive you are a cynic,' – I said – 'Yet surely you believe that there are some things wealth cannot buy, – honour and virtue for example?'

He surveyed me with a whimsical smile.

'I suppose honour and virtue *do* exist –' he answered – 'And when they are existent of course they cannot be bought. But my experience has taught me that I can always buy everything. The sentiments called honour and virtue by the majority of men are the most shifty things imaginable, – set sufficient cash down, and they become bribery and corruption in the twinkling of an eye! Curious – very curious. I confess I found a case of unpurchaseable integrity once, but only once. I may find it again, though I consider the chance a very doubtful one. Now to revert to myself, pray do not imagine I am playing the humbug with you or passing myself off under a *bogus* title. I am a *bona-fide* prince, believe me, and of such descent as none of your oldest families can boast, – but my dominions are long since broken up and my former subjects dispersed among all nations, – anarchy, nihilism, disruption and political troubles generally, compel me to be rather reticent concerning my affairs. Money I fortunately have in plenty, – and with that I pave my way. Some day when we are better acquainted, you shall know more of my private history. I have various other names and titles besides that on my card – but I keep to the simplest of them, because most people are such bunglers at the pronunciation of foreign names. My intimate friends generally drop my title, and call me Lucio simply.'

'That is your christian name –?' I began.

'Not at all – I have no "christian" name,' – he interrupted swiftly and with anger – 'There is no such thing as "christian" in my composition!'

He spoke with such impatience that for a moment I was at a loss for a reply. At last –

'Indeed!' I murmured vaguely.

He burst out laughing.

' "Indeed!" That is all you can find to say! Indeed and again indeed the word "christian" vexes me. There is no such creature alive. *You* are not a Christian, – no one is really, – people pretend to be, – and in so damnable an act of feigning are more blasphemous than any fallen fiend! Now I make no pretences of the kind, – I have only one faith –'

'And that is?' –

'A profound and awful one!' he said in thrilling tones – 'And the worst of it is that it is true, – as true as the workings of the Universe. But of that hereafter, – it will do to talk of when we feel low-spirited and wish to converse of things grim and ghastly, – at present here we are at our destination, and the chief consideration of our lives, (it is the chief consideration of most men's lives) must be the excellence or non-excellence of our food.'

The carriage stopped and we descended. At first sight of the black horses and silver trappings, the porter of the hotel and two or three other servants rushed out to attend upon us; but the prince passed into the hall without noticing any of them and addressed himself to a sober-looking individual in black, his own private valet, who came forward to meet him with a profound salutation. I murmured something about wishing to engage a room for myself in the hotel.

'Oh, my man will see to that for you' – he said lightly – 'The house is not full, – at anyrate all the best rooms are not taken; and of course you want one of the best.'

A staring waiter, who up to that moment, had been noting my shabby clothes with that peculiar air of contempt commonly displayed by insolent menials to those whom they imagine are poor, overheard these words, and suddenly changing the derisive expression of his foxy face, bowed obsequiously as I passed. A thrill of disgust ran through me, mingled with a certain angry triumph, – the hypocritical reflex of this low fellow's countenance, was, I knew, a true epitome of what I should find similarly reflected in the manner and attitude of all 'polite' society. For there the estimate of worth is no higher than a common servant's estimate, and is taken solely from the money standard; – if you are poor and dress shabbily you are thrust aside and ignored, – but if you are rich, you may wear shabby clothes as much as you like, you are still courted and flattered, and invited everywhere, though you may be the greatest fool alive or the worst blackguard unhung. With vague thoughts such as these flitting over my mind, I followed my host to his rooms. He occupied nearly a whole wing of the hotel, having a large drawing-room, dining-room and study *en suite*, fitted up in the most luxurious manner, besides bedroom, bath-room, and dressing-room, with other rooms adjoining, for his valet and two extra personal attendants. The table was laid for supper, and glittered with the costliest glass, silver and china, being furthermore adorned by baskets of the most exquisite fruit and flowers, and in a few moments we were seated. The prince's valet acted as head-waiter, and I noticed that now this man's face, seen in the full light of the electric lamps, seemed very dark and unpleasant, even sinister in expression, – but in the perform-ance of his duties he was unexceptionable, being quick, attentive, and deferential, so much so that I inwardly reproached myself for taking an instinctive dislike to him. His name was Amiel, and I found myself involuntarily watching his movements, they were so noiseless, – his very step suggesting the stealthy gliding of a cat or a tiger. He was assisted in his work by the two other attendants who served as his subordinates, and who were equally active and well-trained, – and presently I found myself enjoying the choicest meal I had tasted for many and many a long day, flavoured with such wine as connoisseurs might be apt to dream of, but never succeed in finding. I began to feel perfectly at my ease, and talked with freedom and confidence, the strong attraction I had for my new friend deepening with every moment I passed in his company.

Marie Corelli, *The Sorrows of Satan*, 1895

Max Beerbohm Meets a Flashy Type

On one side sat a tall, flashy, rather Mephistophelian man whom I had seen from time to time in the domino room and elsewhere. On the other side sat Soames. They made a queer contrast in that sunlit room – Soames sitting haggard in that hat and cape which nowhere at any season had I seen him doff, and this other, this keenly vital man, at sight of whom I more than ever wondered whether he were a diamond merchant, a conjurer, or the head of a private detective agency. I was sure Soames didn't want my company; but I asked, as it would have seemed brutal not to, whether I might join him, and took the chair opposite to his. He was smoking a cigarette, with an untasted salmi of something on his plate and a half-empty bottle of Sauterne before him; and he was quite silent. I said that the preparations for the Jubilee made London impossible. (I rather liked them, really.) I professed a wish to go right away till the whole thing was over. In vain did I attune myself to his gloom. He seemed not to hear me nor even to see me. I felt that his behaviour made me ridiculous in the eyes of the other man. The gangway between the two rows of tables at the Vingtième was hardly more than two feet wide (Rose and Berthe, in their ministrations, had always to edge past each other, quarrelling in whispers as they did so), and any one at the table abreast of yours was practically at yours. I thought our neighbour was amused at my failure to interest Soames, and so, as I could not explain to him that my insistence was merely charitable, I became silent. Without turning my head, I had him well within my range of vision. I hoped I looked less vulgar than he in contrast with Soames. I was sure he was not an Englishman, but what *was* his nationality? Though his jet-black hair was *en brosse*, I did not think he was French. To Berthe, who waited on him, he spoke French fluently, but with a hardly native idiom and accent. I gathered that this was his first visit to the Vingtième; but Berthe was off-hand in her manner to him: he had not made a good impression. His eyes were handsome, but – like the Vingtième's tables – too narrow and set too close together. His nose was predatory, and the points of his moustache, waxed up beyond his nostrils, gave a fixity to his smile. Decidedly, he was sinister. And my sense of discomfort in his presence was intensified by the scarlet waistcoat which tightly, and so unseasonably in June, sheathed his ample chest. This waistcoat wasn't wrong merely because of the heat, either. It was somehow all wrong in itself. It wouldn't have done on Christmas morning. It would have struck a jarring note at the first night of *Hernani*.

Max Beerbohm, *Enoch Soames*, 1912

Ivan Karamazov Meets a Poor Relation

'Hallucinations are quite likely in your condition,' the doctor opined, 'though it would be better to verify them . . . you must take steps at once, without a moment's delay, or things will go badly with you.' But Ivan did not follow this judicious advice and did not take to his bed to be nursed. 'I am walking about, so I am strong enough, if I drop, it'll be different then, anyone may nurse me who likes,' he decided, dismissing the subject.

And so he was sitting almost conscious himself of his delirium and, as I have said already, looking persistently at some object on the sofa against the opposite wall. Someone appeared to be sitting there, though goodness knows how he had come in, for he had not been in the room when Ivan came into it, on his return from Smerdyakov. This was a person or, more accurately speaking, a Russian gentleman of a particular kind, no longer young, *qui faisait la cinquantaine*, as the French say, with rather long, still thick, dark hair, slightly streaked with grey and a small pointed beard. He was wearing a brownish reefer jacket, rather shabby, evidently made by a good tailor though, and of a fashion at least three years old, that had been discarded by smart and well-to-do people for the last two years. His linen and his long scarf-like neck-tie were all such as are worn by people who aim at being stylish, but on closer inspection his linen was not overclean and his wide scarf was very threadbare. The visitor's check trousers were of excellent cut, but were too light in colour and too tight for the present fashion. His soft fluffy white hat was out of keeping with the season.

In brief there was every appearance of gentility on straitened means. It looked as though the gentleman belonged to that class of idle land-owners who used to flourish in the times of serfdom. He had unmistakably been, at some time, in good and fashionable society, had once had good connections, had possibly preserved them indeed, but, after a gay youth, becoming gradually impoverished on the abolition of serfdom, he had sunk into the position of a poor relation of the best class, wandering from one good old friend to another and received by them for his companion-able and accommodating disposition and as being, after all, a gentleman who could be asked to sit down with anyone, though, of course, not in a place of honour. Such gentlemen of accommodating temper and depen-dent position, who can tell a story, take a hand at cards, and who have a distinct aversion for any duties that may be forced upon them, are usually solitary creatures, either bachelors or widowers. Sometimes they have children, but if so, the children are always being brought up at a distance, at some aunt's, to whom these gentlemen never allude in good society, seeming ashamed of the relationship. They gradually lose sight of their children altogether, though at intervals they receive a birthday or Christ-mas letter from them and sometimes even answer it.

The countenance of the unexpected visitor was not so much good-natured, as accommodating and ready to assume any amiable expression as occasion might arise. He had no watch, but he had a tortoise-shell lorgnette on a black ribbon. On the middle finger of his right hand was a massive gold ring with a cheap opal stone in it.

Fyodor Dostoevsky, *The Brothers Karamazov*, 1880; trans. Constance Garnett, 1912

A German Composer Meets a German Bullyboy

I sate alone here, by my lamp, nigh to the windows with shutters closed, before me the length of the hall, and read Kierkegaard on Mozart's *Don Juan*.

Then in a clap I am stricken by a cutting cold, even as though I sat in a winter-warm room and a window had blown open towards the frost. It came not from behind me, where the windows lie; it falls on me from in front. I start up from my boke and look abroad into the hall, belike Sch. is come back for I am no more alone. There is some bodye there in the mirk, sitting on the horse-hair sofa that stands almost in the myddes of the room, nigher the door, with the table and chairs, where we eat our breakfasts. Sitting in the sofa-corner with legs crossed; not Sch., but another, smaller than he, in no wise so imposing and not in truth a gentilman at all. But the cold keeps percing me.

'*Chi e costà?*' is what I shout with some catch in my throat, propping my hands on the chair-arms, in such wise that the book falls from my knees to the floore. Answers the quiet, slow voice of the other, a voice that sounds trained, with pleasing nasal resonance:

'Speak only German! Only good German without feignedness or dissimulation. I understand it. It happens to be just precisely my favoured language. Whiles I understand only German. But fet thee a cloak, a hat and rug. Thou art cold. And quiver and shake thou wilt, even though not taking a cold.'

'Who says *thou* to me?' I ask, chafing.

'I,' he says. 'I, by your leave. Oh, thou meanest because thou sayst to nobody thou, not even to thy jester gentilman, but only to the trusty play-fere, he who clepes thee by the first name but not thou him. No, matter. There is already enough between us for us to say thou. Well then: wilt fet thyself some warm garment?'

I stare into the half-light, fix him angrily in mine eye. A man: rather spindling, not nearly so tall as Sch., smaller even then I. A sports cap over one ear, on the other side reddish hair standing up from the temple; reddish lashes and pink eyes, a cheesy face, a drooping nose with wry tip. Over diagonal-striped tricot shirt a chequer jacket; sleeves too short, with sausage-fingers coming too far out; breeches indecently tight, worn-down yellow shoes. An ugly customer, a bully, a *strizzi*, a rough. And with an actor's voice and eloquence.

'Well?' he says again.

'First and foremost I fain would know,' say I in quaking calm, 'who is bold enough to force himself in to sit down here with me.'

Thomas Mann, *Doctor Faustus*, 1947;
trans. H. T. Lowe-Porter, 1949

Two Moscow Intellectuals Meet a Foreigner

Afterwards, when it was frankly too late, various bodies collected their data and issued descriptions of this man. As to his teeth, he had platinum crowns on his left side and gold ones on his right. He wore an expensive grey suit and foreign shoes of the same colour as his suit. His grey beret was stuck jauntily over one ear and under his arm he carried a walking-stick with a knob in the shape of a poodle's head. He looked slightly over forty. Crooked sort of mouth. Clean-shaven. Dark hair. Right eye black, left eye for some reason green. Eyebrows black, but one higher than the other. In short – a foreigner.

As he passed the bench occupied by the editor and the poet, the foreigner gave them a sidelong glance, stopped and suddenly sat down on the next bench a couple of paces away from the two friends.

'A German,' thought Berlioz. 'An Englishman . . .' thought Bezdomny. 'Phew, he must be hot in those gloves!'

The stranger glanced round the tall houses that formed a square round the pond, from which it was obvious that he was seeing this lo-cality for the first time and that it interested him. His gaze halted on the upper storeys, whose panes threw back a blinding, fragmented re-flection of the sun which was setting on Mikhail Alexandrovich for ever; he then looked downwards to where the windows were turning darker in the early evening twilight, smiled patronisingly at something, frowned, placed his hands on the knob of his cane and laid his chin on his hands.

'You see, Ivan,' said Berlioz, 'you have written a marvellously satirical description of the birth of Jesus, the son of God, but the whole joke lies in the fact that there had already been a whole series of sons of God before Jesus, such as the Phoenician Adonis, the Phrygian Attis, the Persian Mithras. Of course not one of these ever existed, including Jesus, and instead of the nativity or the arrival of the Magi you should have described the absurd rumours about their arrival. But according to your story the nativity really took place . . . !'

Here Bezdomny made an effort to stop his torturing hiccups and held his breath, but it only made him hiccup more loudly and painfully. At that moment Berlioz interrupted his speech because the foreigner suddenly rose and approached the two writers. They stared at him in astonishment.

'Excuse me, please,' said the stranger with a foreign accent, although in correct Russian, 'for permitting myself, without an introduction . . . but the subject of your learned conversation was so interesting that . . .'

Here he politely took off his beret and the two friends had no alternative but to rise and bow.

'No, probably a Frenchman . . .' thought Berlioz.

'A Pole,' thought Bezdomny.

I should add that the poet had found the stranger repulsive from first sight, although Berlioz had liked the look of him, or rather not exactly liked him but, well . . . been interested by him.

'May I join you?' enquired the foreigner politely, and as the two friends moved somewhat unwillingly aside he adroitly placed himself between them and at once joined the conversation. 'If I'm not mistaken, you were saying that Jesus never existed, were you not?' he asked, turning his green left eye on Berlioz.

'No, you were not mistaken,' replied Berlioz courteously. 'I did indeed say that.'

'Ah, how interesting!' exclaimed the foreigner.

'What the hell does he want?' thought Bezdomny and frowned.

'And do you agree with your friend?' enquired the unknown man, turning to Bezdomny on his right.

'A hundred per cent!' affirmed the poet, who loved to use pretentious numerical expressions.

'Astounding!' cried their unbidden companion. Glancing furtively round and lowering his voice he said: 'Forgive me for being so rude, but am I right in thinking that you do not believe in God either?' He gave a horrified look and said: 'I swear not to tell anyone!'

'Yes, neither of us believes in God,' answered Berlioz with a faint smile at this foreign tourist's apprehension. 'But we can talk about it with absolute freedom.'

The foreigner leaned against the backrest of the bench and asked, in a voice positively squeaking with curiosity:

'Are you . . . atheists?'

'Yes, we're atheists,' replied Berlioz, smiling, and Bezdomny thought angrily: 'Trying to pick an argument, damn foreigner!'

'Oh, how delightful!' exclaimed the astonishing foreigner and swivelled his head from side to side, staring at each of them in turn.

'In our country there's nothing surprising about atheism,' said Berlioz with diplomatic politeness. 'Most of us have long ago and quite consciously given up believing in all those fairy-tales about God.'

At this the foreigner did an extraordinary thing – he stood up and shook the astonished editor by the hand, saying as he did so:

'Allow me to thank you with all my heart!'

'What are you thanking him for?' asked Bezdomny, blinking.

'For some very valuable information, which as a traveller I find extremely interesting,' said the eccentric foreigner, raising his forefinger meaningfully.

This valuable piece of information had obviously made a powerful impression on the traveller, as he gave a frightened glance at the houses as though afraid of seeing an atheist at every window.

'No, he's not an Englishman,' thought Berlioz. Bezdomny thought: 'What I'd like to know is – where did he manage to pick up such good Russian?' and frowned again.

'But might I enquire,' began the visitor from abroad after some worried reflection, 'how you account for the proofs of the existence of God, of which there are, as you know, five?'

'Alas!' replied Berlioz regretfully. 'Not one of these proofs is valid, and mankind has long since relegated them to the archives. You must agree that rationally there can be no proof of the existence of God.'

'Bravo!' exclaimed the stranger. 'Bravo! You have exactly repeated the views of the immortal Emmanuel on that subject. But here's the oddity of it: he completely demolished all five proofs and then, as though to deride his own efforts, he formulated a sixth proof of his own.'

'Kant's proof,' objected the learned editor with a thin smile, 'is also unconvincing. Not for nothing did Schiller say that Kant's reasoning on this question would only satisfy slaves, and Strauss simply laughed at his proof.'

As Berlioz spoke he thought to himself: 'But who on earth *is* he? And how does he speak such good Russian?'

'Kant ought to be arrested and given three years in Solovki asylum for that "proof" of his!' Ivan Nikolayich burst out completely unexpectedly.

'Ivan!' whispered Berlioz, embarrassed.

But the suggestion to pack Kant off to an asylum not only did not surprise the stranger but actually delighted him. 'Exactly, exactly!' he cried and his green left eye, turned on Berlioz, glittered. 'That's exactly the place for him! I said to him myself that morning at breakfast: "If you'll forgive me, professor, your theory is no good. It may be clever but it's horribly incomprehensible. People will think you're mad." '

Berlioz's eyes bulged. 'At breakfast ... to Kant? What is he rambling about?' he thought.

'But,' went on the foreigner, unperturbed by Berlioz's amazement and turning to the poet, 'sending him to Solovki is out of the question, because for over a hundred years now he has been somewhere far away from Solovki and I assure you that it is totally impossible to bring him back.'

'What a pity!' said the impetuous poet.

Mikhail Bulgakov, *The Master and Margarita*; trans. Michael Glenny, 1967

Young Lawrie Meets a Salesman at the Fair

Lawrie could hear the sound of sizzling like the noise when Mrs Andrews lowered the basket of chips into the boiling oil at the Fried Fish Shop, and inside he could see flames and billowing smoke. But he did not feel hungry and he wandered on to a booth lit by fish-tail gas-jets.

It was not till he saw these gas-jets that he realised he had passed into a place where it was night – or perhaps he had become so absorbed in his thoughts that he had not noticed the passage of time.

He stopped one of the passers-by, a lugubrious-looking man like a sad cod. 'Excuse me, sir,' he said, 'could you tell me what the time is?'

'It isn't,' the man said, 'not where I come from.'

'What isn't?' Lawrie asked.

'Time,' said the man impatiently. 'I can't waste eternity nattering with you, young man.' He pushed Lawrie to one side and continued on his way.

Lawrie looked round for someone more helpful. Behind the bar of the booth lit by gas-jets, he saw an old gentleman with merrily twinkling eyes. He was almost completely bald, except for a horseshoe of white hair, the ends of which came over the tops of his ears. He was wearing a smart grey linen overcoat, with bright green piping and he looked like a salesman in a large department store. He beckoned and Lawrie went over to him.

'What can I do you for, son?' he asked.

That was a very old joke and Lawrie ignored it. He saw that on the breast pocket of his overcoat was embroidered his name, O.L.D. Scratch. O.L.D. Chestnut, Lawrie thought, would have been more appropriate. 'I wanted to know how long it had been night,' Lawrie said, 'and I'm afraid he wasn't very helpful.'

'I know, I know,' said Mr Scratch. 'But you shouldn't blame him. He's very restless, eternally on the go. You were quite right to come to me. I can give you ages.'

'Then how long has it?' Lawrie asked.

'It always is, here,' Mr Scratch said. 'You see this is a nightspot. I know some people say nightspots are hell. But I must say I like it here. I was lucky to fall into this job. It was made for me.'

Arthur Calder-Marshall, *The Fair to Middling*, 1959

Two

IN THE BEGINNING

God Without the Devil

I *am* the LORD, and *there* is none else, *there is* no God beside me: I girded thee, though thou hast not known me:

That they may know from the rising of the sun, and from the west, that *there is* none beside me. I *am* the LORD, and *there is* none else.

I form the light, and create darkness: I make peace, and create evil: I the LORD do all these *things*.

Drop down, ye heavens, from above, and let the skies pour down righteousness: let the earth open, and let them bring forth salvation, and let righteousness spring up together; I the LORD have created it.

Woe unto him that striveth with his Maker! *Let* the potsherd *strive* with the potsherds of the earth. Shall the clay say to him that fashioneth it, What makest thou? or thy work, He hath no hands?

Woe unto him that saith unto *his* father, What begettest thou? or to the woman, What hast thou brought forth?

Isaiah 45, v.5–10

How the Devil Became: Psychoanalytical

To begin with, we know that God is a father-substitute; or, more correctly, that he is an exalted father; or, yet again, that he is a copy of a father as he is seen and experienced in childhood – by individuals in their own childhood and by mankind in its prehistory as the father of the primitive and primal horde. Later on in life the individual sees his father as something different and lesser. But the ideational image belonging to his childhood is preserved and becomes merged with the inherited memory-traces of the primal father to form the individual's idea of God. We also know, from the secret life of the individual which analysis uncovers, that his relation to his father was perhaps ambivalent from the outset, or, at any rate, soon became so. That is to say, it contained two sets of emotional impulses that were opposed to each other: it contained not only impulses of an affectionate and submissive nature, but also hostile and defiant ones. It is our view that the same ambivalence governs the relations of mankind to its Deity. The unresolved conflict between, on the one hand, a longing for the father and, on the other, a fear of him and a son's defiance of him, has furnished us with an explanation of important characteristics of religion and decisive vicissitudes in it.

Concerning the Evil Demon, we know that he is regarded as the antithesis of God and yet is very close to him in his nature. His history has not been so well studied as that of God; not all religions have adopted the Evil Spirit, the opponent of God, and his prototype in the life of the individual has so far remained obscure. One thing, however, is certain: gods can turn into evil demons when new gods oust them. When one people has been conquered by another, their fallen gods not seldom turn into demons in the eyes of the conquerors. The evil demon of the Christian faith – the Devil of the Middle Ages – was, according to Christian mythology, himself a fallen angel and of a godlike nature. It does not need much analytic perspicacity to guess that God and the Devil were originally identical – were a single figure which was later split into two figures with opposite attributes. In the earliest ages of religion God himself still possessed all the terrifying features which were afterwards combined to form a counterpart of him.

We have here an example of the process, with which we are familiar, by which an idea that has a contradictory – an ambivalent – content becomes divided into two sharply contrasted opposites. The contradictions in the original nature of God are, however, a reflection of the ambivalence which governs the relation of the individual to his personal father. If the benevolent and righteous God is a substitute for his father, it is not to be wondered at that his hostile attitude to his father, too, which is one of hating and fearing him and of making complaints against him, should have come to expression in the creation of Satan. Thus the father, it seems, is the individual prototype of both God and the Devil. But we should expect religions to bear ineffaceable marks of the fact that the primitive primal father was a being of unlimited evil – a being less like God than the Devil.

Sigmund Freud, 'Ein Teufelsneurose im Siebzehnten Jahrhundert' ['A Seventeenth Century Demonological Neurosis'], 1923; trans. James Strachey, 1961

How the Devil Became: Etymological

This conclusion of the original identity of God and Devil receives an interesting confirmation through etymological study of the word 'Devil'. Like the cognate French *diable*, German *Teufel*, Old High German *Tuivel*, as well as the Greek *diabolos*, it is ultimately derived from a primeval root DV, which in Sanscrit is found in two forms, *div* and *dyu*, the original meaning of which was 'to kindle'. From the former come, in addition to our Devil, the Teutonic *Tius* (the god of Tuesday), *Tiwas* or *Zio*, the Greek *theos*, Latin *deus* or *divus*, French *dieu*, Welsh *diw*, Lithuanian *diewas*, Gipsy *dewel*, all of which signify 'God'; further, the word *deva* or *daeva*, which to the Brahmin means God, but to the Persian and Parsee means Devil. From the second form come the Indian *Djaus* (the Brahman sky-god), the Greek *Zeus* (Z = Dj), and the Latin *Jupiter* (old Latin *Diovis*). The same remarkable polarity is shown by the non-personal words derived from the same root. On the one hand there is the Latin *dies* = day, the Keltic *dis* = day-star or day-god, Sanscrit *dyaus* = day, and on the other hand the Aryan *dhvan* (whence the Greek *thanatos*) = death, Teutonic *devan* = to die, Aryan *dvi* = to fear, and the Greek *deos* = dread. Still more remarkable is the fact that the polarity words *par excellence* are of similar origin. The Sanscrit *dva*, Latin *duo*, English *two*, Welsh *deu*, all mean 'two' (compare the English 'double' with the Old High German for devil, *Deudel*), while the Greek *dys* signifies both 'to separate into two' and 'evil'. The primary identity of the ideas of God and Devil can thus be demonstrated quite independently of psychological considerations, though these would in themselves be decisive.

Ernest Jones, On the Nightmare, 1931

How the Devil Became: a Victorian Speculation

I was born in a sweltering vale of Upper Egypt. The date I cannot give, as my chronology goes so much farther back than that of Archbishop Usher, that I have no milestones to take for my measures. Nor can I determine whether my parents belonged to the present geological period, or to one of an earlier date. If now they appear only in a fossil state, they had, at the time I came into existence, much the same qualities as characterize human beings at the present day. Only that those qualities were of a rougher and sterner kind than those that belong to these civilized ages. Indeed, evolution and progress have marked as man's so my steps out of that darkness into this light. The first link of that advancing series I venture not to define. It may have been, as the Scripture says, 'the ground' or 'the dust of the earth' (Gen. ii. 19, iii. 17); it may have been some anthropomorphic organism, which grew into an ape before it became a man. The second source is the more elevated, and as such presupposes the Divine hand more markedly. But as the lower can never produce the higher; since no being can give what he does not possess; so only from the One Perfect and Infinite Will can the human race have sprung, whether in its infancy or in its manhood. Hence as the child of human nature, my origin is divine. Equally certain is it that the moral discipline which I represent has an aim and a tendency no less effectual than benevolent.

It was autumn. The weather had been intensely sultry. The river had inundated the neighbouring plains. The thinly scattered human population were driven into a neighbouring forest. A thunder-storm broke forth, driving husbands, wives and children into the heart of the woods. Then, of a sudden, a flash of lightning set the trees on fire. They blazed up on all sides, and were soon nothing but a mass of burning ashes.

Only one man escaped. It was the chief of the small tribe. He had paid a visit to a neighbour's hunting-ground, and now he slowly made his way back to his covert, in a grove or outpost of the perishing forest. Warned by the intense heat and dazzling glow, he stopped on his approach at a short distance, and watched the rushing flames, stupefied with terror, alarm and grief. Where was his young wife? where his two lovely children? where his little all? and where would the conflagration stop?

He knelt down instinctively in awe and dread before this fell destroyer. He knelt down; his heart was big with a choking emotion; – he knelt down; it was all he could do; but the act was a silent supplication.

In that supplicating act I received life. I was the thunderer, the dark and all but impersonal cause of that wide-spread ruin and woe. I repeat, all but impersonal cause, for that barbarian was hardly self-conscious. As yet he was a constituent part of the outer universe. He went up and down the land and the water; he passed the trees or sat beneath their shadow; he played with the fawn and revelled among the fish; he looked at the stars, and gazed on sun and moon, almost as if he and they were each and all members of the same strange world in and around him. Indeed, the chief was in birth rather than in being. Embryonic himself, he could at best produce only embryos. Already had the prolific earth and the majestic skies quickened his mind with a faint notion of a Good Power who, being good, could not be the author of this terrific destruction. Whence then was it? It came from some Evil Spirit. These were but shadows (one somewhat light, the other very dark) in that infantile mind. Shadows so thin and evanescent were they, that to put them, as I am doing, into words, is to give them form and hue far too real and definite.

And yet something had brought him to his knees. It was for the first time. No! he had not kneeled to the Good Spirit. Only can the terror of the tempest move that hard and unimpressible heart.

Nevertheless, it was chaos, blind, confused, in some sense empty chaos, in the bosom of that wild man of the woods. What may come of that inner whirl, who can tell? It may sink into stolid stupidity. It may emerge into self-consciousness, producing somewhat clear recognitions. At present all is embryonic.

When the flames ceased for want of fuel, our chief was still sitting alone on the summit of a ridge of hills which ran parallel with the stream. There he sat day and night for I know not how long, darkly musing on the disastrous event. At the end of that time he felt as if he had received a blow in his inner nature. Exhausted with fatigue, worn out by intensity of sentiment, unfed, unrefreshed by water or sleep, he fell under the stroke, and lay prostrate on the soil, – a victim to a raging fever.

Days passed and nights passed; the sun and moon rose and set; fair weather returned; the air was alive with the flight and the buzz of insects; and the roar of the lion echoed from a distance: but nothing awoke him from his stupor of mind.

One morning at early dawn he opened his eyes; he opened them only to let the lashes languidly fall. Hours fled away, and he opened them again. The awakening power was his wife, who bent over him, and with her warm breath, her soothing hand, her kindling words, brought back his departing spirit, and he looked as if he saw some one; he looked again, and smiled.

His self-consciousness came and came in a less vague and impersonal form. He knew his wife, and, knowing her, he knew himself.

The knowledge in time gave distinctness to his mental conceptions of outer things, and by and by he knew the Good Spirit, and no less the Bad Spirit. But for the antithesis he could not have known either, and he knew both the better from their contrasted character and reciprocated influence.

In that knowledge I was truly born. I was the dark and evil shadow of that sunny reality. I was the opposite of that bright and pleasing dream. My darkness made the retention of that serene light possible. But for me, the chief must have attributed the devastating storm and the consuming conflagration to the Good Spirit. The act would, with this infant of barbarism, have extinguished the sole glimmer of hope and trust he had. Out of that glimmer, thus preserved, sprang religion. And thus in those primordial days I was not an unessential element in the first acts of worship by which man's spirit lifted itself up toward the descending spirit of God.

I have revealed the secret of my birth. I am a child of the hurricane and the deluge and devastation and fever and suffering and woe. The womb that bore me is the human mind in its half chaotic state, as occasioned by external calamity and internal meditation. Human in my birth, I am human in my character. As the sunderance between evil and good, darkness and light in man, is never exact and complete, I derive from my parentage a streak or two of sunshine; but as I am in virtue of my existence the contradiction of good, I share in all that is bad and dark in human nature. Those evil dispositions are exaggerated by being seen through the darkened medium of fear and dread. A terrified imagination throws my bad qualities into distorted and monstrous proportions. And ever as a period of trouble and distress passes, in tempest, war or famine, over the earth, I am seen by the discoloured eyes of mortals in hues the deepest and features the most repulsive.

John R. Beard, *The Autobiography of Satan*, 1872

God Casts Down the King of Babylon, and Permits the Israelites to Blame Him for their Sorrows

And it shall come to pass in the day that the LORD shall give thee rest from thy sorrow, and from thy fear, and from the hard bondage wherein thou wast made to serve,

That thou shalt take up this proverb against the king of Babylon, and say, How hath the oppressor ceased! the golden city ceased!

The LORD hath broken the staff of the wicked, *and* the sceptre of the rulers.

He who smote the people in wrath with a continual stroke, he that ruled the nations in anger, is persecuted, *and* none hindereth.

The whole earth is at rest, *and* is quiet: they break forth into singing.

Yea, the fir trees rejoice at thee, *and* the cedars of Lebanon, *saying*, Since thou art laid down, no feller is come up against us.

Hell from beneath is moved for thee to meet *thee* at thy coming: it stirreth up the dead for thee, *even* all the chief ones of the earth; it hath raised up from their thrones all the kings of the nations.

All they shall speak and say unto thee, Art thou also become weak as we? art thou become like unto us?

Thy pomp is brought down to the grave, *and* the noise of thy viols: the worm is spread under thee, and the worms cover thee.

How art thou fallen from heaven, O Lucifer, son of the morning! *how* art thou cut down to the ground, which didst weaken the nations!

For thou hast said in thine heart, I will ascend into heaven, I will exalt my throne above the stars of God: I will sit also upon the mount of the congregation, in the sides of the north:

I will ascend above the heights of the clouds; I will be like the most High.

Yet thou shalt be brought down to hell, to the sides of the pit.

They that seek thee shall narrowly look upon thee, *and* consider thee,

saying, *Is* this the man that made the earth to tremble, that did shake
kingdoms;
That made the world as a wilderness, and destroyed the cities thereof;
that opened not the house of his prisoners?
All the kings of the nations, *even* all of them, lie in glory, every one in
his own house.
But thou art cast out of thy grave like an abominable branch, *and as* the
raiment of those that are slain, thrust through with a sword, that go down
to the stones of the pit; as a carcase trodden under feet.

Isaiah 14, v.3–19

God's Servant Satan Performs a Harmless Errand

Rabbi Joshua son of Levi said: After God, blessed be He, had given the
Law to Moses, and Moses had come down from heaven, Satan said: 'Lord
of the universe, where hast Thou put the Torah? To whom hast Thou
given it?' The Lord replied, 'I have given it to the Earth.' So Satan went
to the Earth and said, 'Where hast thou put the Torah which the Lord,
blessed be He, has given thee?' The Earth replied: ' "God understandeth
the way thereof". This means that the Lord, blessed be He, knows everything. But I have not the Torah.' Then Satan went to the Sea and said,
'Oh Sea, where hast thou put the Torah which the Lord, blessed be He,
has given thee?' The Sea replied, ' "The Torah is not with me." ' Then
Satan went to the uttermost depth of the earth and said, 'Where hast thou
put the Torah which the Lord, blessed be He, has given thee?' The abyss
of the earth replied, ' "It is not in me." ' So Satan went all over the earth
searching for the Torah, for the Lord had told him that He had given it
to the earth. Then Satan went to the dead and the lost and asked them:
'Where have you put the Torah which the Lord has given you?' And they
replied, 'Verily we have heard of it with our ears, but we know nothing
more.' Then Satan came again before the Lord, blessed be He, and said,
'Lord of the universe, I have searched the whole earth, but I have not
found the Torah.' Then the Lord said unto him, 'Go to Moses, the son
of Amram, to whom I have given it.' Then Satan went to our master
Moses and said, 'Moses, where hast thou put the Torah which the Lord
has given thee?' And Moses replied, 'How dost thou come to ask me
about the Torah? Who am I and what am I that the Lord should give me
the Torah?' When the Lord, blessed be He, heard that Moses would not
admit that he had received the Torah, He said, 'Thou art a liar. Why dost
thou deny that I have given thee the Torah?' And Moses replied, 'Lord

of the universe, the Torah is a desirable object, it filleth with joy him who is engaged in studying it. Thou rejoicest over it and studiest it Thyself every day. How then can I boast and say that I have received the Torah? It is not seemly for a man to boast of anything, even though he has reason to do so. On the contrary, it is better that he should be humble.' And the Lord said, 'Since thou humblest thyself, and dost not wish to claim the honor of having received the Torah, it shall, as a reward, be called by thy name.' This is why it is written, 'Remember the Law of Moses, My servant, and keep the Law of Moses'.

The Ma'aseh Book, 1602; trans. Moses Gaster, 1934

A Nastier Errand for a Servant on a Longer Rein

Now there was a day when the sons of God came to present themselves before the LORD, and Satan came also among them.

And the LORD said unto Satan, Whence comest thou? Then Satan answered the LORD, and said, From going to and fro in the earth, and from walking up and down in it.

And the LORD said unto Satan, Hast thou considered my servant Job, that *there is* none like him in the earth, a perfect and an upright man, one that feareth God, and escheweth evil?

Then Satan answered the LORD, and said, Doth Job fear God for nought? Hast not thou made an hedge about him, and about his house, and about all that he hath on every side? thou hast blessed the work of his hands, and his substance is increased in the land.

But put forth thine hand now, and touch all that he hath, and he will curse thee to thy face.

And the LORD said unto Satan, Behold, all that he hath *is* in thy power; only upon himself put not forth thine hand. So Satan went forth from the presence of the LORD.

And there was a day when his sons and his daughters *were* eating and drinking wine in their eldest brother's house:

And there came a messenger unto Job, and said, The oxen were plowing, and the asses feeding beside them:

And the Sabeans fell *upon them*, and took them away; yea, they have slain the servants with the edge of the sword; and I only am escaped alone to tell thee.

While he *was* yet speaking, there came also another, and said, The fire of God is fallen from heaven, and hath burned up the sheep, and the servants, and consumed them; and I only am escaped alone to tell thee.

While he *was* yet speaking, there came also another, and said, The Chaldeans made out three bands, and fell upon the camels, and have carried them away, yea, and slain the servants with the edge of the sword; and I only am escaped alone to tell thee.

While he *was* yet speaking, there came also another, and said, Thy sons and thy daughters *were* eating and drinking wine in their eldest brother's house:

And, behold, there came a great wind from the wilderness, and smote the four corners of the house, and it fell upon the young men, and they are dead; and I only am escaped alone to tell thee.

Then Job arose, and rent his mantle, and shaved his head, and fell down upon the ground, and worshipped,

And said, Naked came I out of my mother's womb, and naked shall I return thither: the LORD gave, and the LORD hath taken away; blessed be the name of the LORD.

In all this Job sinned not, nor charged God foolishly.

Again there was a day when the sons of God came to present themselves before the LORD, and Satan came also among them to present himself before the LORD.

And the LORD said unto Satan, From whence comest thou? And Satan answered the LORD, and said, From going to and fro in the earth, and from walking up and down in it.

And the LORD said unto Satan, Hast thou considered my servant Job, that *there is* none like him in the earth, a perfect and an upright man, one that feareth God, and escheweth evil? and still he holdeth fast his integrity, although thou movedst me against him, to destroy him without cause.

And Satan answered the LORD, and said, Skin for skin, yea, all that a man hath will he give for his life.

But put forth thine hand now, and touch his bone and his flesh, and he will curse thee to thy face.

And the LORD said unto Satan, Behold, he *is* in thine hand; but save his life.

So went Satan forth from the presence of the LORD, and smote Job with sore boils from the sole of his foot unto his crown.

And he took him a potsherd to scrape himself withal; and he sat down among the ashes.

Then said his wife unto him, Dost thou still retain thine integrity? curse God, and die.

Job 1, v.6–22; 2, v.1–9

Some of God's Courtiers Desert

And it came to pass when the children of men had multiplied that in those days were born unto them beautiful and comely daughters.

And the angels, the children of the heaven, saw and lusted after them, and said to one another: 'Come, let us choose us wives from among the children of men and beget us children.'

And Semjâzâ, who was their leader, said unto them: 'I fear ye will not indeed agree to do this deed, and I alone shall have to pay the penalty of a great sin.'

And they all answered him and said: 'Let us all swear an oath, and all bind ourselves by mutual imprecations not to abandon this plan but to do this thing.'

Then sware they all together and bound themselves by mutual imprecations upon it.

And they were in all two hundred; who descended [in the days] of Jared on the summit of Mount Hermon, and they called it Mount Hermon, because they had sworn and bound themselves by mutual imprecations upon it.

And these are the names of their leaders: Sêmîazâz, their leader, Arâkîba, Râmêêl, Kôkabîêl, Tâmîêl, Râmîêl, Dânêl, Ezêqêêl, Barâqîjâl, Asâêl, Armârôs, Batârêl, Anânêl, Zaqîêl, Samsâpêêl, Satarêl, Tûrêl, Jômjâêl, Sariêl.

These are their chiefs of tens.

And all the others together with them took unto themselves wives, and each chose for himself one, and they began to go in unto them and to defile themselves with them, and they taught them charms and enchantments, and the cutting of roots, and made them acquainted with plants.

And they became pregnant, and they bare great giants, whose height was three thousand ells:

Who consumed all the acquisitions of men. And when men could no longer sustain them,

The giants turned against them and devoured mankind.

And they began to sin against birds, and beasts, and reptiles, and fish, and to devour one another's flesh, and drink the blood.

Then the earth laid accusation against the lawless ones.

And Azâzêl taught men to make swords, and knives, and shields, and breastplates, and made known to them the metals (of the earth) and the art of working them, and bracelets, and ornaments, and the use of antimony, and the beautifying of the eyelids, and all kinds of costly stones, and all colouring tinctures.

And there arose much godlessness, and they committed fornication, and they were led astray, and became corrupt in all their ways.

Semjâzâ taught enchantments, and root-cuttings, Armârôs the resolving of enchantments, Barâqîjâl (taught) astrology, Kôkabîêl the constellations, Ezêqêêl the knowledge of the clouds, Araqiêl the signs of the earth, Shamsiêl the signs of the sun, and Sariêl the course of the moon.

And as men perished, they cried, and their cry went up to heaven....

And then Michael, Uriel, Raphael, and Gabriel looked down from heaven and saw much blood being shed upon the earth, and all lawlessness being wrought upon the earth.

And they said one to another: 'The earth made without inhabitant cries the voice of their crying up to the gates of heaven.

[And now to you, the holy ones of heaven], the souls of men make their suit, saying, "Bring our cause before the Most High".'

And they said to the Lord of the ages: 'Lord of lords, God of gods, King of kings (and God of the ages), the throne of Thy glory (standeth) unto all the generations of the ages, and Thy name holy and glorious and blessed unto all the ages!

Thou hast made all things, and power over all things hast Thou: and all things are naked and open in Thy sight, and all things Thou seest, and nothing can hide itself from Thee.

Thou seest what Azâzêl hath done, who hath taught all unrighteousness on earth and revealed the eternal secrets which were (preserved) in heaven, which men were striving to learn:

And Semjâzâ, to whom Thou hast given authority to bear rule over his associates.

And they have gone to the daughters of men upon the earth, and have slept with the women, and have defiled themselves, and revealed to them all kinds of sins.

And the women have borne giants, and the whole earth has thereby been filled with blood and unrighteousness.

And now, behold, the souls of those who have died are crying and making their suit to the gates of heaven, and their lamentations have ascended: and cannot cease because of the lawless deeds which are wrought on the earth.

And Thou knowest all things before they come to pass, and Thou seest these things and Thou dost suffer them, and Thou dost not say to us what we are to do to them in regard to these.'

Then said the Most High, the Holy and Great One spake, and sent Uriel to the son of Lamech, and said to him:
'Go to Noah and tell him in my name "Hide thyself", and reveal to him the end that is approaching: that the whole earth will be destroyed, and a deluge is about to come upon the whole earth, and will destroy all that is on it.
And now instruct him that he may escape and his seed may be preserved for all the generations of the world.'
And again the Lord said to Raphael: 'Bind Azâzêl hand and foot, and cast him into the darkness: and make an opening in the desert, which is in Dûdâêl, and cast him therein.
And place upon him rough and jagged rocks, and cover him with darkness, and let him abide there for ever, and cover his face that he may not see light.
And on the day of the great judgement he shall be cast into the fire.
And heal the earth which the angels have corrupted, and proclaim the healing of the earth, that they may heal the plague, and that all the children of men may not perish through all the secret things that the Watchers have disclosed and have taught their sons.
And the whole earth has been corrupted through the works that were taught by Azâzêl: to him ascribe all sin.'

The Book of Enoch, ed. and trans. R. H. Charles, 1912

A Pagan Myth in Parallel

And that the Heauens their safety might suspect,
The Gyants now cœlestiall Thrones affect;
Who to the skies congested mountaines reare.
Then *Ioue* with thunder did *Olympus* teare;
Steepe *Pelion* from vnder *Ossa* throwne.
Prest with their burthen their huge bodies growne;
And with her Childrens blood the Earth imbru'd:
Which shee, scarce throughly cold, with life indu'd;
And gaue thereto, t'vphold her Stock; the face
And forme of Man; a God-contemning Race,

[71]

Greedie of slaughter, not to be withstood;
Such, as well shewes, that they were borne of blood.

George Sandys, *Ovid's Metamorphosis Englished, Mythologiz'd and Represented in Figures*, 1632

The War in Heaven Squeezes into the Last Book of the New Testament

And there was war in heaven: Michael and his angels fought against the dragon; and the dragon fought and his angels,

And prevailed not; neither was their place found any more in heaven.

And the great dragon was cast out, that old serpent, called the Devil, and Satan, which deceiveth the whole world: he was cast out into the earth, and his angels were cast out with him.

And I heard a loud voice saying in heaven, Now is come salvation, and strength, and the kingdom of our God, and the power of his Christ: for the accuser of our brethren is cast down, which accused them before our God day and night.

And they overcame him by the blood of the Lamb, and by the word of their testimony; and they loved not their lives unto the death.

Therefore rejoice, *ye* heavens, and ye that dwell in them. Woe to the inhabiters of the earth and of the sea! for the devil is come down unto you, having great wrath, because he knoweth that he hath but a short time.

And when the dragon saw that he was cast unto the earth, he persecuted the woman which brought forth the man *child*.

And to the woman were given two wings of a great eagle, that she might fly into the wilderness, into her place, where she is nourished for a time, and times, and half a time, from the face of the serpent.

And the serpent cast out of his mouth water as a flood after the woman, that he might cause her to be carried away of the flood.

And the earth helped the woman, and the earth opened her mouth, and swallowed up the flood which the dragon cast out of his mouth.

And the dragon was wroth with the woman, and went to make war with the remnant of her seed, which keep the commandments of God, and have the testimony of Jesus Christ.

And I stood upon the sand of the sea, and saw a beast rise up out of the sea, having seven heads and ten horns, and upon his horns ten crowns, and upon his heads the name of blasphemy.

And the beast which I saw was like unto a leopard, and his feet were as *the feet* of a bear, and his mouth as the mouth of a lion: and the dragon gave him his power, and his seat, and great authority.

And I saw one of his heads as it were wounded to death; and his deadly wound was healed: and all the world wondered after the beast.

And they worshipped the dragon which gave power unto the beast: and they worshipped the beast, saying, Who *is* like unto the beast? who is able to make war with him?

And there was given unto him a mouth speaking great things and blasphemies; and power was given unto him to continue forty *and* two months.

And he opened his mouth in blasphemy against God, to blaspheme his name, and his tabernacle, and them that dwell in heaven.

And it was given unto him to make war with the saints, and to overcome them: and power was given him over all kindreds, and tongues, and nations.

And all that dwell upon the earth shall worship him, whose names are not written in the book of life of the Lamb slain from the foundation of the world.

If any man have an ear, let him hear.

He that leadeth into captivity shall go into captivity: he that killeth with the sword must be killed with the sword. Here is the patience and the faith of the saints.

And I beheld another beast coming up out of the earth; and he had two horns like a lamb, and he spake as a dragon.

And he exerciseth all the power of the first beast before him, and causeth the earth and them which dwell therein to worship the first beast, whose deadly wound was healed.

And he doeth great wonders, so that he maketh fire come down from heaven on the earth in the sight of men.

And deceiveth them that dwell on the earth by *the means of* those miracles which he had power to do in the sight of the beast; saying to them that dwell on the earth, that they should make an image to the beast, which had the wound by a sword, and did live.

And he hath power to give life unto the image of the beast, that the image of the beast should both speak, and cause that as many as would not worship the image of the beast should be killed.

And he causeth all, both small and great, rich and poor, free and bond, to receive a mark in their right hand, or in their foreheads:

And that no man might buy or sell, save he that had the mark, or the name of the beast, or the number of his name.

Here is wisdom. Let him that hath understanding count the number of the beast: for it is the number of a man; and his number *is* Six hundred three-score *and* six.

Revelation 12, v.7–17; 13

Origen Shows Celsus how the Christians Piece it all Together

Some such doctrine is hinted at in the story that the serpent, which was the origin of Pherecydes' Ophioneus, was the cause of man's expulsion from the divine paradise, and deceived the female race with a promise of divine power and of attaining to greater things; and we are told that the man followed her also. And who else could be the destroyer in Exodus, which Moses wrote, except the one who is the cause of destruction to those who obey him and who do not resist and struggle against his wickedness? Further, the averter in Leviticus, which the Hebrew text called Azazel, is none other than he. The goat upon whom the lot fell had to be sent forth in the desert so that it should avert evil. For all who, on account of their sin, belong to the portion of the evil power and who are opposed to the people of God's inheritance, are deserted by God. Moreover, take the sons of Belial in Judges. Who other than he can be the one whose sons they are said to be because of their wickedness? A clearer instance than any of these is that in the book of Job, who was even earlier than Moses himself. It is there written that the devil stands near God, and asks for power against Job that he may encompass him with very severe calamities, first by the destruction of all his possessions and his children, and secondly by afflicting Job's whole body with a violent attack of the disease called elephantiasis. I omit the passages from the gospels about the devil tempting the Saviour, that I may not appear to reply to Celsus with arguments on the question which are drawn from more recent scriptures. Moreover, in the last chapters of Job, where the Lord spoke to Job through a whirlwind and clouds the sayings recorded in the book bearing his name, several passages could be taken which deal with the serpent. I have not yet mentioned also the examples from Ezekiel where he speaks, as it were, of Pharaoh, or of Nebuchadnezzar, or of the prince of Tyre, or the passage from Isaiah where the dirge is sung for the king of Babylon. From these scriptures one would learn not a little about evil, of the character of its origin and beginning, and how that evil came to exist because of some who lost their wings and followed the example of the first being who lost his wings.

Origen, *Contra Celsum*; trans. Henry Chadwick, 1953

Shelley Reflects, Unflatteringly, on the Story the Christians Came Up With

Like panic-stricken slaves in the presence of a jealous and suspicious despot, they have tortured themselves ever to devise any flattering sophism by which they might appease him by the most contradictory praises, endeavoring to reconcile omnipotence, and benevolence, and equity in the Author of an Universe, where evil and good are inextricably entangled, and where the most admirable tendencies to happiness and preservation are forever baffled by misery and decay. The Christians, therefore, invented or adopted the Devil to extricate them from this difficulty.

The account they give us of the origin of the Devil is curious: Heaven, according to the popular creed, is a certain airy region inhabited by the Supreme Being and a multitude of inferior spirits. With respect to the situation of it, theologians are not agreed, but it is generally supposed to be placed beyond that remotest constellation of the visible stars. These spirits are supposed, like those which reside in the bodies of animals and men, to have been created by God with foresight of the consequences which would result from the mechanism of their nature. He made them as good as possible, but the nature of the substance out of which they were formed, or the unconquerable laws according to which that substance when created was necessarily modified, prevented them from being so perfect as he could wish. Some say that he gave them free-will; that is, that he made them without any very distinct apprehension of the results of his workmanship, leaving them an active power which might determine them to this or that action, independently of the motives afforded by the regular operation of those impressions which were produced by the general agencies of the rest of his creation. This he is supposed to have done that he might excuse himself to his own conscience for tormenting and annoying these unfortunate spirits when they provoked him by turning out worse than he expected. This account of the origin of evil, to make the best of it, does not seem more complimentary to the Supreme Being, or less derogatory to his omnipotence and goodness than the Platonic scheme.

They then proceed to relate, gravely, that one fine Morning a chief of these spirits took it into his head to rebel against God, having gained over to his cause a third part of the eternal angels who attended upon the Creator and Preserver of Heaven and Earth. After a series of desperate conflicts between those who remained faithful to the ancient dynasty and the insurgents, the latter were beaten and driven into a place called Hell, which was rather their empire than their prison, and where God reserved them, first to be the tempters and then the jailors and tormentors of a new race of beings whom he created under the same conditions of imperfection and with the same foresight of an unfortunate result. The motive of this insurrection is not assigned by any of the early mythological writers.

Percy Bysshe Shelley, 'Essay on the Devil and Devils', c.1819–20

Three

THE FALL FROM HEAVEN

In a word, Mr Milton has indeed made a fine poem,
but it is the devil of a history.

DANIEL DEFOE

I beheld Satan as lightning fall from heaven.

Luke X, v.18

Enter God

My name is knowyn god *and* kynge
My werk for to make · now wyl I wende
in my self restyth my reynenge
it hath no gynnyng ne non ende
And all þat evyr xal haue beynge
it is closyd in my mende
whan it is made at my lykynge
I may it saue I may it shende
After my plesawns
So gret of myth is my pouste
All thyng xal be wrowth be me
I am oo god · in personys thre
knyt in oo substawns.

I am þe trewe trenyte
here walkyng in þis wone
thre personys myself I se
lokyn in me god Alone
I am þe ffadyr of powste
my sone *with* me gynnyth gon
my gost is grace in mageste
weldyth welthe up in hevyn tron
O god thre · I calle
I am fadyr of myth
my sone kepyth ryth
my gost hath lyth
and grace *with*-alle.

My-self begynnyng nevyr dyd take
And endeles I am thorw my*n* owyn myth
now wole I be-gynne my werke to make
Ffyrst I make hevyn *with* sterrys of lyth
In myrth *and* joy eu*er*more to wake
In hevyn I bylde Angell fful bryth
my servau*ntys* to be *and* for my sake
with merth *and* melody worchepe my myth
I belde them in my blysse
Aungell in hevyn evyr mo*re* xal be

[78]

In lyth ful clere bryth as ble
With myrth and song to worchip me
Of joye þei may not mys.

Ludus Coventriae, ed. K. S. Block, 1922

How it Might Have Been

If the qualifying or fountain Spirits had moved, qualified, or acted gently
and lovely, as they *did* before they became creaturely, as they were *univer-
sally* in God before the Creation, then had they generated also a gentle,
lovely, mild and meek Son in them, which would have been *like* to the
Son of God; and then the Light in *Lucifer* and the Light of the Son of God
had been *one* Thing, one qualifying, operating, acting, and affecting, one
and the same lovely Kissing, Embracing, and Struggling.

For the great Light, which is the Heart of God, would have *played*
meekly, mildly, and lovingly with the *small* Light in *Lucifer*, as with a
young Son, for the *little* Son in *Lucifer* should have been the dear *little*
Brother of the Heart of God.

To this End God the Father has created the Angels, that as he is
manifold and *various* in his Qualities, and in his *Alteration* or Variegation
is incomprehensible in his Sport or *Scene* of Love, so the *little* Spirits also,
or the little Lights of the Angels, which are as the Son of God, should
play or sport very *gently* or lovely in the great Light before the Heart of
God, that the Joy in the Heart of God might here be *increased*, and that
so there might be a holy Sport, Scene, or Play in God.

Jakob Böehme (1575–1624); trans. William Law, 1764

None of Us so Bright as He

Cherubyn. Oure lord god in trynyte,
Myrth and lovyng be to the,
Myrth and lovyng ouer al thyng;
ffor thou has made, with thi bidyng,
Heuen, & erth, and all that is,
and giffen vs Ioy that neuer shall mys.
Lord, thou art full mych of myght,
that has maide lucifer so bright;
we loue the, lord, bright ar we,

bot none of vs so bright as he:
He may well hight lucifere,
ffor lufly light that he doth bere.
He is so lufly and so bright
It is grete ioy to se that sight;
We lofe the, lord, *with* all oure thoght,
that sich thyng can make of noght.

Towneley Plays: I. The Creation, ed. George England, 1897

Lucifer Remembers

For, indeed, I was formed the first angel: for when God made the heavens, he took a handful of fire and formed me first, Michael second, Gabriel third, Uriel fourth, Raphael fifth, Nathanael sixth, and other angels of whom I cannot tell the names.

The Gospel of Bartholomew in *The Apocryphal New Testament*, ed. M. R. James, 1924

God Leaves Lucifer in Charge

LUCIFFER: Lorde, through thy mighte thou hast us wrought,
nine orders here that we maye see:
Cherubyn and Seraphin through thy thought;
Thrones and Dominationes in blisse to bee;

with Principates, that order brighte,
and Potestates in blisfull lighte;
also Vertutes, through thy greate mighte,
Angell and also Arkeangelle.

Nine orders here bene witterlye,
that thou hast made here full right.
In thy blisse full brighte the bee,
and I the principall, lorde, here in thy sight.

DEUS: Here have I you wrought with heavenly mighte,
of angells nine orders of great beautye,

iech one with others, as it is righte,
to walke aboute the Trenitie.

Nowe, Luciffer and Lightborne, loke lowely you bee.
The blessinge of my begyninge I geve to my first operacion.
For crafte nor for cuninge, cast never comprehension;
exsalte you not to exelente into high exaltation.
Loke that you tende righte wisely, for hence I wilbe wendinge.
The worlde that is bouth voyde and vayne, I forme in the
      formacion,
with a dongion of darkenes which never shall have endinge.
This worke is nowe well wrought by my devyne formacion.

This worke is well donne, that is soe cleane and cleare.
As I you made of naughte, my blessinge I geve you here.

ANGELIE: Wee thanke thee, lorde, full soveraignely,
    that us hath formed soe cleane and cleare,
    ever in this blesse to byde thee bye.
    Graunte us thy grace ever to byde here.

DEUS: Nowe seeinge I have formed you soe fayer
    and exalted you so exelente –
    and here I set you nexte my cheare,
    my love to you is soe fervente –
    loke you fall not in noe dispaier.
    Touche not my throne by non assente.
    All your beautie I shall appaier,
    and pride fall oughte in your intente.

LUCIFFER: Ney, lorde, that will we not in deed,
    for nothinge tresspasse unto thee.
    Thy greate godhead we ever dreade,
    and never exsaulte ourselves soe hie.
    Thou hast us marked with greate might and mayne,
    in thy blesse evermore to byde and bee,
    in lastinge life our life to leade.
    And bearer of lighte thou hast made me.

LIGHTEBORNE: And I ame marked of that same moulde.
    Loveinge be to our creator

that us hase made gayer then goulde,
under his dieadem ever to indure.

The Chester Mystery Cycle, ed. R. M. Lumiansky and David Mills, 1974

The Green Apples and the Sweet Water

Just as a sour bitter green Apple is *forced* by the Sun, that it becomes very
pleasant or lovely to he eaten, and yet all its Qualities are tasted; so the
Deity keeps its Qualities also, but strives or struggles gently, like a
pleasant lovely Sport or Scene.

But if the qualifying or fountain Spirits should *extoll* or lift up themselves, and penetrate suddenly one into another, driving hard, rubbing
and thronging, crowding or squeezing, then the sweet Water would be
squeezed out, and the fierce Heat would be kindled, and then would rife
up the *Fire* of the seven Spirits, as in *Lucifer*.

Jakob Böehme (1575–1624); trans. William Law, 1764

How Could the Angels Sin?

Having granted the dignity of his person, and the high station in which
he was placed among the heavenly host, it would come then necessarily
to enquire into the nature of his fall, and, above all, a little into the reason
of it: Certain it is, he did fall, was guilty of rebellion and disobedience,
the just effect of pride; sins, which, in that holy place, might well be called
wonderful.

But what to me is more wonderful, and which, I think, will be very
ill-accounted for, is, How came seeds of crime to rise in the angelic nature,
created in a state of perfect unspotted holiness? How was it first found
in a place where no unclean thing can enter? How came ambition, pride,
or envy, to generate there? Could there be offence where there was
no crime? Could untainted purity breed corruption? Could that nature
contaminate and infect, which was always drinking in principles of
perfection?

Happy it is to me, that writing the history, not solving the difficulties
of Satan's affairs, is my province in this work; that I am to relate the fact,
not give reasons for it, or assign causes: if it was otherwise, I should
break off at this difficulty; for I acknowledge I do not see through it;

neither do I think that the great Milton, after all his fine images and lofty excursions upon the subject, has left it one jot clearer than he found it.

Daniel Defoe, *The History of the Devil*, 1726

Aquinas Answers

I answer that, An angel or any other rational creature considered in his own nature, can sin; and to whatever creature it belongs not to sin, such creature has it as a gift of grace, and not from the condition of nature. The reason of this is, because sinning is nothing else than a deviation from that rectitude which an act ought to have; whether sin be taken in natural, artificial, or moral acts. That act alone can never fall short of rectitude, the rule of which is the very virtue of the agent. Were the carver's hand the rule itself of the act of carving, he could not carve the wood otherwise than rightly; but if the rightness of carving be judged by another rule, then the carving may be right or faulty. Now the Divine will is the sole rule of God's act, because it is not referred to any higher end. But every created will has rectitude of act so far only as it is regulated according to the Divine will, to which the last end is to be referred: as every desire of a subordinate ought to be regulated by the will of his superior; for instance, the soldier's will, according to the will of his commander. Thus only in the Divine will can there be no sin; whereas there can be sin in the will of every creature; considering the condition of its nature.

St Thomas Aquinas, *Summa Theologica*; trans. 'by the
Fathers of the English Dominican Province', 1912

Anselm's Student Presses for a Motive

T: You do not doubt that Satan sinned, since he could not be unjustly damned by a just God; but what you are asking is how he sinned. Is that right?

s: That's right.

T: If he had continually held to justice, he would never have sinned nor have been wretched.

s: We believe this.

T: No one holds to justice except by willing what he ought, and no one deserts it except by willing what he ought not.

S: No doubt.

T: Therefore, by willing something which he ought not to have willed at that time, he deserted justice and thereby sinned.

S: That follows, but I want to know what he willed.

De Casu Diaboli, c.1085–90, by Anselm of Canterbury; trans. Jasper Hopkins and Herbert Richardson, 1967

Was It Pride?

LUCIFER: Cert*ys*, it is a semely sight,
Syn that we ar all angels bright,
    and eu*er* in blis to be;
If that ye will behold me right,
    this mastre long*ys* to me.
I am so fare and bright,
of me *com*mys all this light,
    this gam and all this gle;
Agans my grete myght
    may [no]thyng stand [ne] be.

And ye well me behold
I am a thowsand fold
    bright*er* then is the son;
my strengthe may not be told,
    my myght may no thyng kon;
In heuen, therefor, wit I wold
    Above me who shuld won.

ffor I am lord of blis,
ou*er* all this warld, I-wis,
    My myrth is most of all;
the[r]for my will is this,
    master ye shall me call.

Towneley Plays: I. The Creation, ed. George England, 1897

Was It Feudal Ambition?

The Ruler of all, the holy Lord, by the might of his hand had ordained ten orders of angels in whom he firmly trusted that they would follow in his fealty and work his will since he, the holy Lord, had given them intelligence and shaped them with his hands. So blessedly had he established them, and a certain one he had made so strong and so powerful in his intellect, so much he allowed him to command, the highest after himself in the realm of the heavens, so dazzling had he made him, so winsome was his person in the heavens which came to him from the Lord of the angel multitudes – he was comparable to the incandescent stars – he ought to have done homage to the Lord, he ought to have prized his pleasures in the heavens and he ought to have thanked his Lord for the bounty he had allotted him in that existence: then he would have let him rule it in perpetuity. But he turned it to his own worse purpose: he began to stir up trouble against the supreme Ruler of heaven who sits upon the holy throne.

He was dear to our Lord; it could not be concealed from him that his angel began to grow presumptuous, set himself up against his Master, resorted to malicious talk and boasting against him. He would not wait upon God. He declared that his body was radiant and shining, bright and dazzlingly beautiful. He could not find it in his self-esteem to be willing to wait upon God, his Prince, in a status of fealty. To himself it seemed that he had a greater force and strength of fellow-fighters than the holy God could command. Many words of presumption this angel spoke. He contemplated how, through his sole strength, he might create for himself a more powerful throne, more exalted in the heavens. He declared that his self-esteem persuaded him that he should start building in the west and in the north and fortify the construction. He declared that it seemed to him doubtful that he would remain subordinate to God.

'Why must I labour?' he declared. 'There is no need at all for me to have a master. I can work just as many marvels with my hands. I have plenty of power to furnish a goodlier throne, one more exalted in heaven. Why must I wait upon his favour and defer to him in such fealty? I can be a god as well as he. Strong comrades stand by me, heroes hardy of spirit, who will not fail me in the fight. They have chosen me as their master, those confident warriors; with such fellow-fighters one can think out a strategy and with such achieve it. They are my eager friends, loyal in the

[85]

disposition of their hearts. I can be their master and govern in this realm. So it does not seem to me fitting that I need flatter God at all for any advantage. No longer will I be his subordinate.'

Genesis from *Junius* m.s., 10–11th C.; trans. S. A. J. Bradley, 1982

Did He Wish to be God?

But now seeing he was so beauteously and gloriously imaged, or formed as a King in Nature, his beauteous Form and Feature excited him, and so he thought with himself, *I am now God*, and formed or framed out of God, who can vanquish me? Or who can alter or change me? I *myself* will be Lord, and with my Sharpness rule in all Things, and my *Body* shall be the Image, which shall be worshipped; I will prepare and erect for myself a *new* Kingdom: For the whole Circumference, Extent, or Region is mine, *I am God alone*, and none else.

And in his Pride he struck and smote himself with Darkness and Blindness, and made himself a *Devil*, and that he must be, and abide so *eternally*.

Jakob Böehme (1575–1624); trans. William Law, 1764

Satan Could Will Nothing Unjust

T: But Satan was able to will nothing except what was just or what was beneficial. Happiness, which every rational nature desires, consists in these beneficial things.

S: We can recognize this in ourselves, for we will nothing unless we think it is either just or beneficial.

T: Satan was not able to sin by willing justice.

S: That's true.

T: Therefore, he sinned by willing something beneficial, which he neither possessed nor was supposed to will at that time, even though it was able to increase his happiness.

S: This is clear, since there's no other possibility.

T: So I think you now see that he extended his will beyond justice by a disordered willing of something that was more than he had received.

S: I now see clearly that Satan sinned both by willing what he ought not and by not willing what he ought. And it is evident that he did not will more than he should because he was unwilling to hold to justice, but rather that he did not hold to justice because he willed something else;

[86]

and by willing this, he deserted justice, as you have shown in your example of the miser with his bread and money.

T: And when Satan willed what God did not want him to will, he willed inordinately to be like God.

s: But if God cannot be conceived except as a unique being, so that nothing else can be conceived to be like Him, how was Satan able to will what he could not conceive? He was not so obtuse that he thought something else could be conceived to be like God.

T: Even if he did not will to be completely like God, but willed to be something less than God which was against God's will, then he still willed inordinately to be like God – for he willed something by his own will, which was subject to no one else. For it is supposed to be characteristic of God alone to will something by His own will and to obey no higher will.

s: Yes, that's right.

T: And not only did Satan will to be equal to God because he presumed to have his own will, but he even willed to be greater than God by willing what God did not will for him to will, for he placed his own will above the will of God.

s: This leaves me satisfied.

T: Now then, from the above arguments, I think I have shown you that Satan freely departed from willing what he ought and so justly lost what he had. This is because he freely and unjustly willed what he didn't have and what he wasn't supposed to will.

s: Nothing is more evident.

St Anselm, *De Casu Diaboli*; trans. Jasper Hopkins and Herbert Richardson, 1967

Equality and Likeness

Without doubt the angel sinned by seeking to be as God. This can be understood in two ways: firstly, by equality; secondly, by likeness. He could not seek to be as God in the first way; because by natural knowledge he knew full well that this was impossible: and there was no habit preceding his first sinful act, nor any passion fettering his mind, so as to lead him to choose what was impossible by failing in some particular; as sometimes happens in ourselves. And even supposing it were possible, it would be against the natural desire; because there exists in everything the natural desire of preserving its own nature; which would not be preserved were it to be changed into another nature. Consequently, no creature of a lower order can ever covet the grade of a higher nature; just as an ass does not desire to be a horse: for were it to be so upraised, it would cease to be itself. But herein the imagination plays us false; for one is liable to think that, because a man seeks to occupy a higher grade as to accidentals, which can increase without the destruction of the subject, he can also seek a higher grade of nature, to which he could not attain without ceasing to exist. Now it is quite evident that God surpasses the angels, not merely in accidentals, but also in degree of nature; and one angel, another. Consequently it is impossible for one angel of lower degree to desire equality with a higher; and still more to covet equality with God.

To desire to be as God according to likeness can happen in two ways. In one way, as to that likeness whereby everything is made to be likened unto God. And so, if anyone desire in this way to be Godlike, he commits no sin; provided that he desires such likeness in proper order, that is to say, that he may obtain it of God. But he would sin were he to desire to be like unto God even in the right way, as of his own, and not of God's power. In another way one may desire to be like unto God in some respect which is not natural to one; as if one were to desire to create heaven and earth, which is God's attribute; in which desire there would be sin. It was in this way that the devil desired to be as God. Not that he desired to resemble God by being subject to no one else absolutely; for so he would be desiring his own *not-being*; since no creature can exist except by holding its existence under God. But he desired resemblance with God in this respect, – by desiring, as his last end of beatitude, something which he could attain by the virtue of his own nature, turning his appetite away from supernatural beatitude, which is attained by God's grace.

St Thomas Aquinas, *Summa Theologica*;
trans. 'by the Fathers of the English Dominican Province', 1912

Sufficient Beatitude

He it is that made the world, with all things sensible and intelligible therein, whose chief work the spirits were, to whom He gave an understanding, making them capable of His contemplation, and combining them in one holy and united society, which we call the City of God, holy and heavenly, wherein God is their life, their nutriment, and their beatitude. He gave a free election also unto those intellectual natures, that if they would forsake Him, who was their bliss, they should presently be enthralled in misery. And foreknowing that certain of the angels, proudly presuming that themselves were sufficient beatitude to themselves, would forsake Him, and all good with Him, He did not abridge them of His power, knowing it a more powerful thing to make good use of such as were evil, than to exclude evil for altogether. Nor had there been any evil at all, but that those spirits (though good, yet mutable) which were formed by the omnipotent and unchangeable Deity, procured such evil unto themselves by sin: which very sin, proved that their natures were good in themselves. For if they had not been so (although inferior to the Maker) their apostasy had not fallen so heavily upon them. For as blindness being a defect, proves plainly that the eye was made to see, the excellency of the eye being hereby made more apparent (for otherwise blindness were no defect), so those natures enjoying God, proved themselves to be created good, in their very fall, and that eternal misery that fell upon them for forsaking God, who has given assurance of eternal perseverance unto those that stood firm in Him, as a fit reward for their constancy.

St Augustine, *De Civitate Dei*, c.413–26 AD; trans. John Healey, 1610

Was It Resentment of Adam?

But the devil said: Suffer me, and I will tell thee how I was cast down into this place and how the Lord did make man.

I was going to and fro in the world, and God said unto Michael: Bring me a clod from the four corners of the earth, and water out of the four rivers of paradise. And when Michael brought them *God* formed Adam in the regions of the east, and shaped the clod which was shapeless, and stretched sinews and veins *upon it* and established it with joints; and he worshipped him, himself for his own sake first, because he was the image of God, *therefore* he worshipped him.

And when I came from the ends of the earth Michael said: Worship thou the image of God, which he hath made according to his likeness. But I said: I am fire of fire, I was the first angel formed, and shall I worship clay and matter?

And Michael saith to me: Worship, lest God be wroth with thee. But I said to him: God will not be wroth with me; but I will set my throne over against his throne, and I will be as he is. Then was God wroth with me and cast me down, having commanded the windows of heaven to be opened.

The Gospel of Bartholomew in *The Apocryphal New Testament*,
ed. M. R. James, 1924

Lucifer Now Swelling Against Mankinde

Man, (whom from Dust he did so lately raise)
Subsists of Soule and Body: That which still
Doth comprehend the Vnderstanding, Will,
And Memorie, namely the Soule, (Partaker
Of those great Gifts) is th' Image of the Maker.
    The nature of the Body, though it be
Common with Beasts, yet doth it disagree
In shape and figure; for with Eyes erected
It beholds Heav'n, whilest Brutes haue Looks deiected.
    This compos'd Man is as a ligament,
And folding vp in a small continent,
Some part of all things which before were made;
For in this Microcosme are stor'd and layd
Connexiuely, as things made vp and bound,
Corporeall things with incorporeall. Found
There likewise are in his admired quality,
Things fraile and mortall, mixt with Immortality.
Betweene those Creatures that haue Reason, and
Th' Irrationall, who cannot vnderstand,
There is a Nature intermediate,
That 'twixt them doth of both participate.
For with the blessed Angels, in a kinde,
Man doth partake of an intelligent Minde;
A Body with the Beasts, with Appetite,
It to preserue, feed, cherish, and delight,
And procreate it's like in shapes and features.
    Besides, Man hath aboue all other Creatures,
That whereas they their Appetites pursue,
(As solely sencible of what's in view,
And gouern'd by instinct) Mans eminence
Hath pow'r to sway his Will from common Sence;
And (besides Earthly things) himselfe apply
To contemplate things mysticall and hye.
And though his Excellence doth not extend
To those miraculous Gifts which did commend
Great *Lucifer* at first, in his Majoritie,
Yet in one honour he hath iust prioritie,
Before all Angels to aduance his Seed:

Since God from all eternitie decreed,
That his owne Sonne, the euerlasting *Word*
(Who to all Creatures *Being* doth afford,
By which they first were made) should Heav'n forsake,
And in his Mercy, humane Nature take.
Not that he by so doing should depresse
The Diuine Majestie, and make it lesse;
But Humane frailtie to exalt and raise
From corrupt earth, his glorious Name to praise.
Therefore he did insep'rably vnite
His Goodhood to our Nature, vs t' excite
To magnifie his Goodnesse. This Grace showne
Vnto Mankinde, was to the Angels knowne,
That such a thing should be they all expected,
Not knowing how or when't would be effected.
    With Pride and Enuy *Lucifer* now swelling
Against Mankinde, whom from his heav'nly Dwelling,
He seemes in supernaturall Gifts t' out-shine,
(Man being but Terrene, and himselfe Diuine)
Ambitiously his Hate encreasing still,
Dares to oppose the great Creators Will:
As holding it against his Iustice done,
That th' Almighties sole begotten Sonne,
Mans nature to assume purpos'd and meant,
And not the Angels, much more excellent.
Therefore he to that height of madnesse came,
A stratagem within himselfe to frame,
To hinder this irrevocable Deed,
Which God from all eternitie decreed.
And that which most seem'd to inflame his spleene
And arrogance, was, That he had foreseene,
That many Men by God should be created,
And in an higher eminence instated,
Of place and Glory, than himselfe or those
His Angels, that this great Worke 'gan t' oppose.
Disdaining and repining, that of Men
One should be God Omnipotent; and then,
That others, his Inferiors in degree,
Should out-shine him in his sublimitie.
    In this puft Insolence and timp'anous Pride,
He many Angels drew vnto his side,
(Swell'd with the like thoughts.) Ioyntly these prepare

To raise in Heav'n a most seditious Warre.
He will be the *Trines* Equall, and maintaine,
Ouer the Hierarchies (at least) to raigne.
　'Tis thus in *Esay* read: *I will ascend*
Into the Heav'ns, and there my Pow'r extend;
Exalt my Throne aboue, and my aboad
Shall be made equall with the Stars of God.
Aboue the Clouds I will my selfe apply,
Because I will be like to the Most-Hye.
　To this great Pride, doth the Arch-Angell rise
In boldest opposition, and replies,
(Whose name is *Michael*) Why what is he,
That like the Lord our God aspires to be?
In vaine, *ô Lucifer*, thou striv'st t' assay,
That we thine innovations should obey;
Who know, As God doth purpose, be, it must;
He cannot will, but what is good and iust:
Therefore, with vs, That God and Man adore,
Or in this place thou shalt be found no more.

Thomas Heywood, *The Hierarchie of the Blessed Angells*, 1635

All His Talk About Love

The truth is I slipped by mere carelessness into saying that the Enemy really loves the humans. That, of course, is an impossibility. He is one being, they are distinct from Him. Their good cannot be His. All His talk about Love must be a disguise for something else – He must have some *real* motive for creating them and taking so much trouble about them. The reason one comes to talk as if He really had this impossible Love is our utter failure to find out that real motive. What does He stand to make out of them? That is the insoluble question. I do not see that it can do any harm to tell you that this very problem was a chief cause of Our Father's quarrel with the Enemy. When the creation of man was first mooted and when, even at that stage, the Enemy freely confessed that he foresaw a certain episode about a cross, Our Father very naturally sought an interview and asked for an explanation. The Enemy gave no reply except to produce the cock-and-bull story about disinterested love which He has been circulating ever since. This Our Father naturally could not accept. He implored the Enemy to lay His cards on the table, and gave Him every opportunity. He admitted that he felt a real anxiety to know the secret; the Enemy replied 'I wish with all my heart that you did'. It was, I imagine, at this stage in the interview that Our Father's disgust at such an unprovoked lack of confidence caused him to remove himself an infinite distance from the Presence with a suddenness which has given rise to the ridiculous enemy story that he was forcibly thrown out of Heaven. Since then, we have begun to see why our Oppressor was so secretive. His throne depends on the secret. Members of His faction have frequently admitted that if ever we came to understand what He means by Love, the war would be over and we should re-enter Heaven.

C. S. Lewis, *The Screwtape Letters*, 1942

Satan Gathers His Hosts

> ... but *Satan* with his Powers
> Farr was advanc't on winged speed, an Host
> Innumerable as the Starrs of Night,
> Or Starrs of Morning, Dew-drops, which the Sun
> Impearls on every leaf and every flouer.
> Regions they passd, the mightie Regencies
> Of Seraphim and Potentates and Thrones
> In thir triple Degrees, Regions to which
> All thy Dominion, *Adam*, is no more
> Then what this Garden is to all the Earth,
> And all the Sea, from one entire globose
> Stretcht into Longitude; which having past
> At length into the limits of the North
> They came, and *Satan* to his Royal seat
> High on a Hill, farr blazing, as a Mount
> Rais'd on a Mount, with Pyramids and Towrs
> From Diamond Quarries hewn, and Rocks of Gold,
> The Palace of great *Lucifer*, (so call
> That Structure in the Dialect of men
> Interpreted) which not long after, hee
> Affecting all equality with God,
> In imitation of that Mount whereon
> *Messiah* was declar'd in sight of Heav'n,
> The Mountain of the Congregation calld;
> For thither he assembl'd all his Train,
> Pretending so commanded to consult
> About the great reception of thir King,

Thither to come, and with calumnious Art
Of counterfeted truth thus held thir ears.

    Thrones, Dominations, Princedoms, Vertues, Powers,
If these magnific Titles yet remain
Not meerly titular, since by Decree
Another now hath to himself ingross't
All Power, and us eclipst under the name
Of King anointed, for whom all this haste
Of midnight march, and hurried meeting here,
This onely to consult how we may best
With what may be devis'd of honours new
Receive him coming to receive from us
Knee-tribute yet unpaid, prostration vile,
Too much to one, but double how endur'd,
To one and to his image now proclaimd?
But what if better counsels might erect
Our minds and teach us to cast off this Yoke?
Will ye submit your necks, and chuse to bend
The supple knee? ye will not, if I trust
To know ye right, or if ye know your selves
Natives and Sons of Heav'n possest before
By none, and if not equal all, yet free,
Equally free; for Orders and Degrees
Jarr not with liberty, but well consist.
Who can in reason then or right assume
Monarchie over such as live by right
His equals, if in power and splendor less,
In freedom equal? or can introduce
Law and Edict on us, who without law
Erre not, much less for this to be our Lord,
And look for adoration to th' abuse
Of those Imperial Titles which assert
Our being ordaind to govern, not to serve?

John Milton, *Paradise Lost*, Book V, 1667

Stadtholder Lucifer Stands up for Angels' Rights

LUCIFER: Lord Rafael, I nor threat
  Nor wrath deserve. My heroes both by God
  And Lucifer have sworn, and under oaths

To Heaven have raised this standard thus aloft.
Let rumors, therefore, far and wide be spread
Throughout the Heavens: I battle under God
For the defence of these His choristers,
And for the Charter and the Rights which were
Their lawful heritage ere Adam saw
The rising sun: yea, ere o'er Paradise
The daylight shone. No human power, no yoke
Of man, shall plague the necks of Spirits, nor shall
The Angel world, like any servile slave,
Support the throne of Adam with its neck,
Unfettered now, unless in some abyss
The Heavens shall bury us, together with
The sceptres, crowns, and splendors that to us
The Godhead from His bosom gave, for time
And for eternity! Let burst what will,
I shall maintain the holy Right, compelled
By high necessity, thus urged at length,
Though much against my will, by the complaints
And mournful groans of myriad tongues. Go hence,
This message bear unto the Father, whom
I serve, and under whom I thus unfurl
This warlike standard for our Fatherland.

RAFAEL: O Stadtholder, why thus disguise thy thoughts
Before the all-seeing Eye? Thy purpose thou
Canst not conceal. The rays flashed from His face
Lay bare the darkness, the ambition that
Thy pregnant spirit reveals in all its shape.
And lo! even now its travail hath begun
This monster to bring forth. Where shall I hide
Me in my fright? How rise my hairs with fear!
Thou erring Morning-star, oh! spare thyself!
Thou canst not satisfy Omniscience
With such deceit.

LUCIFER: Ambition? Say me, then,
Where hath my duty suffered through neglect?

RAFAEL: What hast thou in thy heart of hearts resolved! –
'I shall mount up from here beneath, through all
The clouds, aye, even above God's galaxies,
Into the top of Heaven, like unto God
Himself; nor shall the beams of mercy fall
On any Power, unless before my seat

It kneel in homage down! No majesty
Shall sceptre dare, nor crown, unless I shall
First grant it leave out of my towering throne!'
Oh! hide thy face. Fall down and fold thy wings.
Have care to know a higher Power above.

LUCIFER: How now? Am I not then God's Stadtholder?

RAFAEL: That art thou, and from the unbounded Realm
Thou didst receive a power determinate.
Thou rulest in His name.

LUCIFER: Alas! how long?
Until Prince Adam shall make us ashamed:
When he, placed o'er the Angel world, shall from
The bounteous bosom of the Deity
His crown receive, and take his seat by God.

RAFAEL: Even though the sovran Lord should thus divide
His power with His inferiors; though He should
Command that man upon his head shall place
The brightest crown; his consecrate the Chief
Of Spirits, o'er all that crown or sceptre bear,
Or e'er shall bear: learn thou submissively
To bow 'neath God's decree.

LUCIFER: That is the stone
Whereon this battle-axe shall whet its edge.

Joost van den Vondel, *Lucifer*, 1654;
horribly trans. by Leonard Charles Van Noppen, 1898

An Angel Chooses Sides

I knew him. He was the most beautiful of all the Seraphim. He shone
with intelligence and daring. His great heart was big with all the virtues
born of pride: frankness, courage, constancy in trial, indomitable hope.
Long, long ago, ere Time was, in the boreal sky where gleam the seven
magnetic stars, he dwelt in a palace of diamond and gold, where the air
was ever tremulous with the beating of wings and with songs of triumph.
Iahveh, on his mountain was jealous of Lucifer. You both know it: angels
like unto men feel love and hatred quicken within them. Capable, at times,
of generous resolves, they too often follow their own interests and yield
to fear. Then, as now, they showed themselves, for the most part,
incapable of lofty thoughts, and in the fear of the Lord lay their sole
virtue. Lucifer, who held vile things in proud disdain, despised this rabble

of commonplace spirits for ever wallowing in a life of feasts and pleasure. But to those who were possessed of a daring spirit, a restless soul, to those fired with a wild love of liberty, he proffered friendship, which was returned with adoration. These latter deserted in a mass the Mountain of God and yielded to the Seraph the homage which That Other would fain have kept for himself alone.

I ranked among the Dominations, and my name, Alaciel, was not unknown to fame. To satisfy my mind – that was ever tormented with an insatiable thirst for knowledge and understanding – I observed the nature of things, I studied the properties of minerals, air and water. I sought out the laws which govern nature, solid or ethereal, and after much pondering I perceived that the Universe had not been formed as its pretended Creator would have us believe; I knew that all that exists, exists of itself and not by the caprice of Iahveh; that the world is itself its own creator and the spirit its own God. Henceforth I despised Iahveh for his imposture, and I hated him because he showed himself to be opposed to all that I found desirable and good: liberty, curiosity, doubt. These feelings drew me towards the Seraph. I admired him, I loved him. I dwelt in his light. When at length it appeared that a choice had to be made between him and That Other I ranged myself on the side of Lucifer and knew no other aim than to serve him, no other desire than to share his lot.

Anatole France, *La Révolte des Anges*, 1914; trans. Emilie Jackson, 1914

Angry and Irate

Then God grew angry and irate against the multitude whom he had previously dignified with beauty and splendour. He fashioned for the renegade a home – one in exile – as reward for his effort: the howlings of hell and harsh afflictions. That outcasts' prison, deep and cheerless, our Lord commanded the guardians of souls to suffer when he knew it to be ready, enveloped in endless night, filled with torment, inundated with fire and intense cold, smoke and ruddy flame. He then commanded the punitive horrors to multiply throughout that desolate abode. Unrelentingly they had mustered a league of enmity against God, for which an unrelenting reward befell them.

Violent of mood, they declared that they meant to have a kingdom and that they could easily do so. This hope played them false when the Ruler, the high King of the heavens, raised up his most sublime hands against that army. They were not competent, those rash and wicked beings, to share power with the ordaining Lord, but glorious God put a stop to their pride and humbled their bombast. Once he was angered he balked the evil-doers of victory and of rule, of dignity and of wealth, and he despoiled the foe of happiness, of peace and of all pleasure and of shining glory, and by the powers of his own self he vigorously avenged his injury upon his adversaries by forcible dispossession. He had a stern heart, unrelentingly provoked; with hostile hands he snatched up his enemies and crushed them in his grasp, irate in his heart, and cut off his adversaries from their native home, from the heavenly mansions.

Genesis from *Junius* m.s., 10th–11th C.; trans. S. A. J. Bradley, 1982

Michael and Lucifer Cross Swords

They ended parle, and both addressed for fight
Unspeakable; for who, though with the tongue
Of Angels, can relate, or to what things
Lik'n on earth conspicuous, that may lift
Human imagination to such highth
Of Godlike Power: for likest Gods they seemd,
Stood they or mov'd, in stature, motion, arms
Fit to decide the Empire of great Heav'n.
Now wav'd thir fierie Swords, and in the Aire
Made horrid Circles; two broad Suns thir Shields
Blaz'd opposite, while expectation stood
In horror; from each hand with speed retir'd
Where erst was thickest fight, th' Angelic throng,
And left large field, unsafe within the wind
Of such commotion, such as to set forth
Great things by small, if Natures concord broke,
Among the Constellations warr were sprung,
Two Planets rushing from aspect maligne
Of fiercest opposition in mid Skie,
Should combat, and thir jarring Sphears confound.
Together both with next to Almightie Arme,
Uplifted imminent one stroke they aimd
That might determin, and not need repeate,
As not of power, at once; nor odds appeerd
In might or swift prevention; but the sword
Of *Michael* from the Armorie of God
Was giv'n him temperd so, that neither keen

Nor solid might resist that edge: it met
The sword of *Satan* with steep force to smite
Descending, and in half cut sheere, nor staid,
But with swift wheele reverse, deep entring shar'd
All his right side; then *Satan* first knew pain,
And writh'd him to and fro convolv'd; so sore
The griding sword with discontinuous wound
Passd through him, but th' Ethereal substance clos'd
Not long divisible, and from the gash
A stream of Nectarous humor issuing flowd
Sanguin, such as Celestial Spirits may bleed,
And all his Armour staind ere while so bright.
Forthwith on all sides to his aide was run
By Angels many and strong, who interpos'd
Defence, while others bore him on thir Shields
Back to his Chariot, where it stood retir'd
From off the files of Warr; there they him laid
Gnashing for anguish and despite and shame
To find himself not matchless, and his pride
Humbl'd by such rebuke, so farr beneath
His confidence to equal God in power.
Yet soon he heald; for Spirits that live throughout
Vital in every part, not as frail Man
In Entrailes, Heart or Head, Liver or Reines,
Cannot but by annihilating die;
Nor in thir liquid texture mortal wound
Receive, no more then can the fluid Aire:
All Heart they live, all Head, all Eye, all Eare,
All Intellect, all Sense, and as they please,
They Limb themselves, and colour, shape or size
Assume, as likes them best, condense or rare.

John Milton, *Paradise Lost*, Book VI, 1667

This Great Angelomachy

But shall I now tell
The Weapons, Engines, and Artillerie
Vsed in this great Angelomachy.
   No Lances, Swords, nor Bombards they had then,
Or other Weapons now in vse with men;

None of the least materiall substance made,
Spirits by such giue no offence or aid.
Onely spirituall Armes to them were lent,
And these were call'd *Affection* and *Consent*.
Now both of these, in *Lucifer* the Diuell
And his Complyes, immoderate were, and euill.
Those that in *Michael* the Arch-Ange'll raign'd,
And his good Spirits, meekely were maintain'd,
Squar'd and directed by th' Almighties will
(The Rule by which they fight, and conquer still.)
   Lucifer, charg'd with insolence and spleene;
When nothing but Humilitie was seene,
And Reuerence towards God, in *Michaels* brest,
By which the mighty Dragon he supprest.
   Therefore this dreadfull battell fought we finde
By the two motions of the Will and Minde;
Which, as in men, so haue in Angels sway:
Mans motion in his body liues, but they
Haue need of no such Organ. This to be,
Both *Averroes* and *Aristotle* agree.

Thomas Heywood, *The Hierarchie of the Blessed Angells*, 1635

The War Proceeds

For three days our host swept onward over the ethereal plains. Above our heads streamed the black standards of revolt. And now, behold, the Mountain of God shone rosy in the orient sky and our chief scanned with his eyes the glittering ramparts. Beneath the sapphire walls the foe was drawn up in battle array, and, while we marched clad in our iron and bronze, they shone resplendent in gold and precious stones.

Their gonfalons of red and blue floated in the breeze, and lightning flashed from the points of their lances. In a little while the armies were only sundered one from the other by a narrow strip of level and deserted ground, and at this sight even the bravest shuddered as they thought that there in bloody conflict their fate would soon be sealed.

Angels, as you know, never die. But when bronze and iron, diamond point or flaming sword tear their ethereal substance, the pain they feel is more acute than men may suffer, for their flesh is more exquisitely delicate; and should some essential organ be destroyed, they fall inert and, slowly decomposing, are resolved into clouds and during long æons float insensible in the cold ether. And when at length they resume spirit and form they fail to recover full memory of their past life. Therefore it is but natural that angels shrink from suffering, and the bravest among them is troubled at the thought of being reft of light and sweet remembrance. Were it otherwise the angelic race would know neither the delight of battle nor the glory of sacrifice. Those who, before the beginning of Time, fought in the Empyrean for or against the God of Armies, would have taken part without honour in mock battles, and it would not now become me to say to you, my children, with rightful pride:

'Lo, I was there!'

Lucifer gave the signal for the onset and led the assault. We fell upon the enemy, thinking to destroy him then and there and carry the sacred citadel at the first onslaught. The soldiers of the jealous God, less fiery, but no whit less firm than ours, remained immovable. The Archangel Michael commanded them with the calmness and resolution of a mighty spirit. Thrice we strove to break through their lines, thrice they opposed to our ironclad breasts the flaming points of their lances, swift to pierce the stoutest cuirass. In millions the glorious bodies fell. At length our right wing pierced the enemy's left and we beheld the Principalities, the Powers, the Virtues, the Dominations and the Thrones, turn and flee in full career; while the Angels of the Third Choir, flying distractedly above them, covered them with a snow of feathers mingled with a rain of blood. We sped in pursuit of them amid the debris of chariots and broken weapons, and we spurred their nimble flight. Suddenly a storm of cries amazed us. It grew louder and nearer. With desperate shrieks and triumphal clamour the right wing of the enemy, the giant archangels of the Most High, had flung themselves upon our left flank and broken it. Thus we were forced to abandon the pursuit of the fugitives and hasten to the rescue of our own shattered troops. Our prince flew to rally them, and re-established the conflict. But the left wing of the enemy, whose ruin he had not quite consummated, no longer pressed by lance or arrow, regained courage, returned, and faced us yet again. Night fell upon the dubious field. While under the shelter of darkness, in the still, silent air stirred ever and anon by the moans of the wounded, his forces were resting from their toils, Lucifer began to make ready for the next day's battle. Before dawn the trumpets sounded the reveille. Our warriors surprised the enemy at the hour of prayer, put them to rout, and long and fierce was the carnage that ensued. When all had either fallen or fled, the Archangel Michael, none with him save a few companions with four wings of flame, still resisted the onslaughts of a countless host. They fell back ceaselessly opposing their breasts to us, and Michael still displayed an impassible countenance. The sun had run a third of its course when we commenced to scale the Mountain of God. An arduous ascent it was: sweat ran from our brows, a dazzling light blinded us. Weighed down with steel, our feathery wings could not sustain us, but hope gave us wings that bore us up. The beautiful Seraph, pointing with glittering hand, mounting ever higher and higher, showed us the way. All day long we slowly clomb the lofty heights which at evening were robed in azure, rose and violet. The starry host appearing in the sky seemed as the reflection of our own arms. Infinite silence reigned above us. We went on, intoxicated with hope; all at once from the darkened sky lightning darted forth, the thunder muttered, and from the cloudy mountain-top fell fire from Heaven. Our helmets, our breastplates were running with flames, and our bucklers broke under bolts sped by invisible hands. Lucifer, in the storm of fire, retained his haughty mien. In vain the lightning smote him; mightier than ever he stood erect, and still defied the foe.

Anatole France, *La Révolte des Anges*, 1914; trans. Emilie Jackson, 1914

The Rebels Plan to Dislodge God With Cannon-Fire

Whereto with look compos'd *Satan* repli'd.
Not uninvented that, which thou aright
Beleivst so main to our success, I bring;
Which of us who beholds the bright surface
Of this Ethereous mould whereon we stand,
This continent of spacious Heav'n, adornd
With Plant, Fruit, Flour Ambrosial, Gemms and Gold,
Whose Eye so superficially surveyes
These things, as not to mind from whence they grow
Deep under ground, materials dark and crude,
Of spiritous and fierie spume, till toucht
With Heavens ray, and temperd they shoot forth
So beauteous, op'ning to the ambient light.
These in thir dark Nativitie the Deep
Shall yeild us, pregnant with infernal flame,
Which into hollow Engins long and round
Thick-rammd, at th' other bore with touch of fire
Dilated and infuriate shall send forth
From farr with thundring noise among our foes
Such implements of mischief as shall dash
To pieces, and orewhelm whatever stands

Adverse, that they shall fear we have disarmd
The Thunderer of his onely dreaded bolt.
Nor long shall be our labour, yet ere dawne,
Effect shall end our wish. Mean while revive;
Abandon fear; to strength and counsel joind
Think nothing hard, much less to be despaird.
He ended, and his words thir drooping chere
Enlight'nd, and thir languisht hope reviv'd.
Th' invention all admir'd, and each, how hee
To be th' inventer missd, so easie it seemd
Once found, which yet unfound most would have thought
Impossible: yet haply of thy Race
In future dayes, if Malice should abound,
Some one intent on mischief, or inspir'd
With dev'lish machination might devise
Like instrument to plague the Sons of men
For sin, on Warr and mutual slaughter bent.
Forthwith from Councel to the work they flew,
None arguing stood, innumerable hands
Were ready, in a moment up they turnd
Wide the Celestial soile, and saw beneath
Th' originals of Nature in thir crude
Conception; Sulfurous and Nitrous Foame
They found, they mingl'd, and with suttle Art,
Concocted and adjusted they reduc'd
To blackest grain, and into store conveyd:
Part hidd'n veins diggd up (nor hath this Earth
Entrails unlike) of Mineral and Stone,
Whereof to found thir Engins and thir Balls
Of missive ruin; part incentive reed
Provide, pernicious with one touch to fire.

John Milton, *Paradise Lost*, Book VI, 1667

Blake Continues the War in the London Sky

And the clouds & fires pale roll'd round in the night of Enitharmon,
Round Albion's cliffs & London's walls: still Enitharmon slept.
Rolling volumes of grey mist involve Churches, Palaces, Towers;
For Urizen unclasp'd his Book, feeding his soul with pity.

The youth of England, hid in gloom, curse the pain'd heavens, compell'd
Into the deadly night to see the form of Albion's Angel.
Their parents brought them forth, & aged ignorance preaches, canting
On a vast rock, perciev'd by those senses that are clos'd from thought;
Bleak, dark, abrupt it stands & overshadows London city.
They saw his boney feet on the rock, the flesh consum'd in flames;
They saw the Serpent temple lifted above, shadowing the Island white;
They heard the voice of Albion's Angel howling in flames of Orc,
Seeking the trump of the last doom.

Above the rest the howl was heard from Westminster louder & louder:
The Guardian of the secret codes forsook his ancient mansion,
Driven out by the flames of Orc; his furr'd robes & false locks
Adhered and grew one with his flesh, and nerves & veins shot thro' them.
With dismal torment sick, hanging upon the wind, he fled
Groveling along Great George Street thro' the Park gate: all the soldiers
Fled from his sight: he drag'd his torments to the wilderness.

Thus was the howl thro' Europe!
For Orc rejoic'd to hear the howling shadows;
But Palamabron shot his lightnings, trenching down his wide back;
And Rintrah hung with all his legions in the nether deep.

Enitharmon laugh'd in her sleep to see (O woman's triumph!)
Every house a den, every man bound: the shadows are fill'd
With spectres, and the windows wove over with curses of iron:
Over the doors 'Thou shalt not,' & over the chimneys 'Fear' is written:
With bands of iron round their necks fasten'd into the walls
The citizens, in leaden gyves the inhabitants of suburbs
Walk heavy; soft and bent are the bones of villagers.

Between the clouds of Urizen the flames of Orc roll heavy
Around the limbs of Albion's Guardian, his flesh consuming:
Howlings & hissings, shrieks & groans, & voices of despair
Arise around him in the cloudy heavens of Albion.   Furious,

The red limb'd Angel siez'd in horror and torment

The Trump of the last doom; but he could not blow the iron tube!
Thrice he assay'd presumptuous to awake the dead to Judgment.

A mighty Spirit leap'd from the land of Albion,
Nam'd Newton: he siez'd the trump & blow'd the enormous blast!
Yellow as leaves of Autumn, the myriads of Angelic hosts
Fell thro' the wintry skies seeking their graves,
Rattling their hollow bones in howling and lamentation.

William Blake, 'Europe, A Prophecy', 1794

The Son of God in His Chariot

At once the Four spred out thir Starrie wings
With dreadful shade contiguous, and the Orbes
Of his fierce Chariot rowld, as with the sound
Of torrent Floods, or of a numerous Host.
Hee on his impious Foes right onward drove,
Gloomie as Night; under his burning Wheeles
The stedfast Empyrean shook throughout,
All but the Throne it self of God. Full soon
Among them he arriv'd; in his right hand
Grasping ten thousand Thunders, which he sent
Before him, such as in thir Soules infixd
Plagues; they astonisht all resistance lost,
All courage; down thir idle weapons dropd;
Ore Shields and Helmes, and helmed heads he rode
Of Thrones and mighty Seraphim prostrate,
That wishd the Mountains now might be again
Thrown on them as a shelter from his ire.
Nor less on either side tempestuous fell
His arrows, from the fourfold-visag'd Foure,
Distinct with eyes, and from the living Wheels,
Distinct alike with multitude of eyes;
One Spirit in them rul'd, and every eye
Glar'd lightning, and shot forth pernicious fire
Among th' accurst, that witherd all thir strength,
And of thir wonted vigour left them draind,
Exhausted, spiritless, afflicted, fall'n.
Yet half his strength he put not forth, but checkd
His Thunder in mid Volie, for he meant

Not to destroy, but root them out of Heav'n:
The overthrown he rais'd, and as a Herd
Of Goats or timerous flock together throngd
Drove them before him Thunder-strook, persu'd
With terrors and with furies to the bounds
And Crystal wall of Heav'n, which op'ning wide,
Rowld inward, and a spacious Gap disclos'd
Into the wastful Deep; the monstrous sight
Strook them with horror backward, but farr worse
Urg'd them behind; headlong themselves they threw
Down from the verge of Heav'n, Eternal wrauth
Burnd after them to the bottomless pit.

John Milton, *Paradise Lost*, Book VI, 1667

When I Fell Back

LUCIFER: As it is, I know
   Something of pity. When I reeled in Heaven,
   And my sword grew too heavy for my grasp,
   Stabbing through matter, which it could not pierce
   So much as the first shell of, – toward the throne;
   When I fell back, down, – staring up as I fell, –
   The lightnings holding open my scathed lids,
   And that thought of the infinite of God,
   Hurled after to precipitate descent;
   When countless angel faces still and stern
   Pressed out upon me from the level heavens
   Adown the abysmal spaces, and I fell
   Trampled down by your stillness, and struck blind
   By the sight within your eyes, – 'twas then I knew
   How ye could pity, my kind angelhood!

Elizabeth Barrett Browning, 'A Drama of Exile' in *Poems*, 1844

If All the Trees Were Writers

If all Trees were Writers or Clerks, and all Branches were Pens, and all
Hills were Books, and all Waters were Ink, yet they could not *sufficiently
describe* the lamentable Misery which *Lucifer*, together with his Angels, has

brought into his Place, or whole Space of that World wherein he was created.

For he has made the House of *Light* to be a House of *Darkness*, and the House of *Joy* to be a House of Mourning, Lamentation, and *Sadness*; that which was the House of Pleasure, Delight, Vivifying, and *Refreshing*, he has made to be a House of Thirst and *Hunger*; the House of *Love* to be a House of eternal *Enmity*; and the House of *Meekness* to be a House of Knocking, Rumbling, *Thundering* and Lightning; the House of *Peace* to be a House of Lamenting, and eternal *Howling*; the House of *Laughing* to be a House of eternal Trembling and *Horror*; the Birth or Geniture of Light, Munificence, and *Well-doing*, to be an eternal hellish Pain and *Torment*; the *Food of pleasing Relish* to be an eternal Abomination and Stink, a *Loathing* of all Fruits; and the House of *Lebanon* and Cedars to be a stony and *rocky* House of Fire; the *sweet* Scent or Relish to be a *Stink*, and a House of Ruin and Desolation, an End of all Good; the *divine Love* to be a black, cold, hot, eating, *corroding*, and yet not consuming Devil, who is an *Enmity* against God and his Angels; and so he has all the heavenly Hosts or Armies against him.

Jakob Böehme (1575–1624); trans. William Law, 1764

Four

SO GLOZ'D THE TEMPTER

Eve and Adam had a garden
Everything was great
Until one day a voice said, Pardon
Miss, my name is Snake

Forbidden Fruit

Thus he endeavours to entangle Truths: And when he
cannot possibly destroy its substance, he cunningly
confounds its apprehensions; that from the inconsistent
and contrary determinations thereof, collective
impieties, and hopeful conclusions may arise,
there's no such thing at all.

SIR THOMAS BROWNE

Genesis

Now the serpent was more subtil than any beast of the field which the LORD God had made. And he said unto the woman, Yea, hath God said, Ye shall not eat of every tree of the garden?

And the woman said unto the serpent, We may eat of the fruit of the trees of the garden:

But of the fruit of the tree which *is* in the midst of the garden, God hath said, Ye shall not eat of it, neither shall ye touch it, lest ye die.

And the serpent said unto the woman, Ye shall not surely die:

For God doth know that in the day ye eat thereof, then your eyes shall be opened, and ye shall be as gods, knowing good and evil.

And when the woman saw that the tree *was* good for food, and that it *was* pleasant to the eyes, and a tree to be desired to make *one* wise, she took of the fruit thereof, and did eat, and gave also unto her husband with her; and he did eat.

Genesis 3, v.1–6

The Subtle Serpent

EVE: What animal is this that coils and winds
His oblique course toward me?   How he rears
Aloft his scaly mottled head; and forth
Launches his triple tongue: his glittering eye
Glares with an indescribable fire, that burns
And scintillates, and seems to scorch my soul
With horrible fascination.   Now his neck,
Burnished with many-flashing gold, he bends,
And swells his purple breast, whereon bright stars
Flash, dazzling with strange lustre.   Now he rests
His cheek upon his flexile neck, and looks
In cautious calmness round him; while, behind,
His length of tail against the opposing light
Burns like a fallen comet.   Whatsoe'er
His name or nature, this way straight he comes,
And spreads his mazy labyrinths athwart
My chosen path, and with his spiral coils
Surrounds me.   Lo, he lifts his sparkling head,

And doth address himself to motion like
As he would speak; – I wonder if he can!

Hugo Grotius, *Adamus Exul*, 1601;
trans. unreliably by the Rev. Francis Foster Barham, 1839

If Ye Will Bite . . .

SERPENS: Of þis Appyl yf ȝe wyl bute
Evyn as god is so xal ȝe be
wys of Connyng as I ȝow plyte
lyke on to god in al degre
Su*n*ne *and* mone *and* sterrys bryth
ffysch *and* foule boþe sond *and* se
at ȝo*ur* byddyng bothe day *and* nyth
all thynge xal be in ȝowr*e* powste
ȝe xal be goddys per*e*
Take þis appyl in þin hond
and to byte þer of þou ffond
take a nother to þin husbond
þer of haue þou no dwer*e*.
EUA: So wys as god is in his gret mayn
and ffelaw in ku*n*nyng ffayn wold I be.
SERPENS: Ete þis Appyl *and* in certeyn
þ*at* I am trewe sone xalt þou se.

From *Ludus Coventriae*, ed. K. S. Block, 1922

The Serpent Questions God's Generosity

EVE: But thou, mysterious one, whose mental power
Seems conversant with wonders, canst thou tell
What hidden virtues in this tree reside?
SATAN: Its very name may teach thee. Is it not
The immortal, the inexplicable bliss
Of knowledge, perfect knowledge? How divine
To know all good and evil; to discern
All mysteries, like a god, in this new world!
Evil is only evil when unknown;
Known, it refines to good. What happiness,

What intellectual rapture, to compel
Into one gorgeous focus all the charms
Of knowledge, elsewhere scattered, vague, confused!
By this keen sight to make the universe
Transparent as fine ether; by this vision,
To see all causes, all effects conjoined
In their superb complexity!   O Queen
Of Earth! say, is it not the chiefest good
To know all godlike truth, all evil lies,
So as to mock deception, and deride
The assaults of demon tempters?   To the mind
This world is but one glittering mirror, which
Reflects its swift ideas, and refines
And multiplies with Iris-tinctured hues.
Is not the height of strong intelligence
Thus to anatomise all things, and from all
Educe new powers occult?   The more it finds
More earnestly it seeks, and spurns at rest –
That empty, pitiful calmness of content.
It tramples with ambition-wingèd feet
The low, base boundaries of mortality,
Burns to know more, and bursts the bars of fate,
And death itself, to explain the august unknown.
All that it has is nothing to the intense
Glorious concupiscence of all it wants –
Always the greater share.   One God there is,
Whose mind, without this enterprise of toil,
Can form its own ideas, and vindicate,
None daring him to question.   Thus He knows,
Or thinks He knows, all arts and sciences.
Who shall disprove him by the test of fact?
He stands alone.   To other thinking souls,
Either he grants not power to apprehend
The fair discourse of reason, or he grants
This boon of liberal thought, all manacled,
Halt, withered, blind, perplexed with chafing doubts,
Haggard with fears, hoodwinked from heaven's free light,
Masked in incomprehensibility.
By the same words in which he promises
This blessing, in postponed futurity,
Doth he deny it now?   Then break you off
The terms of the agreement, and forestall

At once these promised honours.   What stern heaven
Denies so niggardly this generous tree
Shall instant yield you.   Dare but this one act,
And share the secret of the Deity.
Ay, well he knows, when once this pregnant fruit
Shall pass your lips, therewith your souls shall gain
Such inaccessible brightness, as shall melt
The last faint cloud of error, doubt, and dread.
Then shall ye be as gods, knowing yourselves,
All things which swell magnificence of power,
Beauty, and grace ineffable.   For this
His dark prohibitory law he makes;
For this he cast o'er your imperial heart
This chilling fear of death; that, conscience-smit
With panic terrors at all touch of ill,
You might forego the good, lest you become
Emancipated demi-gods.   Believe
For once in honest counsel, and be sure
No opportunity of fair revenge
Escapes the Thunderer.   That which thou designest
Do quickly, lest you lose your crown for aye;
Perchance e'en now the pole-sustaining king
Meditates revocation of a boon
So full of ominous rivalship.   He thinks
To cheat you of the prize: be not forestalled
In this fair fraud.   To acquire or maintain
Glory and high renown, requires keen wit
And dashing strokes of shrewd finessing art.
Believe me – well to hoard your former store,
And build thereon accumulations fresh
Of glorious superstructure, so secured,
That your aerial castles never fall
By their own weight and crush their dreaming lord –
Gain is the best security 'gainst loss.
One single taste will make the apotheosis,
And raise you from the woman to the goddess.

Hugo Grotius, *Adamus Exul*, 1601;
trans. Rev. Francis Foster Barham, 1839

Satan the Fruiterer Describes the
Forbidden Tree

Can this choyce Tree so great an ill contain?
Pish! don't believ't, for all such thoughts are vain.
No, no, I'le tell you why he did forbid
You to come neer this Tree; such virtue's hid
Within its golden Fruit, should you but tast,
You'd be for ever happy, ever blest;
No longer then in stupid Ignorance
Should you enchained be; then happy glance
From brighter Light, would in your souls arise:
See then would your blind Soul; and dimmer eyes
Made bright, discern betwixt all good, and ill,
Transcendant knowledge then your brains would fill,
You should be wise, and like the Gods; this knew
They well, should happen (if you eat) to you:
Therefore they did prohibit you this Tree,
Lest you by eating like themselves should be.
Thus should you dye, fear not such feare-crows now;
See how the glit'ring Fruit doth lade each bow:
Look how they're painted with Vermilion dye
Like golden starres set in a verdant Skye,
Or like the blushing Roses, which are seen
New peeping forth thorow a verdant Screen.
Look how the Apples blush, see how they stand,
See how the boughs, bow down to kiss thine hand;
All's at thy choyce: which on this fair-spread Tree,
(Come tell me Eve!) most liked is by thee?
See, here's a fine one, this? or this best likes
Thee? do but look what many pretty strikes
Of red, and yellow paint; here's one that skipps
Unto thy mouth: here thine own Cherry lips
Are answered; thy softer skin thou mayst
Here find; but there's a mellow one whose tast
So sweet – delicious that 'twil ravish quite
Thy looser sences with extream delight;
Thou hast such choyce thou knowst not which to choose:
Come take this on my word, try what accrews

By this: here take it, prethee eat, and try
If thou a Goddesse art not by, and by.

Samuel Pordage, *Mundorum Explicatio*, 1661

Look On Me Who Have Touched & Tasted

Lead then, said *Eve*. Hee leading swiftly rowld
In tangles, and made intricate seem strait,
To mischief swift. Hope elevates, and joy
Bright'ns his Crest: as when a wandring Fire
Compact of unctuous vapor, which the Night
Condenses, and the cold invirons round,
Kindl'd through agitation to a Flame,
Which oft, they say, some evil Spirit attends,
Hovering and blazing with delusive Light,
Misleads th' amaz'd Night-wanderer from his way
To Boggs and Mires, and oft through Pond or Poole,
There swallowd up and lost, from succour farr.
So glisterd the dire Snake, and into fraud
Led *Eve* our credulous Mother, to the Tree
Of prohibition, root of all our woe;
Which when she saw, thus to her guide she spake.

Serpent, we might have spar'd our coming hither,
Fruitless to mee, though Fruit be here to excess,
The credit of whose vertue rest with thee,
Wondrous indeed, if cause of such effects.
But of this Tree we may not taste nor touch;
God so commanded, and left that Command
Sole Daughter of his voice; the rest, we live
Law to our selves, our Reason is our Law.

To whom the Tempter guilefully repli'd.
Indeed? hath God then said that of the Fruit
Of all these Garden Trees ye shall not eate,
Yet Lords declar'd of all in Earth or Aire?

To whom thus *Eve* yet sinless. Of the Fruit
Of each Tree in the Garden we may eate,
But of the Fruit of this fair Tree amidst
The Garden, God hath said, Ye shall not eate
Thereof, nor shall ye touch it, least ye die.

She scarse had said, though brief, when now more bold

The Tempter, but with shew of Zeale and Love
To Man, and indignation at his wrong,
New part puts on, and as to passion mov'd,
Fluctuats disturbd, yet comely, and in act
Rais'd, as of som great matter to begin.
As when of old som Orator renound
In *Athens* or free *Rome*, where Eloquence
Flourishd, since mute, to som great cause addrest,
Stood in himself collected, while each part,
Motion, each act won audience ere the tongue,
Somtimes in highth began, as no delay
Of Preface brooking through his Zeal of Right:
So standing, moving, or to highth upgrown
The Tempter all impassiond thus began.

 O Sacred, Wise, and Wisdom-giving Plant,
Mother of Science, Now I feel thy Power
Within me cleere, not onely to discerne
Things in thir Causes, but to trace the wayes
Of highest Agents, deemd however wise.
Queen of this Universe, doe not believe
Those rigid threats of Death; ye shall not Die:
How should ye? by the Fruit? it gives you Life
To Knowledge: By the Threatner? look on mee,
Mee who have toucht and tasted, yet both live,
And life more perfet have attaind then Fate
Meant me, by ventring higher then my Lot.
Shall that be shut to Man, which to the Beast
Is op'n? or will God incense his ire
For such a petty Trespass, and not praise
Rather your dauntless vertue, whom the pain
Of Death denounc't, whatever thing Death be,
Deterrd not from atchieving what might leade
To happier life, knowledge of Good and Evil;
Of good, how just? of evil, if what is evil
Be real, why not known, since easier shunnd?
God therefore cannot hurt ye, and be just;
Not just, not God; not feard then, nor obeid:
Your feare it self of Death removes the feare.
Why then was this forbid? Why but to awe,
Why but to keep ye low and ignorant,
His worshippers; he knows that in the day
Ye Eate thereof, your Eyes that seem so cleere,

[116]

Yet are but dim, shall perfetly be then
Op'nd and cleerd, and yee shall be as Gods,
Knowing both Good and Evil as they know.
That yee should be as Gods, since I as Man,
Internal Man, is but proportion meet,
I of brute human, yee of human Gods.
So ye shall die perhaps, but putting off
Human, to put on Gods, death to be wisht,
Though threat'nd, which no worse then this can bring.
And what are Gods that Man may not become
As they, participating God-like food?
The Gods are first, and that advantage use
On our belief, that all from them proceeds;
I question it, for this fair Earth I see,
Warmd by the Sun, producing every kind,
Them nothing: If they all things, who enclos'd
Knowledge of Good and Evil in this Tree,
That whoso eats thereof, forthwith attains
Wisdom without their leave? and wherein lies
Th' offence, that Man should thus attain to know?
What can your knowledge hurt him, or this Tree
Impart against his will if all be his?
Or is it envie, and can envie dwell
In heav'nly brests? these, these and many more
Causes import your need of this fair Fruit.
Goddess humane, reach then, and freely taste.

   He ended, and his words replete with guile
Into her heart too easie entrance won:
Fixt on the Fruit she gaz'd, which to behold
Might tempt alone, and in her ears the sound
Yet rung of his perswasive words, impregnd
With Reason, to her seeming, and with Truth;
Meanwhile the hour of Noon drew on, and wak'd
An eager appetite, rais'd by the smell
So savorie of that Fruit, which with desire,
Inclinable now grown to touch or taste,
Sollicited her longing eye . . .

John Milton, Paradise Lost, Book IX, 1667

A New Serpent Tempts a New Eve on Venus

'Then listen,' said Weston's body. 'Have you understood that to wait for Maleldil's voice when Maleldil wishes you to walk on your own is a kind of disobedience?'

'I think I have.'

'The wrong kind of obeying itself can be a disobeying.'

The Lady thought for a few moments and then clapped her hands. 'I see,' she said, 'I see! Oh, how old you make me. Before now I have chased a beast for mirth. And it has understood and run away from me. If it had stood still and let me catch it, that would have been a sort of obeying – but not the best sort.'

'You understand very well. When you are fully grown you will be even wiser and more beautiful than the women of my own world. And you see that it might be so with Maleldil's biddings.'

'I think I do not see quite clearly.'

'Are you certain that He really wishes to be always obeyed?'

'How can we not obey what we love?'

'The beast that ran away loved you.'

'I wonder,' said the Lady, 'if that is the same. The beast knows very well when I mean it to run away and when I want it to come to me. But Maleldil has never said to us that any word or work of His was a jest. How could our Beloved need to jest or frolic as we do? He is all a burning joy and a strength. It is like thinking that He needed sleep or food.'

'No, it would not be a jest. That is only a thing like it, not the thing itself. But could the taking away of your hand from His – the full growing up – the walking in your own way – could that ever be perfect unless you had, if only once, *seemed* to disobey Him?'

'How could one *seem* to disobey?'

'By doing what He only *seemed* to forbid. There might be a commanding which He wished you to break.'

'But if He told us we were to break it, then it would be no command. And if He did not, how should we know?'

'How wise you are growing, beautiful one,' said Weston's mouth. 'No. If He told you to break what He commanded, it would be no true command, as you have seen. For you are right, He makes no jests. A real disobeying, a real branching out, this is what He secretly longs for: secretly, because to tell you would spoil all.'

'I begin to wonder,' said the Lady after a pause, 'whether you are so much older than I. Surely what you are saying is like fruit with no taste! How can I step out of His will save into something that cannot be wished? Shall I start trying not to love Him – or the King – or the beasts? It would be like trying to walk on water or swim through islands. Shall I try not to sleep or to drink or to laugh? I thought your words had a meaning. But now it seems they have none. To walk out of His will is to walk into nowhere.'

'That is true of all His commands except one.'

'But can that one be different?'

'Nay, you see of yourself that it is different. These other commands of His – to love, to sleep, to fill this world with your children – you see for yourself that they are good. And they are the same in all worlds. But the command against living on the Fixed Island is not so. You have already learned that He gave no such command to my world. And you cannot see where the goodness of it is. No wonder. If it were really good, must He not have commanded it to all worlds alike? For how could Maleldil not command what was good? There is *no* good in it. Maleldil Himself is showing you that, this moment, through your own reason. It is mere command. It is forbidding for the mere sake of forbidding.'

'But why . . . ?'

'In order that you may break it. What other reason can there be? It is not good. It is not the same for other worlds. It stands between you and all settled life, all command of your own days. Is not Maleldil showing you as plainly as He can that it was set up as a test – as a great wave you have to go over, that you may become really old, really separate from Him.'

'But if this concerns me so deeply, why does He put none of this into my mind? It is all coming from you, Stranger. There is no whisper, even, of the Voice saying Yes to your words.'

'But do you not see that there cannot be? He longs – oh, how greatly He longs – to see His creature become fully itself, to stand up in its own reason and its own courage even against Him. But how can He *tell* it to do this? That would spoil all. Whatever it did after that would only be one more step taken *with* Him. This is the one thing of all the things He desires in which He must have no finger. Do you think He is not weary of seeing nothing but Himself in all that He has made? If that contented Him, why should He create at all? To find the Other – the thing whose will is no longer His – that is Maleldil's desire.'

'If I could but know this –'

'He must not tell you. He cannot tell you. The nearest He can come to telling you is to let some other creature tell it for Him. And behold, He has done so. Is it for nothing, or without His will, that I have journeyed through Deep Heaven to teach you what He would have you know but must not teach you Himself?'

C. S. Lewis, Perelandra, 1943

Corruption Comes to an Indian Isle

He looked at her as she fluttered round him with outspread arms and dancing eyes; and sighed, while she welcomed him in tones of such wild sweetness, as suited a being who had hitherto conversed with nothing but the melody of birds and the murmur of waters. With all her ignorance, however, she could not help testifying her amazement at his arriving at the isle without any visible means of conveyance. He evaded answering her on this point, but said, 'Immalee, I come from a world wholly unlike that you inhabit, amid inanimate flowers, and unthinking birds. I come from a world where all, as I do, think and speak.' Immalee was speechless with wonder and delight for some time; at length she exclaimed, 'Oh, how they must love each other! even I love my poor birds and flowers, and the trees that shade, and the waters that sing to me!' The stranger smiled. 'In all that world, perhaps there is not another being beautiful and innocent as you. It is a world of suffering, guilt, and care.' It was with much difficulty she was made to comprehend the meaning of these words, but when she did, she exclaimed, 'Oh, that I could live in that world, for I would make every one happy!' – 'But you could not, Immalee,' said the stranger; 'this world is of such extent that it would take your whole life to traverse it, and, during your progress, you never could be conversant with more than a small number of sufferers at a time, and the evils they undergo are in many instances such as you or no human power could relieve.' At these words, Immalee burst into an agony of tears. 'Weak, but lovely being,' said the stranger, 'could your tears heal the corrosions of disease? – cool the burning throb of a cancered heart? – wash the pale slime from the clinging lips of famine? – or, more than all, quench the fire of forbidden passion?' Immalee paused aghast at this enumeration, and could only faulter out, that wherever she went, she would bring her flowers and sunshine among the healthy, and they should all sit under the shade of her own tamarind. That for disease and death, she had long been accustomed to see flowers wither and die their beautiful death of nature. 'And perhaps,' she added, after a reflective pause, 'as I have often known them to retain their delicious odour even after they were faded,

[120]

perhaps *what thinks* may live too after the form has faded, and that is a thought of joy.' Of passion, she said she knew nothing, and could propose no remedy for an evil she was unconscious of. She had seen flowers fade with the season, but could not imagine why the flower should destroy itself. 'But did you never trace a worm in the flower?' said the stranger, with the sophistry of corruption. 'Yes,' answered Immalee, 'but the worm was not the native of the flower; its own leaves never could have hurt it.' This led to a discussion, which Immalee's impregnable innocence, though combined with ardent curiosity and quick apprehension, rendered perfectly harmless to her. Her playful and desultory answers, – her restless eccentricity of imagination, – her keen and piercing, though ill-poised intellectual weapons, – and, above all, her instinctive and unfailing *tact* in matters of right and wrong, formed altogether an array that discomfited and baffled the tempter more than if he had been compelled to encounter half the *wranglers* of the European academies of that day. In the logic of the schools he was well-versed, but in this logic of the heart and of nature, he was 'ignorance itself.' It is said, that the 'awless lion' crouches before 'a maid in the pride of her purity.' The tempter was departing gloomily, when he saw tears start from the bright eyes of Immalee, and caught a wild and dark omen from her innocent grief. 'And you weep, Immalee?' 'Yes,' said the beautiful being, 'I always weep when I see the sun set in clouds; and will you, the sun of my heart, set in darkness too? and will you not rise again? will you not?' and, with the graceful confidence of pure innocence, she pressed her red delicious lip to his hand as she spoke. 'Will you not? I shall never love my roses and peacocks if you do not return, for they cannot speak to me as you do, nor can I give them one thought, but you can give me many. Oh, I would like to have many thoughts about *the world that suffers*, from which you came; and I believe you came from it, for, till I saw you, I never felt a pain that was not pleasure; but now, it is all pain when I think you will not return.' – 'I will return,' said the stranger, 'beautiful Immalee, and will shew you, at my return, a glimpse of that world from which I come, and in which you will soon be an inmate.' – 'But shall I see you there,' said Immalee, 'otherwise how shall I *talk thoughts*?' – 'Oh yes, – oh certainly.' – 'But why do you repeat the same words twice; *your once* would have been enough.' – 'Well then, yes.' – 'Then take this rose from me, and let us inhale its odour together, as I say to my friend in the fountain, when I bend to kiss *it*; but my friend withdraws *its* rose before I have tasted it, and I leave mine on the water. Will you not take my rose,' said the beautiful suppliant, bending towards him. 'I will,' said the stranger; and he took a flower from the cluster Immalee held out to him. It was a withered one. He snatched it, and hid it in his breast. 'And will you go without a canoe across that dark sea?' said Immalee. – 'We shall meet again, and meet in the *world of suffering*,' said the stranger. – 'Thank you, – oh, thank you,' repeated Immalee, as she saw him plunge fearless amid the surf. The stranger answered only, 'We shall meet again.' Twice, as he parted, he threw a glance at the beautiful and isolated being; a lingering of humanity trembled round his heart, – but he tore the withered rose from his bosom, and to the waved arm and angel-smile of Immalee, he answered, 'We shall meet again.'

Seven mornings and evenings Immalee paced the sands of her lonely isle, without seeing the stranger. She had still his promise to console her, that they should meet in the world of suffering; and this she repeated to herself as if it was full of hope and consolation. In this interval she tried to educate herself for her introduction into this world, and it was beautiful to see her attempting, from vegetable and animal analogies, to form some image of the incomprehensible destiny of man. In the shade she watched the withering flower. – 'The blood that ran red through its veins yesterday is purple to-day, and will be black and dry to-morrow,' she said; 'but it feels no pain – it dies patiently, – and the ranunculus and tulip near it are untouched by grief for their companion, or their colours would not be so resplendent. But can it be thus in the world that thinks? Could I see *him* wither and die, without withering and dying along with him. Oh no! when that flower fades, I will be the dew that falls over him!'

She attempted to enlarge her comprehension, by observing the animal world. A young loxia had fallen dead from its pendent nest; and Immalee, looking into the aperture which that intelligent bird forms at the lower extremity of the nest to secure it from birds of prey, perceived the old ones with fire-flies in their small beaks, their young one lying dead before them. At this sight Immalee burst into tears. – 'Ah! you cannot weep,' she said, 'what an advantage I have over you! You eat, though your young one, your own one, is dead; but could I ever drink of the milk of the cocoa, if *he* could no longer taste it? I begin to comprehend what he said – to think, then, is to suffer – and a world of thought must be a world of pain! But how delicious are these tears! Formerly I wept for pleasure – but there is a pain sweeter than pleasure, that I never felt till I beheld *him*. Oh! who would not think, to have the joy of tears?'

But Immalee did not occupy this interval solely in reflection; a new anxiety began to agitate her; and in the intervals of her meditation and her tears, she searched with avidity for the most glowing and fantastically wreathed shells to deck her arms and hair with. She changed her drapery of flowers every day, and never thought them fresh after the first hour;

then she filled her largest shells with the most limpid water, and her hollow cocoa nuts with the most delicious figs, interspersed with roses, and arranged them picturesquely on the stone bench of the ruined pagoda. The time, however, passed over without the arrival of the stranger, and Immalee, on visiting her fairy banquet the next day, wept over the withered fruit, but dried her eyes, and hastened to replace them.

She was thus employed on the eighth morning, when she saw the stranger approach; and the wild and innocent delight with which she bounded towards him, excited in him for a moment a feeling of gloomy and reluctant compunction, which Immalee's quick susceptibility traced in his pausing step and averted eye. She stood trembling in lovely and pleading diffidence, as if intreating pardon for an unconscious offence, and asking permission to approach by the very attitude in which she forbore it, while tears stood in her eyes ready to fall at another repelling motion. This sight 'whetted his almost blunted purpose.' She must learn to suffer, to qualify her to become my pupil, he thought. 'Immalee, you weep,' he added, approaching her. 'Oh yes!' said Immalee, smiling like a spring morning through her tears; 'you are to teach me to suffer, and I shall soon be very fit for your world – but I had rather weep for you, than smile on a thousand roses.' – 'Immalee,' said the stranger, repelling the tenderness that melted him in spite of himself, 'Immalee, I come to shew you something of the world of thought you are so anxious to inhabit, and of which you must soon become an inmate. Ascend this hill where the palm-trees are clustering, and you shall see a glimpse of part of it.' – 'But I would like to see the whole, and all at once!' said Immalee, with the natural avidity of thirsty and unfed intellect, that believes it can swallow all things, and digest all things. 'The whole, and all at once!' said her conductor, turning to smile at her as she bounded after him, breathless and glowing with newly excited feeling. 'I doubt the part you will see to-night will be more than enough to satiate even your curiosity.' As he spoke he drew a tube from his vest, and bid her apply it to her sight.

Charles Robert Maturin, *Melmoth the Wanderer*, 1820

A Great Wonder

So he led her on with lies and by cunning coaxed on the woman in that mischief until the snake's thinking began to seethe up inside her – the ordaining Lord had defined for her a frailer resolution – so that she began to let her mind go along with those counsels. Therefore she received from the abhorrent foe, against the word of the Lord, the tree of death's injurious fruit. A deed more evil was not defined for men. It is a great wonder that eternal God, the Prince, would ever tolerate it that so many a servant should be led astray by lies as happened because of those counsels.

Genesis from *Junius* m.s., 10th–11th C., trans. S. A. J. Bradley, 1982

A Devilish Disclaimer

CAIN: Ah! didst *thou* tempt my mother?
LUCIFER: I tempt none,
  Save with the truth: was not the tree, the tree
  Of knowledge? and was not the tree of life
  Still fruitful: Did *I* bid her pluck them not?
  Did *I* plant things prohibited within
  The reach of beings innocent, and curious
  By their own innocence? I would have made ye
  Gods; and even He who thrust ye forth, so thrust ye
  Because 'ye should not eat the fruits of life,
  And become gods as we.' Were those his words?
CAIN: They were, as I have heard from those who heard them,
  In thunder.
LUCIFER: Then who was the demon? He
  Who would not let ye live, or he who would
  Have made ye live for ever in the joy
  And power of knowledge?
CAIN: Would they had snatch'd both
  The fruits, or neither!
LUCIFER: One is yours already,
  The other may be still.
CAIN: How so?
LUCIFER: By being
  Yourselves, in your resistance. Nothing can
  Quench the mind, if the mind will be itself
  And centre of surrounding things – 'tis made
  To sway.
CAIN: But didst thou tempt my parents?
LUCIFER: I?
  Poor clay – what should I tempt them for, or how?
CAIN: They say the serpent was a spirit.
LUCIFER: Who
  Saith that? It is not written so on high:

The proud One will not so far falsify,
Though man's vast fears and little vanity
Would make him cast upon the spiritual nature
His own low failing. The snake *was* the snake –
No more; and yet not less than those he tempted,
In nature being earth also – *more* in *wisdom*,
Since he could overcome them, and foreknew
The knowledge fatal to their narrow joys.
Think'st thou I'd take the shape of things that die?

CAIN: But the thing had a demon?

LUCIFER: He but woke one
In those he spake to with his forky tongue.
I tell thee that the serpent was no more
Than a mere serpent: ask the cherubim
Who guard the tempting tree. When thousand ages
Have roll'd o'er your dead ashes, and your seed's,
The seed of the then world may thus array
Their earliest fault in fable, and attribute
To me a shape I scorn, as I scorn all
That bows to him, who made things but to bend
Before his sullen, sole eternity;
But we, who see the truth, must speak it. Thy
Fond parents listen'd to a creeping thing,
And fell.

Lord Byron, *Cain*, 1822

Thou Wicked Worm

DEUS: Thou wyckyd worm ffull of pryde
ffowle envye syt bi þi syde
Vpon þi gutt þou xalt glyde
As werm wyckyd in kende
tyl a mayden in medyl-erth be born
þou ffende I warn þe be-forn
thorwe here þi hed xal be to-torn
On wombe a-wey þou wende.

DIABOLUS: At þi byddyng ffowle I falle
I krepe hom to my stynkyng stalle
helle pyt *and* hevyn halle
xul do þi byddyng bone

I ffalle down here a ffowle freke
ffor þis ffalle I gynne to qweke
with a ffart my brech I breke
my sorwe comyth ful sone.

Ludus Coventriae, ed. K. S. Block, 1922

If I Was a Serpent

God on this occasion, it is said, assigned a punishment to the Serpent that
its motion should be as it now is along the ground upon its belly. We are
given to suppose that, before this misconduct, it hopped along upon its
tail, a mode of progression which, if I was a serpent, I should think the
severer punishment of the two.

Percy Bysshe Shelley, 'Essay on the Devil and Devils', c.1819–20

A Heretical Version

And I asked of the Lord: When Satan fell, in what place dwelt he? And
he answered me: My Father changed his appearance because of his pride,
and the light was taken from him, and his face became like unto heated
iron, and his face became wholly like that of a man: and he drew with
his tail the third part of the angels of God, and was cast out from the seat
of God and from the stewardship of the heavens. And Satan came down
into this firmament, and he could find (make) no rest for himself nor for
them that were with him. And he asked the Father, saying: Have patience
with me and I will pay thee all. And the Father had mercy on him and
gave him rest and them that were with him, as much as they would even
unto seven days.

And so sat he in the firmament and commanded the angel that was
over the air and him that was over the waters, and they raised the earth
up and it appeared dry: and he took the crown of the angel that was over
the waters, and of the half thereof he made the light of the moon and of
the half the light of the stars: and of the *precious* stones he made all the
hosts of the stars.

And thereafter he made the angels his ministers according to the order
of the form of the Most High, and by the commandment of the invisible
Father *he made* thunder, rain, hail, and snow.

And he sent forth angels to be ministers over them. And he commanded the earth to bring forth every beast for food (fatling), and every creeping thing, and trees and herbs: and he commanded the sea to bring forth fishes, and the fowls of the heaven.

And he devised furthermore and made man in his likeness, and commanded the (*or* an) angel of the third heaven to enter into the body of clay. And he took thereof and made another body in the form of a woman, and commanded the (*or* an) angel of the second heaven to enter into the body of the woman. But the angels lamented when they beheld a mortal shape upon them and that they were unlike in shape. And he commanded them to do the deed of the flesh in the bodies of clay, and they knew not how to commit sin.

Then did the contriver of evil devise in his mind to make paradise, and he brought the man and woman into it. And he commanded to bring a reed, and the devil planted it in the midst of paradise, and so did the wicked devil hide his device that they knew not his deceit. And he came in and spake unto them, saying: Of every fruit which is in paradise eat ye, but of the fruit of the knowledge of good and evil eat not.

And after that I, John, asked of the Lord, saying: How say men that Adam and Eve were created by God and set in paradise to keep the commandments of the Father, and were delivered unto death? And the Lord said to me: Hearken, John, beloved of my Father; foolish men say thus in their deceitfulness that my Father made bodies of clay: but by the Holy Ghost made he all the powers of the heavens, and holy ones were found having bodies of clay because of their transgression, and therefore were delivered unto death.

The Book of John the Evangelist in *The Apocryphal New Testament*,
ed. M. R. James, 1924

The Tempter Recalls His Later Triumphs

By Me *Cain* offer'd up his *Brothers* gore,
A *Sacrifice* far worse then that before;
I saw him fling the *stone*, as if he meant
At once his *Murder*, and his *Monument*,
And laught to see (for 'twas a goodly show)
The *Earth* by her *first Tiller* fatned so.
I drove proud *Pharaoh* to the parted *sea*;
He, and his *Host* drank up cold death by *Mee*;
By *Me* rebellious arms fierce *Corah* took,

And *Moses* (curse upon that *Name!*) forsook;
Hither (ye know) almost *alive* he came
Through the cleft *Earth*; Ours was his *Fun'eral Flame*.
By *Me* – but I lose time, methinks, and should
Perform new acts whilst I relate the old . . .

Abraham Cowley, *Davideis* in *Poems*, 1656

The Tempter, the Prophet, His Wife and Her Hair

And when Satan learned this, he took the guise of a bread-seller, and it was as if by chance that my wife met him and asked him for bread thinking that it was that sort of man.

But Satan said to her: 'Give me the value, and then take what thou wishest'.

Whereupon she answered saying: 'Where shall I get money? Dost thou not know what misfortune happened to me. If thou hast pity, show it to me; if not, thou shalt see'.

And he replied saying: 'If you did not deserve this misfortune, you would not have suffered all this.

Now, if there is no silver piece in thine hand, give me the hair of thine head and take three loaves of bread for it, so that ye may live on these for three days'.

Then said she to herself: 'What is the hair of my head in comparison with my starving husband?'

And so after having pondered over the matter, she said to him: 'Rise and cut off my hair'.

Then he took a pair of scissors and took off the hair of her head in the presence of all, and gave her three loaves of bread.

Then she took them and brought them to me. And Satan went behind her on the road, hiding himself as he walked and troubling her heart greatly.

And immediately my wife came near me, and crying aloud and weeping she said: 'Job! Job! how long wilt thou sit upon the dung-hill outside of the city, pondering yet for a while and expecting to obtain your hoped-for salvation!'

And I have been wandering from place to place, roaming about as a hired servant, behold thy memory has already died away from earth.

And my sons and the daughters that I carried on my bosom and the labors and pains that I sustained have been for nothing?

And thou sittest in the malodorous state of soreness and worms, passing the nights in the cold air.

And I have undergone all trials and troubles and pains, day and night until I succeeded in bringing bread to thee.

For you surplus of bread is no longer allowed to me; and as I can scarcely take my own food and divide it between us, I pondered in my heart that it was not right that thou shouldst be in pain and hunger for bread.

And so I ventured to go to the market without bashfulness, and when the bread-seller told me: 'Give me money, and thou shalt have bread', I disclosed to him our state of distress.

Then I heard him say: 'If thou hast no money, hand me the hair of thy head, and take three loaves of bread in order that ye may live on these for three days'.

And I yielded to the wrong and said to him: 'Rise and cut off my hair!' and he rose and in disgrace cut off with the scissors the hair of my head on the market place while the crowd stood by and wondered.

Who would then not be astonished saying: 'Is this Sitis, the wife of Job, who had fourteen curtains to cover her inner sitting room, and doors within doors so that he was greatly honored who would be brought near her, and now behold, she barters off her hair for bread!

Who had camels laden with goods, and they were brought into remote lands to the poor, and now she sells her hair for bread!

Behold her who had seven tables immovably set in her house at which each poor man and each stranger ate, and now she sells her hair for bread!

Behold her who had the basin wherewith to wash her feet made of gold and silver, and now she walks upon the ground and sells her hair for bread!

Behold her who had her garments made of byssus interwoven with gold, and now she exchanges her hair for bread!

Behold her who had couches of gold and of silver, and now she sells her hair for bread!'

In short then, Job, after the many things that have been said to me, I now say in one word to thee:

'Since the feebleness of my heart has crushed my bones, rise then and take these loaves of bread and enjoy them, and then speak some word against the Lord and die!

For I too, would exchange the torpor of death for the sustenance of my body'.

But I replied to her: 'Behold I have been for these seven years plague-stricken, and I have stood the worms of my body, and I was not weighed down in my soul by all these pains.

And as to the word which thou sayest: "Speak some word against God and die!", together with thee I will sustain the evil which thou seest, and let us endure the ruin of all that we have.

Yet thou desirest that we should say some word against God and that He should be exchanged for the great Pluto.

Why dost thou not remember those great goods which we possessed? If these goods come from the lands of the Lord, should not we also endure evils and be high-minded in everything until the Lord will have mercy again and show pity to us?

Dost thou not see the Seducer stand behind thee and confound thy thoughts in order that thou shouldst beguile me?'

And he turned to Satan and said: 'Why dost thou not come openly to me? Stop hiding thyself, thou wretched one.

Does the lion show his strength in the weasel-cage? Or does the bird fly in the basket? I now tell thee: Go away and wage thy war against me'.

Then he went off from behind my wife and placed himself before me crying and he said: 'Behold, Job, I yield and give way to thee who art but flesh while I am a spirit.

Thou art plague-stricken, but I am in great trouble.

For I am like a wrestler contesting with a wrestler who has, in a single-handed combat, torn down his antagonist and covered him with dust and broken every limb of his, whereas the other one who lies beneath, having displayed his bravery, gives forth sounds of triumph testifying to his own superior excellence.

Thus thou, O Job, art beneath and stricken with plague and pain, and yet thou hast carried the victory in the wrestling-match with me, and behold, I yield to thee'.

Then he left me abashed.

Now my children, do you also show a firm heart in all the evil that happens to you, for greater than all things is firmness of heart.

The Testament of Job, trans. K. Kohler, 1897

Satan Faces a Problem

DIABOLUS: Nowe by my soverayntie I sweare
and principallitye that I beare
in hell-pine, when I am theare,
a gamon I will assaye.
There is a doseberd I would deare
that walkes abroad wydewhere.

Who is his father I wott neare,
the sooth if I should saye.

What maister mon ever be this
that nowe in world commen is?
His mother I wott did never amisse,
and that now mervayles mee.
His [father] cannot I find iwys,
for all my crafte and my couintise.
Hit seemes that heaven all should be his,
so stowte a syre is hee.

He is man from foote to crowne,
and gotten without corruption;
so cleane of conversation
knewe I non before.
All men of him mervayle mone,
for as man hee goeth up and downe;
but as God with devotion
[he has bene honoured yore].

Sythen the world first begane
knewe I never such a man
borne of a deadlych woman,
and hee yet wembles.
Amonge sinfull synne dose hee none,
and cleaner then ever was anyone;
blotles eke of blood and bonne,
and wiser then ever man was.

Avarice nor any envye
in him could I never espie.
He hase no gould in tresorye,
ne tempted ys by no syght.
Pryde hasse he none, ne gluttonye,
ne no likinge of lecherye.
His mouth hard I never lye
neather by day nor night.

My heighnes he puttes aye behynd,
for in him faulte non can I fynd.
If hee be God in mans kinde,

my crafte then fully fayles.
And more then man I wott hee is,
elles somethinge he did amys;
save only [hongarye he is], iwis,
elles wott I not what him ayles.

And this thinge dare I soothly saye:
if that hee be God verey
honger should greeve him by no waye;
that weare agaynst reasoun.
Therfore nowe I would assaye
with speach of bread him to betraye,
for he hasse fast nowe manye a daye;
therfore bread were in seasoun.

The Chester Mystery Cycle,
ed. R. M. Lumiansky and David Mills, 1974

The Temptation in the Wilderness

Then was Jesus led up of the Spirit into the wilderness to be tempted of the devil.

And when he had fasted forty days and forty nights, he was afterward an hungred.

And when the tempter came to him, he said, If thou be the Son of God, command that these stones be made bread.

But he answered and said, It is written, Man shall not live by bread alone, but by every word that proceedeth out of the mouth of God.

Then the devil taketh him up into the holy city, and setteth him on a pinnacle of the temple,

And saith unto him, If thou be the Son of God, cast thyself down: for it is written, He shall give his angels charge concerning thee: and in *their* hands they shall bear thee up, lest at any time thou dash thy foot against a stone.

Jesus said unto him, It is written again, Thou shalt not tempt the Lord thy God.

Again, the devil taketh him up into an exceeding high mountain, and sheweth him all the kingdoms of the world, and the glory of them;

And saith unto him, All these things will I give thee, if thou wilt fall down and worship me.

Then saith Jesus unto him, Get thee hence, Satan: for it is written, Thou shalt worship the Lord thy God, and him only shalt thou serve.
Then the devil leaveth him, and, behold, angels came and ministered unto him.

Matthew 4, v.1–11

Hunger

JHESUS: xl^{ti} days *and* xl^{ti} nyght
  now haue I fastyd for ma*n*nys sake
  A mor*e* grett hungyr had neuyr no wyght
  than I myself be-gynne to take
  Ffor hungyr in peyn stronge am I pyght
  and bred haue I non my*n* hungyr for to slake
  A lytel of a loof relese my*n* hungyr myght
  but mursele haue I non my comforte for to make
  This suffyr I man for the
  Ffor þi glotenye *and* metys wrong
  I suffyr for þe þis hungyr stronge
  I am afferde it wyl be longe
      Or þou do þus for me.

Ludus Coventriae, ed. K. S. Block, 1922

Stones and Bread

SATAN TENTATOR: Now forsoth and God, it is joye of your lyfe,
  That ye take soch paynes, and are in vertu so ryfe,
  Where so small joyes are, to recreate the hart.
JESUS CHRISTUS: Here are for pastyme, the wylde beastes of the
         desart,
  With whom moch better, it is to be conversaunt,
  Than with soch people, as are to God repugnaunt.
SATAN TENTATOR: Ye speake it full well, it is even as ye saye,
  But tell me how longe, ye have bene here, I yow praye.
JESUS CHRISTUS: Fourty dayes and nyghtes, without any sustenaunce.
SATAN TENTATOR: So moch I judged, by your pale countenaunce.
  Then is it no marvele, I trowe, though ye hungrye.
JESUS CHRISTUS: My stomack declareth, the weaknesse of my bodye.

SATAN TENTATOR: Well, to be pleyne with yow, abroade the rumour
    doth ronne,
  Amonge the people, that he shuld be Gods sonne.
  If ye be Gods sonne, as it hath great lykelyhode,
  Make of these stones breade, and geite your bodye hys fode.
JESUS CHRISTUS: No offence is it, to eate whan men be hungrye,
  But to make stones breade, it is unnecessarye.
  He whych in thys fast, hath bene my specyall gyde,
  Fode for my bodye, is able to provyde.
  I thanke my lorde God, I am at no soch nede,
  As to make stones breade, my bodye so to fede.
  Whan I come in place, where God hath appoynted meate,
  Gevynge hym thankes, I shall not spare to eate.

The Temptation of Our Lord, John Bale, 1538

The Pinnacle of the Temple

Well knewe our Sauiour this the Serpent was,
And the old Serpent knewe our Sauiour well,
Neuer did any this in falshood passe,
Neuer did any him in truth excell:
With him we fly to heau'n, from heau'n we fell
    With him: but nowe they both together met
    Vpon the sacred pinnacles, that threat
With their aspiring tops, Astraeas starrie seat.

Here did PRESVMPTION her pauillion spread,
Ouer the Temple, the bright starres among,
(Ah that her foot should trample on the head
Of that most reuerend place!) and a lewd throng
Of wanton boyes sung her a pleasant song
    Of loue, long life, of mercie and of grace,
    And euery one her deerely did embrace,
And she herselfe enamour'd was of her owne face.

A painted face, belied with vermeyl store,
Which light Euëlpis euery day did trimme,
That in one hand a guilded anchor wore,
Not fixed on the rocke, but on the brimme
Of the wide aire she let it loosely swimme:

Her other hand a sprinkle carried,
   And euer, when her Ladie wauered,
Court-holy water all vpon her sprinkeled.

Poore foole, she thought herselfe in wondrous price
With God, as if in Paradise she wear,
But wear shee not in a fooles paradise,
She might haue seene more reason to despere:
But him she, like some ghastly fiend, did feare,
   And therefore as that wretch hew'd out his cell
   Vnder the bowels, in the heart of hell,
So she aboue the Moone, amid the starres would dwell.

Her Tent with sunny cloudes was seel'd aloft,
And so exceeding shone with a false light,
That heau'n it selfe to her it seemed oft,
Heau'n without cloudes to her deluded sight,
But cloudes withouten heau'n it was aright,
   And as her house was built, so did her braine
   Build castles in the aire, with idle paine,
But heart she neuer had in all her body vaine.

Like as a ship, in which no ballance lies,
Without a Pilot, on the sleeping waues,
Fairely along with winde, and water flies,
And painted masts with silken sayles embraues,
That Neptune selfe the bragging vessell saues,
   To laugh a while at her so proud array;
   Her wauing streamers loosely shee lets play,
And flagging colours shine as bright as smiling day:

But all so soone as heau'n his browes doth bend,
Shee veils her banners, and pulls in her beames,
The emptie barke the raging billows send
Vp to th' Olympique waues, and Argus seemes
Again to ride vpon our lower streames:
   Right so PRESVMPTION did her selfe behaue,
   Tossed about with euery stormie waue,
And in white lawne she went, most like an Angel braue.

Gently our Sauiour shee began to shrive,
Whither he wear the Sonne of God, or no:

For any other shee disdeign'd to wive:
And if he wear, shee bid him fearles throw
Himselfe to ground, and thearwithall did show
   A flight of little Angels, that did wait
   Vpon their glittering wings, to latch him strait,
And longed on their backs to feele his glorious weight.

But when she saw her speech preuailed nought,
Her selfe she tombled headlong to the flore:
But him the Angels on their feathers caught,
And to an ayrie mountaine nimbly bore,
Whose snowie shoulders, like some chaulkie shore,
   Restles Olympus seem'd to rest vpon
   With all his swimming globes: so both are gone,
The Dragon with the Lamb. Ah, vnmeet Paragon.

                Giles Fletcher the younger, 'Christs Victorie on Earth', 1610

The High Mountain

DIABOLUS: Yett, fellowe, if it be thy will,
      goe we playe us to a hill;
      another poynte I must fulfill
      for ought that may befall.
      Looke abowte thee nowe and see
      of all this realme the royaltie;
      for to kneele downe and honour me
      thou shall be lord of all.

                The Chester Mystery Cycle,
                ed. R. M. Lumiansky and David Mills, 1974

Why Art Thou Solicitous?

But what concerns it thee when I begin
My everlasting Kingdom, why art thou
Sollicitous, what moves thy inquisition?
Know'st thou not that my rising is thy fall,
And my promotion will be thy destruction?
   To whom the Tempter inly rackt reply'd.

Let that come when it comes; all hope is lost
Of my reception into grace; what worse?
For where no hope is left, is left no fear;
If there be worse, the expectation more
Of worse torments me then the feeling can.
I would be at the worst; worst is my Port,
My harbour and my ultimate repose,
The end I would attain, my final good.
My error was my error, and my crime
My crime; whatever for it self condemnd,
And will alike be punisht; whether thou
Raign or raign not; though to that gentle brow
Willingly I could flye, and hope thy raign,
From that placid aspect and meek regard,
Rather then aggravate my evil state,
Would stand between me and thy Fathers ire,
(Whose ire I dread more then the fire of Hell)
A shelter and a kind of shading cool
Interposition, as a summers cloud.
If I then to the worst that can be hast,
Why move thy feet so slow to what is best,
Happiest both to thy self and all the World,
That thou who worthiest art should'st be thir King?
Perhaps thou linger'st in deep thoughts detain
Of the enterprise so hazardous and high;
No wonder, for though in thee be united
What of perfection can in man be found,
Or human nature can receive, consider
Thy life hath yet been privat, most part spent
At home, scarce viewd the *Gallilean* Towns,
And once a year *Jerusalem*, few days
Short sojourn; and what thence could'st thou observe?
The World thou hast not seen, much less her glory,
Empires, and Monarchs, and thir radiant Courts,
Best school of best experience, quickest insight
In all things that to greatest actions lead.
The wisest, unexperienc't, will be ever
Timorous and loth, with novice modesty,
(As he who seeking Asses found a Kingdom)
Irresolute, unhardy, unadventrous:
But I will bring thee where thou soon shalt quit
Those rudiments, and see before thine eyes

The Monarchies of th' Earth, thir pomp and state,
Sufficient introduction to inform
Thee, of thy self so apt, in regal Arts,
And regal Mysteries; that thou may'st know
How best thir opposition to withstand.

John Milton, *Paradise Regain'd*, Book III, 1671

Mammon Offers Guyon the World

'God of the world and worldlings I me call,
Great *Mammon*, greatest god below the skye,
That of my plenty poure out unto all,
And unto none my graces do envye:
Riches, renowme, and principality,
Honour, estate, and all this worldes good,
For which men swinck and sweat incessantly,
Fro me do flow into an ample flood,
And in the hollow earth have their eternall brood.

'Wherefore, if me thou deigne to serve and sew,
At thy commaund lo all these mountaines bee:
Or if to thy great mind, or greedy vew
All these may not suffise, there shall to thee
Ten times so much be numbred francke and free.'
'Mammon,' (said he) 'thy godheads vaunt is vaine,
And idle offers of thy golden fee;
To them that covet such eye-glutting gaine,
Proffer thy giftes, and fitter servaunts entertaine.

'Me ill besits, that in der-doing armes,
And honours suit my vowed dayes do spend,
Unto thy bounteous baytes, and pleasing charmes,
With which weake men thou witchest, to attend;
Regard of worldly mucke doth fowly blend,
And low abase the high heroicke spright,
That joyes for crownes and kingdomes to contend;
Faire shields, gay steedes, bright armes be my delight:
Those be the riches fit for an advent'rous knight.'

'Vaine glorious Elfe,' (saide he) 'doest not thou weet,

[138]

That money can thy wantes at will supply?
Sheilds, steeds, and armes, and all things for thee meet,
It can purvay in twinckling of an eye;
And crownes and kingdomes to thee multiply.
Do not I kings create, and throw the crowne
Sometimes to him that low in dust doth ly,
And him that raignd, into his rowme thrust downe,
And whom I lust, do heape with glory and renowne?'

'All otherwise' (saide he) 'I riches read,
And deeme them roote of all disquietnesse;
First got with guile, and then preserv'd with dread,
And after spent with pride and lavishnesse,
Leaving behind them griefe and heavinesse:
Infinite mischiefes of them doe arize,
Strife and debate, bloodshed, and bitternesse,
Outrageous wrong, and hellish covetize,
That noble heart as great dishonour doth despize.

'Ne thine be kingdomes, ne the scepters thine;
But realmes and rulers thou doest both confound,
And loyall truth to treason doest incline:
Witnesse the guiltlesse blood pourd oft on ground,
The crowned often slaine, the slayer cround;
The sacred Diademe in peeces rent,
And purple robe gored with many a wound;
Castles surprizd, great cities sackt and brent:
So mak'st thou kings, and gaynest wrongfull governement.'

Edmund Spenser, *The Faerie Queene*, Book II, 1589

All the Kingdoms

To whom the Tempter impudent repli'd.
I see all offers made by me how slight
Thou valu'st, because offerd, and reject'st:
Nothing will please the difficult and nice,
Or nothing more then still to contradict:
On th' other side know also thou, that I
On what I offer set as high esteem,

Nor what I part with mean to give for naught;
All these which in a moment thou behold'st,
The Kingdoms of the World to thee I give;
For giv'n to me, I give to whom I please,
No trifle; yet with this reserve, not else,
On this condition, if thou wilt fall down,
And worship me as thy superior Lord,
Easily done, and hold them all of me;
For what can less so great a gift deserve?
    Whom thus our Saviour answerd with disdain.
I never lik'd thy talk, thy offers less,
Now both abhorr, since thou hast dar'd to utter
Th' abominable terms, impious condition;
But I endure the time, till which expir'd,
Thou hast permission on me. It is writt'n
The first of all Commandments, Thou shalt worship
The Lord thy God, and onely him shalt serve;
And dar'st thou to the Son of God propound
To worship thee accurst, now more accurst
For this attempt bolder then that on *Eve*,
And more blaspheamous? which expect to rue.
The Kingdoms of the World to thee were giv'n,
Permitted rather, and by thee usurpt,
Other donation none thou canst produce:
If giv'n, by whom but by the King of Kings,
God over all supream? if giv'n to thee,
By thee how fairly is the Giver now
Repaid? But gratitude in thee is lost
Long since. Wert thou so void of fear or shame,
As offer them to mee the Son of God,
To mee my own, on such abhorred pact,
That I fall down and worship thee as God?

John Milton, *Paradise Regain'd*, Book IV, 1671

Christ Declares Himself

    To whom the Fiend now swoln with rage reply'd:
Then hear, O Son of *David*, Virgin-born;
For Son of God to me is yet in doubt,
Of the Messiah I have heard foretold

By all the Prophets; of thy birth at length
Announc't by *Gabriel* with the first I knew,
And of the Angelic Song in *Bethlehem* field,
On thy birth-night, that sung thee Saviour born.
From that time seldom have I ceast to eye
Thy infancy, thy childhood, and thy youth,
Thy manhood last, though yet in privat bred;
Till at the Ford of *Jordan* whither all
Flockd to the Baptist, I among the rest,
Though not to be Baptiz'd, by voice from Heav'n
Heard thee pronounc't the Son of God belov'd.
Thenceforth I thought thee worth my nearer view
And narrower Scrutiny, that I might learn
In what degree or meaning thou art calld
The Son of God, which bears no single sense;
The Son of God I also am, or was,
And if I was, I am; relation stands;
All men are Sons of God; yet thee I thought
In some respect far higher so declar'd.
Therefore I watchd thy footsteps from that hour,
And followd thee still on to this wast wild;
Where by all best conjectures I collect
Thou art to be my fatal enemy.
Good reason then, if I before-hand seek
To understand my Adversary, who
And what he is; his wisdom, power, intent,
By parl, or composition, truce, or league
To win him, or win from him what I can.
And opportunity I here have had
To try thee, sift thee, and confess have found thee
Proof against all temptation as a rock
Of Adamant, and as a Center, firm
To th' utmost of meer man both wise and good,
Not more ...

   To whom thus Jesus: also it is writt'n,
Tempt not the Lord thy God; he said and stood.
But Satan smitt'n with amazement fell;
As when Earths Son *Antæus* (to compare
Small things with greatest) in *Irassa* strove
With *Joves Alcides*, and oft foild still rose,
Receiving from his mother Earth new strength,

Fresh from his fall, and fiercer grapple joind,
Throttl'd at length in th' Air, expir'd and fell;
So after many a foil the Tempter proud,
Renewing fresh assaults, amidst his pride
Fell whence he stood to see his Victor fall.

John Milton, *Paradise Regain'd*, Book IV, 1671

The Grand Inquisitor Regrets the Outcome

'The wise and dread spirit, the spirit of self-destruction and non-existence,' the old man goes on, 'the great spirit talked with Thee in the wilderness, and we are told in the books that he "tempted" Thee. Is that so? And could anything truer be said than what he revealed to Thee in three questions and what Thou didst reject, and what in the books is called "the temptation"? And yet if there has ever been on earth a real stupendous miracle, it took place on that day, on the day of the three temptations. The statement of those three questions was itself the miracle. If it were possible to imagine simply for the sake of argument that those three questions of the dread spirit had perished utterly from the books, and that we had to restore them and to invent them anew, and to do so had gathered together all the wise men of the earth – rulers, chief priests, learned men, philosophers, poets – and had set them the task to invent three questions, such as would not only fit the occasion, but express in three words, three human phrases, the whole future history of the world and of humanity – dost Thou believe that all the wisdom of the earth united could have invented anything in depth and force equal to the three questions which were actually put to Thee then by the wise and mighty spirit in the wilderness? From those questions alone, from the miracle of their statement, we can see that we have here to do not with the fleeting human intelligence, but with the absolute and eternal. For in those three questions the whole subsequent history of mankind is, as it were, brought together into one whole, and foretold, and in them are united all the unsolved historical contradictions of human nature. At the time it could not be so clear, since the future was unknown; but now that fifteen hundred years have passed, we see that everything in those three questions was so justly divined and foretold, and has been so truly fulfilled, that nothing can be added to them or taken from them.

'Judge Thyself who was right – Thou or he who questioned Thee then? Remember the first question; its meaning, in other words, was this: "Thou wouldst go into the world, and art going with empty hands, with

[142]

some promise of freedom which men in their simplicity and their natural unruliness cannot even understand, which they fear and dread – for nothing has ever been more insupportable for a man and a human society than freedom. But seest Thou these stones in this parched and barren wilderness? Turn them into bread, and mankind will run after Thee like a flock of sheep, grateful and obedient, though for ever trembling, lest Thou withdraw Thy hand and deny them Thy bread." But Thou wouldst not deprive man of freedom and didst reject the offer, thinking, what is that freedom worth, if obedience is bought with bread? Thou didst reply that man lives not by bread alone. But dost Thou know that for the sake of that earthly bread the spirit of the earth will rise up against Thee and will strive with Thee and overcome Thee, and all will follow him, crying, "Who can compare with this beast? He has given us fire from heaven!" Dost Thou know that the ages will pass, and humanity will proclaim by the lips of their sages that there is no crime, and therefore no sin; there is only hunger? "Feed men, and then ask of them virtue!" that's what they'll write on the banner, which they will raise against Thee, and with which they will destroy Thy temple. Where Thy temple stood will rise a new building; the terrible tower of Babel will be built again, and though, like the one of old, it will not be finished, yet Thou mightest have prevented that new tower and have cut short the sufferings of men for a thousand years; for they will come back to us after a thousand years of agony with their tower. They will seek us again, hidden underground in the catacombs, for we shall be again persecuted and tortured. They will find us and cry to us, "Feed us, for those who have promised us fire from heaven haven't given it!" And then we shall finish building their tower, for he finishes the building who feeds them. And we alone shall feed them in Thy name, declaring falsely that it is in Thy name. Oh, never, never can they feed themselves without us! No science will give them bread so long as they remain free. In the end they will lay their freedom at our feet, and say to us, "Make us your slaves, but feed us." They will understand themselves, at last, that freedom and bread enough for all are inconceivable together, for never, never will they be able to share between them! They will be convinced, too, that they can never be free, for they are weak, vicious, worthless, and rebellious. Thou didst promise them the bread of Heaven, but, I repeat again, can it compare with earthly bread in the eyes of the weak, ever sinful and ignoble race of man? And if for the sake of the bread of Heaven thousands shall follow Thee, what is to become of the millions and tens of thousands of millions of creatures who will not have the strength to forego the earthly bread for the sake of the heavenly? Or dost Thou care only for the tens of thousands of the great and strong, while the millions, numerous as the sands of the sea, who are weak but love Thee, must exist only for the sake of the great and strong? No, we care for the weak too. They are sinful and rebellious, but in the end they too will become obedient. They will marvel at us and look on us as gods, because we are ready to endure the freedom which they have found so dreadful and to rule over them – so awful it will seem to them to be free. But we shall tell them that we are Thy servants and rule them in Thy name. We shall deceive them again, for we will not let Thee come to us again. That deception will be our suffering, for we shall be forced to lie.

'This is the significance of the first question in the wilderness, and this is what Thou has rejected for the sake of that freedom which Thou hast exalted above everything. Yet in this question lies hid the great secret of this world. Choosing "bread," Thou wouldst have satisfied the universal and everlasting craving of humanity – to find someone to worship. So long as man remains free he strives for nothing so incessantly and so painfully as to find someone to worship. But man seeks to worship what is established beyond dispute, so that all men would agree at once to worship it. For these pitiful creatures are concerned not only to find something that all would believe in and worship; what is essential is that all may be *together* in it. This craving for *community* of worship is the chief misery of every man individually and of all humanity from the beginning of time. For the sake of common worship they've slain each other with the sword. They have set up gods and challenged one another, "Put away your gods and come and worship ours, or we will kill you and your gods!" And so it will be to the end of the world, even when gods disappear from the earth; they will fall down before idols just the same. Thou didst know, Thou couldst not but have known, this fundamental secret of human nature, but Thou didst reject the one infallible banner which was offered Thee to make all men bow down to Thee alone – the banner of earthly bread; and Thou hast rejected it for the sake of freedom and the bread of Heaven. Behold what Thou didst further. And all again in the name of freedom! I tell Thee that man is tormented by no greater anxiety than to find someone quickly to whom he can hand over that gift of freedom with which the ill-fated creature is born. But only one who can appease their conscience can take over their freedom. In bread there was offered Thee an invincible banner; give bread, and man will worship Thee, for nothing is more certain than bread. But if someone else gains possession of his conscience – oh! then he will cast away Thy bread and follow after him who has ensnared his conscience. In that Thou wast right. For the secret of man's being is not only to live but to have something to live for. Without a stable conception of the object of life, man would not consent to go on living, and would rather destroy himself than remain on earth, though he had bread in abundance. That is true.

But what happened? Instead of taking men's freedom from them, Thou didst make it greater than ever! Didst Thou forget that man prefers peace, and even death, to freedom of choice in the knowledge of good and evil? Nothing is more seductive for man than his freedom of conscience, but nothing is a greater cause of suffering. And behold, instead of giving a firm foundation for setting the conscience of man at rest for ever, Thou didst choose all that is exceptional, vague and enigmatic; Thou didst choose what was utterly beyond the strength of men, acting as though Thou didst not love them at all – Thou who didst come to give Thy life for them! Instead of taking possession of men's freedom, Thou didst increase it, and burdened the spiritual kingdom of mankind with its sufferings for ever. Thou didst desire man's free love, that he should follow Thee freely, enticed and taken captive by Thee. In place of the rigid ancient law, man must hereafter with free heart decide for himself what is good and what is evil, having only Thy image before him as his guide. But didst Thou not know that he would at last reject even Thy image and Thy truth, if he is weighed down with the fearful burden of free choice? They will cry aloud at last that the truth is not in Thee, for they could not have been left in greater confusion and suffering than Thou hast caused, laying upon them so many cares and unanswerable problems.

'So that, in truth, Thou didst Thyself lay the foundation for the destruction of Thy kingdom, and no one is more to blame for it. Yet what was offered Thee? There are three powers, three powers alone, able to conquer and to hold captive for ever the conscience of these impotent rebels for their happiness – those forces are miracle, mystery and authority. Thou hast rejected all three and hast set the example for doing so. When the wise and dread spirit set Thee on the pinnacle of the temple and said to Thee, "If Thou wouldst know whether Thou art the Son of God then cast Thyself down, for it is written: the angels shall hold him up lest he fall and bruise himself, and Thou shalt know then whether Thou art the Son of God and shalt prove then how great is Thy faith in Thy Father." But Thou didst refuse and wouldst not cast Thyself down. Oh, of course, Thou didst proudly and well, like God; but the weak, unruly race of men, are they gods? Oh, Thou didst know then that in taking one step, in making one movement to cast Thyself down, Thou wouldst be tempting God and have lost all Thy faith in Him, and wouldst have been dashed to pieces against that earth which Thou didst come to save. And the wise spirit that tempted Thee would have rejoiced. But I ask again, are there many like Thee? And couldst Thou believe for one moment that men, too, could face such a temptation? Is the nature of men such, that they can reject miracle, and at the great moments of their life, the moments of their deepest, most agonising spiritual difficulties, cling only to the free verdict of the heart? Oh, Thou didst know that Thy deed would be recorded in books, would be handed down to remote times and the utmost ends of the earth, and Thou didst hope that man, following Thee, would cling to God and not ask for a miracle. But Thou didst not know that when man rejects miracle he rejects God too; for man seeks not so much God as the miraculous. And as man cannot bear to be without the miraculous, he will create new miracles of his own for himself, and will worship deeds of sorcery and witchcraft, though he might be a hundred times over a rebel, heretic and infidel. Thou didst not come down from the Cross when they shouted to Thee, mocking and reviling Thee, "Come down from the cross and we will believe that Thou art He." Thou didst not come down, for again Thou wouldst not enslave man by a miracle, and didst crave faith given freely, not based on miracle. Thou didst crave for free love and not the base raptures of the slave before the might that has overawed him for ever. But Thou didst think too highly of men therein, for they are slaves, of course, though rebellious by nature. Look round and judge; fifteen centuries have passed, look upon them. Whom hast Thou raised up to Thyself? I swear, man is weaker and baser by nature than Thou hast believed him! Can he, can he do what Thou didst? By showing him so much respect, Thou didst, as it were, cease to feel for him, for Thou didst ask far too much from him – Thou who hast loved him more than Thyself! Respecting him less, Thou wouldst have asked less of him. That would have been more like love, for his burden would have been lighter. He is weak and vile. What though he is everywhere now rebelling against our power, and proud of his rebellion? It is the pride of a child and a schoolboy. They are little children rioting and barring out the teacher at school. But their childish delight will end; it will cost them dear. They will cast down temples and drench the earth with blood. But they will see at last, the foolish children, that, though they are rebels, they are impotent rebels, unable to keep up their own rebellion. Bathed in their foolish tears, they will recognise at last that He who created them rebels must have meant to mock at them. They will say this in despair, and their utterance will be a blasphemy which will make them more unhappy still, for man's nature cannot bear blasphemy, and in the end always avenges it on itself. And so unrest, confusion, and unhappiness – that is the present lot of man after Thou didst bear so much for their freedom! The great prophet tells in vision and in image, that he saw all those who took part in the first resurrection and that there were of each tribe twelve thousand. But if there were so many of them, they must have been not men but gods. They had borne Thy cross, they had endured scores of years in the barren, hungry wilderness, living upon locusts and roots – and Thou mayest indeed point with pride at those children of freedom, of free love, of free and splendid sacrifice for Thy name. But remember that they were only some thousands; and what of the rest? And how are the other weak ones to blame, because they could not endure what the strong have endured? How is the weak soul to blame that it is unable to receive such terrible gifts? Canst Thou have simply come to the elect and for the elect? But if so, it is a mystery and we cannot understand it. And if it is a mystery, we too have a right to preach a mystery, and to teach them that it's not the free judgment of their hearts, not love that matters, but a mystery which they must follow blindly, even against their conscience. So we have done. We have corrected Thy work and have founded it upon *miracle*, *mystery* and *authority*.'

Fyodor Dostoevsky, *The Brothers Karamazov*, 1880;
trans. Constance Garnett, 1912

Nothing Daunted

LUCYFER: Owt harow I rore,
  For envy I lore.
  My place to restore
    God hath mad a man.
  All cum þey not thore,
  Woode and þey wore,
  I xall tempte hem so sorre,
    For I am he þat syn begane.

  I was a angell of lyghte;
  Lucyfeer I hyght,
  Presumynge in Godys syght,
    Werfor I am lowest in hell.
  In reformynge of my place ys dyght
  Man, whom I haue in most dyspyght,
  Euer castynge me wyth hem to fyght
    In þat hewynly place he xulde not dwell.

  I am as wyly now as than;
  þe knowynge þat I hade, yet I can;
  I know all compleccyons of a man
    Werto he ys most dysposyde;
  Ande þerin I tempte ay-whan;
  I marre hys myndys to þer wan,

That whoo ys hym þat God hym began;
   Many a holy man wyth me ys mosyde.

Of Gode man ys þe fygure,
Hys symylytude, hys pyctowre,
Gloryosest of ony creature
   þat euer was wrought;
Wyche I wyll dysvygure
Be my fals conjecture;
Yff he tende my reporture
   I xall brynge hym to nought.

In þe soule ben thre partyes iwys:
Mynde, Wyll, Wndyrstondynge of blys,
Fygure of þe Godhede, I know well thys;
   And þe flesche of man þat ys so changeable
That wyll I tempte, as I gees;
Tho þat I perwert, synne non ys
But yff þe Soule consent to mys,
   For in þe Wyll of þe Soule the dedys ben damnable.

To þe Mynde of þe Soule I xall mak suggestyun,
Ande brynge hys Wndyrstondynge to dylectacyon,
So þat hys Wyll make confyrmacyon;
   Than am I sekyr inowe
That dethe xall sew of damnacyon;
Than of þe Sowll þe Dewll hath dominacyon.
I wyll go make hys examynacyon,
   To all þe dewllys of helle I make awow.

For, for to tempte man in my lyknes,
Yt wolde brynge hym to grett feerfullnes,
I wyll change me into bryghtnes,
   And so hym to-begyle,
Sen I xall schew hym perfyghtnes,
And wertu prove yt wykkydnes;
Thus wndyr colors all thynge perverse;
   I xall neuer rest tyll þe Soule I defyle.

Wisdom, c.1465–70 in *The Macro Plays*, ed. M. Eccles, 1969

Manifold Ambushes

Yea, the holy and faithful servants of the true God are in danger of the devil's manifold ambushes: for as long as they live in this frail and foul-browed world, they must be so, and it is for their good, making them more attentive in the quest of that security where their peace is without end, and without want.

St Augustine, *De Civitate Dei*, c.413–26 AD; trans. John Healey, 1610

The Campaign Against St Anthony

But the devil, who hates and envies what is good, could not endure to see such a resolution in a youth, but endeavoured to carry out against him what he had been wont to effect against others. First of all he tried to lead him away from the discipline, whispering to him the remembrance of his wealth, care for his sister, claims of kindred, love of money, love of glory, the various pleasures of the table and the other relaxations of life, and at last the difficulty of virtue and the labour of it; he suggested also the infirmity of the body and the length of the time. In a word he raised in his mind a great dust of debate, wishing to debar him from his settled purpose. But when the enemy saw himself to be too weak for Antony's determination, and that he rather was conquered by the other's firmness, overthrown by his great faith and falling through his constant prayers, then at length putting his trust in the weapons which are 'in the navel of his belly' and boasting in them – for they are his first snare for the young – he attacked the young man, disturbing him by night and harassing him by day, so that even the onlookers saw the struggle which was going on between them. The one would suggest foul thoughts and the other counter them with prayers: the one fire him with lust, the other, as one who seemed to blush, fortify his body with faith, prayers, and fasting. And the devil, unhappy wight, one night even took upon him the shape of a woman and imitated all her acts simply to beguile Antony. But he, his mind filled with Christ and the nobility inspired by Him, and considering the spirituality of the soul, quenched the coal of the other's deceit. Again the enemy suggested the ease of pleasure. But he like a man filled with rage and grief turned his thoughts to the threatened fire and the gnawing worm, and setting these in array against his adversary, passed through the temptation unscathed. All this was a source of shame to his foe. For he, deeming himself like God, was now mocked by a young man; and he who boasted himself against flesh and blood was being put to flight by a man in the flesh. For the Lord was working with Antony – the Lord who for our sake took flesh and gave the body victory over the devil, so that all who truly fight can say, 'not I but the grace of God which was with me.'

At last when the dragon could not even thus overthrow Antony, but saw himself thrust out of his heart, gnashing his teeth as it is written, and as it were beside himself, he appeared to Antony like a black boy, taking a visible shape in accordance with the colour of his mind. And cringing to him, as it were, he plied him with thoughts no longer, for guileful as he was, he had been worsted, but at last spoke in human voice and said, 'Many I deceived, many I cast down; but now attacking thee and thy labours as I had many others, I proved weak.' When Antony asked, 'Who art thou who speakest thus with me?' he answered with a lamentable voice, 'I am the friend of whoredom, and have taken upon me incitements which lead to it against the young. I am called the spirit of lust. How many have I deceived who wished to live soberly, how many are the chaste whom by my incitements I have over-persuaded! I am he on account of whom also the prophet reproves those who have fallen, saying, "Ye have been caused to err by the spirit of whoredom." For by me they have been tripped up. I am he who have so often troubled thee and have so often been overthrown by thee.' But Antony having given thanks to the Lord, with good courage said to him, 'Thou art very despicable then, for thou art black-hearted and weak as a child. Henceforth I shall have no trouble from thee, "for the Lord is my helper, and I shall look down on mine enemies." ' Having heard this, the black one straightway fled, shuddering at the words and dreading any longer even to come near the man.

This was Antony's first struggle against the devil, or rather this victory was the Saviour's work in Antony, 'Who condemned sin in the flesh that the ordinance of the law might be fulfilled in us who walk not after the flesh but after the spirit.' But neither did Antony, although the evil one had fallen, henceforth relax his care and despise him; nor did the enemy as though conquered cease to lay snares for him. For again he went round as a lion seeking some occasion against him. But Antony having learned from the Scriptures that the devices of the devil are many, zealously continued the discipline, reckoning that though the devil had not been able to deceive his heart by bodily pleasure, he would endeavour to ensnare him by other means. For the demon loves sin. Wherefore more and more he repressed the body and kept it in subjection, lest haply having conquered on one side, he should be dragged down on the other.

He therefore planned to accustom himself to a severer mode of life. And many marvelled, but he himself used to bear the labour easily; for the eagerness of soul, through the length of time it had abode in him, had wrought a good habit in him, so that taking but little initiation from others he shewed great zeal in this matter. He kept vigil to such an extent that he often continued the whole night without sleep; and this not once but often, to the marvel of others. He ate once a day, after sunset, sometimes once in two days, and often even in four. His food was bread and salt, his drink, water only. Of flesh and wine it is superfluous even to speak, since no such thing was found with the other earnest men. A rush mat served him to sleep upon, but for the most part he lay upon the bare ground.

Thus tightening his hold upon himself, Antony departed to the tombs, which happened to be at a distance from the village; and having bid one of his acquaintances to bring him bread at intervals of many days, he entered one of the tombs, and the other having shut the door on him, he remained within alone. And when the enemy could not endure it, but was even fearful that in a short time Antony would fill the desert with the discipline, coming one night with a multitude of demons, he so cut him with stripes that he lay on the ground speechless from the excessive pain. For he affirmed that the torture had been so excessive that no blows inflicted by man could ever have caused him such torment. But by the Providence of God – for the Lord never overlooks them that hope in Him – the next day his acquaintance came bringing him the loaves. And having opened the door and seeing him lying on the ground as though dead, he lifted him up and carried him to the church in the village, and laid him upon the ground. And many of his kinsfolk and the villagers sat around Antony as round a corpse. But about midnight he came to himself and arose, and when he saw them all asleep and his comrade alone watching, he motioned with his head for him to approach, and asked him to carry him again to the tombs without waking anybody.

He was carried therefore by the man, and as he was wont, when the door was shut he was within alone. And he could not stand up on account of the blows, but he prayed as he lay. And after he had prayed, he said with a shout, 'Here am I, Antony; I flee not from your stripes, for even if you inflict more nothing shall separate me from the love of Christ.' And then he sang, 'though a camp be set against me, my heart shall not be afraid.' These were the thoughts and words of this ascetic. But the enemy, who hates good, marvelling that after the blows he dared to return, called together his hounds and burst forth, 'Ye see,' said he, 'that neither by the spirit of lust nor by blows did we stay the man, but that he braves us, let us attack him in another fashion.' But changes of form for evil are easy for the devil, so in the night they made such a din that the whole of that place seemed to be shaken by an earthquake, and the demons as if breaking the four walls of the dwelling seemed to enter through them, coming in the likeness of beasts and creeping things. And the place was on a sudden filled with the forms of lions, bears, leopards, bulls, serpents, asps, scorpions, and wolves, and each of them was moving according to his nature. The lion was roaring, wishing to attack, the bull seeming to toss with its horns, the serpent writhing but unable to approach, and the wolf as it rushed on was restrained; altogether the noises of the apparitions, with their angry ragings, were dreadful. But Antony, stricken and goaded by them, felt bodily pains severer still. He lay watching, however, with unshaken soul, groaning from bodily anguish; but his mind was clear, and as in mockery he said, 'If there had been any power in you, it would have sufficed had one of you come, but since the Lord hath made you weak you attempt to terrify me by numbers: and a proof of your weakness is that you take the shapes of brute beasts.' And again with boldness he said, 'If you are able, and have received power against me, delay not to attack; but if you are unable, why trouble me in vain? For faith in our Lord is a seal and a wall of safety to us.' So after many attempts they gnashed their teeth upon him, because they were mocking themselves rather than him.

Athanasius, *Life of St Anthony*, c.356–62 AD; trans. H. Ellershaw, 1892

Rabbi Amram Shouts Fire

Once upon a time women of Nehardea who had been taken captive in battle were brought into the house of a man called Rabbi Amram, the Pious, in order that he might redeem them. For it was the custom in olden times to redeem captives. He put them all in the loft and removed the ladder, so that no one should be able (God forbid!) to go up and commit a sin with them. Among them R. Amram noticed one woman, as she passed by the opening, who was very beautiful. The evil passion took possession of R. Amram and so inflamed him with her beauty that he longed to make her his own. Thereupon he took a ladder, which ordinarily required more than ten persons to carry it, and carried it alone. For his passion was so strong that he wanted to go up and lie with the woman. When he had gone half way up the ladder, he suddenly bethought of the great sin that he was about to commit and began shouting: 'Fire, fire, in R. Amram's house!' When the scholars came to put out the fire, they found none. Then R. Amram said: 'I did this in order to put out the fire of evil passion.' He told them what he had had in mind, for, he said, 'It is better for me to be put to shame in this world than that I should (God forbid!) be put to shame in the world to come.' Then he adjured the evil passion to depart from him, and the evil passion departed in the form of a pillar of fire. Then R. Amram said: 'Behold, you are fire, and I am nothing but flesh and blood, and yet I have subdued you, and I am also better than you, evil passion, you Satan!'

One should therefore not allow oneself to be led astray by the *Yeẓer ha-Ra'* (evil passion), but should put him to shame.

The Ma'aseh Book, 1602; trans. Moses Gaster, 1934

St Anthony Advises

Since the Lord visited earth, the enemy is fallen and his powers weakened. Wherefore although he could do nothing, still like a tyrant, he did not bear his fall quietly, but threatened, though his threats were words only. And let each one of you consider this, and he will be able to despise the demons. Now if they were hampered with such bodies as we are, it would be possible for them to say, 'Men when they are hidden we cannot find, but whenever we do find them we do them hurt.' And we also by lying in concealment could escape them, shutting the doors against them. But if they are not of such a nature as this, but are able to enter in, though the doors be shut, and haunt all the air, both they and their leader the devil, and are wishful for evil and ready to injure; and, as the Saviour said, 'From the beginning the devil is a manslayer and a father of vice;' while we, though this is so, are alive, and spend our lives all the more in opposing him; it is plain they are powerless. For place is no hindrance to their plots, nor do they look on us as friends that they should spare us; nor are they lovers of good that they should amend. But on the contrary they are evil, and nothing is so much sought after by them as wounding them that love virtue and fear God. But since they have no power to effect anything, they do nought but threaten. But if they could, they would not hesitate, but forthwith work evil (for all their desire is set on this), and especially against us. Behold now we are gathered together and speak against them, and they know when we advance they grow weak. If therefore they had power they would permit none of us Christians to live, for godliness is an abomination to a sinner. But since they can do nothing they inflict the greater wounds on themselves; for they can fulfil none of their threats. Next this ought to be considered, that we may be in no fear of them: that if they had the power they would not come in crowds, nor fashion displays, nor with change of form would they frame deceits. But it would suffice that one only should come and accomplish that which he was both able and willing to do: especially as every one who has the power neither slays with display nor strikes fear with tumult, but forthwith makes full use of his authority as he wishes. But the demons as they have no power are like actors on the stage changing their shape and frightening children with tumultuous apparition and various forms: from which they ought rather to be despised as shewing their weakness. At least the true angel of the Lord sent against the Assyrian had no need for tumults, nor displays from without, nor noises nor rattlings, but in quiet he used his power and forthwith destroyed a hundred and eighty-five thousand. But demons like these, who have no power, try to terrify at least by their displays.

Athanasius, *Life of St Anthony*, c.356–62 AD; trans. H. Ellershaw, 1892

Origen Reflects

This leads the simpler sort of believers in Christ the Lord to suppose that all the sins that men have committed come from the persistent influence of the contrary powers on the sinners' minds, because in this invisible contest the powers are found to be superior. But if, so to speak, there were no devil, no man would ever sin at all.

We however, who look more carefully into the reason of things, do not think that this is so; especially when we consider the acts that arise clearly from the necessities of our body. Are we to suppose that the devil is the cause of our being hungry or thirsty? I suppose there is no one who would venture to maintain this. If then he is not the cause of our being hungry or thirsty, what of that condition when an individual has attained the age of puberty and this period has called forth the exciting movements of the natural heat? It follows without a doubt that, as the devil is not the cause of our being hungry or thirsty, so neither is he the cause even of that impulse which is naturally called forth at the time of maturity, that is, of the desire for sexual intercourse. It is certain that this impulse is by no means always aroused by the devil, so as to lead us to suppose that if there were no devil our bodies would not have the desire for such intercourse.

Then again let us consider in regard to food, – if it be true, as we have shown above, that this is not sought for by men at the instance of the devil, but from a natural instinct – whether human experience, supposing there were no devil, could possibly employ such great self-control in partaking of food as absolutely never to exceed the limit, that is, never to take anything but what the occasion demanded or more than reason permitted, and that it should never happen that men went astray in the observance of due measure and moderation in their food. I for my part do not think that, even if there were no impulse from the devil to urge men on, this rule could be so observed by them that no one would exceed due measure and moderation in partaking of food, not at any rate before they had learned this lesson by long practise and experience. What then? In regard to foods and drink it would be possible for us to go wrong even apart from the instigation of the devil, if we happened to be caught at an intemperate or careless moment; and are we to suppose that in regard to the control of the sexual appetite and the natural desires we should not be affected in a similar way? My own opinion is that the same process of reasoning can also be applied to the rest of the natural emotions, such as covetousness, anger, sorrow or any others whatever, which by the fault of intemperance exceed the limits of their natural measure.

The fact is therefore clear that, just as in regard to things that are good the mere human will is by itself incapable of completing the good act, – for this is in all cases brought to perfection by divine help – so also in regard to things of the opposite kind we derive the beginnings and what we may call the seeds of sin from those desires which are given to us naturally for our use. But when we indulge these to excess and offer no resistance to the first movements towards intemperance, then the hostile power, seizing the opportunity of this first offence, incites and urges us on in every way, striving to extend the sins over a larger field; so that while we men supply the occasions and beginnings of our sins, the hostile powers spread them far and wide and if possible endlessly. It is thus that the fall into avarice at last takes place, men first longing for a little money and then increasing in greed as the vice grows. Afterwards their passion is succeeded by a mental blindness and, with the hostile powers stimulating and urging them on, money is now not merely longed for but even seized by force or acquired through the shedding of human blood.

A sure proof that these vast excesses of sin come from the daemons can easily be observed from the following fact, that those who are under the influence of immoderate love or uncontrolled anger or exceptional sorrow suffer no less than those who are tormented in body by daemons. Further, it is related in certain histories that some men have become insane from love, others even for sorrow or excessive joy; and this happens, I think, because these opposing powers, that is, the daemons, have been allowed to occupy a place in their minds, a place which intemperance has first laid open, and have then taken complete possession of their intelligence, especially as no thought of the glory of virtue aroused them to resistance.

Origen, *De Principis*; trans. G. W. Butterworth, 1936

St Francis Rolls in the Snow

He observed great rigour and discipline, and stode with great heedfullnes vpon his owne defence: having an especiall care, for preservation of the puritie of euerie man. Wherefore at the beginning of his conversion, he vsed oftentimes, even in the winter season, to cast himselfe into a watrie pitte, frosen ouer with ice: that so he might both perfectlie overcome his domesticall enemie; and might also preserue the white garment of chastitie, from the raging fire of voluptuouse pleasure. For he thought it more tolierable by much, and without al comparison, for a spirituall man to sustaine great colde, in his body, then to feele neuer so smale a kindling of carnall pleasure, within his minde. But it hapned vpon a certaine night, that as he was praing within his Cell, in the deserte of *Sarthianum*, the ancient enemie did call him three severall times by his name, saying: *Francis, Francis, Francis*, who demanding of him, what he would haue, he craftelie replied in these wordes: *There is no sinner in the worlde, whom God will not pardon, vpon his conversion unto him: but he that shal kill him selfe with harde penance shall neuer finde mercie at his hands.* The servant of God hearing this, had presentlie by revelation discovered vnto him, the whole drifte and devise of the wicked enemie: by what kinde of deciepte he went about to drawe him into a slacknes in devotion, as the event following, did evidently declare. For immediately after this, by the blaste of his mouth, *Whose breath making burning coales to flame*, he was assailed with a great and greivous tentetion, of the fleshe, comming then vpon him. Which so soone as this lover of chastitie did wel forsee, putting of his coate, he beganne very feirclie to beate him selfe with a corde, saying goe to brother Asse, thus doth it beseme thee to continue, thus oughtest thou to indure the scourge. Thy coate serveth for Religion, it beareth the badge of holinesse: for it is lawfull for anie one that is delighted in vnlawful lust, to intrude vpon it: if any whither thou wouldest goe, then goe thy waies. Moreouer also, being animated with a most wonderfull feruour of spirite, opening the doore of his Cell, he went his way forth into the garden: and there casting downe his poore naked bodie, into the deepe snowe, he caught the same in his handes, and made thereof, seauen heapes: which being orderly placed before him, thus did he then speake to his outwarde man: loe here (saith he) the bigger of these is thy wife, these other foure, are thy two sonns, and thy two daughters, and these two that remaine, are thy servantes thy man and thy maied, which thou oughtest to haue to waite vpon thee. Haste thee now therefore, and see thou forslow not to cloth them al, for they are in present danger, to die for colde. But if the manifolde care, of these seaven be over molestful vnto thee: then serue thine one and onely Lord alone, with heedfull diligence. The tempter forthwith perceiving himselfe by this meanes to be subdued: departed straight away, with shame enough, and the holie man, returned with victorie into his Cell againe: for while he exteriourly, afflicted his bodie with the extremitie, of the paineful colde, which he indured, he did so perfectlie extinguishe the heate of his inwarde lust, that never had he after that time, any feeling or touch thereof againe.

The Life of the Holie Father S. Francis Writen by Saint Bonaventure, 1610

A Game of Wrestling

To speke of euery kynd of temptacion particulerly by it selfe, this were ye wot well in maner an infinite thing / for vnder that as I told you fall persecucions & all / And the devill hath of his traynes a thowsand subtill wayes / & of his open fight as many poysenyd dartes.

He tempteth vs by the world / he temptith vs by our own flesh / he temptith vs by pleasure / he temptith vs by payne / he temptith vs by our foes / he temptith vs by our own frendes / & vnder colour of kyndred, he maketh many tymes our next frendes our most foes / For as our saviour sayth, *Inimici hominis domestici eius.*

But in all maner of so diuers temptacions, one mervelous cumfort is this / that with the mo we be temptid, the glader haue we cause to be / for as S Iames sayth, *omne gaudium existimate fratres quum in tentationes varias incideritis* / estime it & take it sayth he my brethren for a thyng of all ioy whan you fall into diuers & sundry maner of temptacions / And no mervel, for there is in this world set vpp as it were a game of wrestelyng, wherin the people of god come in on the tone side, & on the tother side come mighty strong wresteles & wily, that is to wit, the devilles the cursid prowd dampnid sprites. For it is not our flesh alone that we must wrestell with, but with the devill to / *Non est nobis colluctatio aduersus carnem & sanguinem / sed aduersus principes & potestates tenebrarum harum, aduersus spiritalia nequitie in celestibus* / our wrestelyng is not here sayth S paule agaynst flesh and bloude / but agaynst the princes & potestates of these darke regions, agaynst the spirituall wikkid goostes of the ayer.

But as god vnto them that on his part give his aduersary the fall, hath preparid a crowne / so he that will not wrestle shall none haue / for as saynt paule sayth / *Nemo coronabitur nisi qui legitime certauerit* / ther shall no man haue the crown but he that doth his devour therfor icordyng to the law of the game. And than as holy saynt Barnard sayth / how couldest thow fight or wrestell therfor, yf there were no chalenger agaynst the that wold provoke the therto / And therfor may it be a greate comfort / as S Iames sayth, to euery man that seeth hym selfe chalengid & prouokyd by temptacion / For therby percevith he that yt commeth to his course to wrestle / which shalbe / but yf he willyng will play the coward or the fole, the mater of his eternall reward.

Sir Thomas More, *A Dialogue of Comfort*, written 1534, first pub. 1553

Dr Luther's Casebook

When that envious, poisoned spirit, the devil, plagues and torments us, as is his custom, by reason of our sins, intending thereby to lead us into despair, we must meet him in this manner: 'thou deceitful and wicked spirit! how darest thou presume to persuade me to such things? Knowest thou not that Christ Jesus, my Lord and Saviour, who crushed thy head, has forbidden me to believe thee, yea, even when thou speakest the truth, in that he names thee a murderer, a liar, and the father of lies. I do not admit to thee, that I, as thy captive, shall be condemned to everlasting death and hellish torments, by reason of my sins, as thou falsely suggestest; but thou thyself, on the contrary, long since, by Christ my Lord and Saviour, wert stripped, judged, and with everlasting bonds and chains of darkness, art bound, cast down, and delivered to hell, reserved to the judgment of the great day, and finally, with all the ungodly, shalt be thrown into the bottomless pit of hell. Further, I demand of thee, by what authority thou presumest to exercise such power and right against me? whereas thou hast given me neither life, wife, nor child; no, not the least thing that I have; neither art thou my lord, much less the creator of my body and soul; neither hast thou made the members wherewith I have sinned. How, then, thou wicked and false spirit, art thou so insolent as to domineer over that which is mine, as if thou wert God himself.'

The poisonous serpent takes such delight in doing mischief, that he not only deceives secure and proud spirits with his delusions, but also undertakes, through his deceptions, to bring into error those who are well instructed and grounded in God's Word. He vexes me often so powerfully, and assaults me so fiercely with heavy and melancholy thoughts, that I forget my loving Lord and Saviour Christ Jesus, or at least behold him far otherwise than he is to be beheld. There is none of us so free, but that often he is thus deceived and bewitched with false opinions. Therefore we should learn how to know this conjuror, to the end he may not come behind us, being sleepy and secure, and so delude us with his witchcraft. And truly, if he find us not sober and watching, and not armed with spiritual weapons, that is, with God's Word and with faith, then most surely he will overcome us.

When I could not be rid of the devil with sentences out of the Holy Scripture, I made him often fly with jeering words; sometimes I said unto him: Saint Satan! if Christ's blood, which was shed for my sins, be not sufficient, then I desire that thou wouldst pray to God for me. When he finds me idle, with nothing in hand, he is very busy, and before I am aware, he wrings from me a bitter sweat: but when I offer him the pointed spear, God's Word, he flies; yet, before he goes, makes a grievous hurricane.

The devil is like a fowler; of the birds he catches, he wrings most of their necks, but keeps a few alive, to allure other birds to his snare, by singing the song he will have in a cage. I hope he will not get me into his cage.

The devil often casts this into my breast: How if thy doctrine be false and erroneous, wherewith the pope, the mass, friars and nuns are thus dejected and startled? at which the sour sweat has drizzled from me. But at last, when I saw he would not leave, I gave him this answer: Avoid, Satan; address thyself to my God, and talk with him about it, for the doctrine is not mine, but his; he has commanded me to hearken unto this Christ.

Luther's Table-Talk, trans. William Hazlitt the younger

Mistress Stubbes on Her Deathbed

'How now, Satan? what makes thou here? Art thou come to tempt the Lords seruant? I tell thee, thou hel-hound, thou hast no part nor portion in me, nor by the grace of God neuer shalt haue. I was, now am, and shalbe the Lords for euer. Yea, Satan, I was chosen and elected in Christ to euerlasting saluation, before the foundations of the world were laid: and therefore thou maist get the[e] packing, thou damned dog, & go shake thine eares, for in me hast thou nought. But what dost thou lay to my charge, thou foule fiend? Oh, that I am a sinner, and therefore shall be damned: I confesse in deede that I am a sinner, and a grieuous sinner, both by originall sinne, and actuall sinne; and that, I may thanke thee for. And therfore, Satan, I bequeath my sinne to thee, from whome it first proceeded, and I appeale to the mercie of God in Christ Iesus. Christ came to saue sinners (as he saith himselfe) and not the righteous: 'behold the Lambe of God (saith Iohn) that taketh away the sinnes of the world.' And in another place, he crieth out: 'the blood of Iesus Christ doth cleanse vs from al sinne.' And therefore, Satan, I constantly beleeue that my sinnes are washed away in the precious blood of Iesus Christ, and shall neuer be imputed vnto mee. For Christs righteousnesse is my righteousnesse, his holinesse my holines, his innocencie my innocencie, and his blood a full recompence and satisfaction for all my sinnes. But what sayest thou more, Satan? Dost thou aske me how I dare come to him for mercy, he being a righteous God, and I a miserable sinner? I tell the, Satan, I am bolde thorow Christ to come vnto him, being assured and certaine of pardon and remission of all my sinnes for his names sake. For, doth not the Lord bid all that be heauie laden with the burden of sinne, to come vnto him, and he will ease them? Christes armes were spred wide open (Satan) vpon the Crosse (with that she spred her owne armes) to embrace me, and all penitent sinners; and therefore (Satan) I will not feare to present my selfe before his footstoole, in full assurance of his mercie for Christ his sake. What more, Satan? Doest thou say, it is written, that God wil reward euery one according to his works, or according to his deserts? But it is written againe, thou deceitfull deuill, that Christs righteousnesse is my righteousnesse, his works my works, his deserts my deserts, & his precious blood a full satisfaction for all my sinnes. Oh, but God is a iust God, thou saiest, and therefore must needs in iustice condemne me. I grant (Satan) that he is a iust God, and therefore hee cannot in iustice punish me for my sinnes, which hee hath punished alreadie in his sonne. It is against the law of iustice, to punish one fault twice. I was, and am, a great debter vnto God the Father, but Christ Iesus hath paied the debt for me: and therefore it standeth not with the iustice of God to require it againe. And therefore auoid, Satan, auoid, thou firebrande of hell! auoid, thou damned dog, and tempt me no more! for he that is with me is mightier than thou, euen the mightie and victorious Lion of the tribe of *Iuda*, who hath bruized thy head, and hath promised to be with his children to the end of the world. Auoid therfore, thou dastard, auoid, thou cowardly souldier, remooue thy siege, and yeelde the field wonne, & get thee packing, or else I wil cal vpon my grand-captaine Christ Iesus, that valiant *Michael*, who beate thee in heauen, and threw thee downe to hell, with all thy hellish traine, and diuelish crew.' She had scarcely pronounced the last wordes, but she fell suddenly into a sweet smiling laughter, saying,

'Now is he gone, now is he gone! do you not see him flie like a cowarde, and runne away like a beaten cocke?'

Philip Stubbes, *A Christall Glasse for Christian Women*, 1591

Baited Hooks

The *Diuell*, whom our weake *Eyes* cannot view,
Is therefore to be more bewar'd and fear'd,
  As one that *Man* doth night and day pursue;
His wounds (when made) not felt, his voice not heard.
    He baits his hooks with pride, with gold, with treasure.
    A thousand *ginnes* are for our foot-steps layd;
Bird-lime he hath, and that's when aboue measure
We dote on things by which we are betrayd,
    Self-loue, Vain-glory, fleshly Lusts, Ambition,
    All his meere traines to bring vs to perdition.

If I be ignorant, he prompts me then
To dote on *Folly*, *Wisedome* to despise,
To prefer *Ideots* before *Learned* men,
And striue to be sequestred from the *Wise*.
    Or if that I in reading take delight,
    (At sorted leisure my spare houres to spend)
The *Legend* of some strange aduenturous *Knight*,
Or fabulous *Toy*, hee'l to my view commend.
    But from mine eye the sacred *Scriptures* keepe,
    Persuading th' are too plaine, or else to deepe.

Or if I after *Learning* shall enquire,
And to the least perfection can attaine;
Either he makes me mine owne *Gifts* admire,
Or others of lesse knowledge to disdaine.
    Or if my *Talent* to my selfe conceale,
Then to search out things mysticall and hid,
Such as God had no purpose to reueale,
But in his secret *Counsels* hath forbid.
    Assur'd, That 'mongst his other traines and baites,
    None more than *Curiositie* God hates.

Thomas Heywood, *The Hierarchie of the Blessed Angells*, 1635

[161]

The Devil Tempts Sir Thomas Browne with Chemistry

There is, as in philosophy, so in divinity, sturdy doubts and boisterous objections, wherewith the unhappiness of our knowledge too nearly acquainteth us. More of these no man hath known than myself, which I confess I conquered, not in a martial posture, but on my knees. For our endeavours are not only to combat with doubts, but always to dispute with the Devil: the villainy of that spirit takes a hint of infidelity from our studies, and, by demonstrating a naturality in one way, makes us mistrust a miracle in another. Thus, having perused the *Archidoxis*, and read the secret sympathies of things, he would dissuade my belief from the miracle of the brazen serpent; makes me conceit that image worked by sympathy, and was but an Egyptian trick to cure their diseases without a miracle. Again, having seen some experiments of bitumen, and having read far more of naphtha, he whispered to my curiosity the fire of the altar might be natural; and bid me mistrust a miracle in Elias when he entrenched the altar round with water: for that inflammable substance yields not easily unto water, but flames in the arms of its antagonist. And thus would he inveigle my belief to think the combustion of Sodom might be natural, and that there was an asphaltic and bituminous nature in that lake before the fire of Gomorrah. I know that manna is now plentifully gathered in Calabria, and Josephus tells me in his days 'twas as plentiful in Arabia: the Devil therefore made the query, 'Where was then the miracle in the days of Moses? The Israelites saw but that in his time, the natives of those countries behold in ours.' Thus the Devil played at chess with me, and yielding a pawn, thought to gain a queen of me, taking advantage of my honest endeavours; and whilst I laboured to raise the structure of my reason, he strived to undermine the edifice of my faith.

Sir Thomas Browne, *Religio Medici*, 1642

The Tables Are Turned

It may be true, however, that under the powerful guard and protection of the Devil, men do sometimes go a great way in crime, and that perhaps farther in these our days of boasted morals than was known among our fathers; the only difference that I meet with between the sons of Belial in former days, and those of our ages, seems to be in the Devil's management, not in theirs; the sum of which amounts to this, that Satan seems to act with more cunning, and they with less; for in the former ages of Satan's dominion, he had much business upon his hands, all his art and engines, and engineers also, were kept fully employed to wheedle, allure, betray and circumvent people, and draw them into crimes, and they found him, as we may say, a full employment; I doubt not, he was called the Tempter on that very account; but the case seems quite altered now, the tables are turned; then the Devil tempted men to sin. But now, in short, they tempt the Devil; men push into crimes before he pushes them; they out-shoot him in his own bow, out-run him on his own ground, and, as we say of some hot spurs who ride post, they whip the postboy; in a word, the Devil seems to have no business now but to sit still and look on.

This, I must confess, seems to intimate some secret compact between the Devil and them; but then it looks, not as if they had contracted with the Devil for leave to sin, but that the Devil had contracted with them, that they should sin so and so, up to such a degree, and that without giving him the trouble of daily solicitation, private management, and artful screwing up their passions, their affections and their most retired faculties, as he was before obliged to do.

Daniel Defoe, *The History of the Devil*, 1726

Bottled Wickedness

At last, Brother Cyrillus had recourse to an old and strangely carved wooden press, which he carefully unlocked, and out of which he took a small square box. 'Herein, Brother Medardus,' said he, 'is contained the most wonderful and mysterious relic of which our convent is possessed. As long as I have been resident here, no one but the Prior and myself has had this box in his hands. Even the other brethren (not to speak of strangers) are unaware of its existence. For my own part, I cannot even touch this casket without an inward shuddering; for it seems to me as if there were some malignant spell, or rather, some living demon, locked up within it, which, were the bonds broken by which this evil principle is now confined, would bring destruction on all who came within its accursed range.

'That which is therein contained is known to have been derived immediately from the Arch-Fiend, at the time when he was still allowed *visibly*, and in personal shape, to contend against the weal of mankind.'

I looked at Brother Cyrillus with the greatest astonishment; but without leaving me time to answer, he went on.

'I shall abstain, Brother Medardus, from offering you any opinion of my own on this mysterious affair, but merely relate to you faithfully what our documents say upon the subject. You will find the papers in that press, and can read them afterwards at your leisure.

'The life of St Anthony is already well known to you. You are aware, that in order to be completely withdrawn from the distractions of the world, he went out into the desert, and there devoted himself to the severest penitential exercises. The Devil, of course, followed him, and came often in his way, in order to disturb him in his pious contemplations.

'One evening it happened accordingly, that St Anthony was returning home, and had arrived near his cell, when he perceived a dark figure approaching him rapidly along the heath. As his visitant came nearer, he observed with surprise, through the holes in a torn mantle worn by the stranger, the long necks of oddly-shaped bottles, which of course produced an effect the most extraordinary and grotesque. It was the Devil, who, in this absurd masquerade, smiled on him ironically, and inquired if he would not choose to taste of the Elixir which he carried in these bottles? At this insolence, St Anthony was not even incensed, but remained perfectly calm; for the Enemy, having now become powerless and contemptible, was no longer in a condition to venture a real combat, but must confine himself to scornful words.

'The Saint, however, inquired for what reason he carried about so many bottles in that unheard-of manner.

' "For this very reason," said the Devil, "that people may be induced to ask me the question; for as soon as any mortal meets with me, he looks on me with astonishment, makes the same inquiry that you have done, and, in the next place, cannot forbear desiring to taste, and try what sort of elixirs I am possessed of. Among so many bottles, if he finds one which suits his taste, and *drinks it out*, and becomes drunk, he is then irrecoverably mine, and belongs to me and my kingdom for ever."

'So far the story is the same in all legends, though some of them add, that, according to the Devil's confession, if two individuals should drink out of the same flask, they would henceforth become addicted to the same crimes, possessing a wonderful reciprocity of thoughts and feelings, yet mutually and unconsciously acting for the destruction of each other. By our own manuscripts, it is narrated farther, that when the Devil went from thence, he left some of his flasks on the ground, which St Anthony directly took with him into his cave, fearing that they might fall into the way of accidental travellers, or even deceive some of his own pupils, who came to visit him in that retirement. By chance, so we are also told,

St Anthony once opened one of these bottles, out of which there arose directly a strange and stupifying vapour, whereupon all sorts of hideous apparitions and spectral phantoms from hell had environed the Saint, in order to terrify and delude him. Above all, too, there were forms of women, who sought to entice him into shameless indecencies. These altogether tormented him, until, by constant prayer, and severe penitential exercises, he had driven them again out of the field.

'In this very box there is now deposited a bottle of that kind, saved from the relics of St Anthony; and the documents thereto relating, are so precise and complete, that the fact of its having been derived from the Saint is hardly to be doubted. Besides, I can assure you, Brother Medardus, that so often as I have chanced to touch this bottle, or even the box in which it is contained, I have been struck with a mysterious horror. It seems to me also, as if I smelt a peculiar, odoriferous vapour, which stuns the senses, and the effects of which do not stop there, but utterly rob me of composure of spirit afterwards, and distract my attention from devotional exercises.

'Whether I do or not believe in this immediate intercourse with the devil in visible shape, yet, that such distraction proceeds from the direct influence of some hostile power, there can be no doubt. However, I overcame this gradually by zealous and unceasing prayer. As for you, Brother Medardus, whose fervent imagination will colour all things with a strength beyond that of reality, and who, in consequence of youth, also will be apt to trust too much to your own power of resistance, I would earnestly impress on you this advice, – "Never, or at least, for many years, to open the box; and in order that it may not tempt and entice you, to put it as much as possible out of your reach and sight."'

Hereupon Brother Cyrillus shut up the mysterious Box in the press from which it had come, and consigned over to me a large bunch of keys, among which that of the formidable press had its place. The whole story had made on me a deep impression, and the more that I felt an inward longing to contemplate the wonderful relic, the more I was resolved to render this to myself difficult, or even impossible.

When Cyrillus left me, I looked over once more, one by one, the treasures thus committed to my charge; I then returned to my cell, and untied the key of the Devil's press from the bunch to which it belonged, and hid it deeply among the papers in my writing-desk.

One temptation, said I to myself, I have already overcome. I have emancipated myself from the thraldom of Therese. Never more shall the Devil by his insidious artifices, gain ascendancy over me!

E. T. A. Hoffmann, *Die Elixiere des Teufels*, 1815–16; trans. 1824

'La Destruction'

Sans cesse à mes côtés s'agite le Démon;
Il nage autour de moi comme un air impalpable;
Je l'avale et le sens qui brûle mon poumon
Et l'emplit d'un désir éternel et coupable.

Parfois il prend, sachant mon grand amour de l'Art,
La forme de la plus séduisante des femmes,
Et, sous de spécieux prétextes de cafard,
Accoutume ma lèvre à des philtres infâmes.

Il me conduit ainsi, loin du regard de Dieu,
Haletant et brisé de fatigue, au milieu
Des plaines de l'Ennui, profondes et désertes,

Et jette dans mes yeux pleins de confusion
Des vêtements souillés, des blessures ouvertes,
Et l'appareil sanglant de la Destruction!

Charles Baudelaire, 1855

Flaubert Blinds St Anthony with Science

THE DEVIL (*pauses, and rocks Anthony gently in the midst of space*): Nothingness is not – there is no void! Everywhere and forever bodies move upon the immovable deeps of space! Were there boundaries to space, it would not be space, but a body only: it is limitless!

ANTHONY (*stupefied by wonder*): Limitless!

THE DEVIL: Ascend skyward forever and forever, – yet thou wilt not attain the summit. Descend below the earth for billions of billions of centuries: never wilt thou reach the bottom. For there is no summit, there is no bottom; there is no Above, no Below – nor height, nor depth as signified by the terms of human utterance. And Space itself is comprised in God, who is not a portion thereof of such or such a size, – but is Immensity itself!

ANTHONY (*slowly*): Matter ..., then, ... must be a part of God?

THE DEVIL: Why not? Canst thou know the end of God?

ANTHONY: Nay: on the contrary, I prostrate, I crush myself beneath his mightiness!

THE DEVIL: And yet thou dost pretend to move him! Thou dost speak to him, – thou dost even adorn him with virtues, – with goodness, justice, mercy, – in lieu of recognising that all perfections are his!

To conceive aught beyond him is to conceive God above God, the Being above the Being. For He is the only being, the only substance.

If the Substance could be divided, it would not be the Substance, it would lose its nature: God could not exist. He is therefore indivisible as infinite; – and if he had a body, he would be composed of parts, he would not be One – he would not be infinite. Therefore he is not a Person!

ANTHONY: What! my prayers, my sobs, my groans, the sufferings of my flesh, the transports of my love, – have all these things gone out to a lie, – to emptiness, unavailingly – like the cry of a bird, like a whirl of dead leaves?

(*Weeping*): Oh, no! – there is Some One above all things, – a great Soul, a Lord, a Father whom my heart adores and who must love me!

THE DEVIL: Thou dost desire that God were not God; – for did he feel love, or anger, or pity, – he would abandon his perfection for a greater or a lesser perfection. He can stoop to no sentiment, nor be contained in any form.

ANTHONY: One day, nevertheless, I shall see him!

THE DEVIL: With the blessed, is it not? – when the finite shall enjoy the infinite in some restricted place, containing the Absolute!

ANTHONY: Matters not! – there must be a paradise for the good, as there is a hell for the wicked.

THE DEVIL: Can the desire of thy mind create the law of the universe? Without doubt evil is indifferent to God, – forasmuch as the Earth is covered with it!

Is it through impotence that he endures it, or through cruelty that he maintains it?

Dost thou fancy that he is eternally readjusting the world, like an imperfect machine? – that he is forever watching the movements of all beings, from the flight of a butterfly to the thought of a man?

If he have created the universe, his providence is superfluous. If Providence exists, then creation is defective.

But evil and good concern only thee – even like night and day, pleasure and pain, death and birth, which are relative only to one corner of space, to a special centre, to a particular interest. Since the Infinite is permanent, the Infinite is; – and that is all.

(The Devil's wings have been gradually expanding: now they cover all space.)

ANTHONY *(now perceives nothing: a great faintness comes upon him)*: A hideous cold freezes me, even to the depths of my soul! This is beyond the extreme of pain! It is like a death that is deeper than death! I roll in the immensity of darkness; and the darkness itself enters within me. My consciousness bursts beneath this dilation of nothingness!

THE DEVIL: Yet the knowledge of things comes to thee only through the medium of thy mind. Even as a concave mirror, it deforms the objects it reflects; and thou hast no means whatever of verifying their exactitude.

Never canst thou know the universe in all its vastness; consequently it will never be possible for thee to obtain an idea of its cause, to have a just notion of God, nor even to say that the universe is infinite, – for thou must first be able to know what the Infinite is!

May not Form be, perhaps, an error of thy senses, – Substance a figment of thy imagination?

Unless, indeed, that the world being a perpetual flux of things, appearance, on the contrary, be wholly true; illusion the only reality.

But art thou sure thou dost see? – art thou even sure thou dost live? Perhaps nothing exists!

(The Devil has seized Anthony, and, holding him at arms' length, glares at him with mouth yawning as though to devour him): Adore me, then! – and curse the phantom thou callest God!

*(Anthony lifts his eyes with a last effort of hope.
The Devil abandons him.)*

Gustave Flaubert, *La Tentation de St Antoine*, 1874;
trans. Lafcadio Hearn, 1911

The Last Temptation

Lastly, To lead us farther into darkness, and quite to lose us in this maze of Error, he would make men believe there is no such creature as himself: and that he is not only subject unto inferiour creatures, but in the rank of nothing. Insinuating into men's minds there is no Devil at all, and contriveth accordingly, many ways to conceal or indubitate his existency. Wherein beside that, he annihilates the blessed Angels and Spirits in the rank of his Creation; he begets a security of himself, and a careless eye unto the last remunerations.

Sir Thomas Browne, *Pseudodoxia Epidemica*, 1646

Screwtape Concurs

I do not think you will have much difficulty in keeping the patient in the dark. The fact that 'devils' are predominantly *comic* figures in the modern imagination will help you. If any faint suspicion of your existence begins to arise in his mind, suggest to him a picture of something in red tights, and persuade him that since he cannot believe in that (it is an old textbook method of confusing them) he therefore cannot believe in you.

C. S. Lewis, *The Screwtape Letters*, 1942

Five

THE DEVIL AT HOME

One must just be satisfied with symbolism,
my good man, when one is speaking of hell, for there
everything ends – not only the word that describes,
but everything altogether.

THOMAS MANN

Haue good day! I goo to helle.
The Castle of Perseverance, c.1400

A Visitor Calls

Satan the inheritor of darkness cometh and saith unto Hades: O thou that devourest all and art insatiable, hearken to my words. There is one of the race of the Jews, Jesus, who calleth himself the Son of God; but he is a man, and by our contrivance the Jews have crucified him. And now that he hath died, be thou prepared that we may make him fast here. For I know that he is a man, and I have heard him saying: My soul is exceeding sorrowful, even unto death. And he hath done me much hurt in the world that is above while he walked among men. For wheresoever he found my servants he did persecute them, and as many as I caused to be maimed, or blind, or lame, or leprous, or any such thing, he healed them with a word only: and whereas I made ready many to be buried, them also he quickened again only with a word.

Hades saith: And is he indeed so mighty that he can do such things with a word only? or, if he be such, art thou able to withstand him? it seemeth to me, no man will be able to withstand him: but whereas thou sayest that thou hast heard him fearing death, this he said to mock thee and in sport, willing to seize on thee with a mighty hand: and woe, woe unto thee for everlasting! Satan saith: O thou Hades that devourest all and art insatiable, didst thou fear so much at that thou hast heard concerning our common adversary? I feared him not, but I did set on the Jews, and they crucified him and gave him also gall to drink mingled with vinegar. Prepare thyself, therefore, that when he cometh thou mayest hold him fast.

Hades answered: O inheritor of darkness, son of perdition, devil, thou saidst but now unto me that many of them whom thou hadst made ready to be buried he did quicken again with a word only: now if he hath set free many from burial, how and by what strength shall he be held by us? I indeed of late swallowed up a certain dead man named Lazarus, and after a little, one of the living by force snatched him up out of mine entrails by a word only: and I think this is he of whom thou speakest. If, then, we receive him here, I fear lest we be imperilled for the rest also; for I have swallowed up all men from the beginning: behold, I perceive that they are unquiet, and my belly paineth me, and this Lazarus that before was caught away from me I take to be no good sign, for he flew away from me, not like to a dead man, but to an eagle, so instantly did the earth cast him out. Wherefore also I adjure thee by thy gifts and by mine own, that thou bring him not to this place, for I believe that he cometh hither to raise up all the dead. And this I say unto thee: by the outer darkness, if thou bring him hither, not one of all the dead will be left in me.

The Acts of Pilate in *The Apocryphal New Testament*, ed. M. R. James, 1924

I'll Huff and I'll Puff

JESUS: Open up hell-gates anonne,
    ye prynces of pyne everychon,
    that Godes Sonne may in gonne,
    and the kinge of blys.
SECUNDUS DAEMON: Go hense, poplard, owt of thys place
    or thou shalt have a sorye grace.
    For all thy boaste and thy menace
    theise men thou shalt amys.
SATHANAS: Owt, alas, what ys thys?
    Seghe I never so mych blys
    towardes hell come, iwys,
    sythen I was warden here.
    My masterdome fares amys,
    for yonder a stubberne fellowe ys,
    right as wholye hell were his,
    to reave me of my power.

The Chester Mystery Cycle, ed. R. M. Lumiansky and David Mills, 1974

Light into the Dark

Then came there again a voice, saying: Lift up the gates. And when Hades heard the voice the second time, he answered as if he knew it not, and said: Who is this King of glory? The angels of the Lord said: The Lord strong and mighty, the Lord mighty in battle. And straightway at the word the gates of brass were broken in pieces and the bars of iron were ground to powder, and all the dead that were bound were loosed from their chains, and we with them, and the King of glory entered in, *in fashion* as a man, and all the dark places of Hell were enlightened.

The Acts of Pilate in *The Apocryphal New Testament*, ed. M. R. James, 1924

The Exodus to Bliss

JESUS: Þis steede schall stonde no lenger stoken,
    Opynne vppe and latte my pepul passe.
DIABOLUS: Oute! beholdes, oure baill is brokynne,
    And brosten are alle oure bandis of bras.
    Telle lucifer alle is vnlokynne.
BELSABUB: What þanne, is lymbus lorne, allas!
    Garre Satan, helpe þat we were wroken,
    Þis werke is werse þanne euere it was.
SATTAN: I badde ȝe schulde be boune
    If he made maistries more,
    Do dynge þat dastard doune,
    And sette hym sadde and sore.
BELSABUB: Ȝa, sette hym sore, þat is sone saide,
    But come þi selffe and serue hym soo,
    We may not bide his bittir braide,
    He wille vs marre, and we wer moo.
SATTAN: What! faitours, wherfore are ȝe ferde?
    Haue ȝe no force to flitte hym froo?
    Belyue loke þat my gere be grathed,
    Mi selffe schall to þat gedlyng goo.
    [*To Jesus.*] Howe! belamy, a de,
    With al thy booste and bere,
    And telle to me þis tyde,
    What maistries makes þou here?
JESUS: I make no maistries but for myne,
    Þame wolle I saue, I telle þe nowe,
    Þou hadde no poure þame to pyne,
    But as my prisonne for þer prowe.
    Here haue þei soiorned, noght as thyne,
    But in thy warde, þou wote wele howe.
SATTAN: And what deuel haste þou done ay syne
    Þat neuer wolde negh þame nere, or nowe?
JESUS: Nowe is þe tyme certayne
    Mi Fadir ordand be-fore,
    Þat they schulde passe fro payne,
    And wonne in mirthe euer more.

The York Plays, ed. Lucy Toulmin Smith, 1885

A Landlady Is Left Behind

MULIER: Woe be the tyme that I came here,
   I saye to thee nowe, Lucifere,
   with all thy felowshipp in fere
   that present be in place.
   Wofull am I with thee to dwell,
   syr Sathanas, sargeant of hell.
   Endles sorrowe and paynes cruell
   I suffer in this case.

   Sometyme I was a taverner,
   a gentle gossippe and a tapster,
   of wyne and ale a trustie bruer,
   which woe hath me wrought.
   Of kannes I kept no trewe measure.
   My cuppes I sould at my pleasure,
   deceavinge manye a creature,
   thoe my ale were nought.

   And when I was a bruer longe,
   with hoppes I made my alle stronge;
   esshes and hearbes I blend amonge
   and marred so good malt.
   Therfore I may my handes wringe,
   shake my cuppes and kannes ringe.
   Sorrowfull maye I syke and singe
   that ever I so dalt.

   Tavernes, tapsters of this cittye
   shalbe promoted here with mee
   for breakinge statutes of this contrye,
   hurtinge the commonwealth,
   with all typpers-tappers that are cunninge,
   mispendinge much malt, bruynge so thinne,
   sellinge smale cuppes money to wynne,
   agaynst all trueth to deale.

   Therfore this place nowe ordayned ys
   for such yll-doers so mych amysse.

Here shall they have their joye and blys,
exalted by the necke,
with my master, mightie Mahound,
for castinge malt besydes the combes,
myche water takinge for to compound,
and little of the secke.

With all mashers, mengers of wyne, in the night
bruynge so, blendinge agaynst daylight,
sych newe-made claret ys cause full right
of sycknes and disease.
Thus I betake you, more and lesse,
to my sweete mayster, syr Sathanas,
to dwell with him in his place
when hyt shall you please.

SATHANAS: Welcome, dere daughter, to us all three.
Though Jesu be gonne with our meanye,
yett shalt thou abyde here still with mee
in payne withowt ende.

SECUNDUS DAEMON: Welcome, sweete ladye! I will thee wedd,
for manye a heavye and dronken head
cause of thy ale were brougt to bedd
farre worse then anye beaste.

TERTIUS DAEMON: Welcome, dear darlinge, to endles bale.
Usynge cardes, dyce, and cuppes smale,
with many false othes to sell thy ale –
nowe thou shall have a feaste!

The Chester Mystery Cycle, ed. R. M. Lumiansky and David Mills, 1974

The Infernal Fire

But here now is another question: whether this fire, if it plague not
spiritually, but only by a bodily touch, can inflict any torment upon the
devil and his angels? they are to remain in one fire with the damned,
according to our Saviour's own words: 'Depart from Me, ye cursed, into
everlasting fire, which is prepared for the devil and his angels.' But the
devils, according as some learned men suppose, have bodies of condensed

air, such as we feel in a wind; and this air is passible, and may suffer burning, the heating of baths proves, where the air is set on fire to heat the water, and does that which first it suffers. If any will oppose, and say the devils have no bodies at all, the matter is not great, nor much to be stood upon. For why may not unbodied spirits feel the force of bodily fire, as well as man's incorporeal soul is now included in a carnal shape, and shall at that day be bound into a body for ever. These spiritual devils therefore, or those devilish spirits, though strangely, yet shall they be truly bound in this corporeal fire, which shall torment them for all that they are incorporeal. Nor shall they be so bound in it, that they shall give it a soul as it were, and so become both one living creature, but as I said, by a wonderful power shall be so bound that instead of giving it life, they shall from it receive intolerable torment, although the coherence of spirits and bodies, whereby both become one creature, be as admirable, and exceed all human capacity. And surely I should think the devils shall burn them, as the rich glutton did, when he cried saying, 'I am tormented in this flame,' but that I should be answered that that fire was such as his tongue was, to cool which, he seeing Lazarus afar off, entreated him to help him with a little water on the tip of his finger. He was not then in the body but in soul only; such likewise (that is incorporeal) was the fire he burned in, and the water he wished for, as the dreams of those that sleep and the vision of men in ecstasies are, which present the forms of bodies, and yet are not bodies indeed. And though man see these things only in spirit, yet thinks he himself so like to his body, that he cannot discern whether he have it on or no. But that hell, that lake of fire and brimstone, shall be real, and the fire corporeal, burning both men and devils, the one in flesh and the other in air: the one in the body adherent to the spirit, and the other in spirit only adherent to the fire, and yet not infusing life, but feeling torment for one fire shall torment, both men and devils. Christ has spoken it.

St Augustine, *De Civitate Dei*, c.413–26 AD; trans. John Healey, 1610

Down, Down, Down

Beneath the dens where *unfletcht Tempests* lye,
And infant *Winds* their tender *Voyces* try,
Beneath the mighty *Oceans* wealthy caves,
Beneath th'aeternal *Fountain* of all *Waves*,
Where their vast *Court* the *Mother-waters* keep,
And undisturb'd by *Moons* in silence sleep,

There is a place deep, wondrous deep below,
Which genuine *Night* and *Horror* does o'reflow;
No bound controls th'unwearied space, but *Hell*
Endless as those dire *pains* that in it dwell.
Here no dear glimpse of the *Suns* lovely face,
Strikes through the *Solid* darkness of the place;
No dawning *Morn* does her kind reds display;
One slight weak beam would here be thought the *Day*.
No gentle *Stars* with their fair *Gems* of *Light*
Offend the tyr'annous and unquestion'd *Night*.

Abraham Cowley, *Davideis* in *Poems*, 1656

Beyond Hell Gate

A lytull fordermore þey ȝode
And sone at Helle ȝates þey stode.
Ther Tundale sawe a grete pytte,
All þys worlde myghtte it nowt ditte.
'Come hyþer,' sayde þe angell bryȝth,
'Thow shalt se a wonder syȝte:
Stonde ner þys pytte & loke downe
And þou shalte se a fowle dongyone;
This pytte is aye as merke as nyght
And evere shall it bene withowten lyght.
Fendys and sowlys that heerinne es,
Thow shalt hem seen bothe more and les,
And Lucefere that is bownden in fyre
That is prince theer, mayster and syre,
But soo shull they iletted now bee
That none of theym shall see thee.'

Tundale thanne to thee pitte wente
Thorghw thee awngelys comaundement.
Down hee lokede with gret awe,
Lucyfer atte thee grounde he sawe;
Soo ugly was þat lothely syght
Ferde he was for þat foule wyght;
So orryble he was ferede,
Of deuelles he se a foule herde.
Pagh a man hade verrely

A hundred hedis on a body,
And als manye mouthes wythalle
As to ilke a hede shulde falle,
And ilke a mouthe aboue þe chynne
A hundred tongus had wythin,
And ilke a tonge couthe shewe þe wytte
Þat alle men haue þat leuen 3[y]tte,
Were not inoghe, halfe to telle,
Þat he se in þe pytte of Helle.
But Tundale toke full goode kepe
Of Lucyfer that lyes so depe.
Hee auysed hym be his sight
In what wyse descrye hym hee myght;
Hee cowde no wit, hee was so grym,
To what thyng he myghtte lyken hym.
Hym thowghtte hee was full greet to knawe
By any beeste that evere hee sawe;
His body was bothe brode and thicke
And also blak as is any picke;
So blak as he semede was noon thanne,
But hym thoughtte hee hadde the shap of manne.

He was bothe mekyll and therto stronge;
An hundred cubitis hee was longe
Ard twenty cubitis hee was on brade
And ten on thicnesse was hee made.
Whanne hee gapiht or whanne hee gones
A thowsand sowlis hee swolwys attonys.
Byfore and beehynde hee hadde growande
On his body attonys a thowsand hande,
And on every hande theer was sene
Twenty fyngeris with naylis kene,
And like a fynger semede thanne
Thee lengthe of a hunder spanne,
And ten spanne abowte of thiknesse
Was ilke a fynger, and noo lesse.
His nayles semed of irne stronge,
Fulle, scharpe þai were, gret & longe;
Longere þan euer was ony spere
Þat armed knyghtes ar wont to bere;
As mony toes on hym he fande
Wyth nayles on his fete growande;

Hee hade a mekille longe snowte
That was large of brede aboute,
And his mouthe was fulle wyde
Wyth hangynge lyppes on eyther syde;
His tayle was scharpe & of gret lenght,
And in his tayle was greet strenght;
Wyt scharpe hokys þat in his tayle stekyth
Þe sowlis abowte sore hee prekkith;
Upon a gredylle of iren glowande
Þe fowle wyght was ay lyggande.
Brennande koles laye þervnþer,
But þey wer dymme & þat was wonþer.
Mony fendes as hyt were tadered folys
Wyth belewes blewe at þe colys.
So mony abowte hem flowe
In mydwarde þe fyr & in þe lowe,
That Tundale hadde grete ferly
That in þe worlde myȝte haue be so mony.

Lucyfere þat hath ben so grymme
Ther lay bownden in yche a lymme
Wyth iren cheynes brode & longe
Vpon a gredyll þat was full stronge.
Also Tundale þowȝte þe chayne was
Lapped abowte wyth brennande brasse,
And all þe sowles þat he hente
In hys hondes were all toshente.
He þrystede hem in sonder as men doose
Grapys to þryste oute þe wose;
Whenne he hadde þryste hem in sonþer all
Into þe fyre he lette hem fall,
And ȝette keuered þey all aȝeyn
And eftesones þey wer putte in payn.
Tundale herde & sawe also
How Lucyfere sykkede for wo
For þat he was bownden so faste,
And at yche a sykynge þat he kaste
A þowsand sowles fro hym flowe
Out of hys mowþe into þe lowe.
They were sone skatered wyde
Abowte hys mowþe on eche a syde,
But þat payne was not ȝette ynowȝ!

Whenne he aȝeyn hys breth drowȝ
All þe sowles þat were kaste owte
And skatered hym all abowte,
He swolowede hem aȝeyn ylke on.
Wyth þe reke & stynke of brymstone
Tho sowles þat passed owte at hys ende
Fell into þe fyr & brende.
When þey aȝeyn keuered w[o]re
Wyth hys tayle he stroke hem sore;
He pynede þe sowles & dyde hem wo,
And hymselfe was pyned also;
The more payne þat he wrowȝte,
To þe sowles þat were hym browȝte,
The more payne hys owene was,
And fro þat may he neuer passe.

The angell þen sayde to Tundale:
'Her may þou se mykyll bale.
Lucyfer hatte þat vglye wyȝte
That semes so mykyll to þy syȝth.
He was þe fyrste creature
That God made after Hys stature;
Fro Heuen þorow pride he fell downe
Into þys depe fowle dongeoun.
Her ys he bownden as þou mayst se,
And so tyll Domesday shall he be,
For, ȝyf þe cheynes fayled þat do hym holde,
Heuen & Erþe trowbyll he wolde.

Vision of Tundale, Mid. Eng. trans., c.1450–1500, of Lat. *Visio Tnugdali*, c.1150;
ed. Rodney Mearns, 1985

The Prisoner in the Frozen Lake

'Vexilla regis prodeunt inferni
    verso di noi; però dinanzi mira,'
    disse 'l maestro mio, 'se tu 'l discerni.'
Come quando una grossa nebbia spira,
    o quando l'emisperio nostro annotta,
    par di lungi un molin che 'l vento gira,
veder mi parve un tal dificio allotta;

poi per lo vento mi ristrinsi retro
al duca mio, ché no lì era altra grotta.

Già era, e con paura il metto in metro,
là dove l'ombre tutte eran coperte,
e trasparien come festuca in vetro.

Altre sono a giacere; altre stanno erte,
quella col capo e quella con le piante;
altra, com' arco, il volto a' piè rinverte.

Quando noi fummo fatti tanto avante,
ch'al mio maestro piacque di mostrarmi
la creatura ch'ebbe il bel sembiante,

d'innanzi mi si tolse e fé restarmi,
'Ecco Dite,' dicendo, 'ed ecco il loco
ove convien che di fortezza t'armi.'

Com' io divenni allor gelato e fioco,
nol dimandar, lettor, ch'i' non lo scrivo,
però ch'ogne parlar sarebbe poco.

Io non mori' e non rimasi vivo;
pensa oggimai per te, s'hai fior d'ingegno,
qual io divenni, d'uno e d'altro privo.

Lo 'mperador del doloroso regno
da mezzo 'l petto uscia fuor de la ghiaccia;
e più con un gigante io mi convegno,

che i giganti non fan con le sue braccia:
vedi oggimai quant' esser dee quel tutto
ch'a così fatta parte si confaccia.

S'el fu sì bel com' elli è ora brutto,
e contra 'l suo fattore alzò le ciglia,
ben dee da lui procedere ogne lutto.

Oh quanto parve a me gran maraviglia
quand' io vidi tre facce a la sua testa!
L'una dinanzi, e quella era vermiglia;

l'altr' eran due, che s'aggiugnieno a questa
sovresso 'l mezzo di ciascuna spalla,
e sé giugnieno al loco de la cresta:

e la destra parea tra bianca e gialla;
la sinistra a vedere era tal, quali
vegnon di là onde 'l Nilo s'avvalla.

Sotto ciascuna uscivan due grand' ali,
quanto si convenia a tanto uccello:
vele di mar non vid' io mai cotali.

Non avean penne, ma di vispistrello

era lor modo; e quelle svolazzava,
    sì che tre venti si movean da ello:
quindi Cocito tutto s'aggelava.
    Con sei occhi piangëa, e per tre menti
    gocciava 'l pianto e sanguinosa bava.
Da ogne bocca dirompea co' denti
    un peccatore, a guisa di maciulla,
    sì che tre ne facea così dolenti.
A quel dinanzi il mordere era nulla
    verso 'l graffiar, che tal volta la schiena
    rimanea de la pelle tutta brulla.
'Quell' anima là sù c'ha maggior pena,'
    disse 'l maestro, 'è Giuda Scarïotto,
    che 'l capo ha dentro e fuor le gambe mena.
De li altri due c'hanno il capo di sotto,
    quel che pende dal nero ceffo è Bruto:
    vedi come si storce, e non fa motto!;
e l'altro è Cassio, che par sì membruto.
    Ma la notte risurge, e oramai
    è de partir, ché tutto avem veduto.'

'*Vexilla Regis prodeunt Inferni*
    Towards us; therefore look in front of thee,'
    My master said, 'if thou discernest him.'
As, when there breathes a heavy fog, or when
    Our hemisphere is darkening into night,
    Appears far off a mill the wind is turning,
Methought that such a building then I saw;
    And for the wind, I drew myself behind
    My guide, because there was no other shelter.
Now was I, and with fear in verse I put it,
    There where the shades were wholly covered up,
    And glimmered through like unto straws in glass.
Some prone are lying, others stand erect,
    This with the head, and that one with the soles;
    Another, bow-like, face to feet inverts.
When in advance so far we had proceeded,
    That it my master pleased to shew to me
    The creature who once had the beauteous semblance,
He from before me moved and made me stop,
    Saying, 'BEHOLD DIS, and behold the place
    Where thou with fortitude must arm thyself.'

How frozen I became and powerless then,
  Ask it not, reader, for I write it not,
  Because all language would be insufficient.
I did not die, and I alive remained not;
  Think for thyself now, hast thou aught of wit,
  What I became, being of both deprived.
The emperor of the kingdom dolorous
  From his mid-breast forth issued from the ice;
  And better with a giant I compare
Than do the giants with those arms of his;
  Consider now how great must be that whole,
  Which unto such a part conforms itself.
Were he as fair once, as he now is foul,
  And lifted up his brow against his Maker;
  Well may proceed from him all tribulation.
O, what a marvel it appeared to me,
  When I beheld three faces on his head!
  The one in front, and that vermilion was;
Two were the others, that were joined with this
  Above the middle part of either shoulder,
  And they were joined together at the crest;
And the right-hand one seemed 'twixt white and yellow;
  The left was such to look upon as those
  Who came from where the Nile falls valley-ward.
Underneath each came forth two mighty wings,
  Such as befitting were so great a bird;
  Sails of the sea I never saw so large.
No feathers had they, but as of a bat
  Their fashion was; and he was waving them,
  So that three winds proceeded forth therefrom.
Thereby Cocytus wholly was congealed.
  With six eyes did he weep, and down three chins
  Trickled the tear-drops and the bloody drivel.
At every mouth he with his teeth was crunching
  A sinner, in the manner of a brake,
  So that he three of them tormented thus.
To him in front the biting was as naught
  Unto the clawing, for sometimes the spine
  Utterly stripped of all the skin remained.
  'That soul up there which has the greatest pain,'
  The master said, 'is Judas Iscariot;
  With head inside, he plies his legs without.

[184]

Of the two others, who head downwards are,
   The one who hangs from the black jowl is Brutus;
   See how he writhes himself, and speaks no word.
And the other, who so stalwart seems, is Cassius.
   But night is re-ascending, and 'tis time
   That we depart, for we have seen the whole.'

Dante Alighieri, *Inferno*, c.1314; trans. Henry Wadsworth Longfellow

The Throne at the World's Heart

Below the Botome of the great Abysse,
There where one Center reconciles all things;
The worlds profound Heart pants; There placed is
Mischifes old Master, close about him clings
A curl'd knot of embracing Snakes, that kisse
His correspondent cheekes: these loathsome strings
   Hold the perverse Prince in eternall Ties
   Fast bound, since first he forfeited the skies.

The Iudge of Torments, and the King of Teares:
He fills a burnisht Throne of quenchlesse fire:
And for his old faire Roabes of Light, hee weares
A gloomy Mantle of dark flames, the Tire
That crownes his hated head on high appeares;
Where seav'n tall Hornes (his Empires pride) aspire.
   And to make up Hells Majesty, each Horne
   Seav'n crested Hydra's horribly adorne.

His Eyes, the sullen dens of Death and Night,
Startle the dull Ayre with a dismall red:
Such his fell glances as the fatall Light
Of staring Comets, that looke Kingdomes dead.
From his black nostrills, and blew lips, in spight
Of Hells owne stinke, a worser stench is spread.
   His breath Hells lightning is: and each deepe grone
   Disdaines to thinke that Heav'n Thunders alone.

His flaming Eyes dire exhalation,
Vnto a dreadfull pile gives fiery Breath;
Whose unconsum'd consumption preys upon

The never-dying Life, of a long Death.
In this sad House of slow Destruction,
(His shop of flames) hee fryes himselfe, beneath
  A mass of woes, his Teeth for Torment gnash,
  While his steele sides sound with his Tayles strong lash.

Three Rigourous Virgins waiting still behind,
Assist the Throne of th' Iron-Sceptred King.
With whips of Thornes and knotty vipers twin'd
They rouse him, when his ranke Thoughts need a sting.
Their lockes are beds of uncomb'd snakes that wind
About their shady browes in wanton Rings.
  Thus reignes the wrathfull King, and while he reignes
  His Scepter and himselfe both he disdaines.

Giambattista Marini, Le Strage degli Innocenti, 1610;
trans. Richard Crashaw, 1646

The Burning Lake

So stretcht out huge in length the Arch-fiend lay
Chaind on the burning Lake, nor ever thence
Had ris'n or heav'd his head, but that the will
And high permission of all-ruling Heaven
Left him at large to his own dark designs,
That with reiterated crimes he might
Heap on himself damnation, while he sought
Evil to others, and enrag'd might see
How all his malice serv'd but to bring forth
Infinite goodness, grace and mercy shewn
On Man by him seduc't, but on himself
Treble confusion, wrauth and vengeance pourd.
Forthwith upright he rears from off the Pool
His mighty Stature; on each hand the flames
Driv'n backward slope thir pointing spires, and rowld
In billows, leav i' th' midst a horrid Vale.
Then with expanded wings he stears his flight
Aloft, incumbent on the dusky Air
That felt unusual weight, till on dry Land
He lights, if it were Land that ever burnd
With solid, as the Lake with liquid fire,

And such appeard in hue; as when the force
Of subterranean wind transports a Hill
Torn from *Pelorus*, or the shatterd side
Of thundring *Ætna*, whose combustible
And feweld entrals thence conceiving Fire,
Sublim'd with Mineral fury, aid the Winds,
And leave a singed bottom all involv'd
With stench and smoak: Such resting found the sole
Of unblest feet. Him followd his next Mate,
Both glorying to have scap't the *Stygian* flood
As Gods, and by thir own recoverd strength,
Not by the sufferance of supernal Power.

    Is this the Region, this the Soil, the Clime,
Said then the lost Arch-Angel, this the seat
That we must change for Heav'n, this mournful gloom
For that celestial light? Be it so, since hee
Who now is Sovran can dispose and bid
What shall be right: fardest from him is best
Whom reason hath equald, force hath made supream
Above his equals. Farewel happy Fields
Where Joy for ever dwells: Hail horrours, hail
Infernal World, and thou profoundest Hell
Receive thy new Possessor: One who brings
A mind not to be chang'd by Place or Time.
The mind is its own place, and in it self
Can make a Heav'n of Hell, a Hell of Heav'n.
What matter where, if I be still the same,
And what I should be, all but less then hee
Whom Thunder hath made greater? Here at least
We shall be free; th' Almighty hath not built
Here for his envy, will not drive us hence:
Here we may reign secure, and in my choice
To reign is worth ambition though in Hell:
Better to reign in Hell, then serve in Heav'n.

John Milton, *Paradise Lost*, Book I, 1667

Cries and Howls

In Hell is Griefe, Paine, Anguish, and Annoy,
All threatning Death, yet nothing can destroy:

There's Ejulation, Clamor, Weeping, Wailing,
Cries, Yels, Howles, Gnashes, Curses, (neuer failing)
Sighes and Suspires, Woe, and vnpittied Mones,
Thirst, Hunger, Want, with lacerating Grones.
Of Fire or Light no comfortable beames,
Heate not to be endur'd, Cold in extreames.
Torments in ev'ry Artyre, Nerve, and Vaine,
In ev'ry Ioint insufferable paine.
In Head, Brest, Stomake, and in all the Sences,
Each torture suting to the foule offences,
But with more terror than the heart can thinke:
The Sight with Darknesse, and the Smel with Stinke;
The Taste with Gall, in bitternesse extreme;
The Hearing, with their Curses that blaspheme:
The Touch, with Snakes & Todes crauling about them,
Afflicted both within them and without them.

Thomas Heywood, *The Hierarchie of the Blessed Angells*, 1635

Faust Asks the Secrets of Hell

Wherefore in all the hast he calleth unto him his Spirit *Mephostophiles*,
desiring him to tell him some more of the secrets of hell, what paines the
damned were in, and how they were tormented, and whether the damned
soules might get againe the favour of God, and so bee released out of
their torments or not: whereupon the Spirit answered, my *Faustus*, thou
mayst wel leave to question any more of such matters, for they wil but
disquiet thy mind, I pray thee what meanest thou? Thinkest thou through
thy fantasies to escape us? No, for if thou shouldest climb up to heaven,
there to hide thy selfe, yet would I thrust thee downe agayne; for thou
art mine, and thou belongest unto our society: therefore sweete *Faustus*,
thou wilt repent this thy foolish demaund, except thou be content that I
shall tell thee nothing. Quoth *Faustus* ragingly, I will know, or I will not
live, wherefore dispatch and tell me: to whom *Mephostophiles* answered,
Faustus, it is no trouble unto mee at all to tell thee, and therefore sith thou
forcest mee thereto, I will tell thee things to the terror of thy soule, if
thou wilt abide the hearing. Thou wilt have me tel thee of the secrets of
hell, and of the paynes thereof: know *Faustus*, that hell hath many figures,
semblances and names, but it cannot be named nor figured in such sort
unto the living that are damned, as it is unto those that are dead, and doe
both see and feele the torments thereof: for hell is said to bee deadly, out

of the which came never any to life agyne but one, but he is as nothing for thee to reckon upon, hell is blood-thirstie, and is never satisfied: hell is a valley, into the which the damned soules fal: for so soon as the soule is out of mans body, it would gladly goe to the place from whence it came, and climbeth up above the highest hils, even to the heavens; where being by the Angels of the first *Mobile* denied entertainement (in consideration of their evill life spent on the earth) they fall into the deepest pit or valley which hath no bottome, into a perpetuall fire, which shall never bee quenched: for like as the Flint throwne into the water, looseth not his vertue, neither is his fire extinguished; even so the hellish fire is unquenchable: and even as the Flint stone in the fire being burned is red hot, and yet consumeth not: so likewise the damned soules in our hellish fire are ever burning, but their paines never diminishing. Therefore is hell called the everlasting pain, in which is neither hope nor mercy: So is it called utter darknesse, in which we see neither the light of Sunne, Moone, nor Starre: and were our darknesse like the darknes of the night, yet were there hope of mercie, but ours is perpetuall darknesse, cleane exempt from the face of God. Hell hath also a place within it called *Chasma*, out of the which issueth all manner of thunders, lightnings, with such horrible shrikings and waylings, that oft-times the very divels themselves stand in feare thereof: for one while it sendeth foorth windes with exceeding snow, hayle, and raine congealing the water into yce; with the which the damned are frozen, gnash their teeth, howle and cry, and yet cannot die. Otherwhiles, it sendeth foorth most horrible hote mists or fogges, with flashing flames of fire and brimstone, wherein the sorowfull soules of the damned lie broyling in their reiterated torments: yea *Faustus*, hell is called a prison wherein the damned lie continually bound; it is also called *Pernicies*, and *Exitium*, death, destruction, hurtfulnesse, mischiefe, a mischance, a pitifull and an evill thing worlde without end. We have also with us in hell a ladder, reaching of an exceeding height, as though it would touch the heavens, on which the damned ascend to seeke the blessing of God; but through their infidelitie, when they are at the very highest degree, they fall downe againe into their former miseries, complayning of the heate of that unquenchable fire: yea sweete *Faustus*, so must thou understand of hell, the while thou art so desirous to know the secrets of our kingdome. And marke *Faustus*, hell is the nurse of death, the heate of all fire, the shadow of heaven and earth, the oblivion of all goodnes, the paynes unspeakeable, the griefes unremoveable, the dwelling of Divels, Dragons, Serpents, Adders, Toades, Crocodils, and all maner of venymous creatures; the puddle of sinne, the stinking foggs ascending from the Stigian lake, Brimstone, Pitch, and all maner of uncleane mettals, the perpetual and unquenchable fire, the end of whose miseries was never purposed by God: yea, yea *Faustus*, thou sayst, I shall, I must, nay I will tell thee the secrets of our kingdome, for thou buyest it dearely, and thou must also be partaker of our torments, that (as the Lord God sayd) never shall cease: for hell, the womans belly, and the earth are never satisfied; there shalt thou abide horrible torments, trembling, gnashing of teeth, howling, crying, burning, freezing, melting, swimming in a labyrinth of miseries, scalding, burning, smoking in thine eyes, stinking in thy nose, horsenes of thy speech, deafenesse of thine eares, trembling of thy handes, biting thine owne tongue with payne, thy hart crushed as in a presse, thy bones broken, the divels tossing fire brands upon thee, yea thy whole carkasse tossed upon muckforkes from one divel to another, yea *Faustus*, then wilt thou wish for death, and he will flie from thee, thine unspeakable torments shall be every day augmented more and more, for the greater the sinne, the greater is the punishment: howe likest thou this, my *Faustus*, a resolution answerable to thy request?

The Historie of the Damnable Life and Deserved Death
of Doctor John Faustus, 1592

Hell's Architecture

There stood a Hill not farr whose griesly top
Belchd fire and rowling smoak; the rest entire
Shon with a glossie scurff, undoubted sign
That in his womb was hid metallic Ore,
The work of Sulfur. Thither wingd with speed
A numerous Brigad hast'nd. As when bands
Of Pioners with Spade and Pickaxe armd
Forerun the Royal Camp, to trench a Field,
Or cast a Rampart. *Mammon* led them on,
Mammon, the least erected Spirit that fell
From Heav'n, for ev'n in Heav'n his looks and thoughts
Were always downward bent, admiring more
The riches of Heav'ns pavement, trodd'n Gold,
Then aught divine or holy else enjoyd
In vision beatific: by him first
Men also, and by his suggestion taught,
Ransackd the Center, and with impious hands
Rifl'd the bowels of thir mother Earth
For Treasures better hid. Soon had his crew
Op'nd into the Hill a spacious wound
And diggd out ribs of Gold. Let none admire

That riches grow in Hell; that soile may best
Deserve the precious bane. And here let those
Who boast in mortal things, and wondring tell
Of *Babel*, and the works of *Memphian* Kings,
Learn how thir greatest Monuments of Fame
And Strength and Art are easily outdone
By Spirits reprobate, and in an hour
What in an age they with incessant toil
And hands innumerable scarce perform.
Nigh on the Plain in many cells prepar'd,
That underneath had veins of liquid fire
Sluc't from the Lake, a second multitude
With wondrous Art founded the massie Ore,
Severing each kinde, and scummd the Bullion dross:
A third as soon had formd within the ground
A various mould, and from the boiling cells
By strange conveyance filld each hollow nook:
As in an Organ from one blast of wind
To many a row of Pipes the sound-board breathes.
Anon out of the earth a Fabrick huge
Rose like an Exhalation, with the sound
Of Dulcet Symphonies and voices sweet:
Built like a Temple, where *Pilasters* round
Were set, and Doric pillars overlaid
With Gold'n Architrave; nor did there want
Cornice or Freeze, with bossy Sculptures grav'n;
The Roof was fretted Gold. Not *Babilon*,
Nor great *Alcairo* such magnificence
Equald in all thir glories, to inshrine
Belus or *Serapis* thir Gods, or seat
Thir Kings, when *Ægypt* with *Assyria* strove
In wealth and luxurie. Th' ascending pile
Stood fixt her stately highth, and strait the dores
Op'ning thir brazen foulds discover wide
Within, her ample spaces, ore the smooth
And level pavement: from the arched roof
Pendant by suttle Magic many a row
Of Starry Lamps and blazing Cressets fed
With *Naphtha* and *Asphaltus* yeilded light
As from a sky.

John Milton, *Paradise Lost*, Book I, 1667

Another Possibility

In short, the true account of the Devil's circumstances, since his fall from heaven, is much more likely to be thus: That he is more of a vagrant than a prisoner, that he is a wanderer in the wild unbounded waste, where he and his legions, like the hoords of Tartary, who, in the wild countries of Karakathay, the deserts of Barkan, Kassan, and Astracan, live up and down where they find proper: so Satan and his innumerable legions rove about *hic & ubique*, pitching their camps (being beasts of prey) where they find the most spoil; watching over this world, (and all the other worlds for ought we know, and if there be any such,) I say watching, and seeking who they may devour, that is, who they may deceive and delude, and so destroy, for devour they cannot.

Satan being thus confined to a vagabond, wandering, unsettled condition, is without any certain abode; for though he has, in consequence of his angelic nature, a kind of empire in the liquid waste or air, yet, this is certainly part of his punishment, that he is continually hovering over this inhabited globe of earth; swelling with the rage of envy, at the felicity of his rival, man; and studying all the means possible to injure and ruin him; but extremely limited in power, to his unspeakable mortification. This is his present state, without any fixed abode, place, or space, allowed him to rest the sole of his foot upon.

Daniel Defoe, *The History of the Devil*, 1726

Hell Hath No Limits

FAUSTUS: First, I will question with thee about hell:
  Tell me, where is the place that men call Hell?
MEPHOSTOPHILIS: Under the heavens.
FAUSTUS: I, so are all things else; but whereabouts?
MEPHOSTOPHILIS: Within the bowels of these Elements,
  Where we are tortur'd, and remaine for ever.
  Hell hath no limits, nor is circumscrib'd,
  In one selfe place: but where we are is hell,
  And where hell is there must we ever be.
  And to be short, when all the world dissolves,
  And every creature shall be purifi'd,
  All places shall be hell that is not heaven.

FAUSTUS: I thinke Hel's a fable.

MEPHOSTOPHILIS: I, thinke so still, till experience change thy mind.

FAUSTUS: Why, dost thou think that *Faustus* shall be damn'd?

MEPHOSTOPHILIS: I, of necessity, for here's the scrowle
In which thou hast given thy soule to *Lucifer*.

FAUSTUS: I, and body too, but what of that:
Think'st thou that *Faustus*, is so fond to imagine,
That after this life there is any paine
Tush, these are trifles, and meere old wives Tales.

MEPHOSTOPHILIS: But I am an instance to prove the contrary:
For I tell thee I am damn'd, and now in hell.

Christopher Marlowe, *The Tragedie of Doctor Faustus*, 1604

Hell Within

Men commonly set forth the torments of hell by fire and the extremity of corporeal afflictions, and describe hell in the same method that Mahomet doth heaven. This indeed makes a noise, and drums in popular ears; but if this be the terrible piece thereof, it is not worthy to stand in diameter with heaven, whose happiness consists in that part that is best able to comprehend it – that immortal essence, that translated divinity and colony of God, the soul.

Surely, though we place hell under earth, the Devil's walk and purlieu is about it: men speak too popularly who place it in those flaming mountains which to grosser apprehensions represent hell. The heart of man is the place the Devil dwells in: I feel sometimes a hell within myself; Lucifer keeps his court in my breast – Legion is revived within me. There are as many hells as Anaxagoras conceited worlds: there was more than one hell in Magdalen when there were seven devils, for every devil is a hell unto himself – he holds enough of torture in his own *ubi*, and needs not the misery of circumference to afflict him; and thus a distracted conscience here is a shadow of introduction unto hell hereafter. Who can but pity the merciful intention of those hands that do destroy themselves? The Devil, were it in his power, would do the like; which being impossible, his miseries are endless, and he suffers most in that attribute wherein he is impassible, his immortality.

Sir Thomas Browne, *Religio Medici*, 1642

[193]

The Chasm of Orc

'Image of dread, whence art thou? whence is this most woful place?
'Whence these fierce fires, but from thyself? No other living thing
'In all this Chasm I behold. No other living thing
'Dare thy most terrible wrath abide. Bound here to waste in pain
'Thy vital substance in these fires that issue new & new
'Around thee, sometimes like a flood, & sometimes like a rock
'Of living pangs, thy horrible bed glowing with ceaseless fires
'Beneath thee & around. Above, a shower of fire now beats,
'Moulded to globes & arrowy wedges, rending thy bleeding limbs.
'And now a whirling pillar of burning sands to overwhelm thee,
'Steeping thy wounds in salts infernal & in bitter anguish.
'And now a rock moves on the surface of this lake of fire
'To bear thee down beneath the waves in stifling despair.
'Pity for thee mov'd me to break my dark & long repose,
'And to reveal myself before thee in a form of wisdom.
'Yet thou dost laugh at all these tortures, & this horrible place:
'Yet throw thy limbs these fires abroad that back return upon thee
'While thou reposest, throwing rage on rage, feeding thyself
'With visions of sweet bliss far other than this burning clime.
'Sure thou art bath'd in rivers of delight, on verdant fields
'Walking in joy, in bright Expanses sleeping on bright clouds
'With visions of delight so lovely that they urge thy rage
'Tenfold with fierce desire to rend thy chain & howl in fury
'And dim oblivion of all woe, & desperate repose.
'Or is thy joy founded on torment which others bear for thee?'

William Blake, *The Four Zoas*, c.1795–1804

A Brief Explanation by Swedenborg

The manner in which the Lord rules the hells, may be briefly explained.
The hells in general are ruled by the general afflux of Divine Good and
Divine Truth from the heavens, by which the general effort which issues
from the hells is checked and restrained; but they are also ruled by a
specific afflux from each heaven, and from each society of heaven; and in
a more particular sense they are ruled by angels, who are appointed to
inspect them, and to restrain the insanities and disturbances with which

they abound. Sometimes, also, angels are sent thither to moderate those insanities and disturbances by their presence; but in general *all the inhabitants of hell are ruled by fears*. Some are ruled by fears implanted in the world, which still retain their influence; but since these fears are not sufficient, and also because they lose their force by degrees, the fear of punishment is added, and this fear is the chief means of deterring them from doing evils. The punishments of hell are various, and are gentle or severe according to the nature of the evils to be restrained. In most cases the more malignant spirits, who excel the rest in cunning and artifice, and are able to keep them in obedience and slavery by punishments and the terrors which they inspire, are set over their companions; but these governors dare not pass beyond certain prescribed limits. It is worthy to be mentioned again, that the fear of punishment is the only means of restraining the violence and fury of the infernals. There is no other.

It has been hitherto supposed in the world, that there is some one devil who rules over the hells; that he was created an angel of light, and that he was cast down with his crew into hell because he rebelled against God; and this belief has become prevalent, because certain passages of the Word which speak of the Devil and Satan, and also of Lucifer, have been understood according to the sense of the letter; but the Devil and *Satan* mean hell considered under different aspects. The *Devil* means the hell which is at the back, and is inhabited by the very worst spirits, called evil genii; and *Satan* denotes the hell which is in front, the inhabitants of which are not so malignant, and are called evil spirits; and *Lucifer* denotes those who are of Babel or Babylon, and who pretend to have dominion even in heaven. That there is no single devil to whom the hells are subject, is also evident, because all who are in hell, as well as all who are in heaven, are from the human race, and because from the beginning of the creation to the present time, they amount to myriads of myriads, every one of whom is a devil of such a quality as he had acquired by living in the world in opposition to the Divine.

Concerning Heaven and its Wonders, and concerning Hell: Being a Relation of Things Heard and Seen, trans. from Latin of Emmanuel Swedenborg, 1853

Where the Fun Never Stops

THE DEVIL: Curious how these clever men, whom you would have supposed born to be popular here, have turned out social failures, like Don Juan!

DON JUAN: I am really very sorry to be a social failure.

THE DEVIL: Not that we dont admire your intellect, you know. We do. But I look at the matter from your own point of view. You dont get on with us. The place doesnt suit you. The truth is, you have – I wont say no heart; for we know that beneath all your affected cynicism you have a warm one –

DON JUAN [shrinking]: Dont, please dont.

THE DEVIL [nettled]: Well, youve no capacity for enjoyment. Will that satisfy you?

DON JUAN: It is a somewhat less insufferable form of cant than the other. But if youll allow me, I'll take refuge, as usual, in solitude.

THE DEVIL: Why not take refuge in Heaven? Thats the proper place for you. [To Ana] Come, Señora! could you not persuade him for his own good to try a change of air?

ANA: But can he go to Heaven if he wants to?

THE DEVIL: Whats to prevent him?

ANA: Can anybody – can I go to Heaven if I want to?

THE DEVIL [rather contemptuously]: Certainly, if your taste lies that way.

ANA: But why doesnt everybody go to Heaven, then?

THE STATUE [chuckling]: I can tell you that, my dear. It's because heaven is the most angelically dull place in all creation: thats why.

THE DEVIL: His excellency the Commander puts it with military bluntness; but the strain of living in Heaven is intolerable. There is a notion that I was turned out of it; but as a matter of fact nothing could have induced me to stay there. I simply left it and organized this place.

THE STATUE: I dont wonder at it. Nobody could stand an eternity of heaven.

THE DEVIL: Oh, it suits some people. Let us be just, Commander: it is a question of temperament. I dont admire the heavenly temperament: I dont understand it: I dont know that I particularly want to understand it; but it takes all sorts to make a universe. There is no accounting for tastes: there are people who like it. I think Don Juan would like it.

DON JUAN: But – pardon my frankness – could you really go back there if you desired to; or are the grapes sour?

THE DEVIL: Back there! I often go back there. Have you never read the book of Job? Have you any canonical authority for assuming that there is any barrier between our circle and the other one?

ANA: But surely there is a great gulf fixed.

THE DEVIL: Dear lady: a parable must not be taken literally. The gulf is the difference between the angelic and the diabolic temperament. What more impassable gulf could you have? Think of what you have seen on earth. There is no physical gulf between the philosopher's class room and the bull ring; but the bull fighters do not come to the class room for all that. Have you ever been in the country where I have the largest following? England. There they have great racecourses, and also concert rooms where they play the classical compositions of his Excellency's friend Mozart. Those who go to the racecourses can stay away from them and go to the classical concerts instead if they like: there is no law against it; for Englishmen never will be slaves: they are free to do whatever the Government and public opinion allow them to do. And the classical concert is admitted to be a higher, more cultivated, poetic, intellectual, ennobling place than the racecourse. But do the lovers of racing desert their sport and flock to the concert room? Not they. They would suffer there all the weariness the Commander has suffered in heaven. There is the great gulf of the parable between the two places. A mere physical gulf they could bridge; or at least I could bridge it for them (the earth is full of Devil's Bridges); but the gulf of dislike is impassable and eternal. And that is the only gulf that separates my friends here from those who are invidiously called the blest.

ANA: I shall go to heaven at once.

THE STATUE: My child: one word of warning first. Let me complete my friend Lucifer's similitude of the classical concert. At every one of these concerts in England you will find rows of weary people who are there, not because they really like classical music, but because they think they ought to like it. Well, there is the same thing in heaven. A number of people sit there in glory, not because they are happy, but because they think they owe it to their position to be in heaven. They are almost all English.

THE DEVIL: Yes: the Southerners give it up and join me just as you have done. But the English really do not seem to know when they are thoroughly miserable. An Englishman thinks he is moral when he is only uncomfortable.

THE STATUE: In short, my daughter, if you go to Heaven without being naturally qualified for it, you will not enjoy yourself there.

ANA: And who dares say that I am not naturally qualified for it? The most distinguished princes of the Church have never questioned it. I owe it to myself to leave this place at once.

THE DEVIL [*offended*]: As you please, Señora. I should have expected better taste from you.

ANA: Father: I shall expect you to come with me. You cannot stay here. What will people say?

THE STATUE: People! Why, the best people are here – princes of the church and all. So few go to Heaven, and so many come here, that the blest, once called a heavenly host, are a continually dwindling minority. The saints, the fathers, the elect of long ago are the cranks, the faddists, the outsiders of today.

THE DEVIL: It is true. From the beginning of my career I knew that I should win in the long run by sheer weight of public opinion, in spite of the long campaign of misrepresentation and calumny against me. At bottom the universe is a constitutional one; and with such a majority as mine I cannot be kept permanently out of office.

DON JUAN: I think, Ana, you had better stay here.

ANA [*jealously*]: You do not want me to go with you.

DON JUAN: Surely you do not want to enter Heaven in the company of a reprobate like me.

ANA: All souls are equally precious. You repent, do you not?

DON JUAN: My dear Ana, you are silly. Do you suppose heaven is like earth, where people persuade themselves that what is done can be undone by repentance; that what is spoken can be unspoken by withdrawing it; that what is true can be annihilated by a general agreement to give it the lie? No: heaven is the home of the masters of reality: that is why I am going thither.

ANA: Thank you: I am going to heaven for happiness. I have had quite enough of reality on earth.

DON JUAN: Then you must stay here; for hell is the home of the unreal and of the seekers for happiness. It is the only refuge from heaven, which is, as I tell you, the home of the masters of reality, and from earth, which is the home of the slaves of reality. The earth is a nursery in which men and women play at being heroes and heroines, saints and sinners; but they are dragged down from their fool's paradise by their bodies: hunger and cold and thirst, age and decay and disease, death above all, make them slaves of reality: thrice a day meals must be eaten and digested: thrice a century a new generation must be engendered: ages of faith, of romance, and of science are all driven at last to have but one prayer 'Make me a healthy animal.' But here you escape this tyranny of the flesh; for here you are not an animal at all: you are a ghost, an appearance, an illusion, a convention, deathless, ageless: in a word, bodiless. There are no social questions here, no political questions, no religious questions, best of all, perhaps, no sanitary questions. Here you call your appearance beauty, your emotions love, your sentiments heroism, your aspirations virtue, just as you did on earth; but here there are no hard facts to contradict you, no ironic contrast of your needs with your pretensions, no human comedy, nothing but a perpetual romance, a universal melodrama. As our German friend put it in his poem, 'the poetically nonsensical here is good sense; and the Eternal Feminine draws us ever upward and on' – without getting us a step farther. And yet you want to leave this paradise!

ANA: But if Hell be so beautiful as this, how glorious must heaven be!

George Bernard Shaw, *Man and Superman*, 1903

'Hell Gate'

Onward led the road again
Through the sad uncoloured plain
Under twilight brooding dim,
And along the utmost rim
Wall and rampart risen to sight
Cast a shadow not of night,
And beyond them seemed to glow
Bonfires lighted long ago.
And my dark conductor broke
Silence at my side and spoke,
Saying, 'You conjecture well:
Yonder is the gate of hell.'

Ill as yet the eye could see
The eternal masonry,
But beneath it on the dark
To and fro there stirred a spark.
And again the sombre guide
Knew my question, and replied:
'At hell gate the damned in turn
Pace for sentinel and burn.'

Dully at the leaden sky
Staring, and with idle eye
Measuring the listless plain,

I began to think again.
Many things I thought of then,
Battle, and the loves of men,
Cities entered, oceans crossed,
Knowledge gained and virtue lost,
Cureless folly done and said,
And the lovely way that led
To the slimepit and the mire
And the everlasting fire.
And against a smoulder dun
And a dawn without a sun
Did the nearing bastion loom,
And across the gate of gloom
Still one saw the sentry go,
Trim and burning, to and fro,
One for women to admire
In his finery of fire.
Something, as I watched him pace,
Minded me of time and place,
Soldiers of another corps
And a sentry known before.

Ever darker hell on high
Reared its strength upon the sky,
And our footfall on the track
Fetched the daunting echo back.
But the soldier pacing still
The insuperable sill,
Nursing his tormented pride,
Turned his head to neither side,
Sunk into himself apart
And the hell-fire of his heart.
But against our entering in
From the drawbridge Death and Sin
Rose to render key and sword
To their father and their lord.
And the portress foul to see
Lifted up her eyes on me
Smiling, and I made reply:
'Met again, my lass,' said I.
Then the sentry turned his head,
Looked, and knew me, and was Ned.

Once he looked, and halted straight,
Set his back against the gate,
Caught his musket to his chin,
While the hive of hell within
Sent abroad a seething hum
As of towns whose king is come
Leading conquest home from far
And the captives of his war,
And the car of triumph waits,
And they open wide the gates.
But across the entry barred
Straddled the revolted guard,
Weaponed and accoutred well
From the arsenals of hell;
And beside him, sick and white,
Sin to left and Death to right
Turned a countenance of fear
On the flaming mutineer.
Over us the darkness bowed,
And the anger in the cloud
Clenched the lightning for the stroke;
But the traitor musket spoke.

And the hollowness of hell
Sounded as its master fell,
And the mourning echo rolled
Ruin through his kingdom old.
Tyranny and terror flown
Left a pair of friends alone,
And beneath the nether sky
All that stirred was he and I.

Silent, nothing found to say,
We began the backward way;
And the ebbing lustre died
From the soldier at my side,
As in all his spruce attire
Failed the everlasting fire.
Midmost of the homeward track
Once we listened and looked back;

But the city, dusk and mute,
Slept, and there was no pursuit.

A. E. Housman, 1922

'Faust Requires Mephistopheles to Describe Hell and Heaven for Him'

'Tell me, I command you,
What is that place called hell?'

'Hell is grey and has no bottom –
Which reminds me of a joke I heard . . .'

'It was of hell I asked to hear,
Not your stale jokes.'

'But hell is of no substance,
A confused and hence confusing thing – '

'It is yourself that you describe,
I think.'

'So be it – hell is,
Well, it's empty.
Oh there are crowds of people all around.
But hell, you feel, is – empty.
The word is emptiness.'

'Now let us speak of heaven.
What manner of place is that?'

'I lack authority to speak of such.'
(Though not to miss it.)

'Yet you were once in heaven,
Or so I've heard.'

'Some time ago, it may have changed . . .
But – heaven is full.
That's not to say it's chock-a-block with people.

[202]

Simply, full – that's what you feel.
The word is fullness.'

'For one renowned for eloquence
I find you sadly tongue-tied!'

'Whereof one cannot bear to speak,
Thereof one says but little.'

D. J. Enright, A Faust Book, 1979

Six

THE ENEMY

Be sober, be vigilant: because your adversary
the devil, as a roaring lion, walketh about,
seeking whom he may devour.

1 *Peter* 5, v.8

Demonic Possession

And they came over unto the other side of the sea, into the country of the Gadarenes.

And when he was come out of the ship, immediately there met him out of the tombs a man with an unclean spirit,

Who had *his* dwelling among the tombs; and no man could bind him, no, not with chains:

Because that he had been often bound with fetters and chains, and the chains had been plucked asunder by him, and the fetters broken in pieces: neither could any *man* tame him.

And always, night and day, he was in the mountains, and in the tombs, crying, and cutting himself with stones.

But when he saw Jesus afar off, he ran and worshipped him,

And cried with a loud voice, and said, What have I to do with thee, Jesus, *thou* Son of the most high God? I adjure thee by God, that thou torment me not.

For he said unto him, Come out of the man, *thou* unclean spirit.

And he asked him, What *is* thy name? And he answered, saying, My name *is* Legion: for we are many.

And he besought him much that he would not send them away out of the country.

Now there was there nigh unto the mountains a great herd of swine feeding.

And all the devils besought him, saying, Send us into the swine, that we may enter unto them.

And forthwith Jesus gave them leave. And the unclean spirits went out, and entered into the swine: and the herd ran violently down a steep place into the sea, (they were about two thousand;) and were choked in the sea.

And they that fed the swine fled, and told *it* in the city, and in the country. And they went out to see what it was that was done.

And they come to Jesus, and see him that was possessed with the devil, and had the legion, sitting, and clothed, and in his right mind: and they were afraid.

And they that saw *it* told them how it befell to him that was possessed with the devil, and *also* concerning the swine.

And they began to pray him to depart out of their coasts.

And when he was come into the ship, he that had been possessed with the devil prayed him that he might be with him.

Howbeit Jesus suffered him not, but saith unto him, Go home to thy friends, and tell them how great things the Lord hath done for thee, and hath had compassion on thee.

And he departed, and began to publish in Decapolis how great things Jesus had done for him: and all *men* did marvel.

Mark 5, v.1–20

Socks

Some that are yet liuinge with me, affirme this to be true which I wil nowe speake of. A man of holy life there was called *Steuene*, who was a Priest in the prouince of *Valeria*: nighe of kinred to my Deacon *Bonifacius*: who comminge home vpon a tyme from trauaile, spake somewhat negligently to his seruant sayinge. Come Sir deuill and pull of my hoose: at which wordes straight-waies his garters began to loose in great hast, so that he plainely perceiued, that the deuill indeed whom he named, was pulling of his stockinge: whereat beeing muche terrified, he cried out aloude and saide. Away wretched caitiffe, awaye: I spake not to the but to my seruant. Then the deuill gaue ouer, leauing his garters almost quite of. By which we may learne, that yf the deuill be so officious in thinges concerning our bodye, how ready and diligent he is to obserue and note the cogitations of our soule.

The Dialogues of S. Gregorie the Great, trans. into English by 'P.W.', 1608

The Devil's Powers

Thus the Devil reigns, and in a thousand several shapes, as a roaring lion still seeks whom he may devour, by earth, sea, land, air, as yet unconfined, though some will have his proper place the air, all that space betwixt us & the Moon for them that transgressed least, & Hell for the wickedest of them; here, as though in prison to the end of the world, afterwards thrust into the place of doom, as Austin holds in The City Of God. But be [he] where he will, he rageth while he may to comfort himself, as Lactantius thinks, with other men's falls, he labours all he can to bring them into the same pit of perdition with him. For *men's miseries, calamities, and ruins, are the Devil's banqueting dishes*. By many temptations, and several engines, he seeks to captivate our souls. The Lord of lies, saith Austin, *as he was deceived himself, he seeks to deceive others*, the ring-leader to all

[207]

naughtiness, as he did by Eve & Cain, Sodom and Gomorrah, so would he do by all the world. Sometimes he tempts by covetousness, drunkenness, pleasure, pride, &c., errs, dejects, saves, kills, protects, and rides some men, as they do their horses. He studies our overthrow, and generally seeks our destruction; and although he pretend many times human good, and vindicate himself for a God, by curing of several diseases, by restoring health to the sick and sight to the blind, as Austin declares, as Apollo, Æsculapius, Isis, of old have done; divert plagues, assist them in wars, pretend their happiness, yet nothing so impure, nothing so pernicious, as may well appear by their tyrannical and bloody sacrifices of men to Saturn and Moloch, which are still in use amongst those barbarous Indians, their several deceits and cozenings to keep men in obedience, their false oracles, sacrifices, their superstitious impositions of fasts, penury, &c., heresies, superstitious observations of meats, times, &c. by which they crucify the souls of mortal men, as shall be shewed in our Treatise of Religious Melancholy. As Bernard expresseth it, by God's permission he rageth a while, hereafter to be confined to hell and darkness, which is prepared for him and his Angels.

How far their power doth extend, it is hard to determine; what the Ancients held of their effects, force, and operations, I will briefly shew you. Plato in Critias, and after him his followers, gave out that these spirits or devils *were men's governors and keepers, our lords and masters, as we are of our cattle. They govern Provinces and Kingdoms by oracles, auguries,* dreams, rewards and punishments, prophecies, inspirations, sacrifices, and religious superstitions, varied in as many forms as there be diversity of spirits; they send wars, plagues, peace, sickness, health, dearth, plenty, standing near by us, observers & judges, &c., as appears by those histories of Thucydides, Livy, Dionysius Halicarnasseus, with many others that are full of their wonderful stratagems, and were therefore by those Roman and Greek Commonwealths adored and worshipped for gods, with prayers, and sacrifices, &c. In a word, they seek nothing more earnestly than the fear and admiration of mankind; and, as another hath it, it is scarce possible to describe the impotent ardour with which these malign spirits aspire to dominion over men and divine worship. Trithemius, in his book The Lucky Seven, assigns names to such Angels as are Governors of particular Provinces, by what authority I know not, and gives them several jurisdictions. Asclepiades a Grecian, Rabbi Achiba the Jew, Abraham Avenezra, and Rabbi Azariel, Arabians, (as I find them cited by Cicogna) farther add, that they are not our Governors only, but as they agree, so do we and our Princes, or disagree, stand or fall. Juno was a bitter enemy to Troy, Apollo a good friend, Jupiter indifferent, Venus was favorable, Pallas unfavorable; some are for us still, some against us. Religion, policy, publick and private quarrels, wars are procured by them, and they are delighted perhaps to see men fight, as men are with cocks, bulls and dogs, bears, &c. Plagues, dearths, depend on them, our good and evil moods, and almost all our other peculiar actions, (for, as Anthony Rusca contends, every man hath a good and a bad Angel attending of him in particular all his life long, which Iamblicus calls a daimon), preferments, losses, weddings, deaths, rewards, and punishments, and, as Proclus will, all offices whatsoever, motherhood to one, artizanship to another, &c., and several names they give them according to their offices, as *Lares, Indigetes, Præstites, &c.* When the Arcades in that battle at Chæronea, which was fought against King Philip for the liberty of Greece, had deceitfully carried themselves, long after, in the very same place, the gods of Greece being avengers (saith mine Author) they were miserably slain by Metellus the Roman: so likewise, in smaller matters, they will have things fall out, as these good and evil *Genii* favour or dislike us. He that is *Saturnine* shall never likely be preferred. That base fellows are often advanced, undeserving Gnathos, and vicious parasites, when as discreet, wise, virtuous, and worthy men are neglected, and unrewarded, they refer to those domineering spirits, or subordinate *Genii*; as they are inclined, or favour men, so they thrive, are ruled & overcome, for, as Libanius supposeth, in our ordinary conflicts and contentions, one Genius yields and is overcome by another. All particular events almost they refer to these private spirits; & (as Paracelsus adds) they direct, teach, inspire, and instruct men. Never was any man extraordinarily famous in any art, action, or great commander, that had not a familiar to inform him, as Numa, Socrates, and many such, as Cardan illustrates (Secrets of Statesmanship). The magi say (Boissardus), as a special favour from God, they are instructed and taught by the heavenly spirits. But these are most erroneous paradoxes, stupid and fabulous trifles, rejected by our Divines & Christian Churches. 'Tis true they have, by God's permission, power over us, and we find by experience that they can hurt not our fields only, cattle, goods, but our bodies and minds. At Hammel in Saxony, on the 20th of June, 1484, the Devil, in the likeness of a pied piper, carried away 130 children, that were never after seen. Many times men are affrighted out of their wits, carried away quite, as Scheretzius illustrates, and severally molested by his means. Plotinus the Platonist laughs them to scorn that hold the Devil or Spirits can cause any such diseases. Many think he can work upon the body, but not upon the mind. But experience pronounceth otherwise, that he can work both upon body and mind. Tertullian is of this opinion, that he can cause both sickness and health, and that secretly. Taurellus adds, by clancular poisons he can infect the bodies, & hinder the operations of the bowels, though we perceive it not, closely creeping into them, saith

Lipsius, & so crucify our souls, and drive people mad by grievous melancholy. For being a spiritual body, he struggles with our spirits, saith Rogers, and suggests (according to Cardan), words without a voice, apparitions without sight, envy, lust, anger, &c., as he sees men inclined.

Robert Burton, *The Anatomy of Melancholy*, 1621

An Attack of Melancholy

'A person of quality came to my chamber in the Temple, and told me he had two devils in his head (I wondered what he meant), and just at that time one of them bid him kill me. With that I began to be afraid, and thought he was mad. He said he knew I could cure him, and therefore entreated me to give him something, for he was resolved he would go to nobody else. I, perceiving what an opinion he had of me, and that it was only melancholy that troubled him, took him in hand, and warranted him, if he would follow my directions, to cure him in a short time. I desired him to let me be alone about an hour, and then to come again; which he was very willing to. In the meantime I got a card, and wrapped it up handsomely in a piece of taffeta, and put strings to the taffeta; and when he came, gave it to him to hang about his neck; withal charging him that he should not disorder himself either with eating or drinking, but eat very little of supper, and say his prayers duly when he went to bed; and I made no question that he would be well in three or four days. Within that time I went to dinner to his house, and asked him how he did. He said he was much better, but not perfectly well; for in truth he had not dealt clearly with me; he had four devils in his head, and he perceived two of them were gone with that which I had given him, but the other two troubled him still. "Well," said I, "I am glad two of them are gone; I make no doubt to get rid of the other two likewise." So I gave him another thing to hang about his neck. Three days after he came to me to my chamber, and professed he was now as well as he ever was in his life, and did extremely thank me for the great care I had taken of him. I, fearing lest he might relapse into the like distemper, told him that there was none but myself and one physician more in the whole town that could cure the devils in the head, and that was Dr Harvey (whom I had prepared); and wished him, if ever he found himself ill in my absence, to go to him, for he could cure him as well as myself. The gentleman lived many years, and was never troubled after.'

John Selden (1584–1621)

A Warning

For the *human* Flesh is very young and tender, and the *Devil* is rough and hard, also dark, hot, bitter, astringent and cold, and so these *two* are very ill *matched*.

Jakob Böehme (1575–1624); trans. William Law, 1764

The Drunkards Destroyed

On the 8 of February (*saith my Author*) *in the year* 1578, *a company of Drunkards, whose names are recorded as followeth,* Adam Gibbons, George Keepel, John Keysel, Peter Horsdroff, John Warner, Simon Heamkers, Jacob Hermons, *and* Hermon Frow. *These eight Drunkards in contempt of the blessed* Sabbath, *agreed to go to the Tavern on the Lords day to be merry: and coming to the house of one* Antony Hodge, *an honest Godly Man, they called for Burnt-Wine, Sack, Clarat, and what not. The Good-man refusing to give them any, advised them to go to Church to hear the Word of GOD; but they all save* Adam Gibbons, *refused, saying,* they loathed that Exercise. *Whereupon the Host departed, who being gone to Church, they began to curse and ban, wishing, he might brake his neck, ere he returned; and wishing the Devil might brake their own necks, if they went from hence, till they had some Wine.*

Whereupon the Devil in the likeness of a Young-Man appeared unto them, bringing in his hand a Flagon of Wine, and so drank unto them, saying, Good Fellows be merry, you shall have Wine enough, you seem to be lusty Lads, and I hope you will pay me well: who answering said, They would either pay him or engage their Neck for it. *Yea, rather than fail,* their Bodies and Souls. *Thus these men continued drinking, and swilling so long till they could hardly see one another. At last the* Devil *their* Host *told them that now they must pay for all, at which their hearts waxed cold. But the* Devil *bid them be of good chear, for now they must drink Fire and Brimstone with him in the Pit of Hell for ever. At which the Devil breake their Necks assunder and destroyed them. And thus ended these drunkards, their miserable dayes. This by the way, may serve for a Document for all Drunkards for ever, and to perswade folk, that the* Lord *has the* Devil *for his* Executioner, *when he pleases to execute his vengeance upon Notorious Sinners.*

George Sinclair, *Satans Invisible World Discovered*, 1685

Who Shall Defend Us from His Bitings?

He is the Great and Red Dragon, the old Serpent called the Diuell and Sathan, hauing seuen heads and ten hornes; whom thou didst create, a derider and mocker in the great and spacious sea, in which creepe Creatures without number, small and great. These are the seuerall sorts of Diuels, who night and day trauell from place to place, seeking whom they may deuoure, which doubtlesse they would do, didst not thou preserue them. This is the old Dragon who was borne in the Paradise of pleasure, that with his taile sweepes away the third part of the Stars of heauen, and casts them on the earth; who with his poyson infects the waters of the earth, that such men as drinke thereof may die; who prostitutes gold before him as dust; who thinkes hee can drinke Iordan dry at one draught; and is made so that he doth not feare any.

And who shall defend vs from his bitings, and plucke vs out of his jawes, but thou ô Lord, who hast broken the head of the great Dragon? Do thou helpe vs, spread thy wings ouer vs, that vnder them we may fly from this Dragon who pursueth vs, and with thy shield and buckler defend vs from his hornes. It is his sole desire and continuall study, to destroy those Soules whom thou hast created: And therefore, ô God, we call vnto thee, to free vs from our deadly Aduersarie, who whether we wake or sleepe, whether we eat or drinke, or whatsoeuer else wee doe, is always at hand night and day with his craft and fraud, now openly, then secretly, directing his impoysoned shafts to murther our soules.

And yet such is our madnesse, that though we behold this Dragon dayly with open mouth ready to deuoure vs, yet we notwithstanding, wanton in our sloath, are secure, before him who desireth nothing so much as to destroy vs. He always waketh without sleepe, to pursue vs, and we will not awake from sleep to preserue our selues.

Behold, he layeth infinite snares before our feet, and spreadeth ginnes in all our wayes, to intrap our Soules; and who can auoid them? He hath layd snares in our Riches, snares in our Pouertie, in our meat, our drinke, our pleasure, our sleepe, our watching, in our words, our actions, and in all our wayes. But thou, ô Lord, free vs from the snares of the Hunter, that wee may confesse vnto thee and say, Blessed is the Lord, who hath not deliuered vs into his jawes to be deuoured. My Soule hath escaped as the Sparrow from the snare of the Hunter, the snare is destroyed, and I am now set free. Amen.

Thomas Heywood, *The Hierarchie of the Blessed Angells*, 1635

Ruff Handling

The Women there vse great ruffes, & neckerchers of holland, lawne, camerick, and such cloth, as the greatest thred shall not be so bigge as the least haire that is: then, least they should fall down, they are smeared and starched in the deuils liquore, I meane *Starch;* after that, dryed with great diligence, streaked, patted, and rubbed very nicely, and so applyed to their goodly necks, and, withall, vnderpropped with supportasses (as I tolde you before) the statelie arches of pride; beyond all this they haue a further fetch, nothing inferiour to the rest; as, namely, three or foure degrees of *minor* ruffes, placed *gradatim*, step by step, one beneath another, and all vnder *the* Maister deuil ruffe. The skyrts, then, of these great ruffes are long and side euery way, pleted and crested ful curiously, God wot. Then, last of all, they are either clogged *with* golde, siluer, or silk lace of stately price, wrought all ouer with needle woork, speckled and sparkled heer & there with the sonne, the moone, the starres, and many other antiquities straunge to beholde. Some are wrought with open woork down to the midst of the ruffe and further, some with purled lace so cloyd, and other gewgawes so pestred, as the ruffe is the least parte of it self. Sometimes they are pinned vp to their eares, sometimes they are suffered to hang ouer their shoulders, like windmil sayles fluttering in the winde; and thus euery one pleaseth her self with her foolish deuices, for *suus cuiusque crepitus sibi bene olet*, as *the* prouerb saith: euery one thinketh his own wayes best, though they leade to distruction of body and soule, which I wish them to take heed of. And amongest many other fearfull examples of Gods wrathe against Pride, to sett before their eyes, the fearfull Iudgement of God, shewed upon a gentlewoman of Eprautna of late, euen the 27 of Maie 1582, the fearfull sound whereof is blowen through all the worlde, and is yet fresh in euery mannes memorie. This gentlewoman beeyng a very riche Merchaunte mannes daughter: vpon a tyme was inuited to a Bridall, or Weddyng, whiche was solemnized in that Toune, againste whiche daie she made greate preparation, for the plumyng of her self in gorgious arraie, that as her body was moste beautifull, faire, and proper, so her attire in euery respecte might bee corespondent to the same. For the accomplishment whereof, she curled her haire, she died her lockes, and laied them out after the best maner, she coloured her face with waters and Ointmentes: But in no case could she gette any (so curious and daintie she was) that could starche, and sette her Ruffes, and Neckerchers to her mynde: wherefore she sent for a couple of Laundresses, who did the best thei could to please her humors, but in anywise thei could not. Then fell she to sweare and teare, to cursse and banne, castyng the Ruffes vnder feete, and wishyng that the Deuill might take her, when she weare any of those Neckerchers againe. In the meane tyme (through the sufferaunce of God) the Deuill, transformyng himself into the forme of a young man, as braue, and proper as she in euery poincte in outward appearaunce, came in, fainyng hymself to bee a woer or suter vnto her. And seyng her thus agonized, and in suche a peltyng chafe, he demaunded of her the cause thereof, who straight waie tolde hym (as women can conceale no thyng that lieth vppon their stomackes) how she was abused in the settyng of her Ruffes, which thyng beeyng heard of hym, he promised to please her minde, and thereto tooke in hande the setting of her Ruffes, whiche he performed to her greate contentation, and likyng, in so muche as she lokyng her self in a glasse (as the Deuill bad her) became greatly inamoured with hym. This dooen, the yong man kissed her, in the doyng whereof, he writhe her necke in sonder, so she died miserably, her bodie beyng Metamorphosed, into blacke and blewe colours, most vgglesome to behold, and her face (whiche before was so amorous) became moste deformed, and fearfull to look vpon. This being knowen, preparaunce was made for her buriall, a riche coffin was prouided, and her fearfull bodie was laied therein, and it couered verie sumpteously. Foure men immediatly assaied to lifte vp the corps, but could not moue it, then sixe attempted the like, but could not once stirre it from the place, where it stoode. Whereat the standers by marueilyng, caused the Coffin to bee opened, to see the cause thereof. Where thei founde the bodie to be taken awaie, and a black Catte verie leane and deformed sittyng in the Coffin, settting of greate Ruffes, and frizlyng of haire, to the greate feare, and wonder of all the beholders.

Philip Stubbes, The Anatomie of Abuses, 1583

The Possessed Lettuce

Vpon a certaine daye, one of the Nunnes of the same monasterye, goinge into the gardin sawe a lettice that liked her, and forgettinge to blesse it before with the signe of the crosse, greedily did she eate it: where vpon she was suddainly possessed with the deuill, fell downe to the grounde, and was pitifully tormented: worde in all hast was carried to *Equitius*, desiring him quickely to visit the afflicted woman, and to helpe her with his praiers: who so sone as he came into the gardin, the deuill that was entred, began by her tongue as it were to excuse him selfe sayinge: what haue I done? what haue I done? I was fitting there vpon the lettice, and she came and did eat me: But the man of God in great zeale commanded him to departe; and not to tarry any longer in the seruant of almightye God, who straighte waies went out, not presuminge any more to touche her.

The Dialogues of S. Gregorie the Great, trans. into English by 'P.W.', 1608

Faustus Asks the Wrong Question

The spirit replied, my *Faustus*, thou knowest that I was never against thy commaundements as yet, but readie to serve and resolve thy questions, although I am not bound unto thee in such respects as concerne the hurt of our kingdome, yet was I alwaies willing to answere thee, and so I am still: therefore my *Faustus* say on boldly, what is thy will and pleasure? At which words, the spirit stole away the heart of *Faustus*, who spake in this sorte, *Mephostophiles*, tell me how and after what sorte God made the world, and all the creatures in them, and why man was made after the Image of God? The spirit hearing this, answered, *Faustus* thou knowest that all this is in vaine for thee to aske, I knowe that thou art sory for that thou hast done, but it availeth thee not, for I will teare thee in thousands of peeces, if thou change not thy opinions, and hereat he vanished away. Whereat *Faustus* al sorrowful for that he had put forth such a question, fel to weeping and to howling bitterly, not for his sinnes towards God, but for that the Divel was departed from him so sodainely, and in such a rage. And being in this perplexitie, hee was sodainely taken in such an extreame cold, as if he should have frozen in the place where he sate, in which, the greatest Divel in hell appeared unto him, with certaine of his hideous and infernal companie in the most ougliest shapes that it was possible to think upon, and traversing the chamber round about where *Faustus* sate, *Faustus* thought to himselfe, now are they come for me though my time bee not come, and that because I have asked such questions of my servant *Mephostophiles*: at whose cogitations, the chiefest Divel which was his Lord, unto whom he gave his soule, that was *Lucifer*, spake in this sorte: *Faustus*, I have seene thy thoughtes, which are not as thou hast vowed unto me, by vertue of this letter, and shewed him the Obligation that hee had written with his owne blood, wherefore I am come to visite thee and to shewe thee some of our hellish pastimes, in hope that will drawe and confirme thy minde a little more stedfast unto us. Content quoth *Faustus*, goe too, let me see what pastime you can make. At which words, the great Divell in his likenes sate him downe by

Faustus, commanding the rest of the Divels to appear in their forme, as if they were in hel: first entred *Belial* in forme of a Beare, with curled black haire to the ground, his eares standing upright: within the eare was as red as blood, out of which issued flames of fire, his teeth were a foot at least long, as white as snowe, with a tayle three elles long (at the least) having two wings, one behinde each arme, and thus one after another they appeared to *Faustus* in forme as they were in hell. *Lucifer* himselfe sate in manner of a man, all hairie, but of a browne colour like a Squirrell curled, and his tayle turning upwards on his back as the Squirrels use, I thinke hee could cracke nuts too like a Squirrel. After him came *Beelzebub* in curled hayre of hors flesh colour, his head like the head of a Bull, with a mightie payre of hornes, and two long eares downe to the grounde, and two winges on his backe, with pricking stinges like thornes: out of his wings issue flames of fire, his tayle was like a Cowe. Then came *Astaroth* in forme of a worme, going upright on his taile; he had no feete, but a tayle like a glowe-worme: under his chappes grew two shorte hands, and his back was cole blacke, his belly thick in the middle, and yellow like golde, having many bristles on his backe like a Hedgehog. After him came *Chamagosta*, being white and gray mixed, exceeding curled and hayrie: hee had a head like the head of an Asse, the tayle like a Cat, and Cleats like an Oxe, lacking nothing of an ell broade. Then came *Anobis*: this Divell had a head like a Dog, white and black hayre in shape of a Hogge, saving that he had but two feete, one under his throate, the other at his tayle: he was foure elles long, with hanging eares like a Blood-hound. After him came *Dyrhycan*, he was a short theefe in forme of a Frasant, with shining feathers, and foure feete: his neck was greene, his bodie red, and his feete blacke. The last was called *Brachus*, with foure shorte feete like an Hedgehog, yellow and greene: the upper side of his bodie was browne, and the bellie like blewe flames of fire: the tayle redde, like the tayle of a Monkey. The rest of the Divels were in forme of unsensible beasts, as Swine, Harts, Beares, Woolves, Apes, Buffes, Goates, Antelopes, Elephants, Dragons, Horsses, Asses, Lions, Cats, Snakes, Toades, and all manner of ugly odious Serpence and Wormes: yet came in such sorte, that every one at his entrie into the Hall, made their reverence unto *Lucifer*, and so tooke their places, standing in order as they came, untill they has filled the whole Hall: wherewith sodainely fell a most horrible thunder clap, that the house shooke as though it would have fallen to the ground, upon which everie monster had a muck-forke in his hande, holding them towards *Faustus* as though they would have runne a tilt at him: which when *Faustus* perceived, hee thought upon the words of *Mephostophiles*, when he tolde him how the soules in hell were tormented, being cast from Divel to Divel upon muck-forkes, he thought verely to have been tormented chere of them in like sort. But *Lucifer* perceiving his thought, spake to him, my *Faustus*, how likest thou this crewe of mine? Quoth *Faustus*, why came you not in another manner of shape? *Lucifer* replied, wee cannot chaunge our hellish forme. We have shewed our selves heere, as we are there; yet can we blind mens eyes in such sort, that when we will we repayre unto them, as if we were men or Angels of light, although our dwelling bee in darknesse. Then said *Faustus*, I like not so many of you together, whereupon *Lucifer* commaunded them to depart, except seaven of the principall, forthwith they presently vanished, which *Faustus* perceiving, hee was somewhat better comforted, and spake to *Lucifer*, where is my servant *Mephostophiles* let me see if hee can doe the like, whereupon came a fierce Dragon flying and spitting fire round about the house, and comming towards *Lucifer* made reverence, and then changed himself to the forme of a Frier, saying, *Faustus*, what wilt thou? Saith *Faustus*, I will that thou teach me to transforme my selfe in like sort as thou and the rest have done: then *Lucifer* put forth his Pawe, and gave *Faustus* a booke, saying holde, doe what thou wilt, which hee looking upon, straight waies changed himselfe into a Hog, then into a Worme, then into a Dragon, and finding this for his purpose, it liked him well. Quoth he to *Lucifer*, and how commeth it that all these filthy formes are in the world? *Lucifer* answered, they are ordained of God as plagues unto men, and so shalt thou be plagued (quoth he) whereupon, came Scorpions, Waspes, Emits, Bees, and Gnattes, which fell to stinging and biting him, and all the whole house was filled with a most horrible stinking fogge, in so much, that *Faustus* sawe nothing, but still was tormented; wherefore hee cried for helpe saying, *Mephostophiles* my faithfull servant where art thou, helpe, helpe I pray thee: hereat his Spirite answered nothing, but *Lucifer* himself said, ho ho ho *Faustus*, how likest thou the creation of the worlde?

The Historie of the Damnable Life and Deserved Death of Doctor John Faustus, 1592

The Devil by the Bedside

The fact is owned by Richard Baxter, who has recorded a case relative to one Mr White, of Dorchester, assessor to the Westminster Assembly at Lambeth, who being (as the account puts it) honoured with a visit one night from the arch-fiend, treated him with cool contempt. The devil in a light night stood by his bed-side. The assessor looked awhile whether he would say or do anything. Finding that nothing ensued, and annoyed at being thus trifled with, he said, 'If thou hast nothing to do, I have;' and so turned and composed himself to sleep.

John R. Beard, *The Autobiography of Satan*, 1872

In The Minister's House

Anno 1612 *one* Monsieur Perreaud *a* Protestant Ministe *there, being from his own house one night, and his Wife being in bed, she was much troubled with noise, and din in the house: the next night, she felt somewhat that pulled the blankets from the bed; and the same night, all the Pewter Vessel, and Brass Candlesticks were thrown about the Room. The* Minister *coming home, was told this, who carefully searched every corner of the house before he went to bed, and secured all the Doors and Windows, to prevent suspicion of* Imposture: *He was scarce well in bed, when he heard a strange noise in the Kitchen, like the rowling of a great Iron Bullet, beating against a partition of Wanscot: upon this the* Minister *went to the Room, but found nothing; The next morning he made it known to the* Elders *of the* Church, *and a publick* Notary, *one* Francis Tornous, *who sate up with him every night till Midnight, but they heard nothing till* September 20. *At which time about nine a clock at night in the presence of all, who were there, the Devil began to whistle three or four tunes, with a loud and shril voice (though somewhat hoarse) which seemed to be about three or four steps from them, singing a little tune of five notes, which Birds are taught to whistle, and after, he often repeated this word* Minister, Minister, *to which* Master Perreaud said, Yes indeed, I am a Minister, and servant of the living GOD, before whose Majestie thou tremblest. *Said the other, I know nothing to the contrary.* I have no need of thy testimony, *sayes he. This being done, he says over with a loud voice, the* Lords prayer, *the* Creed, *the ten* Commandments, *and the* morning *and evening* Prayers, *and sings the* eighty and first Psalm. *He told the Minister, that his Father had been poysoned, and named the man that did it. He told him, that as he came by his elder brothers house that night, he saluted him, and asked if he had any service to command him with to* Mascon, *to his brother: and told that they were very kind to him, and remembred their* Love *to the* Minister. *It was told him afterwards, by those who were present, that a fellow of strange shape came riding on a very lean horse, hanging down his head and spake to that purpose. At another time the Devil began to mock* GOD, *and all* Religion, *and said over the* Doxology, *but skipped over the* Second Person, *and made a foul horrible, and detestable Equivocation upon the* third Person. *He also earnestly desired them to send for* Mr Du Chaffin *the* Popish Priest *of St* Stevens Parish, *to whom he would confess himself, and withal he desired him to bring some* Holy Water *along with him, for that (said he) will presently send* me a packing. *That great* Mastiff *(said he) dare not bark against me (this was the great* House Dog*)* because I have made the sign of the Cross upon his head.

Then he fell a scoffing and jearing, and told how he did fall off the Ladder into the Ditch *among the* Frogs *while the* Savoyes, *were scalding the walls of* Geneva: *and did most exactly imitate their croaking: At another time, he told them with a lamentable voice, that he had a mind to make his* Latter-Will *and* Testament, *and bid the* Maid *call for Mr* Tornous *the publick Notary, and declared to him what Legacies he would leave, and to one present he said, he would bequeath* five hundred pound; *but he answered,* I will have none of thy money, thy money perisheth with thee.

At another time, while he was speaking, a man who was present rushed into the place, whence the voice seemed to come, and searched it strictly, but found nothing except a small bottle, which he brought forth, at which the Devil *fell a laughing, and said to him,* I was told long since, that thou wast a fool, and I see now thou art one indeed, to believe that I am in the Bottle. I should be a greater Fool my self to go into it; for so I might be catched by stopping the mouth of the Bottle with ones Finger.

At another time, the Minister *said to him,* Go thou cursed into everlasting fire prepared for the Devil and his Angels, *To whom he replyed in great wrath,* Thou lyest I am not cursed, I hope yet for Salvation by the Death and passion of Jesus Christ.

The Devil *threatned the* Minister, *that he would pull him out of his Bed by the feet, and pull the* Blankets *off him. He answered,* I will lay me down and sleep, for the Lord maketh me to dwell in safety, thou canst have no power over me, but what is given thee from above. *Whereupon he said,* it is well for thee, it is good for thee. *And at last he confessed,* that he could not prevail against the Family because they did too much call on the name of God. *And indeed it was observed, that as often as they kneeled down in prayer, the Devil left talking, and often said,* while you are at your prayers, Ile go take a turn in the Street. *But no sooner was prayer ended, but he began as before, which course he continued till the* 25. *of* November, *at which time he spake these last words,* Alas, alas, I shall speake no more.

T*he* Minister *told* Mr Du-Moulin, *that a grave Divine once coming to his house, and hearing the Devil speak profanly, rebuked him sharply for it. Whereupon the Devil answered,* Minister, you are very Holy and Zealous in this Company, but you are not so when you were singing such a baudy song in such a Tavern. *And having said this, he sang the same baudy song over before them all.* The Divine said, it is true, *Satan,* I have been licentious in my younger years, GOD of his mercy hath given me repentance, and pardon for it, but for thy part, thou art hardned in sin, and shall never get Repentance nor Pardon. *After this, the* Devil *said,* O poor Hugonits *(those* of the reformed Religion) you shall suffer much within a few years; O what mischief is intended against you!

A Popish Officer, *that belonged to a* Court of Justice *being a* Lawyer, *came out of curiosity to the* Ministers *house, to ask some Questions concerning many matters. The* Minister *forbad him; but he would not forbear. And after the Devil had resolved him many things, anent* absent Friends, *private Business, News and* State affairs, *and* Questions in Law, *he says to him*, now Sir I have told you all, you have demanded, I must tell you next, what you demanded not, that at this same very time such a man (whom he named) is taking a word of your wife at home. *And then he discovered many secrets and foul practises of the* Lawyer. *And at last sayes,* Now Sir let me correct you for being so bold, as to question with the Devil, you should have taken the Ministers Counsel. *Then upon a sudden, the whole Company saw the* Lawyer *drawn by the Arm into the midst of the room, where the Devil whirled him about, and gave him many turns with great swiftness, touching the ground only with his toe, and then threw him down upon the floor with great violence; and being taken up, and carried to his house, he lay sick and distracted a long time.*

The last ten or twelve dayes, the Devil threw stones about the Ministers *house continually, from morning to evening, and of great quantity, some of them being of two or three pound Weight. One of those dayes, the* publick Notary Mr Tornous *had a great stone thrown at him, which falling at his feet, he took up, and marked it with a coal, and threw it into the backside of the house: but presently the Devil threw it at him again. When he took it up, he found it to be very hot, thinking it had been in Hell, since he handled it last. The next day upon the* 22 *of* December *the Devil went quite away, and to morrow after, there was seen a great* Viper *going out of the* Ministers *house, which the Neighbours about seized upon with a pair of pincers, and carried it all over the town crying,* here is the Devil *that's come out of the* Ministers *house. It was found by an* Apothecary *to be a true and natural* Viper, *a* Serpent *rarely seen in those countreys.*

George Sinclair, *Satans Invisible World Discovered*, 1685

Opposites

For, as to the Life and Temper of the blessed and adorable *JESUS*, we know there was an incomparable *sweetness* in his *Nature*, *Humility* in his *Manners*, *Calmness* in his *Temper*, *Compassion* in his *Miracles*, *Modesty* in his *Expressions*, *Holiness* in all his *Actions*, *Hatred* of *Vice* and *Baseness*, and *Love* to all the World; all which are *essentially contrary* to the Nature and Constitution of *Apostate Spirits*, who abound in *Pride* and *Rancour*, *Insolence* and *Rudeness*, *Tyranny* and *Baseness*, universal *Malice*, and *Hatred* of *Men*.

And their *Designs* are as opposite, as their *Spirit* and their *Genius*. And now, Can the *Sun* borrow its Light from the *bottomless Abyss?* Can *Heat* and *Warmth* flow in upon the World from the Regions of *Snow* and *Ice?* Can *Fire freeze*, and *Water burn?* Can Natures, so infinitely contrary, *communicate*, and jump in *projects* that are *destructive* to each others *known Interests?* Is there any Balsom in the *Cockatrices Egg?* or, Can the *Spirit* of *Life* flow from the *Venome* of the *Asp?*

Joseph Glanvill, *Saducismus Triumphatus*, 1681

The Battle with Apollyon

But now in this Valley of *Humiliation* poor *Christian* was hard put to it, for he had gone but a little way before he espied a foul *Fiend* coming over the field to meet him; his name is *Apollyon*. Then did *Christian* begin to be afraid, and to cast in his mind whether to go back, or to stand his ground. But he considered again, that he had no Armor for his back, and therefore thought that to turn the back to him might give him greater advantage with ease to pierce him with his Darts; therefore he resolved to venture, and stand his ground. For thought he, had I no more in mine eye than the saving of my life, 'twould be the best way to stand.

So he went on, and *Apollyon* met him. Now the Monster was hideous to behold, he was cloathed with scales like a Fish (and they are his pride) he had Wings like a Dragon, feet like a Bear, and out of his belly came Fire and Smoke, and his mouth was as the mouth of a Lion. When he was come up to *Christian*, he beheld him with a disdainful countenance, and thus began to question with him.

APOLLYON: *Whence come you, and whither are you bound?*

CHRISTIAN: I am come from the City of *Destruction*, which is the place of all evil, and am going to the City of *Zion*.

APOLLYON: *By this I perceive thou art one of my Subjects, for all that Country is mine; and I am the Prince and God of it. How is it then that thou hast ran away from thy King? Were it not that I hope thou mayest do me more service, I would strike thee now at one blow to the ground.*

CHRISTIAN: I was born indeed in your Dominions, but your service was hard, and your wages such as a man could not live on, *for the wages of Sin is death*; therefore when I was come to years, I did as other considerate persons do, look out if perhaps I might mend my self.

APOLLYON: *There is no Prince that will thus lightly lose his Subjects, neither will I as yet lose thee. But since thou complainest of thy service and wages be content to go back; what our Country will afford, I do here promise to give thee.*

CHRISTIAN: But I have let myself to another, even to the King of Princes, and how can I with fairness go back with thee?

APOLLYON: *Thou hast done in this, according to the Proverb, changed a bad for a worse: but it is ordinary for those that have professed themselves his Servants, after a while to give him the slip, and return again to me: do thou so to, and all shall be well.*

CHRISTIAN: I have given him my faith, and sworn my Allegiance to him; how then can I go back from this, and not be hanged as a Traitor?

APOLLYON: *Thou didst the same to me, and yet I am willing to pass by all, if now thou wilt yet turn again, and go back.*

CHRISTIAN: What I promised thee was in my nonage; and besides, I count that the Prince under whose Banner now I stand, is able to absolve me; yea, and to pardon also what I did as to my compliance with thee: and besides, (O thou destroying *Apollyon*) to speak truth, I like his Service, his Wages, his Servants, his Government, his Company, and Country better than thine: and therefore leave off to perswade me further, I am his Servant, and I will follow him.

APOLLYON: *Consider again when thou art in cool blood, what thou art like to meet with in the way that thou goest. Thou knowest that for the most part, his Servants come to an ill end, because they are transgressors against me, and my ways. How many of them have been put to shameful deaths! and besides, thou countest his service better than mine, whereas he never came yet from the place where he is, to deliver any that served him out of our hands; but as for me, how many times, as all the World very well knows, have I delivered, either by power or fraud, those that have faithfully served me, from him and his, though taken by them, and so I will deliver thee.*

CHRISTIAN: His forbearing at present to deliver them, is on purpose to try their love, whether they will cleave to him to the end: and as for the ill end thou sayest they come to, that is most glorious in their account. For for present deliverance, they do not much expect it; for they stay for their Glory, and then they shall have it, when their Prince comes in his, and the Glory of the Angels.

APOLLYON: *Thou hast already been unfaithful in thy service to him, and how doest thou think to receive wages of him?*

CHRISTIAN: Wherein, O *Apollyon*, have I been unfaithful to him?

APOLLYON: *Thou didst faint at first setting out, when thou wast almost choked in the Gulf of Dispond; thou didst attempt wrong ways to be rid of thy burden, whereas thou shouldest have stayed till thy Prince had taken it off: thou didst sinfully sleep and lose thy choice thing: thou wast also almost perswaded to go back, at the sight of the Lions; and when thou talkest of thy Journey, and of what thou hast heard, and seen, thou art inwardly desirous of vain-glory in all that thou sayest or doest.*

CHRISTIAN: All this is true, and much more, which thou hast left out; but the Prince whom I serve and honour, is merciful, and ready to forgive: but besides, these infirmities possessed me in thy Country, for there I suckt them in, and I have groaned under them, been sorry for them, and have obtained pardon of my Prince.

APOLLYON: Then *Apollyon* broke out into a grievous rage, saying, *I am an Enemy to this Prince: I hate his Person, his Laws, and People: I am come out on purpose to withstand thee.*

CHRISTIAN: *Apollyon* beware what you do, for I am in the King's Highway, the way of Holiness, therefore take heed to your self.

APOLLYON: Then *Apollyon* straddled quite over the whole breadth of the way, and said, I am void of fear in this matter, prepare thy self to die, for I swear by my Infernal Den, that thou shalt go no further, here will I spill thy soul; and with that, he threw a flaming Dart at his breast, but *Christian* had a Shield in his hand, with which he caught it, and so prevented the danger of that. Then did *Christian* draw, for he saw 'twas time to bestir him; and *Apollyon* as fast made at him, throwing Darts as thick as Hail; by the which, notwithstanding all that *Christian* could do to avoid it, *Apollyon* wounded him in his head, his hand and foot; this made *Christian* give a little back: *Apollyon* therefore followed his work amain, and *Christian* again took courage, and resisted as manfully as he could. This sore combat lasted for above half a day, even till *Christian* was almost quite spent. For you must know that *Christian* by reason of his wounds, must needs grow weaker and weaker.

Then *Apollyon* espying his opportunity, began to gather up close to *Christian*, and wrestling with him, gave him a dreadful fall; and with that, *Christian*'s Sword flew out of his hand. Then said *Apollyon*, *I am sure of thee now*; and with that, he had almost prest him to death, so that *Christian* began to despair of life. But as God would have it, while *Apollyon* was fetching of his last blow, thereby to make a full end of this good Man, *Christian* nimbly reached out his hand for his Sword, and caught it, saying, *Rejoice not against me, O mine Enemy! when I fall, I shall arise*; and with that, gave him a deadly thrust, which made him give back, as one that had received his mortal wound: *Christian* perceiving that, made at him again, saying, *Nay, in all these things we are more than Conquerors, through him that loved us*. And with that, *Apollyon* spread forth his Dragon's wings, and sped him away, that *Christian* saw him no more.

In this Combat no man can imagine, unless he had seen and heard as I did, what yelling, and hideous roaring *Apollyon* made all the time of the fight, he spake like a Dragon: and on the other side, what sighs and groans brast from *Christian*'s heart. I never saw him all the while give so much as one pleasant look, till he perceived he had wounded *Apollyon* with his two edged Sword, then indeed he did smile, and look upward: but 'twas the dreadfullest sight that ever I saw.

So when the Battle was over, *Christian* said, I will here give thanks to him that hath delivered me out of the mouth of the Lion; to him that did help me against *Apollyon*: and so he did, saying

> *Great* Beelzebub, *the Captain of this Fiend,*
> *Design'd my ruin; therefore to this end*
> *He sent him harnest out, and he with rage*
> *That Hellish was, did fiercely me engage:*
> *But blessed* Michael *helped me, and I*
> *By dint of Sword, did quickly make him fly:*
> *Therefore to him let me give lasting praise,*
> *And thank and bless his holy name always.*

Then there came to him an hand, with some of the leaves of the Tree of Life, the which *Christian* took, and applied to the wounds that he had received in the Battle, and was healed immediately. He also sat down in that place to eat Bread, and to drink of the Bottle that was given him a little before; so being refreshed, he addressed himself to his Journey, with his Sword drawn in his hand, for he said, I know not but some other Enemy may be at hand. But he met with no other affront from *Apollyon*, quite through this Valley.

John Bunyan, *The Pilgrim's Progress*, 1678

A Lower Estimate of the Devil's Powers

The fables of Witchcraft have taken so fast hold and deepe root in the heart of man, that fewe or none can (nowadaies) with patience indure the hand and correction of God. For if any adversitie, greefe, sicknesse, losse of children, corne, cattell, or libertie happen unto them; by & by they exclaime uppon witches. As though there were no God in Israel that ordereth all things according to his will; punishing both just and unjust with greefs, plagues, and afflictions in manner and forme as he thinketh good: but that certeine old women heere on earth, called witches, must needs be the contrivers of all mens calamities, and as though they themselves were innocents, and had deserved no such punishments. Insomuch as they sticke not to ride and go to such, as either are injuriouslie tearmed witches, or else are willing so to be accounted, seeking at their hands comfort and remedie in time of their tribulation, contrarie to Gods will and commandement in that behalfe, who bids us resort to him in all our necessities.

Such faithlesse people (I saie) are also persuaded, that neither haile nor snowe, thunder nor lightening, raine nor tempestuous winds come from the heavens at the commandement of God: but are raised by the cunning and power of witches and conjurers; insomuch as a clap of thunder, or a gale of wind is no sooner heard, but either they run to ring bels, or crie out to burne witches; or else burne consecrated things, hoping by the smoke thereof, to drive the divell out of the aire, as though spirits could be fraied awaie with such externall toies: howbeit, these are right inchantments, as *Brentius* affirmeth.

But certeinlie, it is neither a witch, nor divell, but a glorious God that maketh the thunder. I have read in the scriptures, that God maketh the blustering tempests and whirlewinds: and I find that it is the Lord that altogither dealeth with them, and that they blowe according to his will. But let me see anie of them all rebuke and still the sea in time of tempest, as Christ did; or raise the stormie wind, as God did with his word; and I will beleeve in them. Hath anie witch or conjurer, or anie creature entred into the treasures of the snowe; or seene the secret places of the haile, which GOD hath prepared against the daie of trouble, battell, and warre? I for my part also thinke with Jesus Sirach, that at Gods onelie commandement the snowe falleth; and that the wind bloweth according to his will, who onelie maketh all stormes to cease; and who (if we keepe his ordinances) will send us raine in due season, and make the land to bring forth hir increase, and the trees of the field to give their fruit.

But little thinke our witchmongers, that the Lord commandeth the clouds above, or openeth the doores of heaven, as *David* affirmeth; or that the Lord goeth forth in the tempests and stormes, as the Prophet *Nahum* reporteth: but rather that witches and conjurers are then about their businesse.

The *Martionists* acknowledged one God the authour of good things, and another the ordeiner of evill: but these make the divell a whole god, to create things of nothing, to knowe mens cogitations, and to doo that which God never did; as, to transubstantiate men into beasts, &c. Which thing if divels could doo, yet followeth it not, that witches have such power. But if all the divels in hell were dead, and all the witches in *England* burnt or hanged; I warrant you we should not faile to have raine, haile and tempests, as now we have: according to the appointment and will of God, and according to the constitution of the elements, and the course of the planets, wherein God hath set a perfect and perpetual order.

Reginald Scot, *The Discoverie of Witchcraft*, 1584

By Stratagem, Not by Force

See this cunning agent, when he has man's destruction in his view, how securely he acts! he never wants a handle; the best of men have one weak place or other, and he always finds it out, takes the advantage of it, and conquers them by one artifice or another; only take it with you as you go, it is always by stratagem, never by force; a proof that he is not empowered to use violence: He may tempt, and he does prevail; but it is all legerdemain, it is all craft and artifice, he is still *Diabolè*, the calumniator and deceiver, that is, the misrepresenter; he misrepresents man to God, and misrepresents God to man; also he misrepresents things, he puts false colours, and then manages the eye to see them with an imperfect view, raising clouds and fogs to intercept our sight; in short, he deceives all our senses, and imposes upon us in things which otherwise would be the easiest to discern and judge of.

This indeed is in part the benefit of the Devil's history, to let us see that he has used the same method all along; and that ever since he has had any thing to do with mankind, he has practised upon them with stratagem and cunning; also it is observable that he has carried his point better that way than he would have done by fury and violence, if he had been allowed to make use of it; for by his power indeed he might have laid the world desolate, and made a heap of rubbish of it long ago; but, as I have observed before, that would not have answered his ends half so well, for by destroying men he would have made martyrs, and sent abundance of good men to heaven, would much rather have died, than yielded to serve him, and as he aimed to have it, to fall down and worship him; I say, he would have made martyrs, and that not a few: But this was none of Satan's business; his design lies quite another way; his business is to make men sin, not to make them suffer; to make devils of them, not saints; to delude them, and draw them away from their maker, not send them away to him; and therefore he works by stratagem, not by force.

Daniel Defoe, *The History of the Devil*, 1726

Night-Knowledge

The creature is darkness in comparison with the excellence of the Divine light; and therefore the creature's knowledge in its own nature is called *evening* knowledge. For the evening is akin to darkness, yet it possesses some light: but when the light fails utterly, then it is night. So then the knowledge of things in their own nature, when referred to the praise of the Creator, as it is in the good angels, has something of the Divine light, and can be called evening knowledge; but if it be not referred to God, as is the case with the demons, it is not called evening, but *nocturnal* knowledge. Accordingly we read in Gen. i. 5, that the darkness, which God separated from the light, *He called night*.

St Thomas Aquinas, *Summa Theologica*,
trans. 'by the Fathers of the English Dominican Province', 1912

'Lucifer's Letter to the Clergy'

Lucifer, lord and prince of the depe donion of derkenes, rewlour of the regne of the infernall empyre, kyng of the contre of cumbryd, caytifs iustise and iuge of all gehennall subiettes, duke of the dale of dysesse, heer of the erytage of hell, to all our dere, leef and worthi to be lovyd felawes, bretherin and childryn of pryde, universall and singuler, with the froyte of all falsnes fulfillyd of this dayes cherche, as the feute of your obediens to our ymperial magnificens and infernall sovereynte to which evereyet we fynd yow obeysaunt and trewe lieges and subietes, helthe, welthe and gretyng, which as to ourself and oures we coveyte and desire, while ye are to our willes, preceptes and maundementz obedyent, redy and wele willyng, and as to us plesauntly of your lyst bygonne and long lastyngly contynuyd to the lawes of our lordship everlastyngly enduryng and fulfillyng, of wham our adversare, thilk Ihesu Cryst, by his prophete sometyme seyde, *Odivi ecclesiam malignancium*, 'I have hatyd the chirche of mysdoers'. Somtyme some of the vikers, subiettys and disciples of that Ihesu Crist, folowyng his steppis and the tracys of his weyes, stablid in the signes of his vertues, perfourmyng his will in her worchynges, lyvyng undur a pore manere lyf, by her prechynges and werchynges, ynto moost illusion of our tartariall regne and iurisdiccion and contempte of our infernall magestee, alle the world from the yok and servitute of the excellence of our tyrannye turnyd to her doctryne, conversacion and lyf and into grete preiudice, grevaunce and hyndryng of our iehennal iurisdiccion, noght dredyng ne shamyng to hurte, defoyle and greve our fereful powere and to offende the mageste of our infernale estate. In tho dayes, thurgh her wrongful destourblyng, we were violently precludid from the tribute of the dwetes of our subiettes, and to our wepeful paleys of the gehennall empyre concours of our peple was than wrecchidly lettyd and stoppid, and the brode light wey *que ducit ad mortem*, 'that ledith to the dethe', without eny prees or steppys of wrecches of our subiect peple, lay forletyngly undefoulyd, unhauntyd and unusyd. Wherfor al the cravvyd court of our caytif cumpanye with all wepely compleyntes waylid, mornyd and sorowyd, so pytously dispoylid of the right of our rufull regyon, yn so myche that the impacient wodenes of our brest no lenger myght bere hit ne the hard unpite of the herte of our heer and our sorowful subiettes no lenger furthermore myght suffre hit. But now, with forseying from hennys forwarde to mete with our circumspeccion with all suche like perelis, we have avisely purveyd us of an opyn remedy, and in the place and stede of tho our harmeful adversares, that Ihesu Cristes apostles and al her folowers in doctryne or maners, by our myghtfull powere and sotyl boldenes, we have now in thes dayes and moderne tymes made yow which, in the moderne cherche, be presidentes, prelates, and potestates fyctely srutede ynto her place ocupyng substitutes, as thilk Crist Ihesu of you seyde, *Regnaverunt sed non de me*, 'Thei have regnyd but not of me'. Onys yet we behette hym, that Ihesu, al the kyngdoms of the world yf he fallyng on kne had wurshipyd our ryal myght, but he wold noght, seying, *Regnum meum non est de hoc mundo*, 'My kyngdom is not of this world', fleying and voydyng whan the peple wold chose have hym into eny temperall kyngdome or lordship. In yow, which of the grees, steppes and state of grace and trouthe be falle and slyden and to us and to our preceptes, conceils and persuasions in the erthe trewly and continuelly serve, is fulfillyd the promission and byheest, and now by us and of us al that ye of possessioners which we into continuance of your trewe servise have geve ye withholde.

And whan ye to tho profites of worshippes so bene erecte and elate ye be smyte with more houndship hungre than byfor, the pore and al your lower unpitously with an houndisshe rage oppressyng, al that ye cacche and hold ravisshyng, al thing out of his kynd, as yt may best lyke us, pervertyng with inflacion of all manere of pryde, the curis and thoghtis of your hertys pyttyng yn all lustis of lecherous lyvyng, in all delices and bodyly lustys, confortes and fedynges your dayes of this lyf leding and expendyng, takyng on you on erthe names of goddis, and holy under dissimulid face of holynes and visage of goodnes the privehyd supersticious pride as our predilecte childrin of wikkidnes with all the craft of our cautels curiosly and ypocrytly coveryng, the world but noght that Ihesu deceyvyng, and the wele willyng of our tartareal mageste pleasauntly and continuelly fulfillyng.

Mid. Eng. trans. of *Epistola Luciferi* by Peter Ceffons of Clairvaux, 1352

Sleight of Hand

There lived in the parish of St Bennet Fynk, near the Royal Exchange, an honest poor widow woman, who, her husband being lately dead, took lodgers into her house; that is, she let out some of her rooms in order to lessen her own charge of rent; among the rest, she let her garrets to a working watch-wheel maker, or one some way concerned in making the movements of watches, and who worked for those shop-keepers who sell watches, as is usual.

It happened that a man and woman went up, to speak with this move-ment maker upon some business which related to his trade, and when they were near the top of the stairs, the garret door where he usually worked being wide open, they saw the poor man (the watch maker, or wheel maker) had hanged himself upon a beam which was left open in the room a little lower than the plaister, or ceiling: Surprized at the sight, the woman stopped, and cried out to the man who was behind her on the stairs, to run up, and cut the poor creature down.

At that very moment comes a man hastily from another part of the room which they upon the stairs could not see, bringing a joint-stool in his hand, as if in great haste, and sets it down just by the wretch that was hanged, and getting up as hastily upon it pulls a knife out of his pocket, and taking hold of the rope with one of his hands, beckoned to the woman and the man behind her with his head, as if to stop and not come up, shewing them the knife in his other hand, as if he was just going to cut the poor man down.

Upon this, the woman stopped awhile, but the man who stood on the joint-stool continued with his hand and knife, as if fumbling at the knot, but did not yet cut the man down; at which the woman cried out again, and the man behind her called to her, Go up, says he, and help the man upon the stool! supposing something hindered. But the man upon the stool made signs to them again to be quiet, and not come on, as if saying, I shall do it immediately; then he made two strokes with his knife, as if cutting the rope, and then stopped again; and still the poor man was hanging, and consequently dying: Upon this, the woman on the stairs cried out to him, What ails you? why don't you cut the poor man down? and the man behind her having no more patience, thrusts her by, and said to her, let me come, I'll warrant you I'll do it; and with that runs up and forward into the room to the man; but when he came there, behold, the poor man was there hanging; but no man with a knife, or joint-stool, or any such thing to be seen, all that was spectre and delusion, in order, no doubt, to let the poor creature that had hanged himself perish and expire.

The man was so frighted and surprized, that with all the courage he had before, he dropped on the floor as one dead, and the woman at last was fain to cut the poor man down with a pair of scissars, and had much to do to effect it.

As I have no room to doubt the truth of this story, which I had from persons on whose honesty I could depend, so I think it needs very little trouble to convince us who the man upon the stool must be, and that it was the Devil who placed himself there, in order to finish the murder of the man who he had, devil-like, tempted before, and prevailed with to be his own executioner.

Daniel Defoe, *The History of the Devil*, 1726

A Call at the Mad-House

'Listen to me, Stanton; nay, wrap not yourself in that miserable blanket, – that cannot shut out my words. Believe me, were you folded in thunder-clouds, you must hear *me*! Stanton, think of your misery. These bare walls – what do they present to the intellect or to the senses? – White-wash, diversified with the scrawls of charcoal or red chalk, that your happy predecessors have left for you to trace over. You have a taste for drawing, – I trust it will improve. And here's a grating, through which the sun squints on you like a step-dame, and the breeze blows, as if it meant to tantalize you with a sigh from that sweet mouth, whose kiss you must never enjoy. And where's your library, – intellectual man, – travelled man?' he repeated in a tone of bitter derision; 'where be your companions, your peaked men of countries, as your favourite Shakespeare has it? You must be content with the spider and the rat, to crawl and scratch round your flock-bed! I have known prisoners in the Bastile to feed them for companions, – why don't you begin your task? I have known a spider to descend at the tap of a finger, and a rat to come forth when the daily meal was brought, to share it with his fellow-prisoner! – How delightful to have vermin for your guests! Aye, and when the feast fails them, they make a meal at their entertainer! – You shudder – Are you, then, the first

[230]

prisoner who has been devoured alive by the vermin that infested his cell? – Delightful banquet, not "where you eat, but where you are eaten!" Your guests, however, will give you one token of repentance while they feed; there will be *gnashing of teeth*, and you shall hear it, and feel it too perchance! – And then for meals – Oh you are daintily off! – The soup that the cat has lapped; and (as her progeny has probably contributed to the hell-broth) why not? – Then your hours of solitude, deliciously diversified by the yell of famine, the howl of madness, the crash of whips, and the broken-hearted sob of those who, like you, are supposed, or *driven* mad by the crimes of others! – Stanton, do you imagine your reason can possibly hold out amid such scenes? – Supposing your reason was unimpaired, your health not destroyed, – suppose all this, which is, after all, more than fair supposition can grant, guess the effect of the continuance of these scenes on your senses alone. A time will come, and soon, when, from mere habit, you will echo the scream of every delirious wretch that harbours near you; then you will pause, clasp your hands on your throbbing head, and listen with horrible anxiety whether the scream proceeded from *you* or *them*. The time will come, when, from the want of occupation, the listless and horrible vacancy of your hours, you will feel as anxious to hear those shrieks, as you were at first terrified to hear them, – when you will watch for the ravings of your next neighbour, as you would for a scene on the stage. All humanity will be extinguished in you. The ravings of these wretches will become at once your sport and your torture. You will watch for the sounds, to mock them with the grimaces and bellowings of a fiend. The mind has a power of accommodating itself to its situation, that you will experience in its most frightful and deplorable efficacy. Then comes the dreadful doubt of one's own sanity, the terrible announcer that *that* doubt will soon become fear, and *that* fear certainty. Perhaps (still more dreadful) the *fear* will at last become a *hope*, – shut out from society, watched by a brutal keeper, writhing with all the impotent agony of an incarcerated mind without communication and without sympathy, unable to exchange ideas but with those whose ideas are only the hideous spectres of departed intellect, or even to hear the welcome sound of the human voice, except to mistake it for the howl of a fiend, and stop the ear desecrated by its intrusion, – then at last your fear will become a more fearful hope; you will wish to become one of them, to escape the agony of consciousness. As those who have long leaned over a precipice, have at last felt a desire to plunge below, to relieve the intolerable temptation of their giddiness, you will hear them laugh amid their wildest paroxysms; you will say, "Doubtless those wretches have some consolation, but I have none; my sanity is my greatest curse in this abode of horrors. They greedily devour their miserable meals, while I loathe mine. They sleep sometimes soundly, while my sleep is – worse than their waking. They are revived every morning by some delicious illusion of cunning madness, soothing them with the hope of escaping, baffling or tormenting their keeper; my sanity precludes all such hope. *I know I never can escape*, and the preservation of my faculties is only an aggravation of my sufferings. I have all their miseries, – I have none of their consolations. They laugh, – I hear them; would I could laugh like them." You will try, and the very effort will be an invocation to the demon of insanity to come and take full possession of you from that moment for ever.'

Charles Robert Maturin, Melmoth the Wanderer, 1820

An Intolerable Presence

At the extremity of the Colwan wood, I perceived a figure approaching me with slow and dignified motion. The moment that I beheld it, my whole frame received a shock as if the ground on which I walked had sunk suddenly below me. Yet, at that moment, I knew not who it was; it was the air and motion of some one that I dreaded, and from whom I would gladly have escaped; but this I even had not power to attempt. It came slowly onward, and I advanced as slowly to meet it; yet when we came within speech, I still knew not who it was. It bore the figure, air, and features of my late brother, I thought, exactly; yet in all these there were traits so forbidding, so mixed with an appearance of misery, chagrin, and despair, that I still shrunk from the view, not knowing on whose face I looked. But when the being spoke, both my mental and bodily frame received another shock more terrible than the first, for it was the voice of the great personage I had so long denominated my friend, of whom I had deemed myself for ever freed, and whose presence and counsels I now dreaded more than hell. It was his voice, but so altered – I shall never forget it till my dying day. Nay, I can scarce conceive it possible that any earthly sounds could be so discordant, so repulsive to every feeling of a human soul, as the tones of the voice that grated on my ear at that moment. They were the sounds of the pit, wheezed through a grated cranny, or seemed so to my distempered imagination.

'So! Thou shudderest at my approach now, dost thou?' said he. 'Is this all the gratitude that you deign for an attachment of which the annals of the world furnish no parallel? An attachment which has caused me to forego power and dominion, might, homage, conquest and adulation, all that I might gain one highly valued and sanctified spirit, to my great and true principles of reformation among mankind. Wherein have I offended? What have I done for evil, or what have I not done for your good, that you would thus shun my presence?'

'Great and magnificent prince,' said I humbly, 'let me request of you to abandon a poor worthless wight to his own wayward fortune, and return to the dominion of your people. I am unworthy of the sacrifices you have made for my sake; and after all your efforts, I do not feel that you have rendered me either more virtuous or more happy. For the sake of that which is estimable in human nature, depart from me to your own home, before you render me a being either altogether above, or below the rest of my fellow creatures. Let me plod on towards heaven and happiness in my own way, like those that have gone before me, and I promise to stick fast by the great principles which you have so strenuously inculcated, on condition that you depart and leave me for ever.'

'Sooner shall you make the mother abandon the child of her bosom; nay, sooner cause the shadow to relinquish the substance, than separate me from your side. Our beings are amalgamated, as it were, and consociated in one, and never shall I depart from this country until I can carry you in triumph with me.'

I can in nowise describe the effect this appalling speech had on me. It was like the announcement of death to one who had of late deemed himself free, if not of something worse than death, and of longer continuance. There was I doomed to remain in misery, subjugated, soul and body, to one whose presence was become more intolerable to me than ought on earth could compensate: And at that moment, when he beheld the anguish of my soul, he could not conceal that he enjoyed it. I was troubled for an answer, for which he was waiting: it became incumbent on me to say something after such a protestation of attachment; and, in some degree to shake the validity of it, I asked, with great simplicity, where he had been all this while?

'Your crimes and your extravagancies forced me from your side for a season,' said he; 'but now that I hope the day of grace is returned, I am again drawn towards you by an affection that has neither bounds nor interest; an affection for which I receive not even the poor return of gratitude, and which seems to have its radical sources in fascination. I have been far, far abroad, and have seen much, and transacted much, since I last spoke with you. During that space, I grievously suspect that you have been guilty of great crimes and misdemeanours, crimes that would have sunk an unregenerated person to perdition; but as I knew it to be only a temporary falling off, a specimen of that liberty by which the chosen and elected ones are made free, I closed my eyes on the wilful debasement of our principles, knowing that the transgressions could never be accounted to your charge, and that in good time you would come to your senses, and throw the whole weight of your crimes on the shoulders that had voluntarily stooped to receive the load.'

'Certainly I will,' said I, 'as I and all the justified have a good right to do. But what crimes? What misdemeanours and transgressions do you talk about? For my part, I am conscious of none, and am utterly amazed at insinuations which I do not comprehend.'

'You have certainly been left to yourself for a season,' returned he, 'having gone on rather like a person in a delirium, than a Christian in his sober senses. You are accused of having made away with your mother privately; as also of the death of a beautiful young lady, whose affections you had seduced.'

'It is an intolerable and monstrous falsehood!' cried I, interrupting him; 'I never laid a hand on a woman to take away her life, and have even shunned their society from my childhood: I know nothing of my mother's exit, nor of that young lady's whom you mention – Nothing whatever.'

'I hope it is so,' said he. 'But it seems there are some strong presumptuous proofs against you, and I came to warn you this day that a precognition is in progress, and that unless you are perfectly convinced, not only of your innocence, but of your ability to prove it, it will be the safest course for you to abscond, and let the trial go on without you.'

'Never shall it be said that I shrunk from such a trial as this,' said I. 'It would give grounds for suspicions of guilt that never had existence, even in thought. I will go and show myself in every public place, that no slanderous tongue may wag against me. I have shed the blood of sinners, but of these deaths I am guiltless; therefore, I will face every tribunal, and put all my accusers down.'

'Asseveration will avail you but little,' answered he, composedly: 'It is, however, justifiable in its place, although to me it signifies nothing, who know too well that you *did* commit both crimes, in your own person, and with your own hands. Far be it from me to betray you; indeed, I would rather endeavour to palliate the offences; for though adverse to nature, I can prove them not to be so to the cause of pure Christianity, by the mode of which we have approved of it, and which we wish to promulgate.'

'If this that you tell me be true,' said I, 'then is it as true that I have two souls, which take possession of my bodily frame by turns, the one being all unconscious of what the other performs; for as sure as I have at this moment a spirit within me, fashioned and destined to eternal felicity, as sure am I utterly ignorant of the crimes you now lay to my charge.'

'Your supposition may be true in effect,' said he. 'We are all subjected to two distinct natures in the same person. I myself have suffered grievously in that way. The spirit that now directs my energies is not that with which I was endowed at my creation. It is changed within me, and so is my whole nature. My former days were those of grandeur and felicity. But, would you believe it? *I was not then a Christian.* Now I am. I have been converted to its truths by passing through the fire, and since my final conversion, my misery has been extreme. You complain that I have not been able to render you more happy than you were. Alas! do you expect it in the difficult and exterminating career which you have begun. I, however, promise you this – a portion of the only happiness which I enjoy, sublime in its motions, and splendid in its attainments – I will place you on the right hand of my throne, and show you the grandeur of my domains, and the felicity of my millions of true professors.'

James Hogg, *Private Memoirs and Confessions of a Justified Sinner*, 1824

'The Devil's Walk' (1)

From his brimstone bed at break of day
    A walking the Devil is gone,
To look at his little snug farm of the World,
    And see how his stock went on.

Over the hill and over the dale,
    And he went over the plain;
And backward and forward he swish'd his tail,
    As a gentleman swishes a cane.

How then was the Devil drest?
    Oh, he was in his Sunday's best,
His coat was red and his breeches were blue,
And there was a hole where his tail came through.

A lady drove by in her pride,
In whose face an expression he spied
    For which he could have kiss'd her;
Such a flourishing, fine, clever creature was she,
With an eye as wicked as wicked can be,
I should take her for my Aunt, thought he,
    If my dam had had a sister.

He met a lord of high degree,
No matter what was his name;
Whose face with his own when he came to compare
The expression, the look, and the air,
And the character too, as it seem'd to a hair, –
Such a twin-likeness there was in the pair
That it made the Devil start and stare,
For he thought there was surely a looking-glass there,
But he could not see the frame.

He saw a Lawyer killing a viper
On a dunghill beside his stable;
Ho! quoth he, thou put'st me in mind
Of the story of Cain and Abel.

An Apothecary on a white horse
Rode by on his vocation;
And the Devil thought of his old friend
Death in the Revelation.

He pass'd a cottage with a double coach-house,
A cottage of gentility!
And he own'd with a grin
That his favourite sin
Is pride that apes humility.

He saw a pig rapidly
Down a river float;
The pig swam well, but every stroke
Was cutting his own throat;

And Satan gave thereat his tail
A twirl of admiration;
For he thought of his daughter War
And her suckling babe Taxation . . .

He entered a thriving bookseller's shop;
Quoth he, We are both of one college,
For I myself sate like a Cormorant once
Upon the Tree of Knowledge.

As he passed through Cold-Bath Fields he look'd
     At a solitary cell;
And he was well-pleased, for it gave him a hint
For improving the prisons of Hell.

He saw a turnkey tie a thief's hands
     With a cordial tug and jerk;
Nimbly, quoth he, a man's fingers move
     When his heart is in his work.

He saw the same turnkey unfettering a man
     With little expedition;
And he chuckled to think of his dear slave trade,
And the long debates and delays that were made
     Concerning its abolition.

He met one of his favourite daughters
     By an Evangelical Meeting;
And forgetting himself for joy at her sight,
He would have accosted her outright,
     And given her a fatherly greeting.

But she tipt him a wink, drew back, and cried,
     Avaunt! my name's Religion!
And then she turn'd to the preacher
     And leer'd like a love-sick pigeon . . .

Now the morning air was cold for him
     Who was used to a warm abode;
And yet he did not immediately wish
     To set out on his homeward road.

For he had some morning calls to make
     Before he went back to Hell;
So, thought he, I'll step into a gaming-house,
     And that will do as well;
But just before he could get to the door
     A wonderful chance befell.

     For all on a sudden, in a dark place,
He came upon General —'s burning face;
     And it struck him with such consternation,

That home in a hurry his way did he take,
Because he thought by a slight mistake
  'Twas the general conflagration.

Robert Southey, 1799

'The Devil's Walk' (2)

Once, early in the morning,
  Beelzebub arose,
With care his sweet person adorning,
  He put on his Sunday clothes.

He drew on a boot to hide his hoof,
  He drew on a globe to hide his claw,
His horns were concealed by a *Bras Chapeau*,
And the Devil went forth as natty a *Beau*
  As Bond-street ever saw.

He sate him down, in London town,
    Before earth's morning ray;
With a favourite imp he began to chat,
On religion, and scandal, this and that,
    Until the dawn of day.

And then to St James's Court he went,
  And St Paul's Church he took on his way;
He was mighty thick with every Saint,
  Though they were formal and he was gay.

The Devil was an agriculturist,
  And as bad weeds quickly grow,
In looking over his farm, I wist,
  He wouldn't find cause for woe.

He peeped in each hole, to each chamber stole,
    His promising live-stock to view;
Grinning applause, he just showed them his claws,
And they shrunk with affright from his ugly sight
    Whose work they delighted to do.

Satan poked his red nose into crannies so small
    One would think that the innocents fair,
Poor lambkins! were just doing nothing at all
But settling some dress or arranging some ball,
    But the Devil saw deeper there.

A Priest, at whose elbow the Devil during prayer
    Sate familiarly, side by side,
Declared that, if the Tempter were there,
    His presence he would not abide.
Ah! ah! thought Old Nick, that's a very stale trick,
For without the Devil, O favourite of Evil,
    In your carriage you would not ride.

Satan next saw a brainless King,
    Whose house was as hot as his own;
Many Imps in attendance were there on the wing,
They flapped the pennon and twisted the sting,
    Close by the very Throne.

Ah! ah! thought Satan, the pasture is good,
    My Cattle will here thrive better than others;
They dine on news of human blood,
They sup on the groans of the dying and dead,
And supperless never will go to bed;
    Which will make them fat as their brothers.

Fat as the Fiends that feed on blood,
    Fresh and warm from the fields of Spain,
        Where Ruin ploughs her gory way,
Where the shoots of earth are nipped in the bud,
        Where Hell is the Victor's prey,
Its glory the meed of the slain.

Fat – as the Death-birds on Erin's shore,
That gutted themselves in her dearest gore,
        And flitted round Castlereagh,
When they snatched the Patriot's heart, that *his* grasp
Had torn from its widow's maniac clasp,
        And fled at the dawn of day.

Fat – as the Reptiles of the tomb,
    That riot in corruption's spoil,

That fret their little hour in gloom,
    And creep, and live the while.

Fat as that Prince's maudlin brain,
    Which, addled by some gilded toy,
Tired, gives his sweetmeat, and again
    Cries for it, like a humoured boy.

For he is fat, – his waistcoat gay,
When strained upon a levee day,
    Scarce meets across his princely paunch;
And pantaloons are like half-moons
        Upon each brawny haunch.

How vast his stock of calf! when plenty
    Had filled his empty head and heart,
Enough to satiate foplings twenty,
    Could make his pantaloon seams start.

The Devil (who sometimes is called Nature),
    For men of power provides thus well,
Whilst every change and every feature,
    Their great original can tell.

Satan saw a lawyer a viper slay,
    That crawled up the leg of his table,
It reminded him most marvellously
    Of the story of Cain and Abel.

The wealthy yeoman, as he wanders
        His fertile fields among,
And on his thriving cattle ponders,
    Counts his sure gains, and hums a song;
Thus did the Devil, through earth walking,
        Hum low a hellish song.

For they thrive well whose garb of gore
    Is Satan's choicest livery,
And they thrive well who from the poor
    Have snatched the bread of penury,
And heap the houseless wanderer's store
    On the rank pile of luxury.

The Bishops thrive, though they are big;
    The Lawyers thrive, though they are thin;
For every gown, and every wig,
    Hides the safe thrift of Hell within.

Thus pigs were never counted clean,
    Although they dine on finest corn;
And cormorants are sin-like lean,
    Although they eat from night to morn.

Oh! why is the Father of Hell in such glee,
    As he grins from ear to ear?
Why does he doff his clothes joyfully,
    As he skips, and prances, and flaps his wing,
    As he sidles, leers, and twirls his sting,
        And dares, as he is, to appear?

A statesman passed – alone to him,
    The Devil dare his whole shape uncover,
To show each feature, every limb,
    Secure of an unchanging lover.

At this known sign, a welcome sight,
    The watchful demons sought their King,
And every Fiend of the Stygian night,
    Was in an instant on the wing.

Pale Loyalty, his guilt-steeled brow,
    With wreaths of gory laurel crowned:
The hell-hounds, Murder, Want and Woe,
    Forever hungering, flocked around;
From Spain had Satan sought their food,
'Twas human woe and human blood!

Hark! the earthquake's crash I hear, –
    Kings turn pale, and Conquerors start,
Ruffians tremble in their fear,
    For their Satan doth depart.

This day Fiends give to revelry
    To celebrate their King's return,

And with delight its Sire to see
  Hell's adamantine limits burn.

But were the Devil's sight as keen
  As Reason's penetrating eye,
His sulphurous Majesty I ween,
  Would find but little cause for joy.

For the sons of Reason see
  That, ere fate consume the Pole,
The false Tyrant's cheek shall be
  Bloodless as his coward soul.

Percy Bysshe Shelley, 1812

Whipping Pigs to Death

The Devil is *diabolos*, an Accuser. In this character he presented himself among the other sons of God before his Father's throne to request to be allowed to tempt Job by tormenting him so that God might damn him. God, it seems, had some special reason for patronizing Job; and one does not well see why he spared him at last. The expostulations of Job with God are of the most daring character; it is certain he would not bear them from a Christian. If God were a refined critic, which from his inspiration of Ezechiel would never have been suspected, one might imagine that the profuse and sublime strain of poetry, not to be surpassed by ancient literature, much less modern, had found favor with him. In this view he [the Devil] is at once the informer, the attorney general, and the jailor of the celestial tribunal. It is not good policy, or at least cannot be considered as constitutional practice, to unite these characters. The Devil must have a great interest to exert himself to procure a sentence of guilty from the judge; for I suppose there will be no jury at the resurrection – at least if there is it will be so overawed by the bench and the counsel for the Crown as to ensure whatever verdict the court shall please to recommend. No doubt that as an incentive to his exertions, half goes to the informer. What an army of spies and informers all Hell must afford, under the direction of that active magistrate, the Devil! How many plots and conspiracies and . . .

If the Devil takes but half the pleasure in tormenting a sinner which

God does, who took the trouble to create him, and then to invent a system of casuistry by which he might excuse himself for devoting him to eternal torment, this reward must be considerable. Conceive how the enjoyment of one half of the advantages to be derived from their ruin, whether in person or property, must irritate the activity of a delator. Tiberius, or Bonaparte, or Lord Castlereagh, never affixed any reward to the disclosure or the creation of conspiracies equal to that which God's government has attached to the exertions of the Devil, to tempt, betray, and accuse unfortunate man. These two considerable personages are supposed to have entered into a sort of partnership in which the weaker has consented to bear all the odium of their common actions and to allow the stronger to talk of himself as a very honorable person, on condition of having a participation in what is the especial delight of both of them, burning men to all eternity. The dirty work is done by the Devil in the same manner as some starving wretch will hire himself out to a King or Minister to work with a stipulation that he shall have some portion of the public spoil as an instrument to betray a certain number of other starving wretches into circumstances of capital punishment, when they may think it convenient to edify the rest by hanging up a few of those whose murmurs are too loud.

It is far from inexplicable that earthly tyrants should employ this kind of agents, or that God should have done so with regard to the Devil and his angels; or that any depositary of power should take these measures with respect to those by whom he fears lest that power should be wrested from him. But to tempt mankind to incur everlasting damnation must, on the part of God and even on the part of the Devil, arise from that very disinterested love of tormenting and annoying which is seldom observed on earth except from the very old. . . . The thing that comes nearest to it is a troop of idle dirty boys baiting a cat; cooking, skinning eels, and boiling lobsters alive, and bleeding calves, and whipping pigs to death; naturalists anatomizing dogs alive (a dog has as good a right and a better excuse for anatomizing a naturalist) are nothing compared to God and the Devil judging, damning, and then tormenting the soul of a miserable sinner. It is pretended that God dislikes it, but this is mere shamefacedness and coquetting, for he has everything his own way and he need not damn unless he likes. The Devil has a better excuse, for, as he was entirely made by God, he can have no tendency or disposition the seeds of which were not originally planted by his creator; and as everything else was made by God, those seeds can only have developed themselves in the precise degree and manner determined by the impulses arising from the agency of the rest of his creation. It would be as unfair to complain of the Devil for acting ill, as of a watch for going badly; the defects are to be imputed as much to God in the former case, as to the watchmaker in the latter.

Percy Bysshe Shelley, 'Essay on the Devil and Devils', c.1819-20

Crusoe Explains the Conflict

I had been talking a great deal to him of the power of God, His omnipotence, His dreadful nature to sin, His being a consuming fire to the workers of iniquity; how, as He had made us all, He could destroy us and all the world in a moment; and he listened with great seriousness to me all the while.

After this, I had been telling him how the devil was God's enemy in the hearts of men, and used all his malice and skill to defeat the good designs of Providence, and to ruine the kingdom of Christ in the world; and the like. 'Well,' says Friday, 'but you say, God is so strong, so great, is He not much strong, much might as the devil?' 'Yes, yes,' says I, 'Friday, God is stronger than the devil, God is above the devil, and therefore we pray to God to tread him down under our feet, and enable us to resist his temptations and quench his fiery darts.' 'But,' says he again, 'if God much strong, much might as the devil, why God no kill the devil, so make him no more do wicked?'

Daniel Defoe, *Robinson Crusoe*, 1719

George III Meets the Accuser (1)

On the cerulean floor by that dread circle surrounded,
Stood the soul of the King alone.   In front was the Presence
Veil'd with excess of light; and behind was the blackness of darkness.
Then might be seen the strength of holiness, then was its triumph,
Calm in his faith he stood, and his own clear conscience upheld him.

When the trumpet was blown, and the Angel made proclamation –
Lo, where the King appears! Come forward ye who arraign him!
Forth from the lurid cloud a Demon came at the summons.
It was the Spirit by which his righteous reign had been troubled;
Likest in form uncouth to the hideous Idols whom India

(Long by guilty neglect to hellish delusions abandon'd,)
Worships with horrible rites of self-immolation and torture.
Many-headed and monstrous the Fiend; with numberless faces,
Numberless bestial ears erect to all rumours, and restless,
And with numberless mouths which were fill'd with lies as with
    arrows.
Clamours arose as he came, a confusion of turbulent voices,
Maledictions, and blatant tongues, and viperous hisses;
And in the hubbub of senseless sounds the watchwords of
    faction,
Freedom, Invaded Rights, Corruption, and War, and Oppression,
Loudly enounced were heard.
                         But when he stood in the Presence,
Then was the Fiend dismay'd, though with impudence clothed as a
    garment;
And the lying tongues were mute, and the lips which had scatter'd
Accusation and slander, were still.

Robert Southey, 'A Vision of Judgement', 1822

George III Meets the Accuser (2)

The spirits were in neutral space, before
    The gate of heaven; like eastern thresholds is
The place where Death's grand cause is argued o'er,
    And souls dispatched to that world or to this;
And therefore Michael and the other wore
    A civil aspect: though they did not kiss,
Yet still between his Darkness and his Brightness
There passed a mutual glance of great politeness.

The Archangel bowed, not like a modern beau,
    But with a graceful Oriental bend,
Pressing one radiant arm just where below
    The heart in good men is supposed to tend.
He turned as to an equal, not too low,
    But kindly; Satan met his ancient friend
With more hauteur, as might an old Castilian
Poor noble meet a mushroom rich civilian.

He merely bent his diabolic brow
  An instant; and then raising it, he stood
In act to assert his right or wrong, and show
  Cause why King George by no means could or should
Make out a case to be exempt from woe
  Eternal, more than other kings endued
With better sense and hearts, whom history mentions,
Who long have 'paved hell with their good intentions.'

Michael began: 'What wouldst thou with this man,
  Now dead, and brought before the Lord? What ill
Hath he wrought since his mortal race began,
  That thou can'st claim him: Speak! and do thy will,
If it be just: if in this earthly span
  He hath been greatly failing to fulfil
His duties as a king and mortal, say,
And he is thine; if not, let him have way.'

'Michael!' replied the Prince of Air, 'even here,
  Before the gate of him thou servest, must
I claim my subject; and will make appear
  That as he was my worshipper in dust,
So shall he be in spirit, although dear
  To thee and thine, because nor wine nor lust
Were of his weaknesses; yet on the throne
He reign'd o'er millions to serve me alone.

'Look to *our* earth, or rather *mine*; it was,
  Once, more thy master's: but I triumph not
In this poor planet's conquest, nor, alas!
  Need he thou servest envy me my lot:
With all the myriads of bright worlds which pass
  In worship round him, he may have forgot
Yon weak creation of such paltry things;
I think few worth damnation save their kings,

'And these but as a kind of quit-rent, to
  Assert my right as lord; and even had
I such an inclination, 'twere (as you
  Well know) superfluous; they are grown so bad,
That hell has nothing better left to do
  Than leave them to themselves: so much more mad

And evil by their own internal curse,
Heaven cannot make them better, nor I worse.

'Look to the earth, I said, and say again:
  When this old, blind, mad, helpless, weak, poor worm,
Began in youth's first bloom and flush to reign,
  The world and he both wore a different form,
And much of earth and all the watery plain
  Of ocean call'd him king: through many a storm
His isles had floated on the abyss of Time;
For the rough virtues chose them for their clime.

'He came to his sceptre, young; he leaves it, old:
  Look to the state in which he found his realm,
And left it; and his annals too behold,
  How to a minion first he gave the helm;
How grew upon his heart a thirst for gold,
  The beggar's vice, which can but overwhelm
The meanest hearts; and for the rest, but glance
Thine eye along America and France!

' 'Tis true, he was a tool from first to last
  (I have the workmen safe); but as a tool
So let him be consumed! From out the past
  Of ages, since mankind have known the rule
Of monarchs – from the bloody rolls amass'd
  Of sin and slaughter – from the Caesar's school,
Take the worst pupil; and produce a reign
More drench'd with gore, more cumber'd with the slain!

'He ever warr'd with freedom and the free:
  Nations as men, home subjects, foreign foes,
So that they utter'd the word "Liberty!"
  Found George the Third their first opponent. Whose
History was ever stain'd as his will be
  With national and individual woes?
I grant his household abstinence; I grant
His neutral virtues, which most monarchs want;

'I know he was a constant consort; own
  He was a decent sire, and middling lord.
All this is much, and most upon a throne;
  As temperance, if at Apicius' board,

Is more than at an anchorite's supper shown.
   I grant him all the kindest can accord;
And this was well for him, but not for those
Millions who found him what oppression chose.

'The new world shook him off; the old yet groans
   Beneath what he and his prepared, if not
Completed: he leaves heirs on many thrones
   To all his vices, without what begot
Compassion for him – his tame virtues; drones
   Who sleep, or despots who have now forgot
A lesson which shall be re-taught them, wake
Upon the throne of Earth; but let them quake!

Lord Byron, 'A Vision of Judgement', 1822

The Spirit which Eternally Denies

FAUST: What are you called?
MEPHISTOPHELES: For one so down on the word,
   Who, so remote from everything external,
   Past all appearance seeks the inmost kernel,
   This question seems a bit absurd.
FAUST: With gentry such as you, their nature
   Is aptly gathered from the nomenclature,
   Whence all too clearly it transpires
   When you are labeled Lord of Flies, corrupters, liars.
   All right – who are you, then?
MEPHISTOPHELES: Part of that force which would
   Do ever evil, and does ever good.
FAUST: And that conundrum of a phrase implies?
MEPHISTOPHELES: The spirit which eternally denies!
   And justly so; for all that which is wrought
   Deserves that it should come to naught;
   Hence it were best if nothing were engendered.
   Which is why all things you have rendered
   By terms like sin, destruction – evil, in brief
   Are my true element-in-chief.
FAUST: You call yourself a part, yet whole you stand in view?
MEPHISTOPHELES: I speak a modest truth for you.
   Whereas your Man, that microcosmic fool,

Regards himself an integer as a rule,
I am but part of the part that was the whole at first,
Part of the dark which bore itself the light,
That supercilious light which lately durst
Dispute her ancient rank and realm to Mother Night;
And yet to no avail, for strive as it may,
It cleaves in bondage to corporeal clay.
It streams from bodies, bodies it lends sheen,
A body can impede its thrust,
And so it should not be too long, I trust,
Before with bodies it departs the scene.

FAUST: Now I perceive your worthy role!
Unable to destroy on the scale of the whole,
You now attempt it in the little way.

MEPHISTOPHELES: It does not come to much, I'm bound to say.
What bids defiance to the Naught,
The clumsy lumber of the Aught,
Endeavor what I would against it,
I never have discountenanced it
By waves or tempests, quake or firebrand –
Sedately rest at last both sea and land!
As for that scum of beast- and humanhood,
There's just no curbing it, no quelling,
I've buried them in droves past telling,
Yet ever newly circulates fresh blood.
And so it goes, it drives one to distraction!
From air, from water, as from soil
A thousand germinating seeds uncoil,
In warm or cold, in moist or dry-as-bone!
Had I not fire for my preserve of action,
I should not have a place to call my own.

FAUST: And so against the ever sanely,
Benignantly creative might
You clench your devil's fist, inanely
Upraising it in frigid spite!
Come, seek another occupation,
Hoar Chaos's fantastic son!

MEPHISTOPHELES: It merits earnest contemplation;
We shall talk more of this anon!

J. W. von Goethe, *Faust*, 1770–1831;
trans. Walter Arndt, 1976

Blake Praises Contraries

Without Contraries is no progression. Attraction and Repulsion, Reason and Energy, Love and Hate, are necessary to Human existence.

From these contraries spring what the religious call Good & Evil. Good is the passive that obeys Reason. Evil is the active springing from Energy.

Good is Heaven. Evil is Hell.

William Blake, *The Marriage of Heaven and Hell*, 1790–3

Screwtape Hates his Contrary

He's a hedonist at heart. All those fasts and vigils and stakes and crosses are only a façade. Or only like foam on the sea shore. Out at sea, out in His sea, there is pleasure, and more pleasure. He makes no secret of it; at His right hand are 'pleasures for evermore'. Ugh! I don't think He has the least inkling of that high and austere mystery to which we rise in the Miserific Vision. He's vulgar, Wormwood. He has a bourgeois mind. He has filled His world full of pleasures. There are things for humans to do all day long without His minding in the least – sleeping, washing, eating, drinking, making love, playing, praying, working. Everything has to be *twisted* before it's any use to us. We fight under cruel disadvantages. Nothing is naturally on our side. . . .

To us a human is primarily food; our aim is the absorption of its will into ours, the increase of our own area of selfhood at its expense. But the obedience which the Enemy demands of men is quite a different thing. One must face the fact that all the talk about His love for men, and His service being perfect freedom, is not (as one would gladly believe) mere propaganda, but an appalling truth. He really *does* want to fill the universe with a lot of loathsome little replicas of Himself – creatures whose life, on its miniature scale, will be qualitatively like His own, not because He has absorbed them but because their wills freely conform to His. We want cattle who can finally become food; He wants servants who can finally become sons. We want to suck in, He wants to give out. We are empty and would be filled; He is full and flows over. Our war aim is a world in which Our Father Below has drawn all other beings into himself: the Enemy wants a world full of beings united to Him but still distinct.

C. S. Lewis, *The Screwtape Letters*, 1942

Woland Revels in his Contrariness

At sunset, high above the town, on the stone roof of one of the most beautiful buildings in Moscow, built about a century and a half ago, stood two figures – Woland and Azazello. They were invisible from the street below, hidden from the vulgar gaze by a balustrade adorned with stucco flowers in stucco urns, although they could see almost to the limits of the city.

Woland was sitting on a folding stool, dressed in his black soutane. His long, broad-bladed sword had been rammed vertically into the cleft between two flagstones, making a sundial. Slowly and inexorably the shadow of the sword was lengthening, creeping towards Satan's black slippers. Resting his sharp chin on his fist, hunched on the stool with one leg crossed over the other, Woland stared unwaveringly at the vast panorama of palaces, huge blocks of flats and condemned slum cottages.

Azazello, without his usual garb of jacket, bowler and patent-leather shoes and dressed instead like Woland in black, stood motionless at a short distance from his master, also staring at the city.

Woland remarked:

'An interesting city, Moscow, don't you think?'

Azazello stirred and answered respectfully:

'I prefer Rome, messire.'

'Yes, it's a matter of taste,' replied Woland. . . .

There was silence again and both figures on the roof stood watching the setting sun reflected in all the westward-facing windows. Woland's eyes shone with the same fire, even though he sat with his back to the sunset.

Then something made Woland turn his attention to a round tower behind him on the roof. From its walls appeared a grim, ragged, mud-spattered man with a beard, dressed in a chiton and home-made sandals.

'Ha!' exclaimed Woland, with a sneer at the approaching figure. 'You are the last person I expected to see here. What brings you here, of all people?'

'I have come to see you, spirit of evil and lord of the shadows,' the man replied with a hostile glare at Woland.

'Well, tax-gatherer, if you've come to see me, why don't you wish me well?'

'Because I have no wish to see you well,' said the man impudently.

'Then I am afraid you will have to reconcile yourself to my good health,' retorted Woland, his mouth twisted into a grin. 'As soon as you appeared on this roof you made yourself ridiculous. It was your tone of voice. You spoke your words as though you denied the very existence of the shadows or of evil. Think, now: where would your good be if there were no evil and what would the world look like without shadow? Shadows are thrown by people and things. There's the shadow of my sword, for instance. But shadows are also cast by trees and living things. Do you want to strip the whole globe by removing every tree and every creature to satisfy your fantasy of a bare world? You're stupid.'

'I won't argue with you, old sophist,' replied Matthew the Levite.

'You are incapable of arguing with me for the reason I have just mentioned – you are too stupid,' answered Woland and enquired: 'Now tell me briefly and without boring me why you are here?'

'He has sent me.'

'What message did he give you, slave?'

'I am not a slave,' replied Matthew the Levite, growing angrier, 'I am his disciple.'

'You and I are speaking different languages, as always,' said Woland, 'but that does not alter the things we are talking about. Well?'

Mikhail Bulgakov, *The Master and Margarita*; trans. Michael Glenny, 1967

Seven

THE BUYER OF SOULS

And the days keep on 'minding me
There's a hellhound on my trail

ROBERT JOHNSON

There is an infernal irony in the discourses of
Mephistopheles, which extends itself to the whole
creation, and criticises the universe like a bad book
of which the devil has made himself the censor.

MADAME DE STÄEL

The Party of the First Part

For he will oblish himselfe to teach them artes and sciences, which he may easelie doe, being so learned a knaue as he is: To carrie them newes from anie parte of the worlde, which the agilitie of a Spirite may easelie performe: to reueale to them the secretes of anie persons, so being they bee once spoken, for the thought none knowes but GOD; except so far as yee may ghesse by their countenance, as one who is doubtleslie learned inough in the *Physiognomie*: Yea, he will make his schollers to creepe in credite with Princes, by fore-telling them manie greate thinges; parte true, parte false: For if all were false, he would tyne credite at all handes; but alwaies doubtsome, as his Oracles were. And he will also make them to please Princes, by faire banquets and daintie dishes, carryed in short space fra the farthest part of the worlde. For no man doubts but he is a thiefe, and his agilitie (as I spake before) makes him to come suche speede. Such-like, he will guard his schollers with faire armies of horsemen and foote-men in appearance, castles and fortes: Which all are but impressiones in the aire, easelie gathered by a spirite, drawing so neare to that substance himselfe . . .

For it is no wonder, that the Deuill may delude our senses, since we see by common proofe, that simple juglars will make an hundreth thinges seeme both to our eies and eares otherwaies then they are. Now as to the *Magicians* parte of the contract, it is in a word that thing, which I said before, the Deuill hunts for in all men.

King James I, *Daemonologie*, 1597

A Selection of Useful Demons

Shax, alias Scox, is a darke and a great marquesse, like unto a storke, with a hoarse and subtill voice: he dooth marvellouslie take awaie the sight, hearing and understanding of anie man, at the commandement of the conjuror: he taketh awaie monie out of everie kings house, and carrieth it backe after 1200. yeares, if he be commanded, he is a horssestealer, he is thought to be faithfull in all commandements: and although he promise to be obedient to the conjuror in all things; yet is he not so, he is a lier, except he be brought into a triangle and there he speaketh divinelie, and telleth of things which are hidden, and not kept of wicked spirits, he promiseth good familiars, which are accepted if they be not deceivers, he hath thirtie legions.

Procell is a great and a strong duke, appearing in the shape of an angell, but speaketh verie darklie of things hidden, he teacheth geometrie and all the liberall arts, he maketh great noises, and causeth the waters to rore, where are none, he warmeth waters, and distempereth bathes at certeine times, as the exorcist appointeth him, he was of the order of potestats, and hath fourtie eight legions under his power.

Furcas is a knight and commeth foorth in the similitude of a cruell man, with a long beard and a hoarie head, he sitteth on a pale horsse, carrieng in his hand a sharpe weapon, he perfectlie teacheth practike philosophie, rhetorike, logike, astronomie, chiromancie, pyromancie, and their parts: there obeie him twentie legions.

Murmur is a great duke and an earle, appearing in the shape of a souldier, riding on a griphen, with a dukes crowne on his head; there go before him two of his ministers, with great trumpets, he teacheth philosophie absolutelie, he constraineth soules to come before the exorcist, to answer what he shall aske them, he was of the order partlie of thrones, and partlie of angels, and ruleth thirtie legions.

Caim is a great president, taking the forme of a thrush, but when he putteth on man's shape, he answereth in burning ashes, carrieng in his hand a most sharpe swoord, he maketh the best disputers, he giveth men the understanding of all birds, of the lowing of bullocks, and barking of dogs, and also of the sound and noise of waters, he answereth best of things to come, he was of the order of angels, and ruleth thirtie legions of divels.

Remark on the Foregoing

He that can be persuaded that these things are true, or wrought indeed according to the assertion of couseners, or according to the supposition of witchmongers & papists, may soone be brought to beleeve that the moone is made of greene cheese. You see in this which is called *Salomons* conjuration, there is a perfect inventarie registred of the number of divels, of their names, of their offices, of their personages, of their qualities, of their powers, of their properties, of their kingdomes, of their governments, of their orders, of their dispositions, of their subjection, of their submission, and of the waies to bind or loose them; with a note what wealth, learning, office, commoditie, pleasure, &c: they can give, and may be forced to yeeld in spight of their harts, to such (forsooth) as are cunning in this art: of whome yet was never seene any rich man, or at least that gained any thing that waie; or any unlearned man, that became learned by that meanes; or any happie man, that could with the helpe of this art either deliver himselfe, or his freends, from adversitie, or adde unto his estate any point of felicitie: yet these men, in all worldlie happinesse, must needs exceed all others; if such things could be by them accomplished, according as it is presupposed. For if they may learne of *Marbas*, all secrets, and to cure all diseases; and of *Furcas*, wisdome, and to be cunning in all mechanicall arts; and to change anie mans shape, of *Zepar*: if *Bune* can make them rich and eloquent, if *Beroth* can tell them of all things, present, past, and to come; if *Asmodaie* can make them go invisible and shew them all hidden treasure; if *Salmacke* will afflict whom they list, & *Allocer* can procure them the love of any woman; if *Amy* can provide them excellent familiars, if *Caym* can make them understand the voice of all birds and beasts, and *Buer* and *Bifrons* can make them live long; and finallie, if *Orias* could procure unto them great friends, and reconcile their enimies, & they in the end had all these at commandement; should they not live in all worldlie honor and felicitie? whereas contrariwise they lead their lives in all obloquie, miserie, and beggerie, and in fine come to the gallowes; as though they had chosen unto themselves the spirit *Valefer*, who they saie bringeth all them with whom he entreth into familiaritie, to no better end than the gibet or gallowes.

Reginald Scot, *The Discoverie of Witchcraft*, 1584

Faustus, Begin Thine Incantations

FAUSTUS: Now that the gloomy shadow of the night,
Longing to view *Orions* drisling looke,
Leapes from th'Antarticke world unto the skie,
And dyms the *Welkin*, with her pitchy breathe:
Faustus, begin thine Incantations,
And try if devils will obey thy Hest,
Seeing thou hast pray'd and sacrific'd to them.
Within this circle is *Jehova*'s Name,
Forward, and backward, *Anagramatis'd*:
Th'abreviated names of holy Saints,
Figures of every adjunct to the heavens,
And Characters of Signes, and erring Starres,
By which the spirits are inforc'd to rise:
Then feare not *Faustus* to be resolute
And try the utmost Magicke can performe.

Christopher Marlowe, *The Tragedie of Doctor Faustus*, 1604

Faustus Interviews Candidates

ALEKSO, VITZLIPUTZLI, AUERHAHN, MEXICO, *rush in amid violent thunder and lightning. Lastly,* MEPHISTOPHILIS.

FAUST: A pretty company! But how dilatory ye are! Pray do not let this occur again in future. Tell me, thou first hell-fury, what is thy name?

MEXICO: Mexico.

FAUST: And how fleet art thou?

MEXICO: As fleet as the bullet from the gun.

FAUST: Thou hast a marvellous speed, but not enough for me. Hence! (MEXICO *flies through the air.*) What is thy name, hell-fury! and how fleet art thou?

AUERHAHN: Auerhahn; and I am as fleet as the wind.

FAUST: That is a marvellous speed, but it satisfies me not. Hence! (AUERHAHN *departs like* MEXICO.) How art thou named, hell-fury?

VITZLIPUTZLI: Vitzliputzli!

FAUST: And how fleet art thou?

VITZLIPUTZLI: As fleet as the ship on the sea.

FAUST: As the ship on the sea? That is a notable velocity; yet through unfavourable winds the ship does not always reach its port. – Hence! (VITZLIPUTZLI *departs.*) Say on, hell-fury! who art thou?

ALEKSO: Alexo.

FAUST: Alexo? And what fleetness may'st thou possess?

ALEKSO: I am as fleet as a snail.

FAUST: As a snail! – Then art thou the most leaden-paced of all the spirits of hell; for thee I have no use whatever. Hence! (ALEKSO *sails slowly off.*) A trifle slow!

      MEPHISTOPHILIS *enters, in the dress of a huntsman.*

Ha! what do I behold! a hell-fury in a human form?

MEPHISTOPHILIS: Thou must know, Faust! that I am a prince of hell, and have the power to assume and to appear in any shape I please.

FAUST: Thou a prince of hell! – How namest thou thyself?

MEPHISTOPHILIS: Mephistophilis.

FAUST: Mephistophilis! The name sounds well; and how fleet art thou?

MEPHISTOPHILIS: As fleet as human thought.

Das Puppenspiel vom Doctor Faust, trans. T. C. H. Hedderinck, 1887

The Deal

MEPHOSTOPHILIS: Now *Faustus* what wouldst thou have me do?

FAUSTUS: I charge thee waite upon me whilst I live
   To do what ever *Faustus* shall command:
   Be it to make the Moone drop from her Sphere,
   Or the Ocean to overwhelme the world.

MEPHOSTOPHILIS: I am a servant to great *Lucifer*,
   And may not follow thee without his leave;
   No more then he commands, must we performe.

FAUSTUS: Did not he charge thee to appeare to me?

MEPHOSTOPHILIS: No, I came now hether of mine owne accord.

FAUSTUS: Did not my conjuring speeches raise thee? speake.

MEPHOSTOPHILIS: That was the cause, but yet *per accidens*:
   For when we heare one racke the name of God,
   Abjure the Scriptures, and his Saviour Christ;
   We flye in hope to get his glorious soule:
   Nor will we come unlesse he use such meanes,
   Whereby he is in danger to be damn'd:
   Therefore the shortest cut for conjuring
   Is stoutly to abjure the Trinity,
   And pray devoutely to the Prince of hell.

FAUSTUS: So *Faustus* hath already done, and holds this principle,
   There is no chiefe but onely *Beelzebub*:
   To whom *Faustus* doth dedicate himselfe.
   This word Damnation, terrifies not me,
   For I confound hell in *Elizium*:
   My Ghost be with the old Phylosophers.
   But leaving these vaine trifles of mens soules,
   Tell me, what is that *Lucifer*, thy Lord?

MEPHOSTOPHILIS: Arch-regent and Commander of all Spirits.

FAUSTUS: Was not that *Lucifer* an Angell once?

MEPHOSTOPHILIS: Yes *Faustus*, and most deerely lov'd of God.

FAUSTUS: How comes it then that he is Prince of Devils?

MEPHOSTOPHILIS: O: by aspiring pride and insolence,
   For which God threw him from the face of heaven.

FAUSTUS: And what are you that live with *Lucifer*?

MEPHOSTOPHILIS: Unhappy spirits that fell with *Lucifer*,
   Conspir'd against our God with *Lucifer*,
   And are for ever damn'd with *Lucifer*.

FAUSTUS: Where are you damn'd?

MEPHOSTOPHILIS: In hell.

FAUSTUS: How comes it then that thou art out of hell?

MEPHOSTOPHILIS: Why this is hell: nor am I out of it.
Think'st thou that I who saw the face of God,
And tasted the eternall Joyes of heaven,
Am not tormented with ten thousand hels,
In being depriv'd of everlasting blisse?
O *Faustus* leave these frivolous demandes,
Which strike a terror to my fainting soule.

FAUSTUS: What, is great *Mephostophilis* so passionate
For being deprived of the Joyes of heaven?
Learne thou of *Faustus* manly fortitude,
And scorne those Joyes thou never shalt possesse.
Go beare these tydings to great *Lucifer*,
Seeing *Faustus* hath incur'd eternall death,
By desperate thoughts against *Joves* Deity:
Say he surrenders up to him his soule,
So he will spare him foure and twenty yeares,
Letting him live in all voluptuousnesse,
Having thee ever to attend on me,
To give me whatsoever I shall aske;
To tell me whatsoever I demand:
To slay mine enemies, and aid my friends,
And alwaies be obedient to my will.

Christopher Marlowe, *The Tragedie of Doctor Faustus*, 1604

'Faust grows impatient with his companion's dark mutterings'

'You're forever talking rot,' snapped Faust.
'*Which way you fly is hell*, and suchlike ...'

'And what do you intend,' he groused,
'By *this is hell and you are in it?* –

This is the University Senior Common Room,
And you are in it as my guest!'

[259]

'I do repeat myself, I fear,'
His hamefaced friend confessed.

D. J. Enright, *A Faust Book*, 1979

Great Time, Mad Time, Quite Bedevilled Time

I: 'So you would sell me time?'

HE: 'Time? Simple time? No, my dear fere, that is not devyll's ware. For that we should not earn the reward, namely that the end belongs to us. What manner of time, that is the heart of the matter! Great time, mad time, quite bedivelled time, in which the fun waxes fast and furious, with heaven-high leaping and springing – and again, of course, a bit miserable, very miserable indeed, I not only admit that, I even emphasize it, with pride, for it is sitting and fit, such is artist-way and artist-nature. That, as is well knowen, is given at all times to excess on both sides and is in quite normal way a bit excessive. Alway the pendulum swings very wide to and fro between high spirits and melancholia, that is usual, is so to speak still according to moderate bourgeois Nueremberg way, in comparison with that which we purvey. For we purvey the uttermost in this direction; we purvey towering flights and illuminations, experiences of upliftings and unfetterings, of freedom, certainty, facility, feeling of power and triumph, that our man does not trust his wits – counting in besides the colossal admiration for the made thing, which could soon bring him to renounce every outside, foreign admiration – the thrills of self-veneration, yes, of exquisite horror of himself, in which he appears to himself like an inspired mouthpiece, as a godlike monster. And correspondingly deep, honourably deep, doth he sink in between-time, not only into void and desolation and unfruitful melancholy but also into pains and sicknesse – familiar incidentally, which had alway been there, which belong to his character, yet which are only most honorably enhanced by the illumination and the well-known "sack of heyre". Those are pains which a man gladly pays, with pleasure and pride, for what he has so much enjoyed, pains which he knows from the fairy-tale, the pains which the little sea-maid, as from sharp knives, had in her beautiful human legs she got herself instead of her tail. You know Andersen's Little Sea-maid? She would be a sweetheart for you! Just say the word and I will bring her to your couch.'

Thomas Mann, *Doctor Faustus*, 1947; trans. H. T. Lowe-Parker, 1949

A Side-bet and a Signature

FAUST: And for my part – what is it you require?

MEPHISTOPHELES: Never you mind, it's much too soon to worry.

FAUST: No, no! Old Nick's an egoist – it's hard
To picture him in any special hurry
To be of service for the love of God.
Spell out just what the bargain turns upon;
Not safely is such servant taken on.

MEPHISTOPHELES: I shall be at your service by this bond
Without relief or respite here on earth;
And if or when we meet again beyond,
You are to give me equal worth.

FAUST: Beyond to me makes little matter;
If once this earthly world you shatter,
The next may rise when this has passed.
It is from out this earth my pleasures spring,
It is this sun shines on my suffering;
If once from these I draw asunder,
Then come to pass what will and must.
I do not further choose to wonder
If hate may then be felt or love,
Or whether in those regions yonder
They still know nether or above.

MEPHISTOPHELES: So minded, you may dare with fitness.
Engage yourself; these days you are to witness
Examples of my pleasing arts galore.
I'll give you what no man has seen before.

FAUST: What is, poor devil, in your giving?
Has ever human mind in its high striving
Been comprehended by the likes of you?
What's yours but food unsating, the red hue
Of gold which, shifting and untrue,
Quicksilverlike will through the fingers run,
A game which always stays unwon,
A girl who at my very breast
Trades winks already with another's eyes,
But honor's fair and godly zest
Which like a meteor flares and dies?
Show me the fruit which, still unplucked, will rot,

Trees freshly green, with every day's renewal!

MEPHISTOPHELES: Such a commission daunts me not,
  I can provide that sort of jewel.
  But nonetheless, there comes a time, my friend,
  When good things savored at our ease give pleasure.

FAUST: Should ever I take ease upon a bed of leisure,
  May that same moment mark my end!
  When first by flattery you lull me
  Into a smug complacency,
  When with indulgence you can gull me,
  Let that day be the last for me!
  This is my wager!

MEPHISTOPHELES: Done!

FAUST: And beat for beat!
  If the swift moment I entreat:
  Tarry a while! you are so fair!
  Then forge the shackles to my feet,
  Then I will gladly perish there!
  Then let them toll the passing-bell,
  Then of your servitude be free,
  The clock may stop, its hands fall still,
  And time be over then for me!

MEPHISTOPHELES: Reflect upon this – we shall not forget it.

FAUST: That is your right, by no means to be waived!
  My stake was in no wanton spirit betted.
  Once come to rest, I am enslaved –
  To you, whomever – why regret it?

MEPHISTOPHELES: This very evening, at the doctoral feast,
  Watch me my servant's duty plying.
  Just one more thing – for living or for dying,
  I'd like a line or two at least.

FAUST: Cannot you pedant do without a screed?
  Have you not met a man, not found his word his deed?
  What, is it not enough my spoken word should force
  My days into eternal peonage?
  Does not the world rush on with brimming course,
  And I am to be prisoned by a pledge?
  Yet this conceit is lodged within our breast,
  And who would gladly see it leave him?
  Who bears good faith in his pure soul is blessed,
  No sacrifice will ever grieve him!
  A square of parchment, though, all writ and stamped,

Becomes a specter that repels all men.
Still in the pen, the word is cramped,
And wax and leather lord it then.
What, evil spirit, say your rules?
Parchment or paper? Marble? Brass? What tools,
The stylus, chisel, pen? How shall I write it?
You are at liberty to choose.

MEPHISTOPHELES: How can you with so puny a fuse
Get such hot rhetoric ignited?
Just any slip will do, it's all the same.
You draw a drop of blood and sign your name.

FAUST: On with the hocus-pocus – I am game,
If this is all you need to be requited.

MEPHISTOPHELES: Blood is a very special juice.

FAUST: Oh, never fear my promise might be broken!
My utmost striving's fullest use
Is just the part I have bespoken.
I sought to puff myself too high,
Your rank is all I may attain.
The lofty Spirit spurned me, and I pry
At Nature's bolted doors in vain.
The web of thought is all in slashes,
All knowledge long turned dust and ashes.
Let in the depths of sensual life
The blaze of passions be abated!
May magic shrouds unpenetrated
With every miracle be rife!
Let's hurl ourselves in time's on-rushing tide,
Occurrence's on-rolling stride!
So may then pleasure and distress,
Failure and success,
Follow each other as they please;
Man's active only when he's never at ease.

MEPHISTOPHELES: No bars or bounds are set for you.
If anywhere you feel like snatching
Chance relish, sweets of passage catching,
May what delights prove wholesome too.
Just help yourself and don't be coy.

FAUST: You heard me, there can be no thought of joy.
Frenzy I choose, most agonizing lust,
Enamored enmity, restorative disgust.
Henceforth my soul, for knowledge sick no more,

Against no kind of suffering shall be cautioned,
And what to all of mankind is apportioned
I mean to savor in my own self's core,
Grasp with my mind both highest and most low,
Weigh down my spirit with their weal and woe,
And thus my selfhood to their own distend,
And be, as they are, shattered in the end.

MEPHISTOPHELES: Oh, take my word, who for millennia past
Has had this rocky fare to chomp,
That from his first breath to his last
No man digests that ancient sourdough lump!
Believe the likes of us: the whole
Is made but for a god's delight!
He dwells in an eternal aureole,
Us he committed to the depth of night,
And you make do with dark and light.

FAUST: And yet I choose it!

J. W. von Goethe, *Faust*, 1770–1831; trans. Walter Arndt, 1976

Matilda Helps a Friend

She had quitted her religious habit: She was now cloathed in a long sable
Robe, on which was traced in gold embroidery a variety of unknown
characters: It was fastened by a girdle of precious stones, in which was
fixed a poignard. Her neck and arms were uncovered. In her hand She
bore a golden wand. Her hair was loose and flowed wildly upon her
shoulders: Her eyes sparkled with terrific expression; and her whole
Demeanour was calculated to inspire the beholder with awe and
admiration.

'Follow me!' She said to the Monk in a low and solemn voice; 'All is
ready!'

His limbs trembled, while He obeyed her. She led him through various
narrow passages; and on every side as they past along, the beams of the
Lamp displayed none but the most revolting objects; Skulls, Bones,
Graves, and Images whose eyes seemed to glare on them with horror and
surprize. At length they reached a spacious Cavern, whose lofty roof the
eye sought in vain to discover. A profound obscurity hovered through
the void. Damp vapours struck cold to the Friar's heart; and He listened
sadly to the blast, while it howled along the lonely Vaults. Here Matilda
stopped. She turned to Ambrosio. His cheeks and lips were pale with

apprehension. By a glance of mingled scorn and anger She reproved his pusillanimity, but She spoke not. She placed the Lamp upon the ground, near the Basket. She motioned that Ambrosio should be silent, and began the mysterious rites. She drew a circle round him, another round herself, and then taking a small Phial from the Basket, poured a few drops upon the ground before her. She bent over the place, muttered some indistinct sentences, and immediately a pale sulphurous flame arose from the ground. It increased by degrees, and at length spread its waves over the whole surface, the circles alone excepted in which stood Matilda and the Monk. It then ascended the huge Columns of unhewn stone, glided along the roof, and formed the Cavern into an immense chamber totally covered with blue trembling fire. It emitted no heat: On the contrary, the extreme chillness of the place seemed to augment with every moment. Matilda continued her incantations: At intervals She took various articles from the Basket, the nature and name of most of which were unknown to the Friar: But among the few which He distinguished, He particularly observed three human fingers, and an Agnus Dei which She broke in pieces. She threw them all into the flames which burned before her, and they were instantly consumed.

The Monk beheld her with anxious curiosity. Suddenly She uttered a loud and piercing shriek. She appeared to be seized with an access of delirium; She tore her hair, beat her bosom, used the most frantic gestures, and drawing the poignard from her girdle plunged it into her left arm. The blood gushed out plentifully, and as She stood on the brink of the circle, She took care that it should fall on the outside. The flames retired from the spot on which the blood was pouring. A volume of dark clouds rose slowly from the ensanguined earth, and ascended gradually, till it reached the vault of the Cavern. At the same time a clap of thunder was heard: The echo pealed fearfully along the subterraneous passages, and the ground shook beneath the feet of the Enchantress.

It was now that Ambrosio repented of his rashness. The solemn singularity of the charm had prepared him for something strange and horrible. He waited with fear for the Spirit's appearance, whose coming was announced by thunder and earthquakes. He looked wildly round him, expecting that some dreadful Apparition would meet his eyes, the sight of which would drive him mad. A cold shivering seized his body, and He sank upon one knee, unable to support himself.

'He comes!' exclaimed Matilda in a joyful accent.

Ambrosio started, and expected the Dæmon with terror. What was his surprize, when the Thunder ceasing to roll, a full strain of melodious Music sounded in the air. At the same time the cloud dispersed, and He beheld a Figure more beautiful, than Fancy's pencil ever drew. It was a

Youth seemingly scarce eighteen, the perfection of whose form and face was unrivalled. He was perfectly naked: A bright Star sparkled upon his fore-head; Two crimson wings extended themselves from his shoulders; and his silken locks were confined by a band of many-coloured fires, which played round his head, formed themselves into a variety of figures, and shone with a brilliance far surpassing that of precious Stones. Circlets of Diamonds were fastened round his arms and ankles, and in his right hand He bore a silver branch, imitating Myrtle. His form shone with dazzling glory: He was surrounded by clouds of rose-coloured light, and at the moment that He appeared, a refreshing air breathed perfumes through the Cavern. Enchanted at a vision so contrary to his expectations, Ambrosio gazed upon the Spirit with delight and wonder: Yet however beautiful the Figure, He could not but remark a wildness in the Dæmon's eyes, and a mysterious melancholy impressed upon his features, betraying the Fallen Angel, and inspiring the Spectators with secret awe.

The Music ceased. Matilda addressed herself to the Spirit: She spoke in a language unintelligible to the Monk, and was answered in the same. She seemed to insist upon something, which the Dæmon was unwilling to grant. He frequently darted upon Ambrosio angry glances, and at such times the Friar's heart sank within him. Matilda appeared to grow incensed. She spoke in a loud and commanding tone, and her gestures declared, that She was threatening him with her vengeance. Her menaces had the desired effect: The Spirit sank upon his knee, and with a submissive air presented to her the branch of Myrtle. No sooner had She received it, than the Music was again heard; A thick cloud spread itself over the Apparition; The blue flames disappeared, and total obscurity reigned through the Cave. The Abbot moved not from his place: His faculties were all bound up in pleasure, anxiety, and surprize. At length the darkness dispersing, He perceived Matilda standing near him in her religious habit, with the Myrtle in her hand. No traces of the incantation, and the Vaults were only illuminated by the faint rays of the sepulchral Lamp.

'I have succeeded,' said Matilda, 'though with more difficulty than I expected. Lucifer, whom I summoned to my assistance, was at first unwilling to obey my commands: To enforce his compliance I was constrained to have recourse to my strongest charms. They have produced the desired effect, but I have engaged never more to invoke his agency in your favour. Beware then, how you employ an opportunity which never will return. My magic arts will now be of no use to you: In future you can only hope for supernatural aid, by invoking the Dæmons yourself, and accepting the conditions of their service. This you will never do: You want strength of mind to force them to obedience, and unless you pay their established price, they will not be your voluntary Servants. In this one instance they consent to obey you: I offer you the means of enjoying your Mistress, and be careful not to lose the opportunity. Receive this constellated Myrtle: While you bear this in your hand, every door will fly open to you. It will procure you access tomorrow night to Antonia's chamber: Then breathe upon it thrice, pronounce her name, and place it upon her pillow. A death-like slumber will immediately seize upon her, and deprive her of the power of resisting your attempts. Sleep will hold her till break of Morning. In this state you may satisfy your desires without danger of being discovered; since when day-light shall dispel the effects of the enchantment, Antonia will perceive her dishonour, but be ignorant of the Ravisher. Be happy then, my Ambrosio, and let this service convince you, that my friendship is disinterested and pure.

Matthew Lewis, *The Monk*, 1796

Christoph Haizmann's Motive

In return for an immortal soul, the Devil has many things to offer which are highly prized by men: wealth, security from danger, power over mankind and the forces of nature, even magical arts, and, above all else, enjoyment – the enjoyment of beautiful women. These services performed or undertakings made by the Devil are usually mentioned specifically in the agreement made with him. What, then, was the motive which induced Christoph Haizmann to make his pact?

Curiously enough, it was none of these very natural wishes. To put the matter beyond doubt, one has only to read the short remarks attached by the painter to his illustrations of the apparitions of the Devil. For example, the caption to the third vision runs: 'On the third occasion within a year and a half, he appeared to me in this loathsome shape, with a book in his hand which was full of magic and black arts . . .' But from the legend attached to a later apparition we learn that the Devil reproached him violently for having 'burnt his before-mentioned book', and threatened to tear him to pieces if he did not give it back.

At his fourth appearance the Devil showed him a large yellow money-bag and a great ducat and promised him to give him as many of these as he wanted at any time. But the painter is able to boast that he 'had taken nothing whatever of the kind'.

Another time the Devil asked him to turn to enjoyment and entertainment, and the painter remarks that 'this indeed came to pass at his desire; but I did not continue for more than three days and it was then brought to an end'.

Since he rejected magical arts, money and pleasures when they were offered him by the Devil, and still less made them conditions of the pact, it becomes really imperative to know what the painter in fact wanted from the Devil when he signed a bond with him. *Some* motive he must have had for his dealings with the Devil.

On this point, too, the *Trophaeum* provides us with reliable information. He had become low-spirited, was unable or unwilling to work properly and was worried about making a livelihood; that is to say, he was suffering from melancholic depression, with an inhibition in his work and (justified) fears about his future. We can see that what we are dealing with really is a case history. We learn, too, the exciting cause of the illness, which the painter himself, in the caption to one of his pictures of the Devil, actually calls a melancholia ('that I should seek diversion and banish melancholy'). The first of our three sources of information, the village priest's letter of introduction, speaks, it is true, only of the state of depression ('*dum artis suae progressum emolumentumque secuturum* pusillanimis *perpenderet*'), but the second source, the Abbot Franciscus's report, tells us the cause of this despondency or depression as well. He says: '*acceptâ aliquâ pusillanimitate* ex morte parentis'; and in the compiler's preface the same words are used, though in a reversed order: ('*ex morte parentis acceptâ aliquâ pusillanimitate*'). His father, then, had died and he had in consequence fallen into a state of melancholia; whereupon the Devil had approached him and asked him why he was so downcast and sad, and had promised 'to help him in every way and to give him support'.

Here was a person, therefore, who signed a bond with the Devil in order to be freed from a state of depression. Undoubtedly an excellent motive, as anyone will agree who can have an understanding sense of the torments of such a state and who knows as well how little medicine can do to alleviate this ailment. Yet no one who has followed the story so far as this would be able to guess what the wording of this bond (or rather, of these two bonds) with the Devil actually was.

These bonds bring us two great surprises. In the first place, they mention no *undertaking* given by the Devil in return for whose fulfilment the painter pledges his eternal bliss, but only a *demand* made by the Devil which the painter must satisfy. It strikes us as quite illogical and absurd that this man should give up his soul, not for something he is to *get* from the Devil but for something he is to *do* for him. But the undertaking given by the *painter* seems even stranger.

The first 'syngrapha' [bond], written in ink, runs as follows:

'Ich Christoph Haizmann vndterschreibe mich disen Herrn sein leibeigener Sohn auff 9. Jahr. 1669 Jahr.'*

The second, written in blood, runs:

'Anno 1669.

'Christoph Haizmann. Ich verschreibe mich disen Satan ich sein leibeigner Sohn zu sein, und in 9. Jahr ihm mein Leib und Seel zuzugeheren.'†

All our astonishment vanishes, however, if we read the text of the bonds in the sense that what is represented in them as a demand made by the Devil is, on the contrary, a service performed by him – that is to say, it is a demand made by the *painter*. The incomprehensible pact would in that case have a straightforward meaning and could be paraphrased thus. The Devil undertakes to replace the painter's lost father for nine years. At the end of that time the painter becomes the property, body and soul, of the Devil, as was the usual custom in such bargains. The train of thought which motivated the painter in making the pact seems to have been this: his father's death had made him lose his spirits and his capacity to work; if he could only obtain a father-substitute he might hope to regain what he had lost.

A man who has fallen into a melancholia on account of his father's death must really have been fond of him. But, if so, it is very strange that such a man should have hit upon the idea of taking the Devil as a substitute for the father whom he loved.

* 'I, Christoph Haizmann, subscribe myself to this Lord as his bounden son till the ninth year. Year 1669.'
† 'Christoph Haizmann. I sign a bond with this Satan, to be his bounden son and in the ninth year to belong to him body and soul.'

Sigmund Freud, 'Eine Teufelsneurose in Siebzehnten Jahrhundert'
['A Seventeenth Century Demonological Neurosis'] 1922,
trans. James Strachey, 1961

Ade Davie's Story

One *Ade Davie*, the wife of *Simon Davie*, husbandman, being reputed a right honest bodie, and being of good parentage, grew suddenlie (as hir husband informed mee, and as it is well knowne in these parts) to be somewhat pensive and more sad than in times past. Which thing though it greeved him, yet he was loth to make it so appeere, as either his wife might be troubled or discontented therewith, or his neighbours informed thereof; least ill husbandrie should be laid to his charge (which in these quarters is much abhorred). But when she grew from pensivenes, to some perturbation of mind; so as hir accustomed rest began in the night season to be withdrawne from hir, through sighing and secret lamentation; and that, not without teares, hee could not but demand the cause of hir conceipt and extraordinarie moorning. But although at that time she covered the same, acknowledging nothing to be amisse with hir: soone after notwithstanding she fell downe before him on hir knees, desiring him to forgive hir, for she had greevouslie offended (as she said) both God & him. Hir poore husband being abashed at this hir behaviour, comforted hir, as he could; asking hir the cause of hir trouble & greefe: who told him, that she had, (contrarie to Gods lawe) & to the offense of all good christians, to the injurie of him, & speciallie to the losse of hir owne soule, bargained and given hir soule to the divell, to be delivered unto him within short space. Whereunto hir husband answered, saieng; Wife, be of good cheere, this thy bargaine is void and of none effect: for thou hast sold that which is none of thine to sell; sith it belongeth to Christ, who hath bought it, and deerelie paid for it, even with his bloud, which he shed upon the crosse; so as the divell hath no interest in thee. After this, with like submission, teares, and penitence, she said unto him; Oh husband, I have yet committed another fault, and doone you more injurie: for I have bewitched you and your children. Be content (quoth he) by the grace of God, Jesus Christ shall unwitch us: for none evill can happen to them that feare God.

And (as trulie as the Lord liveth) this was the tenor of his words unto me, which I knowe is true, as proceeding from unfeigned lips, and from one that feareth God. Now when the time approched that the divell should come, and take possession of the woman, according to his bargaine, he watched and praied earnestlie, and caused his wife to read psalmes and praiers for mercie at God's hands: and suddenlie about midnight, there was a great rumbling beelowe under his chamber windowe, which amazed them exceedinglie. For they conceived, that the divell was beelowe, though he had no power to come up, bicause of their fervent praiers.

He that noteth this womans first and second confession, freelie and voluntarilie made, how everie thing concurred that might serve to adde credit thereunto, and yeeld matter for hir condemnation, would not thinke, but that if *Bodin* were foreman of hir inquest, he would crie; Guiltie: & would hasten execution upon hir; who would have said as much before any judge in the world, if she had beene examined; and have confessed no lesse, if she had beene arraigned therupon. But God knoweth, she was innocent of anie these crimes: howbeit she was brought lowe and pressed downe with the weight of this humor, so as both hir rest and sleepe were taken awaie from hir; & hir fansies troubled and disquieted with despaire, and such other cogitations as grew by occasion thereof. And yet I beleeve, if any mishap had insued to hir husband, or his children; few witchmongers would have judged otherwise, but that she had bewitched them. And she (for hir part) so constantlie persuaded hir selfe to be a witch, that she judged hir selfe worthie of death; insomuch as being reteined in hir chamber, she sawe not anie one carrieng a faggot to the fier, but she would saie it was to make a fier to burne hir for witcherie. But God knoweth she had bewitched none, neither insued there anie hurt unto anie, by hir imagination, but unto hir selfe.

And as for the rumbling, it was by occasion of a sheepe, which was flawed, and hoong by the wals, so as a dog came and devoured it; whereby grew the noise which I before mentioned: and she being now recovered, remaineth a right honest woman, far from such impietie, and shamed of hir imaginations, which she perceiveth to have growne through melancholie.

Reginald Scot, *The Discoverie of Witchcraft*, 1584

Pierce Penilesse Fails to Find a Buyer

'I was informed of layte dayes that a certaine blinde retayler, called the Diuell, used to lend money upon pawnes or anie thing, and would let one have a thousand poundes vppon a statute merchant of his soule; or if a man plyde him throughly, would trust him vppon a bill of his hand, without anie more circumstance. Besides he was noted for a priuie bene-factor to traytors and parasites, and to aduance fooles and asses farre sooner than anie; to be a greedie pursuer of newes; and so famous a politician in purchasing, that Hel, which at the beginning was but an obscure village, is now become a huge citie, wherevnto all countreys are tributarie.

'These manifest conjectures of plentie, assembled in one common-place of abilitie, I determined to clawe Avarice by the elboe, till his full belly gave me a full hand; and let him blood with my pen (if it might be) in the veyne of Liberality; and so (in short time) was this paper monster, Pierce Penilesse, begotten.

'But written and all, here lies the question; where shall I find this old asse that I may deliuer it? They say the lawyers have the Diuel and all, and it is like enough he is playing ambitexter amongst them. "Fie! fie! the Diuell a driver in Westminster Hall? it can never be."

'Now, I pray, what do you imagine him to be? Perhaps you think it is not possible for him to be so grave. Oh! then you are in an errour, for hee is as formale as the best scriuener of them all. Marry, hee doth not vse to weare a night-cap, for his hornes will not let him; and yet I know a hundred, as well headed as he, that will make a jolly shift with a court-cap on their crownes, if the weather be colde.

'To proceed with my tale. To Westminster Hall I went, and made a search of enquirie, from the black gowne to the buckram bag, if there were anie such serjeant, bencher, counsailer, attorney, or pettifogger as *Signior Cornuto Diabolo*, with the good face? But they all (*una voce*) affirmed that he was not there; marry, whether hee were at the Exchange or no, amongst the ritch merchants, that they could not tell; but it was the likelier of the two that I should meete with him, or heare of him in those quarters. "I' faith, and say you so?" quoth I; "and Ile bestow a little labour more, but Ile hunt him out."

'Without more circumstance thether came I; and thrusting myselfe amongst the confusion of languages, I askt whether he were there extant or no? But from one to another, *Non novi Dæmonem*, was all the answere I could get. At length (as fortune serued) I lighted vppon an old, straddling usurer, clad in a damaske cassocke. Of him I demanded if hee could tell me anie tidings of the partie I sought for. "By my troth," quoth he, "stripling (and then he cought), I saw him not lately, nor know I certainly where he keepes; but thus much I heard by a broker, a friend of mine, that hath had some dealings with him in his time, that hee is at home sick of the goute, and will not be spoken withall under more than thou art able to giue, some two or three hundred angels, if thou hast anie suite to him; and then perhaps hele straine curtesie with his legges in child-bed, and come forth and talk with thee; but otherwise *non est domi* – he is busy with Mammon and the Prince of the North, howe to build vp his king-dome, or sending his sprites abroad to vndermine the maligners of his government."'

Thomas Nash, *Pierce Penilesse His Supplication to the Devil*, 1592

The Connoisseur of Souls

'But if I *have* a *penchant*, Monsieur Bon-Bon – if I *have* a *penchant*, it is for a philosopher. Yet, let me tell you, sir, it is not every dev – I mean it is not every gentleman who knows how to *choose* a philosopher. Long ones are *not* good; and the best, if not carefully shelled, are apt to be a little rancid on account of the gall.'

'Shelled!!'

'I mean taken out of the carcass.'

'What do you think of a – hic-cup! – physician?'

'*Don't* mention them! – ugh! ugh!' (Here his Majesty retched violently.) 'I never tasted but one – that rascal Hippocrates! – smelt of asafœtida –

ugh! ugh! ugh! – caught a wretched cold washing him in the Styx – and after all he gave me the cholera morbus.'

'The – hiccup! – wretch!' ejaculated Bon-Bon, 'the – hiccup! – abortion of a pill-box!' – and the philosopher dropped a tear.

'After all,' continued the visiter, 'after all, if a dev – if a gentleman wishes to *live*, he must have more talents than one or two; and with us a fat face is an evidence of diplomacy.'

'How so?'

'Why we are sometimes exceedingly pushed for provisions. You must know that, in a climate so sultry as mine, it is frequently impossible to keep a spirit alive for more than two or three hours; and after death, unless pickled immediately, (and a pickled spirit is *not* good,) they will – smell – you understand, eh? Putrefaction is always to be apprehended when the souls are consigned to us in the usual way.'

'Hiccup! – hiccup! – good God! how *do* you manage?'

Here the iron lamp commenced swinging with redoubled violence, and the devil half started from his seat; – however, with a slight sigh, he recovered his composure, merely saying to our hero in a low tone, 'I tell you what, Pierre Bon-Bon, we *must* have no more swearing.'

The host swallowed another bumper, by way of denoting thorough comprehension and acquiescence, and the visiter continued:

'Why there are *several* ways of managing. The most of us starve: some put up with the pickle: for my part I purchase my spirits *vivente corpore*, in which case I find they keep very well.'

'But the body! – hiccup! – the body!!!'

'The body, the body – well, what of the body? – oh! ah! I perceive. Why, sir, the body is not *at all* affected by the transaction. I have made innumerable purchases of the kind in my day, and the parties never experienced any inconvenience. There were Cain and Nimrod, and Nero, and Caligula, and Dionysius, and Pisistratus, and – and a thousand others, who never knew what it was to have a soul during the latter part of their lives; yet, sir, these men adorned society. Why is n't there A—, now, whom you know as well as I? Is *he* not in possession of all his faculties, mental and corporeal? Who writes a keener epigram? Who reasons more wittily? Who – but, stay! I have his agreement in my pocket-book.'

Thus saying, he produced a red leather wallet, and took from it a number of papers. Upon some of these Bon-Bon caught a glimpse of the letters *Machi – Maza – Robesp* – with the words *Caligula, George, Elizabeth*. His Majesty selected a narrow slip of parchment, and from it read aloud the following words:

'In consideration of certain mental endowments which it is unnecessary to specify, and in farther consideration of one thousand louis d'or, I, being aged one year and one month, do hereby make over to the bearer of this agreement all my right, title, and appurtenance in the shadow called my soul.' (Signed) A.... (Here his Majesty repeated a name which I do not feel myself justified in indicating more unequivocally.)

'A clever fellow that,' resumed he; 'but like you, Monsieur Bon-Bon, he was mistaken about the soul. The soul a shadow truly! The soul a shadow! Ha! ha! ha! – he! he! he! – hu! hu! hu! Only think of a fricasséed shadow!'

'*Only* think – hiccup! – of a fricasséed shadow!' exclaimed our hero, whose faculties were becoming much illuminated by the profundity of his Majesty's discourse.

'Only think of a – hiccup! – fricasséed shadow!! Now, damme! – hiccup! – humph! If *I* would have been such a – hiccup! – nincompoop. *My* soul, Mr – humph!'

'*Your* soul, Monsieur Bon-Bon?'

'Yes, sir – hiccup! – *my* soul is' –

'What, sir?'

'*No* shadow, damme!'

'Did not mean to say' –

'Yes, sir, *my* soul is – hiccup! – humph! – yes, sir.'

'Did not intend to assert' –

'*My* soul is – hiccup! – peculiarly qualified for – hiccup! – a' –

'What, sir?'

'Stew.'

'Ha!'

'Soufflée.'

'Eh?'

'Fricassée.'

'Indeed!'

'Ragoût and fricandeau – and see here, my good fellow! I'll let you have it – hiccup! – a bargain.' Here the philosopher slapped his Majesty upon the back.

'Could n't think of such a thing,' said the latter calmly, at the same time rising from his seat. The metaphysician stared.

'Am supplied at present,' said his Majesty.

'Hiccup! – e-h?' said the philosopher.

'Have no funds on hand.'

'What?'

'Besides, very unhandsome in me' –

'Sir!'

'To take advantage of' –

'Hiccup!'
'Your present disgusting and ungentlemanly situation.'

Edgar Allan Poe, 'Bon-Bon', 1835

Faustus' Comic Servant (1)

CASPER (*comes against Mephistophilis*): Now, who are we, then, mon cher ami? Is it the fashion also to present yourself in his Insolence's chamber with your hat on your head?

MEPHISTOPHILIS: Don't you know who I am, then? I am the Master of the Chase.

CASPER: Master of the Chase! What use has master, then, for a hunter, when he is a theologian?

MEPHISTOPHILIS: But a great lover of the chase. I stand very high in his favour, too, for I catch all the foxes and hares with my hands.

CASPER: Sapperment! You must be a smart one. You'll save powder at that rate. What's your name, then?

MEPHISTOPHILIS: Mephistophilis!

CASPER: Eh! Are you called Stoffelfuss?

MEPHISTOPHILIS: Mephistophilis! Mangle not my name, or –

CASPER: Well, well; but don't shout like that, and don't be so easily offended. I misunderstood.

MEPHISTOPHILIS: Have you heard yet whither our master is about to wend?

CASPER: Who is he going to rend?

MEPHISTOPHILIS: Wend!

Das Puppenspiel vom Doctor Faust, trans. T. C. H. Hedderinck, 1887

Mephistopheles Smiles

Faustus said, I would gladly know of thee, if thou wert a man in manner and forme as I am; what wouldest thou doe to please both God and man? Whereat the Spirit smiled saying: my Faustus, if I were a man as thou art, and that God had adorned me with those gifts of nature as thou once haddest; even so long as the breath of God were by, & within me, would I humble my selfe unto his Maiestie, indevouring in all that I could to keepe his Commaundements, prayse him, glorifie him, that I might continue in his favour, so were I sure to enjoy the eternall joy and felicity of his kingdome. *Faustus* said, but that have I not done. No, thou sayest true (quoth *Mephostophiles*) thou hast not done it, but thou hast denied thy Lord and maker, which gaveth thee the breath of life, speech, hearing, sight, and all other thy reasonable senses that thou mightest understand his will and pleasure, to live to the glory and honour of his name, and to the advancement of thy body and soule, him I say being thy maker hast thou denied and defied, yea wickedly thou hast applyed that excellent gift of thine understanding, and given thy soule to the Divell: therefore give none the blame but thine owne selfe will, thy proude and aspiring minde, which hath brought thee into the wrath of God and utter damnation. This is most true (quoth *Faustus*) but tell me *Mephostophiles*, wouldst thou be in my case as I am nowe? Yea, saith the Spirite (and with that fetcht a great sigh) for yet would I so humble my selfe, that I would winne the favour of God. Then (said Doctor *Faustus*) it were time enough for me if I amended. True (said *Mephostophiles*) if it were not for thy great sinnes, which are so odious and detestable in the sight of God, that it is too late for thee, for the wrath of God resteth upon thee. Leave off (quoth *Faustus*) and tell me my question to my greater comfort.

The Historie of the Damnable Life and Deserved Death of
Doctor John Faustus, 1592

Faustus' Comic Servant (2)

CASPER: So, he will get me something to ride on! If he would only fetch me a little Polish or Hungarian pony! for I am very fond of riding, and – (*Here a dragon comes on the stage and, thrusting him in the back, knocks him down.*) Now what sort of flail is that? (*Rises.*) Hey! hey! help! help! Stoffelfuss! Stoffelfuss! Is this the riding-horse you promised me?

MEPHISTOPHILIS (*inside*): Only get up on it; it won't hurt you.

CASPER: Only get up on it, say you? – It's quite a new-fangled sort of horse. I must take a look at it first. Sapperment! but it has a walking-stick standing out behind there; if the beast strikes me with that on my nose it would go to pot. And if it hasn't got wings, too! I only hope I may not come to grief if it should burst! Courage. I'll get on its back. (*He gets upon it.*) What a delicious seat this is! Hy! hy! hy! (*The beast hits him on the head from behind with its tail.*) Now then, what clown strikes me on the head, as if I had lost my four senses? Please don't do that again. – Now Füchsel, let us be moving, hy! hy! (*The beast strikes him again.*) Donnerwetter! somebody has just struck me again. (*He turns round.*) I believe it was you with your walking-stick. Wait a bit though, wait a bit, I'll take another seat where I shall be out of your line of action. (*He sits further forward.*) For one just learning to ride, the beast is very well adapted, for if one were to tumble off one hasn't very far to fall. But bad weather had better not come on to-day, or I shall lose more in shoe-leather on this journey than I earn in wages. – Now then, Füchsel, hy! hy! (*The beast suddenly ascends and flies through the air with him amid thunder and lightning; he shrieks.*) Hey! hey! help! help! Stoffelfuss! Stoffelfuss! the beast is going through the air! Hey! hey! hey! (*He is carried off.*)

Das Puppenspiel vom Doctor Faust, trans. T. C. H. Hedderinck, 1887

Pope Alexander Borgia's Time Runs Out

ALEXANDER: Rest with this answer, that my soule is Gods
   Whose habitacle is prepar'd in heauen.
   First it doth know God being figured
   According to that Image of himselfe,
   And then the world whose liuely shape it beares,
   And to conclude, the soule of man knowes all,
   Because with all things it doth simbolize,
   For in this Man there is a minde intelligent,
   A quickning word and a celestiall spirit,
   That like a lightning euery way diffused,
   All things which are made by the mighty power,
   Vniteth, moueth, and replenisheth.
DIVIL: These things should haue been thought vpon before,
   The *summum bonum* which liues in the soule,
   Is an eternall pleasure to behold,
   And haue fruition of the mightie power,
   Which thou didst neuer see, nor canst enjoy.
ALEXANDER: Pawse yet a little, let me meditate.
   Alexander holdeth up his hands wringing and softly crying.
   Mercy, mercy, mercy; arise arise: vp, vp, vp: fy, fy: no, no? stirre
   stubburne, stonie, stiff indurate heart. not yet, vp. why, what? wilt
   thou not foule traytor? to my soule? not yet?
   The Diuill laugheth.
   Arise, arise, aduance heart clogg'd with sinne,
   Oppressed with damnation: vp aduaunce yet.
   Wilt thou not stirre stiffe heart? what am I damn'd?
   Yet a little, yet a little, oh yet: not yet? alas.

High God of heauens and earth if thou beare loue,
Vnto the soule of sinfull man shew mercy,
Mercy good Lord, oh mercy, mercy, mercy.
Oh saue my soule out of the Lyons pawes,
My darling from the denne of blacke damnation,
My soule, my doue, couer with siluer wings,
Her downe and plumage make of fine tryed gould,
Help, help, help, aboue. stirre, stirre, stupiditie.

DIVIL: He charmes in *Dauids* words with *Iudas spirit*,

ALEXANDER: It will not, no it will not, yet alas, no, no, no? is that my
    sentence to damnation?

I am vndone, vndone.

DIVIL: He shall dispaire, vassall of sinne and hell,
Prouide thy selfe in black dispaire to dwell.
He cea{z}eth on his face.

ALEXANDER: I tell thee I cannot be resolu'd,
To dwell in darkenesse breake black soule dissolue,
And poyson all this Hemisphere with sinne . . .
*Here Alexander is in extreame torment and groneth whilst the diuill laugheth
    at him.*

Learne miserable wretched mortall men,
By this example of a sinfull soule,
What are the fruits of pride and Auarice,
Of cruell Empire and impietie,
Of prophanation and Apostacie,
Of brutish lust, falsehood, and perfidie,
Of deepe dissembling and hypocrisie,
Learne wicked worldlings, learne, learne, learne by me
To saue your soules, though I condemned be.
Sound a Horne within, enter a Diuill like a Poast.

1. DIVIL: Here comes a fatall message, I must hence.   *Exit.*

ALEXANDER: My roabes, my roabes, he robs me of my roabes,
Bring me my roabes, or take away my life,
My roabes, my life, my soule and all is gone.
Alexander falleth in an extasie vpon the ground.

2. DIVIL: From the pale horror of eternall fire,
Am I sent with the wagon of blacke *Dis*,
To guide thy spirit to the gates of death,
Therefore I summon thee to come with speed,
For horrizons now stand thee not insteed.
Alexander aduanceth a little.

ALEXANDER: Horror and horror, feare ensueth feare,
  Torment with tormentes is Incompassed:
  Dispaire vpon dispaire, damnation
  Vpon damnation, hell and consience,
  Murther, lust, auarice, impiety,
  Vaine prophanation and apostacie,
  Rage and distraction tiranize: away,
  Away proud *Lucifer*, away.
DIVILL: Away, away.

The Diuill windeth his horne in his eare and there more diuills enter with a noise incompassing him, Alexander starteth.

ALEXANDER: Holla, holla, holla, come, come, come, what, when, where,
  when, why, deaf, strike, dead, aliue, oh alas, oh alas, alwaies
  burning, alwayes freezing, always liuing, tormented, neuer ending,
  neuer, neuer, neuer mending, out, out, out, out, why, why,
  whether, whether, thether.
DIVILLS: Thether, thether, thether.

Thunder and lightning with fearefull noise the diuells thrust him downe and goe Triumphing.

Barnabe Barnes, *The Divils Charter*, 1607

The Devil Collects

. . . the Students wondered greatly thereat, that he was so blinded, for knavery, conjuration, and such like foolish things, to give his body and soule unto the divell: for they loved him entirely, and never suspected any such thing before he had opened his mind to them: wherefore one of them sayd unto him; ah, friend *Faustus*, what have you done to conceale this matter so long from us, we would by the help of good Divines, and the grace of God, have brought you out of this net, and have torne you out of the bondage and chaynes of Sathan, whereas nowe we feare it is too late, to the utter ruine of your body and soule? Doctor *Faustus* answered, I durst never doo it, although I often minded, to settle my selfe unto godly people, to desire counsell and helpe, as once mine olde neighbour counsailed mee, that I shoulde follow his learning, and leave all my conjurations, yet when I was minded to amend, and to followe that good mans counsell, then came the Divell and would have had me away, as this night he is like to doe, and sayd so soone as I turned againe to God, he would dispatch me altogether. Thus, even thus, (good Gentlemen, and my deare friends) was I inthralled in that Satanicall band, all good desires drowned, all pietie banished, al purpose of amendment utterly exiled, by the tyranous threatnings of my deadly enemy. But when the Students heard his words, they gave him counsaile to doo naught else but call upon God, desiring him for the love of his sweete Sonne Jesus Christes sake, to have mercy upon him, teaching him this forme of prayer. O God bee mercifull unto me, poore and miserable sinner, and enter not into judgement with me, for no flesh is able to stand before thee. Although, O Lord, I must leave my sinfull body unto the Divell, being by him deluded, yet thou in mercy mayest preserve my soule.

This they repeated unto him, yet it could take no holde, but even as *Caine* he also said his sinnes were greater than God was able to forgive; for all his thought was on his writing, he meant he had made it too filthy in writing it with his owne blood. The Students & the other that were there, when they had prayed for him, they wept, and so went foorth, but *Faustus* taryed in the hall: and when the Gentlemen were laid in bed, none of them could sleepe, for that they attended to heare if they might be privy of his ende. It happened between twelve and one a clock at midnight, there blewe a mighty storme of winde against the house, as though it would have blowne the foundation thereof out of his place. Hereupon the Students began to feare, and got out of their beds, comforting one another, but they would not stirre out of the chamber: and the Host of the house ran out of doores, thinking the house would fall. The Students lay neere unto that hall wherein Doctor *Faustus* lay, and they heard a mighty noyse and hissing, as if the hall had beene full of Snakes and Adders: with that the hall doore flew open wherein Doctor *Faustus* was, then he began to crie for helpe, saying: murther, murther, but it came foorth with halfe a voice hollowly: shortly after they heard him no more. But when it was day, the Students that had taken no rest that night, arose and went into the hall in the which they left Doctor *Faustus*, where notwithstanding they found no *Faustus*, but all the hall lay besprinckled with blood, his braines cleaving to the wall: for the Divel had beaten him from one wall against another, in one corner lay his eyes, in another his teeth, a pitifull and fearefull sight to beholde. Then began the Students to bewayle and weepe for him, and sought for his body in many places: lastly they came into the yarde where they found his bodie lying on the horse dung, most monstrously torne, and fearefull to beholde, for his head and all his joynts were dasht in peeces.

*The Historie of the Damnable Life and Deserved Death of
Doctor John Faustus*, 1592

The Clock Strikes

FAUSTUS: Ah *Faustus*,
Now hast thou but one bare houre to live,
And then thou must be damn'd perpetually.
Stand still you ever moving Spheares of heaven,
That time may cease, and midnight never come.
Faire natures eye, rise, rise againe and make
Perpetuall day: or let this houre be but
A yeare, a month, a weeke, a naturall day,
That *Faustus* may repent, and save his soule.
O lente lente currite noctis equi:
The Stars move still, Time runs, the Clocke will strike,
The devill will come, and *Faustus*, must be damn'd.
O I'le leape up to my God: who puls me downe?
See see where Christs bloud streames in the firmament,
One drop would save my soule, halfe a drop, ah my Christ.
Rend not my heart, for naming of my Christ,
Yet will I call on him: O spare me *Lucifer.*
Where is it now? 'tis gone. And see where God
Stretcheth out his Arme, and bends his irefull Browes:
Mountaines and Hills, come, come, and fall on me,
And hide me from the heavy wrath of God.
No, no?
Then will I headlong run into the earth:
Gape earth; O no, it will not harbour me.
You Starres that raign'd at my nativity,
Whose influence hath allotted death and hell;
Now draw up *Faustus* like a foggy mist,
Into the entrals of yon labouring cloud,
That when you vomite forth into the aire,
My limbes may issue from your smoky mouthes,
So that my soule may but ascend to heaven.
The Watch strikes.
Ah halfe the houre is past: 'twill all be past anone:
O God, if thou wilt not have mercy on my soule,
Yet for Christs sake, whose bloud hath ransom'd me,
Impose some end to my incessant paine:
Let *Faustus* live in hell a thousand yeares,
A hundred thousand, and at last be sav'd.

No end is limited to damned soules.
Why wert thou not a creature wanting soule?
Or why is this immortall that thou hast?
Ah *Pythagoras Metemsycosis*; were that true,
This soule should flie from me, and I be chang'd
Unto some brutish beast.
All beasts are happy, for when they die,
Their soules are soone dissolv'd in elements,
But mine must live still to be plagu'd in hell.
Curst be the parents that ingendred me;
No *Faustus*, curse thy selfe, curse *Lucifer*,
That hath depriv'd thee of the joies of heaven.
The clocke striketh twelve.
It strikes, it strikes; now body turne to aire,
Or *Lucifer* will beare thee quicke to hell.
O soule be chang'd into little water drops,
And fall into the Ocean, ne're be found.
Thunder, and enter the devils.
My God, my God, looke not so fierce on me;
Adders and serpents, let me breathe a while:
Ugly hell gape not; come not *Lucifer*,
I'le burne my bookes; ah *Mephostophilis*.
Exeunt with him.

Christopher Marlowe, *The Tragedie of Doctor Faustus*, 1604

Eight

THE DEMON LOVER

The Devil, Exorcised, Makes a Surprising Statement

And having said this the devil wept, saying: I leave thee, my fairest consort, whom long since I found and rested in thee; I forsake thee, my sure sister, my beloved in whom I was well pleased. What I shall do I know not, or on whom I shall call that he may hear me and help me. I know what I will do: I will depart unto some place where the report of this man hath not been heard, and peradventure I shall call thee, my beloved, by another name. And he lifted up his voice and said: Abide in peace, for thou hast taken refuge with one greater than I, but I will depart and seek for one like thee, and if I find her not, I will return unto thee again: for I know that whilst thou art near unto this man thou hast a refuge in him, but when he departeth thou wilt be such as thou wast before he appeared, and him thou wilt forget, and I shall have opportunity and confidence: but now I fear the name of him that hath saved thee. And having so said the devil vanished out of sight: only when he departed fire and smoke were seen there: and all that stood there were astonished.

The Acts of Thomas in *The Apocryphal New Testament*,
ed. M. R. James, 1924

Diverse Carnal Instances

Iacobus Rufus writeth of a woman who had congresse with one of these Spirits; and when her time of childing came, after infinite pangs and throwes, she was deliuered of nothing saue keyes, chips, pieces of iron, and fragments of old leather. Another thing much more admirable hapned (saith he) in the Diocesse of Cullein. Diuers Princes and Noblemen, being assembled in a beautifull and faire Pallace which was scituate vpon the Riuer Rhine, they beheld a boat or small barge make toward the shore, drawne by a Swain in a siluer chain, the one end fastened about her necke, the other to the Vessell; and in it an vnknowne souldier, a man of a comely personage, and gracefull presence, who stept vpon the shore: which done, the boat guided by the Swan left him and floted downe the Riuer. This man fell afterward in league with a faire gentlewoman, maried her, and by her had many children. After some yeares, the same Swanne came with the same barge vnto the same place; the souldier entring into it, was caried thence the way he came, after disappeared, left wife, children, and family, and was neuer seen amongst them after. Now who can iudge this to be other than one of those Spirits that are named *Incubi*.

In Brasilia, a barbarous woman by accompanying with one of these Dæmons, brought forth a Monster, which in a few houres grew to be sixteen handfuls high, whose backe was couered with the skin of a Lisard, with big and swolne breasts; his hands like the pawes of a Lyon, with eyes staring, and seeming to sparkle fire; all his other members being deformed and horrible to behold. *Alexander* remembreth vs of a woman called *Alcippe*, who in the time of the Marsicke war, by companying with an *Incubus* brought forth an Elephant. *Aumosius* writeth, That in Heluetia, in the yeare 1278, a woman brought forth a Lion. In Ficinum, *Anno* 1370, a woman was deliuered of Cats. And at Brixium, another of a Dog. Licosthenes writeth of one at Augusta, who was first deliuered of a mans head wrapt vp in skinnes and parchment, then of a Serpent with two feet, last of an Hog; and all at one birth, &c.

Hector Boëthius writeth, That in Scotland in the County of Marr, a Maid of a noble Family, of great beautie, but altogether auerse from mariage was found with child. At which the Parents much grieued, were importunat to know by whom she was vitiated. To whom she ingeniously confessed, That a beautifull young man had nightly conuersation and company with her, but from whence he was she was altogether ignorant. They, though they held this answer to be but an excuse, and therefore gaue smal credit vnto it, yet because she told them, the third night after, he had appointed to lodge with her, kept the houre, and with swords candles, and torches, brake open the dores of her chamber, where they might espy an hideous Monster, and (beyond humane capacitie) terrible, in the close embraces of their daughter. They stand stupified, feare makes them almost without motion: The clamor flies abroad, the neighbours come in to be spectators of the wonderment, and amongst them the Parson of the parish, who was a Scholler, and a man of vnblemisht life and conuersation; who seeing this prodigious spectacle, broke out into those words of Saint *Iohn* the Euangelist, *Et Verbum Caro factum est*, And the Word was made Flesh which was no sooner spoke, but the Diuel arose, and suddenly vanished in a terrible storme, carrying with him the roofe of the chamber, and setting fire on the bed wherein he had lien, which was in a moment burned to ashes. Shee was within three dayes after deliuered of a Monster, such as the Father appeared vnto them; of so odible an aspect, that the Midwiues caus'd it instantly to be burnt, lest the infamy of the daughter might too much reflect vpon the innocencie of the Noble Parents.

The same Author recordeth the like wonderment in a Ship of passengers, who tooke in their lading at Fortha, to land in the Low-Countries: which being in the middest of Sommer, there grew so sudden a storme, that the main-mast was split, the sailes rent, the Tacles torne in pieces, and nothing but imminent shipwracke was expected. The Pilot cries out, (in regard the storme was intempestiue, it being then the Summer Solstice, when the Seas are for the most part temperat and calme) that it must needs be the worke of the Diuell. When suddenly was heard a lamentable complaint of a woman passenger below the Decke, confessing that all this disaster was for her sake, for hauing often carnal company with the diuel, he at that time was tempting her to that abhominable act: which a Priest (a passenger then among them) hearing, persuaded her to repentance, and not to despaire, but to call vpon God for mercy: which she did, with many sighes and teares; when presently they might espy a cloud or darke shadow in the shape of a man, to ascend from the Hold of the ship, with a great sound, fire, smoke, and stench, to vanish: after which the tempest ceased, and they in a calme sea arriued safe at their expected Harbor.

Thomas Heywood, *The Hierarchie of the Blessed Angells*, 1635

'The Demon Lover'

O where have you been, my long, long love,
    This long seven years and mair?
O I'm come to seek my former vows
    Ye granted me before.

O hold your tongue of your former vows,
    For they will breed sad strife;
O hold your tongue of your former vows,
    For I am become a wife.

He turned him right and round about,
    And the tear blinded his ee:
I wad never hae trodden on Irish ground,
    If it had not been for thee.

I might hae had a king's daughter,
    Far, far beyond the sea;
I might have had a king's daughter,
    Had it not been for love o thee.

If ye might have had a king's daughter,
 Yer sel ye had to blame;
Ye might have taken the king's daughter,
 For ye kend that I was nane.

If I was to leave my husband dear,
 And my two babes also,
O what have you to take me to,
 If with you I should go?

I hae seven ships upon the sea –
 The eighth brought me to land –
With four-and-twenty bold mariners,
 And music on every hand.

She has taken up her two little babes,
 Kissd them baith cheek and chin:
O fair ye weel, my ain two babes,
 For I'll never seen you again.

She set her foot upon the ship,
 No mariners could she behold;
But the sails were o the taffetie,
 And the masts o the beaten gold.

They had not sailed a league, a league,
 A league but barely three,
When dismal grew his countenance,
 And drumlie grew his ee.

They had not sailed a league, a league,
 A league but barely three,
Until she espied his cloven foot,
 And she wept right bitterlie.

O hold your tongue of your weeping, says he,
 Of your weeping now let me be;
I will shew you how lilies grow
 On the banks of Italy.

O what hills are yon, yon pleasant hills,
 That the sun shines sweetly on?

O yon are the hills of heaven, he said,
  Where you will never win.

O whaten mountain is yon, she said,
  All so dreary wi frost and snow?
O yon is the mountain of hell, he cried
  Where you and I will go.

He strack the tap-mast wi his hand,
  The fore-mast wi his knee,
And he brake that gallant ship in twain,
  And sank her in the sea.

James Harris

Oh Who Can Be Mine and Live!

There was no light, but a livid grey that sickened the eye to behold, except when the bright red lightning burst out like the eye of a fiend, glancing over the work of ruin, and closing as it beheld it completed.

'Amid this scene stood two beings, one whose appealing loveliness seemed to have found favour with the elements even in their wrath, and one whose fearless and obdurate eye appeared to defy them. "Immalee," he cried, "is this a place or an hour to talk of love! – all nature is appalled – heaven is dark – the animals have hid themselves – and the very shrubs, as they wave and shrink, seem alive with terror." – "It is an hour to implore protection," said the Indian, clinging to him timidly. "Look up," said the stranger, while his own fixed and fearless eye seemed to return flash for flash to the baffled and insulted elements; "Look up, and if you cannot resist the impulses of your heart, let me at least point out a fitter object for them. Love," he cried, extending his arm towards the dim and troubled sky, "love the storm in its might of destruction – seek alliance with those swift and perilous travellers of the groaning air, – the meteor that rends, and the thunder that shakes it! Court, for sheltering tenderness, those masses of dense and rolling cloud, – the baseless mountains of heaven! Woo the kisses of the fiery lightnings, to quench themselves on your smouldering bosom! Seek all that is terrible in nature for your companions and your lover! – woo them to burn and blast you – perish in their fierce embrace, and you will be happier, far happier, than if you lived in mine! *Lived!* – Oh who can be mine and live! Hear me, Immalee!" he cried, while he held her hands locked in his – while his eyes, rivetted on her, sent forth a light of intolerable lustre – while a new feeling of indefinite enthusiasm seemed for a moment to thrill his whole frame, and new-modulate the tone of his nature; "Hear me! If you will be mine, it must be amid a scene like this for ever – amid fire and darkness – amid hatred and despair – amid – " and his voice swelling to a demoniac shriek of rage and horror, and his arms extended, as if to grapple with the fearful objects of some imaginary struggle, he was rushing from the arch under which they stood, lost in the picture which his guilt and despair had drawn, and whose images he was for ever doomed to behold.

'The slender form that had clung to him was, by this sudden movement, prostrated at his feet; and, with a voice choked with terror, yet with that perfect devotedness which never issued but from the heart and lip of woman, she answered his frightful questions with the simple demand, "*Will you be there?*" – "Yes! – THERE I must be, and for ever! And *will* you, and *dare* you, be with me?" And a kind of wild and terrible energy nerved his frame, and strengthened his voice, as he spoke and cowered over pale and prostrate loveliness, that seemed in profound and reckless humiliation to court its own destruction, as if a dove exposed its breast, without flight or struggle, to the beak of a vulture. "Well, then," said the stranger, while a brief convulsion crossed his pale visage, "amid thunder I wed thee – bride of perdition! mine shalt thou be for ever! Come, and let us attest our nuptials before the reeling altar of nature, with the lightnings of heaven for our bed-lights, and the curse of nature for our marriage-benediction!" The Indian shrieked in terror, not at his words, which she did not understand, but at the expression which accompanied them. "Come," he repeated, "while the darkness yet is witness to our ineffable and eternal union." Immalee, pale, terrified, but resolute, retreated from him.

'At this moment the storm, which had obscured the heavens and ravaged the earth, passed away with the rapidity common in those climates, where the visitation of an hour does its work of destruction unimpeded, and is instantly succeeded by the smiling lights and brilliant skies of which mortal curiosity in vain asks the question, Whether they gleam in triumph or in consolation over the mischief they witness?

'As the stranger spoke, the clouds passed away, carrying their diminished burden of wrath and terror where sufferings were to be inflicted, and terrors to be undergone, by the natives of other climes – and the bright moon burst forth with a glory unknown in European climes. The heavens were as blue as the waves of the ocean, which they seemed to reflect; and the stars burst forth with a kind of indignant and aggravated brilliancy, as if they resented the usurpation of the storm, and asserted the eternal predominance of nature over the casual influences of the storms that obscured her. Such, perhaps, will be the development of the moral world. We shall be told why we suffered, and for what; but a bright and blessed lustre shall follow the storm, and all shall yet be light.

'The young Indian caught from this object an omen alike auspicious to her imagination and her heart. She burst from him – she rushed into the light of nature, whose glory seemed like the promise of redemption, gleaming amid the darkness of the fall. She pointed to the moon, that sun of the eastern nights, whose broad and brilliant light fell like a mantle of glory over rock and ruin, over tree and flower.

' "Wed me by this light," cried Immalee, "and I will be yours for ever!" And her beautiful countenance reflected the full light of the glorious planet that rode bright through the cloudless heaven – and her white and naked arms, extended towards it, seemed like two pure attesting pledges of the union. "Wed me by this light," she repeated, sinking on her knees, "and I will be yours for ever!"

'As she spoke, the stranger approached, moved with what feelings no mortal thought can discover. At that moment a trifling phenomenon interfered to alter her destiny. A darkened cloud at that moment covered the moon – it seemed as if the departed storm collected in wrathful haste the last dark fold of its tremendous drapery, and was about to pass away for ever.

'The eyes of the stranger flashed on Immalee the brightest rays of mingled fondness and ferocity. He pointed to the darkness, – "WED ME BY THIS LIGHT!" he exclaimed, *"and you shall be mine for ever and ever!"* Immalee, shuddering at the grasp in which he held her, and trying in vain to watch the expression of his countenance, yet felt enough of her danger to tear herself from him. "Farewell for ever!" exclaimed the stranger, as he rushed from her.

'Immalee, exhausted by emotion and terror, had fallen senseless on the sands that filled the path to the ruined pagoda. He returned – he raised her in his arms – her long dark hair streamed over them like the drooping banners of a defeated army – her arms sunk down as if declining the support they seemed to implore – her cold and colourless cheek rested on his shoulder.

' "Is she dead?" he murmured. "Well, be it so – let her perish – let her be any thing *but mine!*" He flung his senseless burden on the sands, and departed – nor did he ever revisit the island.'

Charles Robert Maturin, *Melmoth the Wanderer*, 1820

Presque Charmé

Le Tentateur lui-même était presque charmé,
Il avait oublié son art et sa victime,
Et son cœur un moment se reposa du crime.
Il répétait tout bas, et le front dans ses mains:
«Si je vous connaissais, ô larmes des humains!»
Ah! si dans ce moment la Vierge eût pu l'entendre,
Si la céleste main qu'elle eût osé lui tendre
L'eût saisi repentant, docile à remonter...
Qui sait? le mal peut-être eût cessé d'exister.
Mais sitôt qu'elle vit sur sa tête pensive
De l'Enfer décelé la douleur convulsive,
Étonnée et tremblante, elle éleva ses yeux;
Plus forte, elle parut se souvenir des Cieux
Et souleva deux fois ses ailes argentées,
Entr'ouvrant pour gémir ses lèvres enchantées,
Ainsi qu'un jeune enfant, s'attachant aux roseaux,
Tente de faibles cris étouffés sous les eaux.
Il la vit prête à fuir vers les Cieux de lumière.
Comme un tigre éveillé bondit dans la poussière,
Aussitôt en lui-même, et plus fort désormais,
Retrouvant cet esprit qui ne fléchit jamais,
Ce noir esprit du mal qu'irrite l'innocence,
Il rougit d'avoir pu douter de sa puissance,
Il rétablit la paix sur son front radieux.
Rallume tout à coup l'audace de ses yeux,
Et longtemps en silence il regarde et contemple
La victime du Ciel qu'il destine à son temple,
Comme pour lui montrer qu'elle résiste en vain,
Et s'endurcir lui-même à ce regard divin.
Sans amour, sans remords, au fond d'un cœur de glace,
Des coups qu'il va porter il médite la place,
Et pareil au guerrier qui, tranquille à dessein,
Dans les défauts du fer cherche à frapper le sein,
Il compose ses traits sur les désirs de l'Ange;
Son air, sa voix, son geste et son maintien, tout change;
Sans venir de son cœur, des pleurs fallacieux
Paraissent tout à coup sur le bord de ses yeux.
La Vierge dans le Ciel n'avait pas vu de larmes

Et s'arrête; un soupir augmente ses alarmes.
Il pleure amèrement comme un homme exilé,
Comme une veuve auprès de son fils immolé;
Ses cheveux dénoués sont épars; rien n'arrête
Les sanglots de son sein qui soulèvent sa tête.
Éloa vient et pleure; ils se parlent ainsi:

«Que vous ai-je donc fait? Qu'avez-vous? Me voici.
– Tu cherches à me fuir, et pour toujours peut-être.
Combien tu me punis de m'être fait connaître!
– J'aimerais mieux rester; mais le Seigneur m'attend.
Je veux parler pour vous, souvent il nous entend.
– Il ne peut rien sur moi, jamais mon sort ne change,
Et toi seule es le Dieu qui peut sauver un Ange.
– Que puis-je faire? Hélas! dites, faut-il rester?
– Oui, descends jusqu'à moi, car je ne puis monter.
– Mais quel don voulez-vous? – Le plus beau, c'est nous-mêmes.
Viens. – M'exiler du Ciel? – Qu'importe, si tu m'aimes?
Touche ma main. Bientôt dans un mépris égal
Se confondront pour nous et le bien et le mal.
Tu n'as jamais compris ce qu'on trouve de charmes
A présenter son sein pour y cacher des larmes.
Viens, il est un bonheur que moi seul t'apprendrai;
Tu m'ouvriras ton âme, et je l'y répandrai;
Comme l'aube et la lune au couchant reposée
Confondent leurs rayons, ou comme la rosée
Dans une perle seule unit deux de ses pleurs
Pour s'empreindre du baume exhalé par les fleurs,
Comme un double flambeau réunit ses deux flammes.
Non moins étroitement nous unirons nos âmes.
– Je t'aime et je descends. Mais que diront les Cieux?»

En ce moment passa dans l'air, loin de leurs yeux,
Un des célestes chœurs où, parmi les louanges,
On entendit ces mots que répétaient des Anges:
«Gloire dans l'Univers, dans les Temps, à celui
Qui s'immole à jamais pour le salut d'autrui!»
Les Cieux semblaient parler. C'en était trop pour elle.

Deux fois encor levant sa paupière infidèle,
Promenant des regards encore irrésolus,
Elle chercha ses Cieux qu'elle ne voyait plus.

Des Anges au Chaos allaient puiser des mondes.
Passant avec terreur dans ses plaines profondes,
Tandis qu'ils remplissaient les messages de Dieu,
Ils ont tous vu tomber un nuage de feu.
Des plaintes de douleurs, des réponses cruelles
Se mêlaient dans la flamme au battement des ailes:
«Où me conduisez-vous, bel Ange? – Viens toujours.
– Que votre voix est triste, et quel sombre discours!
N'est-ce pas Éloa qui soulève ta chaîne?
J'ai cru t'avoir sauvé. – Non, c'est moi qui t'entraîne.
– Si nous sommes unis, peu m'importe en quel lieu!
Nomme-moi donc encore ou ta Sœur ou ton Dieu!
– J'enlève mon esclave et je tiens ma victime.
– Tu paraissais si bon! Oh! qu'ai-je fait? – Un crime.
– Seras-tu plus heureux du moins, es-tu content?
– Plus triste que jamais. – Qui donc es-tu? – Satan.»

Alfred de Vigny, *Eloa ou La Soeur des Anges*, 1824

The Devil's Wooing

TAMARA: Deceitful spirit, you must leave me!
    Be still, I'll not believe the foe . . .
    Oh, my Creator . . . grief and woe!
    no prayer comes out . . . my wits deceive me,
    they falter, gripped by venom's ire!
    Listen, you pile up doom above me
    with words of poison and of fire . . .
    Tell me the reason why you love me!
DEMON: The reason why, fair one, you said?
    Alas, I know it not! . . . elated
    with new life, from my guilty head
    the thorny crown I relegated,
    threw in the ashes all my days:
    my heaven, my hell are in your gaze.
    I love you with no earthly passion,
    such love that *you* could never find:
    with rapture, in the towering fashion
    of an immortal heart and mind.
    On my sad soul, from world's first aeon.
    deeply your image was impressed;

ever before me it progressed
through wastes of timeless empyrean.
My thoughts had long been stirred and racked
by just one name of passing sweetness:
my days in paradise had lacked
just your perfection for completeness.
If you could guess, if you could know
how much it costs in tribulation
throughout the ages' long gradation
to take one's pleasure, suffer woe,
to expect no praise for evil, no
prize for good deeds; what condemnation
to live for self, by self be bored
in endless struggle – no reward,
no crown, no reconciliation!
To regret all, to seek no prize,
to know, feel, see all things for ever,
to seek to hate the world – whatever
there may be in it, to despise! . . .
As soon as I from heaven's employment
was banned by curses, from that day
all nature's warmth and sweet enjoyment
grew chilled for ever, froze away;
bluer before me stretched the spaces;
I saw apparelled in their places,
like wedding guests, the lights I knew . . .
crowned, gliding one behind another;
and yet their former friend and brother
not one would recognise anew.
So, in despair, the expatriated,
the outcasts I began to call,
but faces, words, and looks that hated,
I failed to recognise them all.
And so, in horror, wings inflected,
I swooped away – but whither? why?
I know not . . . I had been rejected
by my old friends; like Adam I
found the world gone deaf-mute and dry.
So, at the current's free impulsion,
a helpless and storm-crippled boat,
sailless and rudderless, will float,
knowing no goal for its propulsion;

so at the earliest morning-tide
a scrap of thunder-cloud will ride,
in heaven's azure vaults the only
visible speck, unhalting, lonely,
will without trace and without sense
fly God knows whither, God knows whence!
Briefly I guided mankind's thought,
briefly the ways of sin I taught,
discredited what's noble, brought
everything beautiful to nought;
briefly ... the flame of all committed
belief in man I firmly drowned ...
but was it worthwhile to confound
just hypocrites and the half-witted?
I hid where the ravines run deep;
I started, meteor-like, to sweep
on course through midnight's darkest glooming ...
A lonely wayfarer was looming,
enticed by a near lamp – to fall
over the cliff-edge, horse and all;
vainly he called out – bloody traces
followed him down the mountain-side ...
but hatred's tricks, its sad grimaces,
brought me a solace that soon died!
How often, locked in dusty battle
with some great hurricane, in shroud
of mist and lightning I would rattle
and swoop and storm amid the cloud,
and hope in elemental churning
to stifle all my heart's regret,
to escape from thoughts that kept returning,
the unforgotten to forget!
What is the sum of the privations,
the labours and the grief of man,
of past, of future generations,
compared with just one minute's span
of all my untold tribulations?
What is man's life? his labour? why –
he's passed, he's died, he'll pass and die ...
his hopes on Judgment Day rely:
sure judgment, possible forgiving!
but *my* sorrow is endless, I

am damned to sorrow everliving;
for it, no grave in which to doze!
sometimes, snakelike, it creeps, or glows
like flame, it crackles, blazes, rushes,
or, like a tomb, for the repose
of ruined passions, hopes and woes.

TAMARA: Why should I share your griefs, your inner torments? why
listen to your moan?
You've sinned ...

DEMON: Towards you, I'm no sinner.

TAMARA: Someone will hear us! ...

DEMON: We're alone.

TAMARA: And God?

DEMON: Won't glance at us: eternal for heaven, but not for earth, his
care.

TAMARA: And punishment, and pains infernal?

DEMON: What of them, if we both are there?

TAMARA: Sufferer, stranger-friend, unwilling –
whoever you may be – I find
your words set secret pleasure thrilling,
ceaselessly they disturb my mind.
But if there's cunning in your story,
if there's a secret, wicked goal ...
oh, have some mercy! where's the glory
to you, what value is my soul?
In heaven's eye could I be reckoned
dearer than those you spurned instead?
they too are beauties, though unbeckoned!
as here, no mortal for a second
has dared defile their maiden bed ...
Swear me a fateful oath ... in anguish
I bid you swear ... see how I languish;
you know the stuff of women's dreams!
instinctively you soothe my terrors ...
you understand my ways, my errors –
and you'll have pity that redeems!
Swear it ... from evil machinations
you'll cease for ever, swear it now.
Have you no oaths, no adjurations,
have you no single sacred vow? ...

DEMON: By the first day of our creation
I swear, and by its final night,

[296]

I swear by evil's condemnation
and by the triumph of the right,
by downfall, with its bitter smarting,
by victories I dream to score,
by bliss of seeing you once more
and by the threat of once more parting.
I swear by all the souls of those
who serve me in predestined fashion,
I swear by my unsleeping foes;
by heaven, by hell, by earth's profession
of holiness, and by your head,
I swear by your last look's expression,
I swear by the first tear you shed,
the air your sweet lips are inhaling,
those silky curls that wave above,
I swear by bliss and by travailing,
I swear, believe it, by my love.
Old plans of vengeance and destruction
I have renounced, and dreams of pride;
henceforth, by evil's sly seduction
no human spirit shall be tried;
with heaven I seek to end my warring,
to live for praying and adoring,
to live for faith in all that's good.
Tears of repentance, as they should,
will from my forehead, thus deserving
your virtues, wash off heaven's brand,
and may the world, calm, unobserving,
flourish untroubled by my hand!
Till now, you've found appreciation
at your true worth from me alone:
I chose you for my adoration,
laid at your feet my realms, my throne.
I need your love, my benefaction
to you will be eternal life;
in love, just as in evil action,
I'm strong and quite unmoved by strife.
With me, free son of the ethereal,
to stellar regions you'll be whirled;
you're fated to be my imperial
consort, and first queen of the world.
Then without pity, without caring,

you'll learn to look down at the earth,
where no true bliss and no long-wearing
beauty exist, which brings to birth
only misdeeds and retribution,
where only paltry passions live;
where love and hate, without dilution
by fear, are past man's power to give.
Surely you know how short and fleeting
is human love's ephemeral rule?
just for a flash, young blood is heating –
then days go flying, blood runs cool!
Who can stand up to pain of parting,
or to new beauty's tempting gleams,
to weariness or boredom starting,
or to the waywardness of dreams?
Be sure that you were never fated,
my consort, to destroy your bloom
and fade away incarcerated,
enslaved in envy's narrow room,
amongst the cold and the small-minded,
the false friends and the open foes,
the fears, the toils that vainly grinded,
the fruitless hopes, the crushing woes.
No, pitifully, without passion,
you'll not expire, in prayer, behind
high walls, removed in equal fashion
from God, and from all human kind.
Oh, no, you wonder of creation,
a different destiny is yours;
you face a different tribulation
and different bliss in bounteous stores;
give up all previous ambition,
renounce the fate of this sad world:
instead, a lofty, splendid mission
before your eyes will be unfurled.
A host of souls who owe me duty
I'll bring, I'll throw them at your feet;
magically for you, my beauty,
handmaids will labour, deft and fleet;
for you from the eastern star I'll ravish
a golden crown; I'll take for you
from flowers the midnight dew, and lavish

upon your crown that selfsame dew;
I'll bring a sunset ray; ecstatic,
I'll clasp it, belt-like, round your waist,
with breath of healing aromatic
the airs around you will be laced;
all day the strains of heavenly playing
will lull your hearing with their tune;
I'll build you halls with an inlaying
of turquoise, rooms with amber strewn;
I'll sound the bottom of the ocean,
high up above the clouds I'll climb,
all, all, that's earthly, my devotion
will give you – love me! ...

                    And this time
with ardent lips so lightly grazing
he kissed her trembling mouth, and then
answered her pleas, in language dazing
with sweet temptation; once again
those mighty eyes were fixed and gazing
deep into hers. He set her blazing.
He gleamed above her like a spark
or like a knife that finds its mark.
That devil triumphed! In the dark,
alas, to her bosom the infernal
poison of his embrace could pierce.
A cry resounded, tortured, fierce.
troubling the stillnesses nocturnal.
In it were love, and pain's hard kernel,
reproaches, a last desperate prayer,
and then a hopeless, an eternal
farewell to life – all these were there.

Mikhail Lermontov, *The Demon*, 1831–41; trans. Charles Johnston, 1980

'The Devil at Little Dunkeld Manse'

A long time ago there was a servant lassie, who worked for the Minister at Little Dunkeld. She was a quiet lass, who had no mind for dances and such follies, and she liked fine to go for long walks on Birnam Hill.

After a time she told the Minister that she had met a grand gentleman there, who used to walk and talk with her, and he was courting her. The Minister thought that a fine gentleman would be dangerous company for the lass, and he told her to bring him to the Manse, and let him see what kind of a man he was.

The lassie was pleased enough, and next Saturday she brought in her jo.

He was a grand-looking gentleman, sure enough, and pleasant spoken, but when the Minister looked down at his feet, the blood ran cold in his veins, for he saw that he had cloven hoofs, and he knew that there was just one person that had that. So, when the stranger had gone, he said to the lassie: 'That's a braw man, yon, but did you see the feet of him?'

'Aye, did I,' said the lass, 'and bonnie feet he has, with braw shining boots.'

'Take another look on them, when you see him again,' said the Minister.

But nothing he could say made any difference. She was still terribly taken up with him. At last it came to this, that the braw gentleman asked her to marry him. When the Minister heard that, he was sorely put about, but at length he said: 'Well, you may be married on one condition, that none shall wed you but me, and that the wedding shall be in the Manse.'

The lassie was well enough pleased at that, for it would be a grand wedding for her, and when the day came, half the parish came to see it. All the guests were waiting, and the bride in her bonnie new gown, and there was no sign of the bridegroom. But at length they heard a great rumbling, and a chariot drove up to the door, with six black horses. In comes my fine gentleman, bowing and smiling around him. The guests were terribly taken up with him, but the Minister saw the cloven hoofs of him as plain as ever.

So the Minister took a candle, and he lighted it at both ends, as they do for the bidding at a roup [auction], and he said: 'Now, when this candle is burnt out I'll marry you, and not a minute before.'

The stranger looked black at this; but the Minister held the candle steadily between his two fingers, while the bride cried, and the bridegroom scowled, and the guests shuffled their feet and whispered. The wax dripped and dripped, and the candle burnt and burnt, till the one flame was about two inches from the other. Then, whilst it was still burning, the Minister put it into his mouth and swallowed it.

'Now,' he said, 'the candle will never burn out, and you will never be married.'

With that the stranger gave a most awesome shriek, and leaped out of the window, and vanished into the earth, and his coach and six with him.

[300]

And outside Little Dunkeld Manse there is a black spot of earth where they say no grass will grow to this day.

K. M. Briggs, *Dictionary of British Folk-Tales*, 1971

'Amoureuse du Diable'

A Stéphane Mallarmé

Il parle italien avec un accent russe.
Il dit: «Chère, il serait précieux que je fusse
«Riche, et seul, tout demain et tout après-demain.
«Mais riche à paver d'or monnayé le chemin
«De l'Enfer, et si seul qu'il vous va falloir prendre
«Sur vous de m'oublier jusqu'à ne plus entendre
«Parler de moi sans vous dire de bonne foi:
«Qu'est-ce que ce monsieur Félice? Il vend de quoi?»
Cela s'adresse à la plus blanche de comtesses.

Hélas! toute grandeur, toutes délicatesses,
Cœur d'or, comme l'on dit, âme de diamant,
Riche, belle, un mari magnifique et charmant
Qui lui réalisait toute chose rêvée,
Adorée, adorable, une Heureuse, la Fée,
La Reine, aussi la Sainte, elle était tout cela,
Elle avait tout cela.
           Cet homme vint, vola
Son cœur, son âme, en fit sa maîtresse et sa chose
Et ce que la voilà dans ce doux peignoir rose
Avec ses cheveux d'or épars comme du feu,
Assise, et ses grands yeux d'azur tristes un peu.

Ce fut une banale et terrible aventure
Elle quitta de nuit l'hôtel. Une voiture
Attendait. Lui dedans. Ils restèrent six mois
Sans que personne sût où ni comment. Parfois
On les disait partis à toujours. Le scandale
Fut affreux. Cette allure était par trop brutale
Aussi pour que le monde ainsi mis au défi
N'eût pas frémi d'une ire énorme et poursuivi
De ses langues les plus agiles l'insensée.

Elle, que lui faisait? Toute à cette pensée,
Lui, rien que *lui*, longtemps avant qu'elle s'enfuît,
Ayant réalisé son avoir (sept ou huit
Millions en billets de mille qu'on liasse
Ne pèsent pas beaucoup et tiennent peu de place.)
Elle avait tassé tout dans un coffret mignon
Et le jour du départ, lorsque son compagnon
Dont du rhum bu de trop rendait la voix plus tendre
L'interrogea sur ce colis qu'il voyait pendre
A son bras qui se lasse, elle répondit: «Ça
C'est notre bourse.»
    O tout ce qui se dépensa!
Il n'avait rien que sa beauté problématique
(D'autant pire) et que cet esprit dont il se pique
Et dont nous parlerons, comme de sa beauté.
Quand il faudra . . . Mais quel bourreau d'argent! Prêté,
Gagné, volé! Car il volait à sa manière,
Excessive, partant respectable en dernière
Analyse, et d'ailleurs respectée, et c'était
Prodigieux la vie énorme qu'il menait
Quand au bout de six mois ils revinrent.

       Le coffre
Aux millions (dont plus que quatre) est là qui s'offre
A sa main. Et pourtant cette fois – une fois
N'est pas coutume – il a gargarisé sa voix
Et remplacé son geste ordinaire de prendre
Sans demander, par ce que nous venons d'entendre.
Elle s'étonne avec douceur et dit: «Prends tout
«Si tu veux.»
    Il prend tout et sort.
        Un mauvais goût
Qui n'avait de pareil que sa désinvolture
Semblait pétrir le fond même de sa nature,
Et dans ses moindres mots, dans ses moindres clins d'yeux,
Faisait luire et vibrer comme un charme odieux.
Ses cheveux noirs étaient trop bouclés pour un homme,
Ses yeux très grands, tout verts, luisaient comme à Sodome.
Dans sa voix claire et lente, un serpent s'avançait,
Et sa tenue était de celles que l'on sait:
Du vernis, du velours, trop de linge, et des bagues.
D'antécédents, il en avait de vraiment vagues

Ou pour mieux dire, pas. Il parut un beau soir,
L'autre hiver, à Paris, sans qu'aucun pût savoir
D'où venait ce petit monsieur, fort bien du reste
Dans son genre et dans son outrecuidance leste.
Il fit rage, eut des duels célèbres et causa
Des morts de femmes par amour dont on causa.
Comment il vint à bout de la chère comtesse,
Par quel philtre ce gnome insuffisant qui laisse
Une odeur de cheval et de femme après lui
A-t-il fait d'elle cette fille d'aujourd'hui?
Ah, ça, c'est le secret perpétuel que berce
Le sang des dames dans son plus joli commerce,
A moins que ce ne soit celui du DIABLE aussi.
Toujours est-il que quand le tour eut réussi
Ce fut du propre!

        Absent souvent trois jours sur quatre,
Il rentrait ivre, assez lâche et vil pour la battre,
Et quand il voulait bien rester près d'elle un peu,
Il la martyrisait, en manière de jeu,
Par l'étalage de doctrines impossibles.

«*Mia*, je ne suis pas d'entre les irascibles,
«Je suis le doux par excellence, mais tenez,
«Ça m'exaspère, et je le dis à votre nez,
«Quand je vous vois l'œil blanc et la lèvre pincée,
«Avec je ne sais quoi d'étroit dans la pensée
«Parce que je reviens un peu soûl quelquefois.
«Vraiment, en seriez-vous à croire que je bois
«Pour boire, pour licher, comme vous autres chattes,
«Avec vos vins sucrés dans vos verres à pattes
«Et que l'Ivrogne est une forme du Gourmand?
«Alors l'instinct qui vous dit ça ment plaisamment
«Et d'y prêter l'oreille un instant, quel dommage!
«Dites, dans un bon Dieu de bois est-ce l'image
«Que vous voyez et vers qui vos vœux vont monter?
«L'Eucharistie est-elle un pain à cacheter
«Pur et simple, et l'amant d'une femme, si j'ose
«Parler ainsi, consiste-t-il en cette chose
«Unique d'un monsieur qui n'est pas son mari
«Et se voit de ce chef tout spécial chéri?
«Ah, si je bois c'est pour me soûler, non pour boire.
«Être soûl, vous ne savez pas quelle victoire

«C'est qu'on remporte sur la vie, et quel don c'est!
«On oublie, on revoit, on ignore et l'on sait;
«C'est des mystères pleins d'aperçus, c'est du rêve
«Qui n'a jamais eu de naissance et ne s'achève
«Pas, et ne se meut pas dans l'essence d'ici;
«C'est une espèce d'autre vie en raccourci,
«Un espoir actuel, un regret qui «rapplique»,
«Que sais-je encore? Et quant à la rumeur publique,
«Au préjugé qui hue un homme dans ce cas,
«C'est hideux, parce que bête, et je ne plains pas
«Ceux ou celles qu'il bat à travers son extase,
«O que nenni!
                    «Voyons, l'amour, c'est une phrase
«Sous un mot, – avouez, un écoute-s'il-pleut,
«Un calembour dont un chacun prend ce qu'il veut,
«Un peu de plaisir fin, beaucoup de grosse joie
«Selon le plus ou moins de moyens qu'il emploie,
«Ou pour mieux dire, au gré de son tempérament,
«Mais, entre nous, le temps qu'on y perd! Et comment!
«Vrai, c'est honteux que des personnes sérieuses
«Comme nous deux, avec ces vertus précieuses
«Que nous avons, du cœur, de l'esprit, – de l'argent,
«Dans un siècle que l'on peut dire intelligent
«Aillent!...»
                    Ainsi de suite, et sa fade ironie
N'épargnait rien de rien dans sa blague infinie.
Elle écoutait le tout avec les yeux baissés
Des cœurs aimants à qui tous torts sont effacés,
Hélas!
          L'après-demain et le demain se passent.
Il rentre et dit: «*Altro!* que voulez-vous que fassent
«Quatre pauvres petits millions contre un sort?
«Ruinés, ruinés, je vous dis! C'est la mort
«Dans l'âme que je vous le dis.»
                                        Elle frissonne
Un peu, mais *sait* que c'est arrivé.
                                        – «Ça, personne,
«Même vous, *diletta*, ne me croit assez sot
«Pour demeurer ici dedans le temps d'un saut
«De puce.»
          Elle pâlit très fort et frémit presque,
Et dit: «Va, je sais tout.» – «Alors c'est trop grotesque

Et vous jouez là sans atouts avec le feu.
– «Qui dit non?» – Mais JE SUIS SPÉCIAL à ce jeu.»
– «Mais si je veux, exclame-t-elle, être damnée?»
– «C'est différent, arrange ainsi ta destinée,
Moi, je sors.» – «Avec moi!» – «Je ne puis *aujourd'hui*.»
Il a disparu sans autre trace de lui
Qu'une odeur de soufre et qu'un aigre éclat de rire.
Elle tire un petit couteau.
                    Le temps de luire
Et la lame est entrée à deux lignes du cœur.
Le temps de dire, en renfonçant l'acier vainqueur:
«A toi, je t'aime!» et la JUSTICE la recense.

Elle ne savait pas que l'Enfer c'est l'absence.

Paul Verlaine, 1874

Prince Lucio Resorts to a Drastic Expedient

'When I know who you are!' she repeated wonderingly – 'Do I not know? You are Lucio, – Lucio Rimânez – my love, – my love! – whose voice is my music, – whose beauty I adore, – whose looks are my heaven' . . .

'And Hell!' he interposed, with a low laugh – 'Come here!'

She went towards him eagerly, yet falteringly. He pointed to the ground, – I saw the rare blue diamond he always wore on his right hand, flash like a flame in the moonrays.

'Since you love me so well,' – he said – 'Kneel down and worship me!'

She dropped on her knees – and clasped her hands, – I strove to move, – to speak, – but some resistless force held me dumb and motionless; – the light from the stained glass window fell upon her face, and showed its fairness illumined by a smile of perfect rapture.

'With every pulse of my being I worship you!' she murmured passionately – 'My king! – my god! The cruel things you say but deepen my love for you, – you can kill, but you can never change me! For one kiss of your lips I would die, – for one embrace from you I would give my soul! . . .'

'Have you one to give?' he asked derisively – 'Is it not already disposed of? You should make sure of that first! Stay where you are and let me look at you! So! – a woman, wearing a husband's name, holding a husband's honour, clothed in the very garments purchased with a husband's money, and newly risen from a husband's side, steals forth thus in the night, seeking to disgrace him and pollute herself by the vulgarest unchastity! And this is all that the culture and training of nineteenth-century civilization can do for you? Myself, I prefer the barbaric fashion of old times, when rough savages fought for their women as they fought for their cattle, treated them as cattle, and kept them in their place, never dreaming of endowing them with such strong virtues as truth and honour! If women were pure and true, then the lost happiness of the world might return to it, – but the majority of them are like you, liars, ever pretending to be what they are not. I may do what I choose with you, you say? torture you, kill you, brand you with the name of outcast in the public sight, and curse you before Heaven – if I will only love you! – all this is melodramatic speech, and I never cared for melodrama at any time. I shall neither kill you, brand you, curse you, nor love you; – I shall simply – call your husband!'

Marie Corelli, *The Sorrows of Satan*, 1895

Nine

THE DEVIL'S DISCIPLES

Blues is like the devil
They'll have me hell-bound soon
SARA MARTIN

Witches

One sort of such as are said to bee witches, are women which be commonly old, lame, bleare-eied, pale, fowle, and full of wrinkles; poore, sullen, superstitious, and papists; or such as knowe no religion: in whose drousie minds the divell hath goten a fine seat; so as, what mischeefe, mischance, calamitie, or slaughter is brought to passe, they are easilie persuaded the same is doone by themselves; imprinting in their minds an earnest and constant imagination hereof. They are leane and deformed, shewing melancholie in their faces, to the horror of all that see them. They are doting, scolds, mad, divelish; and not much differing from them that are thought to be possessed with spirits; so firme and stedfast in their opinions, as whosoever shall onelie have respect to the constancie of their words uttered, would easilie beleeve they were true indeed.

These miserable wretches are so odious unto all their neighbors, and so feared, as few dare offend them, or denie them anie thing they aske: whereby they take upon them; yea, and sometimes thinke, that they can doo such things as are beyond the abilitie of humane nature. These go from house to house, and from doore to doore for a pot full of milke, yest, drinke, pottage, or some such releefe; without the which they could hardlie live: neither obtaining for their service and paines, nor by their art, nor yet at the divels hands (with whome they are said to make a perfect and visible bargaine) either beautie, monie, promotion, welth, worship, pleasure, honor, knowledge, learning, or anie other benefit whatsoever.

It falleth out many times, that neither their necessities, nor their expectation is answered or served, in those places where they beg or borrowe; but rather their lewdnesse is by their neighbors reprooved. And further, in tract of time the witch waxeth odious and tedious to hir neighbors; and they againe are despised and despited of hir: so as sometimes she cursseth one, and sometimes another; and that from the maister of the house, his wife, children, cattell, &c. to the little pig that lieth in the stie. Thus in processe of time they have all displeased hir, and she hath wished evill lucke unto them all; perhaps with cursses and imprecations made in forme. Doubtlesse (at length) some of hir neighbors die, or fall sicke; or some of their children are visited with diseases that vex them strangelie: as apoplexies, epilepsies, convulsions, hot fevers, wormes, &c. Which by ignorant parents are supposed to be the vengeance of witches. Yea and their opinions and conceits are confirmed and maintained by unskilfull physicians: according to the common saieng; *Inscitiæ pallium maleficium &*

incantatio, Witchcraft and inchantment is the cloke of ignorance: whereas indeed evill humors, & not strange words, witches, or spirits are the causes of such diseases. Also some of their cattell perish, either by disease or mischance. Then they, upon whom such adversities fall, weighing the fame that goeth upon this woman (hir words, displeasure, and cursses meeting so justlie with their misfortune) doo not onelie conceive, but also are resolved, that all their mishaps are brought to pass by hir onelie meanes.

The witch on the other side exspecting hir neighbours mischances, and seeing things sometimes come to passe according to hir wishes, cursses, and incantations (for *Bodin* himselfe confesseth, that not above two in a hundred of their witchings or wishings take effect) being called before a Justice, by due examination of the circumstances is driven to see hir imprecations and desires, and hir neighbors harmes and losses to concurre, and as it were to take effect: and so confesseth that she (as a goddes) hath brought such things to passe. Wherein, not onelie she, but the accuser, and also the Justice are fowlie deceived and abused; as being thorough hir confession and other circumstances persuaded (to the injurie of Gods glorie) that she hath doone, or can doo that which is proper onelie to God himselfe.

Reginald Scot, *The Discoverie of Witchcraft*, 1584

A Piece of Dark Practice

There is another piece of dark practice here, which lies between Satan and his particular agents, and which they must give us an answer to, when they can, which I think will not be in haste; and that is about the obsequious Devil submitting to be called up into visibility, whenever an old woman has her hand crossed with a white sixpence, as they call it: One would think that instead of these vile things called witches, being sold to the Devil, the Devil was really sold for a slave to them; for how far soever Satan's residence is off from this state of life, they have power, it seems, to fetch him from home, and oblige him to come at their call.

I can give little account of this, only that indeed so it is; nor is the thing so strange in itself, as the methods to do it are mean, foolish, and ridiculous; as making a circle and dancing in it, pronouncing such and such words, saying the Lord's prayer backward, and the like; now is this agreeable to the dignity of the prince of the air or atmosphere, that he should be commanded forth with no more pomp or ceremony than that

of muttering a few words, such as the old witches and he agree about?
Or is there something else in it, which none of us or themselves understand?

Daniel Defoe, *The History of the Devil*, 1726

Stranger Still

For alas! What an unapt instrument is a toothles, old, impotent, and
unweldie woman to flie in the aier? Truelie, the divell little needs such
instruments to bring his purposes to passe. It is strange, that we should
suppose, that such persons can worke such feates: and it is more strange,
that we will imagine that to be possible to be doone by a witch, which
to nature and sense is impossible; speciallie when our neighbours life
dependeth upon our credulitie therein.

Reginald Scot, *The Discoverie of Witchcraft*, 1584

Dancing with the Gentleman in Black

Elizabeth Styles her Confession of her Witchcrafts, *Jan.* 26. and 30. and
Feb. 7. 1664. before *Rob. Hunt* Esq; She then confessed, that the Devil
about Ten years since appeared to her in the Shape of a handsome Man,
and after of a black Dog. That he promised her Money, and that she
should live gallantly, and have the Pleasure of the World for twelve years,
if she would with her Blood sign his Paper, which was to give her Soul
to him, and observe his Laws, and that he might suck her Blood. This
after Four Sollicitations, the Examinant promised him to do. Upon which
he prickt the fourth Finger of her right hand, between the middle and
upper Joynt (where the Sign at the Examination remained) and with a
Drop or two of her Blood, she signed the Paper with an [O.] Upon this
the Devil gave her Sixpence, and vanished with the Paper.

That since he hath appeared to her in the Shape of a *Man*, and did so
on *Wednesday* seven-night past, but more usually he appears in the Likeness of a *Dog*, and *Cat*, and a *Fly* like a Millar, in which last he usually
sucks in the Poll about four of the Clock in the Morning, and did so *Jan.*
27. and that it usually is Pain to her to be so suckt.

That when she hath a desire to do harm, she calls the Spirit by the
name of *Robin*, to whom when he appeareth, she useth these words, *O
Sathan, give me my purpose.* She then tells him what she would have done.

And that he should so appear to her, was part of her Contract with him.

That about a Month ago he appearing, she desired him to torment one *Elizabeth Hill*, and to thrust Thorns into her Flesh, which he promised to do, and the next time he appeared, he told her he had done it.

That a little above a Month since this Examinant, *Alice Duke*, *Anne Bishop* and *Mary Penny*, met about Nine of the Clock in the Night, in the Common near *Trister* Gate, where they met a Man in black Cloths with a little Band, to whom they did Courtesie and due observance, and the Examinant verily believes that this was the Devil. At that time *Alice Duke* brought a Picture in Wax, which was for *Elizabeth Hill*. The Man in black took it in his Arms, anointed its Fore-head, and said, *I baptize thee with this Oyl*, and used some other words. He was Godfather, and the Examinant and *Anne Bishop* Godmothers. They called it *Elizabeth* or *Bess*. Then the Man in Black, this Examinant, *Anne Bishop*, and *Alice Duke* stuck Thorns into several places of the Neck, Hand-Wrists, Fingers, and other parts of the said Picture. After which they had Wine, Cakes and Rost Meat (all brought by the Man in black) which they did eat and drink. They danced and were merry, were bodily there, and in their Cloths.

She further saith, that the same persons met again, at or near the same place about a Month since, when *Anne Bishop* brought a Picture in Wax, which was Baptized *John*, in like manner as the other was, the Man in black was Godfather, and *Alice Duke*, and this Examinant Godmothers. As soon as it was Baptized, *Anne Bishop* stuck two Thorns into the Arms of the Picture, which was for one *Robert Newman*'s Child of *Wincaunton*. After they had eaten, drank, danced, and made merry, they departed.

That she with *Anne Bishop*, and *Alice Duke*, met at another time in the Night, in a ground near *Marnhul*, where also met several other persons. The Devil then also there in the former shape, Baptized a Picture by the name of *Anne* or *Rachel Hatcher*. The Picture one *Durnford*'s Wife brought, and stuck Thorns in it. Then they also made merry with Wine and Cakes, and so departed.

She saith, before they are carried to their meetings, they anoint their Foreheads, and Hand-Wrists, with an Oyl the Spirit brings them (which smells raw) and then they are carried in a very short time, using these words as they pass. *Thout, tout a tout, tout, throughout and about.* And when they go off from their Meetings, they say, *Rentum Tormentum.*

That at their first meeting, the Man in black bids them welcome, and they all make low obeysance to him, and he delivers some Wax Candles like little Torches, which they give back again at parting. When they anoint themselves, they use a long form of words, and when they stick in Thorns into the Picture of any they would torment, they say, *A Pox on thee, I'le spite thee.*

That at every meeting before the Spirit vanisheth away, he appoints the next meeting place and time, and at his departure there is a foul smell. At their meeting they have usually Wind or good Beer, Cakes, Meat or the like. They eat and drink really when they meet in their Bodies, dance also and have Musick. The Man in black sits at the higher end, and *Anne Bishop* usually next him. He useth some words before meat, and none after, his Voice is audible, but very low.

That they are carried sometimes in their Bodies and their Cloths, sometimes without, and as the Examinant thinks their Bodies are sometimes left behind. When only their Spirits are present, yet they know one another.

When they would bewitch Man, Woman or Child, they do it sometimes by a *Picture* made in Wax, which the Devil formally Baptizeth. Sometimes they have an *Apple, Dish, Spoon*, or other thing from their evil Spirit, which they give the party to whom they would do harm. Upon which they have power to hurt the person that eats or receives it. Sometimes they have power to do mischief by a touch or curse, by these they can mischief Cattle, and by cursing without touching; but neither without the Devils leave.

That she hath been at several general meetings in the night at High Common, and a Common near *Motcombe*, at a place near *Marnhull*, and at other places where have met *John Combes, John Vining, Richard Dickes, Thomas Boster* or *Bolster, Thomas Dunning, James Bush* a lame Man, *Rachel King, Richard Lannen*, a Woman called *Durnford, Alice Duke, Anne Bishop, Mary Penny* and *Christopher Ellen*, all which did obeysance to the Man in black, who was at every one of their meetings. Usually they have at them some Picture Baptized.

The Man in black, sometimes plays on a Pipe or Cittern, and the Company dance. At last the Devil vanisheth, and all are carried to their several homes in a short space. At their parting they say [*A Boy! merry meet, merry part.*]

Joseph Glanvill, *Saducismus Triumphatus*, 1681

Nanny Howe

Tradition affirms, that in days of yore his Satanic majesty, with a sporting company of favourite imps, was accustomed, like the stout Percy of Northumberland,

> His pleasure in the 'Kildale' woods
> Three summer days to take.

A worthy named Stephen Howe, incensed at his highness for poaching on his manor, had the effrontery to boast, on one occasion, that if he again caught him hunting without license, he would not only discharge him from his liberty, but chastise him for his insolence. Hearing of this, Satan, whose courage has never been impeached, seated in a magnificent car, drawn by six coal-black steeds, drove down boldly, at his next visit, to Stephen Howe's small cot, on the brink of Court Moor. 'Hah, hah!' shouted Lucifer; 'I have found you at last!' Upon which poor Stephen took to his heels, being mightily afraid. Not so his wife, Nanny Howe, who being reputed a famous witch, did not fear even the devil himself, and boldly saluted him with her broom, which caused him to scratch his head with his claws. Soon rallying, with a powerful switch of his tail he capsized poor Nanny, who was thus compelled to own the superior skill and agility of her antagonist. 'Ah!' quoth the devil, 'you have both grievously offended me; one of you at least must accompany me, – see I have brought you a carriage and horses: say which of you will go!' 'I, I' said Nanny and, shouldering her broom, leapt into the coach without waiting further invitation, and away they drove in gallant style. Midway up the hill the devil, who felt thirsty alighted and at one draught drank dry the church-well, which formerly supplied the holy water for baptism.

We were further informed, that during the last century, a certain youth, who, like Tam O'Shanter, had been 'getting fou' and unco happy,' in crossing the wild heaths and moorlands above Kildale, actually beheld Nanny riding on her broomstick over the 'Devil's Court.' The fright occasioned by this incident induced the youth to become ever afterwards a very zealous tee-totaller. Nanny Howe is still sometimes to be seen gaily frolicking through the air at the awful hour of midnight.

County Folklore, 'Examples of Printed Folk-Lore concerning the N. Riding of Yorkshire . . .', coll. and ed. by Eliza Gutch, 1901

An Upset at the Hell-Fire Club

It was about four o'clock in the afternoon when my master [John Montagu, Lord Sandwich] arrived at the verge of the lake, where he no sooner made the concerted signal, than a boat was sent to ferry him over. On his landing on the island, he went to the monastery, where he found the society just sitting down to dinner, at which he took his place among them. When they had made a short meal, and drank their spirits up to a proper pitch, they retired to their respective cells, to prepare for the solemnity they were going to celebrate. My master, then clad in a milk-white robe of the finest linen, that flowed loosely round him, repaired, at the tolling of the bell, to the chapel, the scene of all their mysterious rites, and knocking gently thrice at the door, it was opened to him, to the sound of soft and solemn music. On his entrance he made a most profound obeisance; and, advancing slowly towards a table that stood against the wall in the upper end of the chapel, as soon as he came to the rails by which it was surrounded, he fell upon his knees, and making a profession of his principles nearly in the words, but with the most gross perversion of the sense of the articles of faith of the religion established in the country, demanded admission within the rails, the peculiar station of the upper order, where the superior and eleven of the fraternity – the twelfth place was vacant, and now to be filled up – stood arrayed in the habits of those whose names and characters they profaned by their assumption.

When he had finished, another candidate [John Wilkes] advanced in the like manner, and making his profession, also preferred the same claim; as there were more who had a right to do, but, discouraged by the superior merit of these two, they had declined their pretensions for this time.

The brotherhood, having heard the competitors with attention, retired to the table, and kneeling around it, the superior repeated a prayer, in the same strain and manner with the profession of the candidates, to the Being whom they served, to direct their choice to him of the two most worthy of his service. The superior then proceeded to take the suffrages of the rest, with the same mimic solemnity; when my master being found to have the majority, his election was exultingly attributed to immediate inspiration; and he was accordingly admitted within the rails, where he received the name and character which he was to bear in the society, in a manner not proper to be described, every most sacred rite and ceremony of religion being profaned; all the prayers and hymns of praise appointed for the worship of the Deity burlesqued by a perversion to the horrid occasion. In this manner the evening was wasted till supper-time, when they sat down to a banquet in the chapel, in honour of the occasion, at which nothing that the most refined luxury, the most lascivious imagination could suggest to kindle loose desire, and provoke and gratify appetite was wanting; both the superiors and inferiors – who were permitted to take their places at the lower end of the table, as soon as they had served in the banquet, vying with each other in loose songs, and dissertations of such gross lewdness and daring impiety, as despair may be supposed to dictate to the damned; in both which my master shone so unrivalled, as to bear down the superior sprightliness, wit, and humour, of all the rest; and compensate for the want of every companionable merit. But while they were in the height of their festivity, an affair happened that interrupted it for a time, and showed their resolution, particularly that of my master, in a proper light.

The person who had that day been his competitor for the honour of admission into the higher order of society, possessed the qualifications which he wanted in the most eminent degree. He had such a flow of spirits that it was impossible ever to be a moment dull in his company. His wit gave charms to every subject he spoke upon; and his humour displayed the foibles of mankind in such colours, as to put folly even out of countenance. But the same vanity which had first made him ambitious of entering into this society, only because it was composed of persons of a rank superior to his own in life, and still kept him in it, though upon acquaintance he despised them, sullied all these advantages. His spirits were often stretched to extravagance, to overpower competition. His humour was debased into buffoonery; and his wit was so prostituted to the lust of applause, that he would sacrifice his best friend for a scurvy jest; and wound the heart of him whom he would at that very moment hazard his life and fortune to serve, only to raise a laugh; in which he was also assisted by a peculiar archness of disposition, and an unlucky expertness at carrying his jests into practice, as he proved upon this occasion. Though he disdained to decline the late competition, as the others did, he had been well aware that my master's higher rank in life would carry the point in dispute against him; for which injustice he resolved to revenge himself in the most signal manner. For this purpose, he had contrived the night before to bring into his cell a great baboon, which he had provided for the occasion. When the brotherhood retired to their cells after dinner, as I have told you, to prepare for the ceremony, he availed himself of the office of keeper of the chapel, which he then filled, to convey this creature, dressed up in the fantastic garb, in which childish imagination clothes devils, into the chapel; where he shut him up in a large chest that stood there to hold the ornaments and utensils of the table, when the society was away. To the spring of the lock of this chest he fastened a cord, which he drew under the carpet that was on the floor to his own seat, and there brought the end of it through a hole made for that purpose, in such a manner that he could readily find it; and, by giving it a pull, open the chest, and let the baboon loose whenever he pleased, without being perceived by any of the rest of the company. Accordingly, when they were all in the height of their mirth, on my master's kneeling down, and with hands and eyes raised towards heaven, repeating an invocation, in the perverted phrase of Holy Writ, to the Being whom they served, to come among them, and receive their adorations in person, he pulled the cord, and let the animal loose, who, glad to be delivered from his confinement, gave a sudden spring upon the middle of the table.

The effect which the sight of such a visitor had upon them may be better conceived than expressed. Their attention had been so fixed upon what my master was saying, that they perceived not from whence he came; and his appearing so critically at the invocation, and in such a shape, made them conclude he was the Being invoked. Terrified out of their senses by this thought, they all roared out with one voice, 'The devil! the devil!' and starting from their seats, made directly towards the door, tumbling over one another, and oversetting everything in their way.

In the height of this uproar and confusion, the baboon, frightened at the effects of their fear, happened to leap upon my master's shoulders, as he lay sprawling on the floor; who, turning about his head at feeling the shock, saw the animal grinning horribly at him, and concluded the devil had obeyed his summons in good earnest, and come to carry him bodily away. Driven as he was to despair by this thought, he strove, however, in the instinctive impulse of self-preservation, to shake off the invader; but he, instead of loosing his hold on his repeated efforts, only clung to him the closer, clasping his paws around his neck, and chattering with spite at his ear. This completed the caitiff's distress. Every shadow of spirit failed him, and conscious guilt suggesting to him the meaning of this unintelligible jargon, he attempted, in the blindness of fear, to move the very devil to pity, by his pathetic wailings and supplications.

'Spare me, gracious devil!' said he; 'spare a wretch who never was sincerely your servant! I sinned only from vanity of being in the fashion! Thou knowest I never have been half so wicked as I pretended; never have been able to commit the thousandth part of the vices which I have boasted of. Take not, then, the advantage of that vanity; but judge me only from my actions. I knew not that thou wouldst have come, or I should never have invoked thee! leave me, therefore, and go to those who are more truly devoted to thy service. I am but half a sinner. My conscience always flew in my face when I commited any crime! my heart gave the lie to my tongue, when I gloried in my vices; and I trembled at the damnation I affected to brave! Oh, spare me, therefore, at least for this time, till I have served thee better. I am as yet but half a sinner.'

Charles Johnstone, *Chrysal, Or the Adventures of A Guinea*, 1760–65

The Coven

In the interval of silence, he stole forward, until the light glared full upon his eyes. At one extremity of an open space, hemmed in by the dark wall of the forest, arose a rock, bearing some rude, natural resemblance either to an altar or a pulpit, and surrounded by four blazing pines, their tops aflame, their stems untouched, like candles at an evening meeting. The mass of foliage, that had overgrown the summit of the rock, was all on fire, blazing high into the night, and fitfully illuminating the whole field. Each pendent twig and leafy festoon was in a blaze. As the red light arose and fell, a numerous congregation alternately shone forth, then disappeared in shadow, and again grew, as it were, out of the darkness, peopling the heart of the solitary woods at once.

'A grave and dark-clad company!' quoth Goodman Brown.

In truth, they were such. Among them, quivering to-and-fro, between gloom and splendor, appeared faces that would be seen, next day, at the council-board of the province, and others which, Sabbath after Sabbath, looked devoutly heavenward, and benignantly over the crowded pews, from the holiest pulpits in the land. Some affirm, that the lady of the governor was there. At least, there were high dames well known to her, and wives of honored husbands, and widows, a great multitude, and ancient maidens, all of excellent repute, and fair young girls, who trembled, lest their mothers should espy them. Either the sudden gleams of light, flashing over the obscure field, bedazzled Goodman Brown, or he recognized a score of the church-members of Salem village, famous for their especial sanctity. Good old Deacon Gookin had arrived, and waited at the skirts of that venerable saint, his revered pastor. But, irreverently consorting with these grave, reputable, and pious people, these elders of the church, these chaste dames and dewy virgins, there were men of dissolute lives and women of spotted fame, wretches given over to all mean and filthy vice, and suspected even of horrid crimes. It was strange to see, that the good shrank not from the wicked, nor were the sinners abashed by the saints. Scattered, also, among their pale-faced enemies, were the Indian priests, or powows, who had often scared their native forest with more hideous incantations than any known to English witchcraft.

'But, where is Faith?' thought Goodman Brown; and, as hope came into his heart, he trembled.

Another verse of the hymn arose, a slow and mournful strain, such as the pious love, but joined to words which expressed all that our nature can conceive of sin, and darkly hinted at far more. Unfathomable to mere mortals is the lore of fiends. Verse after verse was sung, and still the chorus of the desert swelled between, like the deepest tone of a mighty organ. And, with the final peal of that dreadful anthem, there came a sound, as if the roaring wind, the rushing streams, the howling beasts, and every other voice of the unconverted wilderness, were mingling and according with the voice of guilty man, in homage to the prince of all.

The four blazing pines threw up a loftier flame, and obscurely discovered shapes and visages of horror on the smoke-wreaths, above the impious assembly. At the same moment, the fire on the rock shot redly forth, and formed a glowing arch above its base, where now appeared a figure. With reverence be it spoken, the figure bore no slight similitude, both in garb and manner, to some grave divine of the New-England churches.

'Bring forth the converts!' cried a voice, that echoed through the field and rolled into the forest.

At the word, Goodman Brown stept forth from the shadow of the trees, and approached the congregation, with whom he felt a loathful brotherhood, by the sympathy of all that was wicked in his heart. He could have well nigh sworn, that the shape of his own dead father beckoned him to advance, looking downward from a smoke-wreath, while a woman, with dim features of despair threw out her hand to warn him back. Was it his mother? But he had no power to retreat one step, nor to resist, even in thought, when the minister and good old Deacon Gookin seized his arms, and led him to the blazing rock. Thither came also the slender form of a veiled female, led between Goody Cloyse, that pious teacher of the catechism, and Martha Carrier, who had received the devil's promise to be queen of hell. A rampant hag was she! And there stood the proselytes, beneath the canopy of fire.

'Welcome, my children,' said the dark figure, 'to the communion of your race! Ye have found, thus young, your nature and your destiny. My children, look behind you!'

They turned; and flashing forth, as it were, in a sheet of flame, the fiend-worshippers were seen; the smile of welcome gleamed darkly on every visage.

'There,' resumed the sable form, 'are all whom ye have reverenced from youth. Ye deemed them holier than yourselves, and shrank from your own sin, contrasting it with their lives of righteousness, and prayerful aspirations heavenward. Yet, here are they all, in my worshipping assembly! This night it shall be granted you to know their secret deeds; how hoary-bearded elders of the church have whispered wanton words to the young maids of their households; how many a woman, eager for widow's weeds, has given her husband a drink at bed-time, and let him sleep his last sleep in her bosom; how beardless youths have made haste to inherit their fathers' wealth; and how fair damsels – blush not, sweet ones! – have dug little graves in the garden, and bidden me, the sole guest, to an infant's funeral. By the sympathy of your human hearts for sin, ye shall scent out all the places – whether in church, bed-chamber, street, field, or forest – where crime has been committed, and shall exult to behold the whole earth one stain of guilt, one mighty blood-spot. Far more than this! It shall be yours to penetrate, in every bosom, the deep mystery of sin, the fountain of all wicked arts, and which inexhaustibly supplies more evil impulses than human power – than my power, at its utmost! – can make manifest in deeds. And now, my children, look upon each other.'

They did so; and, by the blaze of the hell-kindled torches, the wretched man beheld his Faith, and the wife her husband, trembling before that unhallowed altar.

'Lo! there ye stand, my children,' said the figure, in a deep and solemn tone, almost sad, with its despairing awfulness, as if his once angelic nature could yet mourn for our miserable race. 'Depending upon one another's hearts, ye had still hoped, that virtue were not all a dream. Now are ye undeceived! Evil is the nature of mankind. Evil must be your only happiness. Welcome, again, my children, to the communion of your race!'

'Welcome!' repeated the fiend-worshippers, in one cry of despair and triumph.

Nathaniel Hawthorne, 'Young Goodman Brown', 1835

'Les Litanies de Satan'

Ô toi, le plus savant et le plus beau des Anges,
Dieu trahi par le sort et privé de louanges,

Ô Satan, prends pitié de ma longue misère!

Ô Prince de l'exil, à qui l'on a fait tort,
Et qui, vaincu, toujours te redresses plus fort,

Ô Satan, prends pitié de ma longue misère!

Toi qui sais tout, grand roi des choses souterraines,
Guérisseur familier des angoisses humaines,

Ô Satan, prends pitié de ma longue misère!

Toi qui, même aux lépreux, aus parias maudits,
Enseignes par l'amour le goût du Paradis,

Ô Satan, prends pitié de ma longue misère!

Ô toi qui de la Mort, ta vieille et forte amante,
Engendras l'Espérance, – une folle charmante!

Ô Satan, prends pitié de ma longue misère!

Toi quis fais au proscrit ce regard calme et haut
Qui damne tout un peuple autour d'un échafaud,

Ô Satan, prends pitié de ma longue misère!

Toi qui sais en quels coins des terres envieuses
La Dieu jaloux cacha les pierres précieuses,

Ô Satan, prends pitié de ma longue misère!

Toi dont l'œil clair connaît les profonds arsenaux
Où dort enseveli le peuple des métaux,

Ô Satan, prends pitié de ma longue misère!

Toi dont la large main cache les précipices
Au somnambule errant au bord des édifices,

Ô Satan, prends pitié de ma longue misère!

Toi qui, magiquement, assouplis les vieux os
De l'ivrogne attardé foulé par les chevaux,

Ô Satan, prends pitié de ma longue misère!

Toi qui, pour consoler l'homme frêle qui souffre,
Nous appris à mêler le salpêtre et le soufre,

Ô Satan, prends pitié de ma longue misère!

Toi qui poses ta marque, ô complice subtil,
Sur le front du Crésus impitoyable et vil,

Ô Satan, prends pitié de ma longue misère!

Toi qui mets dans les yeux et dans le cœur des filles
Le culte de la plaie et l'amour des guenilles,

Ô Satan, prends pitié de ma longue misère!

Bâton des exilés, lampe des inventeurs,
Confesseur des pendus et des conspirateurs,

Ô Satan, prends pitié de ma longue misère!

Père adoptif de ceux qu'en sa noire colère
Du paradis terrestre a chassés Dieu le Père,

Ô Satan, prends pitié de ma longue misère!

PRIÈRE

Gloire et louange à toi, Satan, dans les hauteurs
Du Ciel, où tu régnas, et dans les profondeurs
De l'Enfer, où, vaincu, tu rêves en silence!
Fais que mon âme un jour, sous l'Arbre de Science,
Près de toi se repose, à l'heure où sur ton front
Comme un Temple nouveau ses rameaux s'épandront!

Charles Baudelaire, *Les Fleurs du Mal*, 1857

Glimpses of the Yezidis

As night advanced, those who had assembled – they must now have amounted to nearly five thousand persons – lighted torches, which they carried with them as they wandered through the forest. The effect was magical; the varied groups could be faintly distinguished through the darkness; men hurrying to and fro; women, with their children, seated on the house-tops; and crowds gathering round the pedlars who exposed their wares for sale in the court-yard. Thousands of lights were reflected in the fountains and streams, glimmered amongst the foliage of the trees, and danced in the distance. As I was gazing on this extraordinary scene, the hum of human voices was suddenly hushed, and a strain, solemn and melancholy, arose from the valley. It resembled some majestic chant which years before I had listened to in the cathedral of a distant land. Music so pathetic and so sweet I had never before heard in the East. The voices of men and women were blended in harmony with the soft notes of many flutes. At measured intervals the song was broken by the loud crash of cymbals and tambourines; and those who were without the precincts of the tomb then joined in the melody . . .

The Yezidis recognise one Supreme Being; but, as far as I could learn, they do not offer up any direct prayer or sacrifice to him. Sheikh Nasr endeavoured to evade my questions on the subject; and appeared to shun, with superstitious awe, every topic connected with the existence and attributes of the Deity. The common Mohammedan forms of expression – half oath, half ejaculation – are nevertheless frequently in the mouths of the people, but probably from mere habit. The name of the Devil is, however, never mentioned; and any allusion to it by others so vexes and irritates them, that it is said they have put to death persons who have wantonly outraged their feelings by its use. So far is their dread of offend-ing the Evil Spirit carried, that they carefully avoid every expression which may resemble in sound the name of Satan, or the Arabic word for 'accursed.' When they speak of the Devil, they do so with reverence, as *Melek el Kout*, the mighty angel.

Sheikh Nasr distinctly admitted that they possessed a bronze or copper figure of a bird, which, however, he was careful in explaining was only looked upon as a symbol, or banner, of the house of Hussein Bey and not as an idol. There are four of these figures. One always remains with the great Sheikh, and is carried with him wherever he may journey. When deputies are sent to any distance to collect money for the support of the tomb and the priests, they are furnished with one of these images, which is shown to those amongst whom they go as an authority for their mission. This symbol is called the Melek Taous (King Peacock), and is held in great reverence.

On a subsequent occasion, when travelling in the district of Redwan with Cawal Yusuf, one of the principal priests of the Yezidis, I had an opportunity of seeing this mysterious figure. The Cawals who are sent yearly by Hussein Bey and Sheikh Nasr to instruct the Yezidis in their faith, and to collect the revenues of their chief, and of the tomb of Sheikh Adi, were in that district. On these visits they carry with them the Melek Taous. I asked Cawal Yusuf to permit me to see it. He at once acceded to my request, and the other Cawals and the elders offering no objection, I was conducted with much mystery into an inner room of the house of the chief of the village in which the brazen peacock was deposited. It was some time before my eyes had been sufficiently accustomed to the dim light to distinguish an object from which a large red coverlet had been raised on my entry. The Cawals drew near with every sign of respect, bowing and kissing the corner of the cloth on which it was placed. A stand of bright copper or brass, in shape like the candlesticks in common use in Mosul and Baghdad, was surmounted by the rude image of a bird in the same metal, more like an Indian or Mexican idol than a peacock. Its peculiar workmanship indicated some antiquity, but I could see no traces of inscription upon it. Before it stood a copper bowl to receive contributions, and a bag to contain the image and stand, which takes to pieces, when carried from place to place. The Yezidis declare that, notwithstanding the frequent wars and massacres to which they have been exposed, and the plunder and murder of their priests during their journeys, no Melek Taous has ever fallen into the hands of the Mohammedans.

The Yezidis believe Satan to be the chief of the Angelic host, now suffering punishment for his rebellion against the divine will; but still all-powerful, and to be restored hereafter to his high estate in the celestial hierarchy. He must be conciliated and reverenced, they say; for as he now has the means of doing evil to mankind, so will he hereafter have the power of rewarding them. Next to Satan, but inferior to him in might and wisdom, are seven archangels, who exercise a great influence over the world; they are Gabrail, Michail, Raphail, Azrail, Dedrail, Azrapheel, and Shemkeel. Christ, according to the Yezidis, was also a great angel, who had taken the form of man. He did not die on the cross, but ascended to heaven.

They hold the Old Testament in great reverence, and believe in the cosmogony of Genesis, the Deluge, and other events recorded in the Bible. They do not reject the New Testament, nor the Koran; but consider them less entitled to their veneration. Still they always select passages from the latter for their tombs and holy places; but this may be done to preserve them from violation and defacement by the Mohammedans. Mohammed they look upon as a prophet; as they do Abraham and the patriarchs.

They believe that Christ will come to govern the world, but that, after him, Sheikh (the Imaum) Mehdi will appear, to whom will be given special jurisdiction over those speaking the Kurdish language, including the Yezidis. This appears to be a modern interpolation in their creed; perhaps invented to conciliate the Mohammedans. All who go to heaven must first pass an expiatory period in hell, but no one will be punished eternally. Mohammedans they exclude from all future life, but not Christians. This may have been said to me to avoid giving offence . . .

I was awakened in the afternoon by that shrill cry of the women, which generally announces some happy event. The youthful chief entered soon afterwards, followed by a long retinue. It was evident, from the smile upon his features that he had joyful news to communicate. He seated himself on my carpet, and thus addressed me:– 'O Bey, your presence has brought happiness on our house. At your hands we receive nothing but good. We are all your servants; and, praise be to the Highest! in this house another servant has been born to you. The child is yours; he is our first-born, and he will grow up under your shadow. Let him receive his name from you, and be hereafter under your protection.' The assembly joined in the request, and protested that this event, so interesting to all the tribe, was solely to be attributed to my fortunate visit. I was not quite aware of the nature of the ceremony, if any, in which I might be expected to join on naming the new-born chief. Notwithstanding my respect and esteem for the Yezidis, I could not but admit that there were some doubts as to the propriety of their tenets and form of worship; and I was naturally anxious to ascertain the amount of responsibility which I might incur, in standing godfather to a devil-worshipping baby.

Austen Henry Layard, *Nineveh and Its Remains*, 1849

'The Devil's Sooty Brother'

A disabled soldier had nothing to live on, and did not know how to get on. So he went out into the forest, and when he had walked for a short time, he met a little man who was, however, the Devil. The little man said to him, 'What ails you, you seem so very sorrowful?' Then the soldier said, 'I am hungry, but have no money.' The Devil said, 'If you hire yourself to me, and be my serving-man, you shall have enough for all your life. You shall serve me for seven years, and after that you shall again be free. But one thing I must tell you, and that is, you must not wash, comb, or trim yourself, or cut your hair or your nails, or wipe the water from your eyes.' The soldier said, 'All right, if there is no help for it,' and went off with the little man, who straightway led him down into hell. Then he told him what he had to do, he was to poke the fire under the kettles wherein the hell-broth was stewing, keep the house clean, drive all the sweepings behind the doors, and see that everything was in order, but if he once peeped into the kettles, it would go ill with him. The soldier said, 'Good, I will take care.' And then the old Devil went out again on his wanderings, and the soldier entered upon his new duties, made the fire, and swept the dirt well behind the doors, just as he had been bidden. When the old Devil came back again, he looked to see if all had been done, appeared satisfied, and went forth a second time. The soldier now took a good look on every side; the kettles were standing all round hell with a mighty fire below them, and inside they were boiling and sputtering. He would have given anything to look inside them, if the Devil had not so particularly forbidden him: at last, he could no longer restrain himself, and slightly raised the lid of the first kettle, and peeped in, and there he saw his former corporal shut in. 'Aha, old bird!' said he. 'Do I meet you here? You once had me in your power, now I have you,' and he quickly let the lid fall, poked the fire, and added a fresh log. After that, he went to the second kettle, raised its lid also a little, and peeped in; his former ensign was inside that. 'Aha, old bird, so I find you here! You once had me in your power, now I have you.' He closed the lid again, and fetched yet another log to make it really hot. Then he wanted to see who might be shut up in the third kettle – it was actually a general. 'Aha, old bird, do I meet you here? Once you had me in your power, now I have you,' and he fetched the bellows and made hell-fire flare well up under him. So he did his work seven years in hell, did not wash, comb, or trim himself, or cut his hair or his nails or wash the water out of his eyes, and the seven years seemed so short to him that he thought he had only been half a year. Now when the time had fully gone by, the Devil came and said, 'Well Hans, what have you done?' 'I have poked the fire under the kettles, and I have swept all the dirt well behind the doors.'

'But you have peeped into the kettles as well; it is lucky for you that you added fresh logs to them, or else your life would have been forfeited; now that your time is up, will you go home again?' 'Yes,' said the soldier, 'I should very much like to see what my father is doing at home.' The Devil said, 'In order that you may receive the wages you have earned, go and fill your knapsack full of the sweepings, and take it home with you. You must go unwashed and uncombed, with long hair on your head and beard, and with uncut nails and dim eyes, and when you are asked whence you came, you must say, "From hell," and when you are asked who you are, you are to say, "The Devil's sooty brother, and my King as well."' The soldier held his peace, and did as the Devil bade him, but he was not at all satisfied with his wages. Then as soon as he was up in the forest again, he took his knapsack from his back, to empty it, but on opening it, the sweepings had become pure gold. 'I should never have expected that,' said he, and was well pleased, and entered the town. The landlord was standing in front of the inn, and when he saw the soldier approaching, he was terrified, because Hans looked so horrible, worse than a scare-crow. He called to him and asked, 'Whence comest thou?' 'From hell.' 'Who art thou?' 'The Devil's sooty brother, and my King as well.' Then the host would not let him enter, but when Hans showed him the gold, he came and unlatched the door himself. Hans then ordered the best room and attendance, ate, and drank his fill, but neither washed nor combed himself as the Devil had bidden him, and at last lay down to sleep. But the knapsack full of gold remained before the eyes of the landlord, and left him no peace, and during the night he crept in and stole it away. Next morning, however, when Hans got up and wanted to pay the landlord and travel further, behold, his knapsack was gone! But he soon composed himself and thought, 'Thou hast been unfortunate from no fault of thine own,' and straightway went back again to hell, complained of his misfortune to the old Devil, and begged for his help. The Devil said, 'Seat yourself, I will wash, comb, and trim you, cut your hair and nails, and wash your eyes for you,' and when he had done with him, he gave him the knapsack back again full of sweepings, and said, 'Go and tell the landlord that he must return you your money, or else I will come and fetch him, and he shall poke the fire in your place.' Hans went up and said to the landlord, 'Thou hast stolen my money; if thou dost not return it, thou shalt go down to hell in my place, and wilt look as horrible as I.' Then the landlord gave him his money, and more besides, only begging him to keep it secret, and Hans was now a rich man.

He set out on his way home to his father, bought himself a shabby smock-frock to wear, and strolled about making music, for he had learned to do that while he was with the Devil in hell. There was, however, an old King in that country, before whom he had to play, and the King was so delighted with his playing, that he promised him his eldest daughter in marriage. But when she heard that she was to be married to a common fellow in a smock-frock, she said, 'Rather than do it, I would go into the deepest water,' and then the King gave him the youngest, who was quite willing to do it to please her father, and thus the Devil's sooty brother got the king's daughter, and when the aged King died, the whole kingdom likewise.

From *Grimm's Household Tales*, trans. from the German
by Margaret Hunt, 1884

The Devil's Disciple

RICHARD: Essie: did you ever hear of a person called the devil?

ANDERSON [*revolted*]: Shame on you, sir, with a mere child —

RICHARD: By your leave, Minister: I do not interfere with your sermons: do not you interrupt mine. [*To Essie*] Do you know what they call me, Essie?

ESSIE: Dick.

RICHARD [*amused: patting her on the shoulder*]: Yes, Dick; but something else too. They call me the Devil's Disciple.

ESSIE: Why do you let them?

RICHARD [*seriously*]: Because it's true. I was brought up in the other service; but I knew from the first that the Devil was my natural master and captain and friend. I saw that he was in the right, and that the world cringed to his conqueror only through fear. I prayed secretly to him; and he comforted me, and saved me from having my spirit broken in this house of children's tears. I promised him my soul, and swore an oath that I would stand up for him in this world and stand by him in the next. [*Solemnly*] That promise and that oath made a man of me. From this day this house is his home; and no child shall cry in it: this hearth is his altar; and no soul shall ever cower over it in the dark evenings and be afraid. Now [*turning forcibly on the rest*] which of you good men will take this child and rescue her from the house of the devil?

JUDITH [*coming to Essie and throwing a protecting arm about her*]: I will. You should be burnt alive.

ESSIE: But I don't want to.

George Bernard Shaw, *The Devil's Disciple*, 1901

The Black Mass

'But what is it they burn to stink like that?'

'Rue, henbane and thorn-apple leaves, dried nightshade and myrtle; they are perfumes beloved of Satan, our master!'

She said this in the gutteral, unnatural voice that on certain emotional occasions characterized her.

He looked hard at her; her face was pale, her teeth clenched, the lids flickering over her stormy eyes.

'Here he is!' she cried suddenly, while the women hurried across to kneel at the chairs in front.

Preceded by two acolytes and wearing a scarlet biretta decorated with a pair of bison's horns of red material, the Canon entered.

Durtal watched him as he advanced to the altar. He was tall, but ill proportioned, all head and shoulders; a bald forehead ran down in one unbroken line to a straight nose; lips and cheeks showed the harsh, dry stubble common to ecclesiastics who have shaved for years; the features were irregular and coarse; the eyes, like apple-pips, small, black, and close together either side the nose, had a phosphorescent glitter. Taken all together, the expression was thoroughly bad and untrustworthy, but full of fire and energy, and those hard, steady eyes had none of the sly, shifty look Durtal had expected to see.

He bowed solemnly before the altar, mounted the steps and began his mass.

Durtal then saw that, under his sacrificial robes, he was naked. The chasuble was of the usual shape, but of a dark blood-red colour, and in the middle, within a triangle, surrounded by a tangled growth of meadow-saffron, sorrel-apple and spurge, a black he-goat stood, butting with its horns.

Docre made the genuflexions and bowings, less or more profound, as specified in the ritual; the servers kneeling intoned the Latin responses in clear, ringing voices, dwelling long on the final syllables of the words.

'Why, it is just an ordinary low mass,' Durtal observed to Mme. Chantelouve.

She shook her head. In fact, at that moment the two servers passed behind the altar and brought back with them, the one copper chafing dishes, the other small censers, which they distributed among the congregation. Soon all the women were wrapped in clouds of smoke; some of them dropped their heads over the chafing-dishes and eagerly inhaled the fumes, emitting hoarse gasps.

At this point the office was suspended. The priest descended the altar steps backwards and in a quavering, high-pitched voice cried:

'Lord of evil, thou who dost reward sins and heinous vices, Satan, it is thou whom we adore, God of reason, God of Justice!

'Suzerain of the scornful, Defence of the down-trodden. Depositary of cherished hatreds, thou only dost make fertile the brain of the man crushed by injustice; thou dost whisper in his ears ideas of long-meditated vengeance and sure retaliation! thou dost incite him to murder and give him the exuberant joy of reprisals inflicted, the glorious intoxication of punishments he has accomplished and tears he has caused to flow!

'Master, thy faithful servants implore thee on their knees. They beseech thee grant them assurance of those sweet sins Justice takes no heed of; they beseech thee assist the spells whose unrecognised traces baffle human reason. Fame, fortune, power they ask of thee, King of the disinherited whom the inexorable Father drove forth from heaven!'

Then Docre got to his feet and, with outstretched arms, in a ringing voice of hate vociferated:

'And Thou, Thou, whom by right of my priesthood I force to come down and enter into this host and become transubstantiated in this bread . . .'

Then followed a litany of insults, of invective that was almost insane in its vileness and its hate.

'Amen,' shrilled the clear voice of the acolytes.

Durtal, listening to this torrent of blasphemies and abuse, was astounded at the foul profanity of the priest. A silence ensued after his ravings; the Chapel was misty with the smoke of censers. The women, hitherto silent stirred restlessly when, mounting again to the altar, the Canon turned towards them and blessed them with a sweeping gesture of the left hand.

And suddenly the servers tinkled little bells. This seemed to be a signal; women fell to the floor and rolled on the carpets. One, her eyes suddenly convulsed in a horrible squint, clucked like a hen, then, fallen dumb, gaped with wide open jaws, the tongue retracted till its tip touched the palate high up; another, her face puffed and livid, pupils dilated, lolled back her head on her shoulders, then stiffened in a sudden spasm and tore at her bosom with her nails; another, grimacing horribly, shot out a white tongue, which she could not draw in again, from a bleeding mouth guarded by a portcullis of red teeth.

At that moment Durtal stood up to get a better view and could plainly see and hear the Canon.

He was gazing at the Crucifix surmounting the tabernacle and with outspread arms was belching forth appalling outrages, using what strength was left him to bellow a torrent of obscenities which would have shamed a drunken gangster. One of the servers knelt before him, turning his back on the altar. A shudder ran through the priest's limbs. Solemnly, but in a quavering voice, he pronounced the words: *Hoc est enim corpus meum*, then instead of genuflecting after the consecration before the Sacred Body, he faced round to the congregation and stood there bloated, haggard and dripping with sweat.

He was staggering between the two acolytes, while the host he held in his hands tumbled, defiled and filthy, on the altar steps.

Then Durtal felt a shudder run through him, for a wind of madness shook the assemblage. The breath of high hysteria succeeded the profane outrage and bowed the women's heads; they fell upon the Eucharistic bread, clawed at it and tearing off fragments, ate this filth.

One woman burst out in a strident laugh and insanely yelled: 'Father, Father!' An old beldam wrenched out handfuls of her hair, leapt high in the air, spun round on her heels, stood on one leg and collapsed beside a girl who, crouching against one wall, was writhing in convulsions, slavering at the mouth, weeping as she spat out hideous blasphemies. And Durtal, appalled, saw through the smoke as in a fog the red horns on Docre's head.

Then, at the back of the Chapel in the shadows a little girl, who had not stirred till that moment, reeled forward and began to howl like a rabid bitch!

Overwhelmed with disgust and almost stifled, Durtal longed to escape. He looked for Hyacinthe, but she was not there. At last he saw her beside the Canon; stepping over the bodies on the carpets, he approached her.

With quivering nostrils she was inhaling the odours of the perfumes.

'The savour of the Witches' Sabbath!' she said to him in a low voice through clenched teeth.

'Are you coming?' he said sharply.

J.-K. Huysmans, *Là-bas*, 1891; trans. A. Allison, 1930

Margarita Acts Hostess at Satan's Ball

Margarita was standing at the head of a vast carpeted staircase stretching downwards in front of her. At the bottom, so far away that she seemed to be looking at it through the wrong end of a telescope, she could see a vast hall with an absolutely immense fireplace, into whose cold, black maw one could easily have driven a five-ton lorry. The hall and the staircase, bathed in painfully bright light, were empty. Then Margarita heard the sound of distant trumpets. For some minutes they stood motionless.

'Where are the guests?' Margarita asked Koroviev.

'They will be here at any moment, your majesty. There will be no lack of them. I confess I'd rather be sawing logs than receiving them here on this platform.'

'Sawing logs?' said the garrulous cat. 'I'd rather be a tram-conductor and there's no job worse than that.'

'Everything must be prepared in advance, your majesty,' explained Koroviev, his eye glittering behind the broken lens of his monocle. 'There can be nothing more embarrassing than for the first guest to wait around uncomfortably, not knowing what to do, while his lawful consort curses him in a whisper for arriving too early. We cannot allow that at our ball, queen Margot.'

'I should think not,' said the cat.

'Ten seconds to midnight,' said Koroviev, 'it will begin in a moment.'

Those ten seconds seemed unusually long to Margarita. They had obviously passed but absolutely nothing seemed to be happening. Then there was a crash from below in the enormous fireplace and out of it sprang a gallows with a half-decayed corpse bouncing on its arm. The corpse jerked itself loose from the rope, fell to the ground and stood up as a dark, handsome man in tailcoat and lacquered pumps. A small, rotting coffin then slithered out of the fireplace, its lid flew off and another corpse jumped out. The handsome man stepped gallantly towards it and offered his bent arm. The second corpse turned into a nimble little woman in black slippers and black feathers on her head and then man and woman together hurried up the staircase.

'The first guests!' exclaimed Koroviev. 'Monsieur Jacques and his wife. Allow me to introduce to you, your majesty, a most interesting man. A confirmed forger, a traitor to his country but no mean alchemist. He was famous,' Koroviev whispered into Margarita's ear, 'for having poisoned the king's mistress. Not everybody can boast of that, can they? See how good-looking he is!'

Turning pale and open-mouthed with shock, Margarita looked down and saw gallows and coffin disappear through a side door in the hall.

'We are delighted!' the cat roared to Monsieur Jacques as he mounted the steps.

Just then a headless, armless skeleton appeared in the fireplace below, fell down and turned into yet another man in a tailcoat.

Monsieur Jacques' wife had by now reached the head of the staircase where she knelt down, pale with excitement, and kissed Margarita's foot.

'Your majesty . . .' murmured Madame Jacques.

'Her majesty is charmed!' shouted Koroviev.

'Your majesty . . .' said Monsieur Jacques in a low voice.

'We are charmed!' intoned the cat. The young men beside Azazello, smiling lifeless but welcoming smiles, were showing Monsieur and Madame Jacques to one side, where they were offered goblets of champagne by the Negro attendants. The single man in tails came up the staircase at a run.

'Count Robert,' Koroviev whispered to Margarita. 'An equally interesting character. Rather amusing, your majesty – the case is reversed: he was the queen's lover and poisoned his own wife.'

'We are delighted, Count,' cried Behemoth.

One after another three coffins bounced out of the fireplace, splitting and breaking open as they fell, then someone in a black cloak who was immediately stabbed in the back by the next person to come down the chimney. There was a muffled shriek. When an almost totally decomposed corpse emerged from the fireplace, Margarita frowned and a hand, which seemed to be Natasha's, offered her a flacon of sal volatile.

The staircase began to fill up. Now on almost every step there were men in tailcoats accompanied by naked women who only differed in the colour of their shoes and the feathers on their heads.

Margarita noticed a woman with the downcast gaze of a nun hobbling towards her, thin, shy, hampered by a strange wooden boot on her left leg and a broad green kerchief round her neck.

'Who's that woman in green?' Margarita enquired.

'A most charming and respectable lady,' whispered Koroviev. 'Let me introduce you – Signora Toffana. She was extremely popular among the young and attractive ladies of Naples and Palermo, especially among those who were tired of their husbands. Women do get bored with their husbands, your majesty . . .'

'Yes,' replied Margarita dully, smiling to two men in evening dress who were bowing to kiss her knee and her foot.

'Well,' Koroviev managed to whisper to Margarita as he simultaneously cried: 'Duke! A glass of champagne? We are charmed! . . . Well, Signora Toffana sympathised with those poor women and sold them some liquid in a bladder. The woman poured the liquid into her husband's soup, who ate it, thanked her for it and felt splendid. However, after a few hours he would begin to feel a terrible thirst, then lay down on his bed and a day later another beautiful Neapolitan lady was as free as air.'

'What's that on her leg?' asked Margarita, without ceasing to offer her hand to the guests who had overtaken Signora Toffana on the way up. 'And why is she wearing green round her neck? Has she a withered neck?'

'Charmed, Prince!' shouted Koroviev as he whispered to Margarita: 'She has a beautiful neck, but something unpleasant happened to her in prison. The thing on her leg, your majesty, is a Spanish boot and she wears a scarf because when her jailers found out that about five hundred ill-matched husbands had been dispatched from Naples and Palermo for ever, they strangled Signora Toffana in a rage.'

'How happy I am, your majesty, that I have the great honour . . .' whispered Signora Toffana in a nun-like voice, trying to fall on one knee but hindered by the Spanish boot. Koroviev and Behemoth helped Signora Toffana to rise.

'I am delighted,' Margarita answered her as she gave her hand to the next arrival.

People were now mounting the staircase in a flood. Margarita ceased to notice the arrivals in the hall. Mechanically she raised and lowered her hand, bared her teeth in a smile for each new guest. The landing behind her was buzzing with voices, and music like the waves of the sea floated out from the ballrooms.

'Now this woman is a terrible bore.' Koroviev no longer bothered to whisper but shouted it aloud, certain that no one could hear his voice over the hubbub. 'She loves coming to a ball because it gives her a chance to complain about her handkerchief.'

Among the approaching crowd Margarita's glance picked out the woman at whom Koroviev was pointing. She was young, about twenty, with a remarkably beautiful figure but a look of nagging reproach.

'What handkerchief?' asked Margarita.

'A maid has been assigned to her,' Koroviev explained, 'who for thirty years has been putting a handkerchief on her bedside table. It is there every morning when she wakes up. She burns it in the stove or throws it in the river but every morning it appears again beside her.'

'What handkerchief?' whispered Margarita, continuing to lower and raise her hand to the guests.

'A handkerchief with a blue border. One day when she was a waitress in a café the owner enticed her into the storeroom and nine months later she gave birth to a boy, carried him into the woods, stuffed a handkerchief into his mouth and then buried him. At the trial she said she couldn't afford to feed the child.'

'And where is the café-owner?' asked Margarita.

'But your majesty,' the cat suddenly growled, 'what has the café-owner got to do with it? It wasn't he who stifled the baby in the forest, was it?'

Without ceasing to smile and to shake hands with her right hand, she dug the sharp nails of her left hand into Behemoth's ear and whispered to the cat:

'If you butt into the conversation once more, you little horror . . .'

Behemoth gave a distinctly unfestive squeak and croaked: 'Your majesty . . . you'll make my ear swell . . . why spoil the ball with a swollen ear? I was speaking from the legal point of view . . . I'll be quiet, I promise, pretend I'm not a cat, pretend I'm a fish if you like but please let go of my ear!'

Margarita released his ear.

The woman's grim, importunate eyes looked into Margarita's:

'I am so happy, your majesty, to be invited to the great ball of the full moon.'

'And I am delighted to see you,' Margarita answered her, 'quite delighted. Do you like champagne?'

'Hurry up, your majesty!' hissed Koroviev quietly but desperately. 'You're causing a traffic-jam on the staircase.'

'Yes, I like champagne,' said the woman imploringly, and began to repeat mechanically: 'Frieda, Frieda, Frieda! My name is Frieda, your majesty!'

'Today you may get drunk, Frieda, and forget about everything,' said Margarita.

Frieda stretched out both her arms to Margarita, but Koroviev and Behemoth deftly took an arm each and whisked her off into the crowd.

By now people were advancing from below like a phalanx bent on assaulting the landing where Margarita stood. The naked women mounting the staircase between the tail-coated and white-tied men floated up in a spectrum of coloured bodies that ranged from white through olive, copper and coffee to quite black. In hair that was red, black, chestnut or flaxen, sparks flashed from precious stones. Diamond-studded orders glittered on the jackets and shirt-fronts of the men. Incessantly Margarita felt the touch of lips to her knee, incessantly she offered her hand to be kissed, her face stretched into a rigid mask of welcome.

'Charmed,' Koroviev would monotonously intone. 'We are charmed . . . her majesty is charmed . . .'

'Her majesty is charmed,' came a nasal echo from Azazello, standing behind her.

'I am charmed!' squeaked the cat.

'Madame la marquise,' murmured Koroviev, 'poisoned her father, her two brothers and two sisters for the sake of an inheritance . . . Her majesty is delighted, Mme. Minkin! . . . Ah, how pretty she is! A trifle nervous, though. Why *did* she have to burn her maid with a pair of curling-tongs? Of course, in the way she used them it was bound to be fatal . . . Her majesty is charmed! . . . Look, your majesty – the Emperor Rudolf – magician and alchemist . . . Another alchemist – he was hanged . . . Ah, there she is! What a magnificent brothel she used to keep in Strasbourg! . . . We are delighted, madame! . . . That woman over there was a Moscow dressmaker who had the brilliantly funny idea of boring two peep-holes in the wall of her fitting-room . . .'

'And didn't her lady clients know?' enquired Margarita.

'Of course, they all knew, your majesty,' replied Koroviev.

'Charmed! . . . That young man over there was a dreamer and an eccentric from childhood. A girl fell in love with him and he sold her to a brothel-keeper . . .'

On and on poured the stream from below. Its source – the huge fireplace – showed no sign of drying up. An hour passed, then another. Margarita felt her chain weighing more and more. Something odd was happening to her hand: she found she could not lift it without wincing. Koroviev's remarks ceased to interest her. She could no longer distinguish between slant-eyed Mongol faces, white faces and black faces. They all merged into a blur and the air between them seemed to be quivering. A sudden sharp pain like a needle stabbed at Margarita's right hand, and clenching her teeth she leaned her elbow on the little pedestal. A sound like the rustling of wings came from the rooms behind her as the horde of guests danced, and Margarita could feel the massive floors of marble, crystal and mosaic pulsating rhythmically.

Mikhail Bulgakov, *The Master and Margarita*; trans. Michael Glenny, 1967

The Black Sabbath

If it had been possible for any stranger to enter that locked room in the middle of his journeying they would have found his body lying there still. By no broomstick flight over the lanes of England did Gregory Persimmons attend the Witches' Sabbath, nor did he dance with other sorcerers upon some blasted heath before a goat-headed manifestation of the Accursed. But scattered far over the face of the earth, though not so far in the swiftness of interior passage, those abandoned spirits answered one another that night; and That beyond them (which some have held to be but the precipitation and tendency of their own natures, and others for the equal and perpetual co-inheritor of power and immortality with God) – That beyond them felt them and shook and replied, sustained and nourished and controlled.

After Gregory had laid himself upon the bed he made the usual attempt at excluding from the attention all his surroundings. But to-night the powerful ointment worked so swiftly upon him, stealing through all his flesh with a delicious venom and writhing itself into his blood and heart, that he had scarcely come to rest before the world was shut out. He was being made one with something beyond his consciousness; he accepted the union in a deep sigh of pleasure.

When it had approached a climax it ceased suddenly. There passed through him a sense of lightness and airy motion; his body seemed to float upwards, so unconscious had it become of the bed on which it rested. He knew now that he must begin to exercise his own intention, and in a depth beyond thought he did so. He commanded and directed himself towards the central power which awaited him. Images floated past him; for his mind, rising as it were out of the faintness which had overcome it, now began to change his experiences into such sounds and shapes as it knew; so that he at once experienced and expressed experience to himself intellectually, and could not generally separate the two. At this beginning, for example, as he lay given up to that sensation of swift and easy motion towards some still hidden moment of exquisite and destructive delight, it seemed to him that at a great distance he heard faint and lovely voices, speaking to him or to each other, and that out of him in turn went a single note of answering glee.

And now he was descending; lower and lower, into a darker and more heavy atmosphere. His intention checked his flight, and it declined almost into stillness; night was about him, and more than night, a heaviness which was like that felt in a crowd, a pressure and intent expectation of relief. As to the mind of a man in prayer might come sudden reminders of great sanctities in other places and other periods, so now to him came the consciousness, not in detail, but as achievements, of far-off masteries of things, multitudinous dedications consummating themselves in That which was already on its way. But that his body was held in a trance by the effect of the ointment, the smell of which had long since become part of his apprehension, he would have turned his head one way or the other to see or speak to those unseen companions.

Suddenly, as in an excited crowd a man may one minute be speaking and shouting to those near him, and the next, part of the general movement directed and controlled by that to which he contributes, there rose within him the sense of a vast and rapid flow, of which he was part, rushing and palpitating with desire. He desired – the heat about his heart grew stronger – to give himself out, to be one with something that should submit to him and from which he should yet draw nourishment; but something beyond imagination stupendous. He was hungry – but not for food; he was thirsty – but not for drink; he was filled with passion – but not for flesh. He expanded in the rush of an ancient desire; he longed to be married to the whole universe for a bride. His father appeared before him, senile and shivering; his wife, bewildered and broken; his son, harassed and distressed. These were his marriages, these his bridals. The bridal dance was beginning; they and he and innumerable others were moving to the wild rhythm of that aboriginal longing. Beneath all the little cares and whims of mankind the tides of that ocean swung, and those who had harnessed them and those who had been destroyed by them were mingled in one victorious catastrophe. His spirit was dancing with his peers, and yet still something in his being held back and was not melted.

There was something – from his depths he cried to his mortal mind to recall it and pass on the message – some final thing that was needed still; some offering by which he might pierce beyond this black drunkenness and achieve a higher reward. What was the sacrifice, what the oblation that was greater than the wandering and unhappy souls whose ruin he had achieved? Heat as from an immense pyre beat upon him, beat upon him with a demand for something more; he absorbed it, and yet, his ignorance striking him with fear, shrunk from its ardent passions. It was not heat only, it was sound also, a rising tumult, acclamation of shrieking voices, thunder of terrible approach. It came, it came, ecstasy of perfect mastery, marriage in hell, he who was Satan wedded to that beside which was Satan. And yet one little thing was needed and he had it not – he was an outcast for want of that one thing. He forced his interior mind to stillness for a moment only, and in that moment recollection came.

From the shadowy and forgotten world the memory of the child Adrian floated into him, and he knew that this was what was needed. All gods had their missionaries, and this god also who was himself and not himself demanded neophytes. Deeply into himself he drew that memory; he gathered up its freshness and offered it to the secret and infernal powers. Adrian was the desirable sacrifice, an unknowing initiate, a fated candidate. To this purpose the man lying still and silent on the bed, or caught up before some vast interior throne where the masters and husbands and possessors of the universe danced and saw immortal life decay before their subtle power, dedicated himself. The wraith of the child drifted into the midst of the dance, and at the moment when Adrian far away in London stirred in his sleep with a moan a like moan broke out in another chamber. For the last experience was upon the accepted devotee; there passed through him a wave of intense cold, and in every chosen spot where the ointment had been twice applied the cold concentrated and increased. Nailed, as it were, through feet and hands and head and genitals, he passed utterly into a pang that was an ecstasy beyond his dreams. He was divorced now from the universe; he was one with a rejection of all courteous and lovely things; by the oblation of the child he was made one with that which is beyond childhood and age and time – the reflection and negation of the eternity of God. He existed supernaturally, and in Hell . . .

When the dissolution of this union and the return began, he knew it as an overwhelming storm. Heat and cold, the interior and exterior world, images and wraiths, sounds and odours, warred together within him. Chaos broke upon him; he felt himself whirled away into an infinite desolation of anarchy. He strove to concentrate, now on that which was within, now on some detail of the room which was already spectrally apparent to him; but fast as he did so it was gone. Panic seized him; he would have screamed, but to scream would be to be lost. And then again the image of Adrian floated before him, and he knew that much was yet to be done. With that image in his heart, he rose slowly and through many mists to the surface of consciousness, and as it faded gradually to a name and a thought he knew that the Sabbath was over and the return accomplished.

Charles Williams, *War in Heaven*, 1930

Ten

SYMPATHY FOR
THE DEVIL

When charmed by the beauty of that viper, did it never
occur to you to change personalities with him? to feel
what it was to be a snake? to glide unsuspected in grass?
to sting, to kill at a touch; your whole beautiful body
one iridescent scabbard of death?

HERMAN MELVILLE

I feel confident I should have been a rebel Angel
had the opportunity been mine.

JOHN KEATS

The Petition of the Fallen Angels

Then I went and spoke to them all together, and they were all afraid, and fear and trembling seized them.

And they besought me to draw up a petition for them that they might find forgiveness, and to read their petition in the presence of the Lord of heaven.

For from thenceforward they could not speak (with Him) nor lift up their eyes to heaven for shame of their sins for which they had been condemned.

Then I wrote out their petition, and the prayer in regard to their spirits and their deeds individually and in regard to their requests that they should have forgiveness and length.

And I went off and sat down at the waters of Dan, in the land of Dan, to the south of the west of Hermon: I read their petition till I fell asleep.

And behold a dream came to me, and visions fell down upon me, and I saw visions of chastisement, and a voice came bidding (me) to tell it to the sons of heaven, and reprimand them.

And when I awaked, I came unto them, and they were all sitting gathered together, weeping in 'Abelsjâil, which is between Lebanon and Sênêsêr, with their faces covered.

And I recounted before them all the visions which I had seen in sleep, and I began to speak the words of righteousness, and to reprimand the heavenly Watchers.

The book of the words of righteousness, and of the reprimand of the eternal Watchers in accordance with the command of the Holy Great One in that vision.

I saw in my sleep what I will now say with a tongue of flesh and with the breath of my mouth: which the Great One has given to men to converse therewith and understand with the heart.

As He has created and given to man the power of understanding the word of wisdom, so hath He created me also and given me the power of reprimanding the Watchers, the children of heaven. I wrote out your petition, and in my vision it appeared thus, that your petition will not be granted unto you throughout all the days of eternity, and that judgement has been finally passed upon you: yea (your petition) will not be granted unto you. And from henceforth you shall not ascend into heaven unto all eternity, and in bonds of the earth the decree has gone forth to bind you for all the days of the world.

And (that) previously you shall have seen the destruction of your beloved sons and ye shall have no pleasure in them, but they shall fall before you by the sword.

And your petition on their behalf shall not be granted, nor yet on your own: even though you weep and pray and speak all the words contained in the writing which I have written.

The Book of Enoch, ed. and trans. R. H. Charles, 1912

Why Do They Blame Me?

Once some one knocked at the door of my cell, and going forth I saw one who seemed of great size and tall. Then when I enquired, 'Who art thou?' he said, 'I am Satan.' Then when I said, 'Why art thou here?' he answered, 'Why do the monks and all other Christians blame me undeservedly? Why do they curse me hourly?' Then I answered, 'Wherefore dost thou trouble them?' He said, 'I am not he who troubles them, but they trouble themselves, for I am become weak. Have they not read, "The swords of the enemy have come to an end, and thou hast destroyed the cities?" I have no longer a place, a weapon, a city. The Christians are spread everywhere, and at length the desert is filled with monks. Let them take heed to themselves, and let them not curse me undeservedly.' Then I marvelled at the grace of the Lord, and said to him: 'Thou who art ever a liar and never speakest the truth, this at length, even against thy will, thou hast truly spoken. For the coming of Christ hath made thee weak, and He hath cast thee down and stripped thee.' But he having heard the Saviour's name, and not being able to bear the burning from it, vanished.

Athanasius, *Life of St Anthony*, c.356–62 AD; trans. H. Ellershaw, 1892

'Sinne (II)'

O that I could a sinne once see!
We paint the devil foul, yet he
Hath some good in him, all agree.
Sinne is flat opposite to th' Almighty, seeing
It wants the good of *vertue*, and of *being*.

But God more care of us hath had:
If apparitions make us sad,

By sight of sinne we should grow mad.
Yet as in sleep we see foul death, and live:
So devils are our sinnes in perspective.

George Herbert (1593–1633)

Come On You Philosophers

1. Here, *King Lucifer*, pull thy Hat down over thy Eyes, lest thou shouldst see how Man will take off thy Crown away from thee, thou canst *no more* rule in Heaven; stand still a little While, we must first *view* thee, and observe what a beauteous fair Bride thou art, and whether the Filth of thy Whoredom may *not* be cleansed and washed away from thee, that thou mayest be fair again; we will a little describe thy *Chastity* and Virtue.

2. *Come on* you Philosophers, and you Lawyers and Advocates, that justify and defend King *Lucifer!* Come near and bring him to the *Bar*, whilst he has yet the *Crown upon him*, for here we will hold a *Court* of Judgment against Malefactors for him; if you can *maintain* his Cause to be right, then he shall be your King; if not, then he shall be turned out and cast down into Hell; and another shall get his royal Crown, who will *govern* better than he.

Jakob Böehme (1575–1624); trans. William Law, 1764

The Speech to the Sun

Somtimes towards *Eden* which now in his view
Lay pleasant, his grievd look he fixes sad,
Somtimes towards Heav'n and the full-blazing Sun,
Which now sat high in his Meridian Towre:
Then much revolving, thus in sighs began.
  O thou that with surpassing Glory crownd,
Look'st from thy sole Dominion like the God
Of this new World; at whose sight all the Starrs
Hide thir diminisht heads; to thee I call,
But with no friendly voice, and add thy name
O Sun, to tell thee how I hate thy beams
That bring to my remembrance from what state
I fell, how glorious once above thy Spheare;
Till Pride and worse Ambition threw me down

Warring in Heav'n against Heav'ns matchless King:
Ah wherefore? he deservd no such return
From mee, whom he created what I was
In that bright eminence, and with his good
Upbraided none; nor was his service hard.
What could be less then to afford him praise,
The easiest recompence, and pay him thanks,
How due! yet all his good prov'd ill in me,
And wrought but malice; lifted up so high
I sdeind subjection, and thought one step higher
Would set me highest, and in a moment quit
The debt immense of endless gratitude,
So burdensom, still paying, still to ow;
Forgetful what from him I still receivd,
And understood not that a grateful mind
By owing owes not, but still pays, at once
Indebted and discharg'd; what burden then?
O had his powerful Destiny ordaind
Mee some inferiour Angel, I had stood
Then happie; no unbounded hope had rais'd
Ambition. Yet why not? som other Power
As great might have aspir'd, and mee though mean
Drawn to his part: but other Powers as great
Fell not, but stand unshak'n, from within
Or from without, to all temptations armd.
Hadst thou the same free Will and Power to stand?
Thou hadst: whom hast thou then or what to accuse,
But Heav'ns free Love dealt equally to all?
Be then his Love accurst, since love or hate,
To mee alike, it deals eternal woe.
Nay curst be thou; since against his thy will
Chose freely what it now so justly rues.
Mee miserable! which way shall I flie
Infinite wrauth, and infinite despaire?
Which way I flie is Hell; my self am Hell;
And in the lowest deep a lower deep
Still threatning to devour me op'ns wide,
To which the Hell I suffer seems a Heav'n.
O then at last relent: is there no place
Left for Repentance, none for Pardon left?
None left but by submission; and that word
Disdain forbids me, and my dread of shame

Among the Spirits beneath, whom I seduc'd
With other promises and other vaunts
Then to submit, boasting I could subdue
Th' Omnipotent. Ay me, they little know
How dearly I abide that boast so vaine,
Under what torments inwardly I groane:
While they adore me on the Throne of Hell,
With Diadem and Scepter high advanc't
The lower still I fall, onely supream
In miserie: such joy Ambition findes.
But say I could repent and could obtaine
By Act of Grace my former state; how soon
Would highth recall high thoughts, how soon unsay
What feignd submission swore: ease would recant
Vows made in pain, as violent and void.
For never can true reconcilement grow
Where wounds of deadly hate have peirc't so deep:
Which would but lead me to a worse relapse,
And heavier fall: so should I purchase deare
Short intermission bought with double smart.
This knows my punisher; therefore as farr
From granting hee, as I from begging peace:
All hope excluded thus, behold in stead
Of us out-cast, exil'd, his new delight,
Mankind created, and for him this World.
So farwel Hope, and with Hope farwel Fear,
Farwel Remorse: all Good to me is lost;
Evil be thou my Good; by thee at least
Divided Empire with Heav'ns King I hold,
By thee, and more then half perhaps will reigne;
As Man ere long, and this new World shall know.

John Milton, Paradise Lost, Book IV, 1667

Sympathy Denied

He sees the Sun; it makes him think of his own position. He spies on the human lovers; and states his position. In Book IX he journeys round the whole earth; it reminds him of his own position. The point need not be laboured. Adam, though locally confined to a small park on a small planet, has interests that embrace 'all the choir of heaven and all the furniture of earth.' Satan has been in the Heaven of Heavens and in the abyss of Hell, and surveyed all that lies between them, and in that whole immensity has found only one thing that interests Satan. It may be said that Adam's situation made it easier for him, than for Satan, to let his mind roam. But that is just the point. Satan's monomaniac concern with himself and his supposed rights and wrongs is a necessity of the Satanic predicament. Certainly, he has no choice. He has chosen to have no choice. He has wished to 'be himself', and to be in himself and for himself, and his wish has been granted. The Hell he carries with him is, in one sense, a Hell of infinite boredom. Satan ... is interesting to read about; but Milton makes plain the blank uninterestingness of *being* Satan.

To admire Satan, then, is to give one's vote not only for a world of misery, but also for a world of lies and propaganda, of wishful thinking, of incessant autobiography. Yet the choice is possible. Hardly a day passes without some slight movement towards it in each one of us. That is what makes *Paradise Lost* so serious a poem. The thing is possible, and the exposure of it is resented. Where *Paradise Lost* is not loved, it is deeply hated. As Keats said more rightly than he knew, 'there is death' in Milton. We have all skirted the Satanic island closely enough to have motives for wishing to evade the full impact of the poem. For, I repeat, the thing is possible; and after a certain point it is prized ... Satan *wants* to go on being Satan. That is the real meaning of his choice 'Better to reign in Hell, than serve in Heav'n.' Some, to the very end, will think this a fine thing to say; others will think that it fails to be roaring farce only because it spells agony. On the level of literary criticism the matter cannot be argued further. Each to his taste.

C. S. Lewis, *A Preface to Paradise Lost*, 1942

Grand Fellows

Certainly there is a dreary, melancholic grandeur, a fine overwhelming association, with ruined greatness. You see millions of heroic angels, faithfully adhering to their leader, wither'd, dusky, singed, scarred! – the consequences of their dreadful defeat. You see them drawn up, in endless line, illumined by the gleaming fiery flame of glimmering hell, and the recollection of their former glory, when virtuous, weighs down your faculties, when you reflect on their present misery. You admire their faith, their firmness, their adherence; you lament with their ingratitude, their infatuation, but it is the faith of bad minds, and yet, such is the power of their qualities, that it is only on reflection the perversion of their powers and the justness of their present state have any strength to cool your enthusiasm. You weep with Satan, at their hopeless, endless prospect, yet you must acknowledge the justice.

Satan! grand, terrific, revengeful, daring Satan! What terms can express the admiration, the enthusiasm, the grief, the detestation of thy diabolic and tremendous Soul. Rebellion seems sanctioned by such a Leader, and fit for such followers in their blaze of enthusiasm. You would glory to be of such a band, and it is only when you recollect the attempt and consider against Whom, that you tremble at your temerity and suffer your feelings to evaporate with almost an unwilling sullenness. To the energy of perseverance, to the firmness of an unsubdued mind, dark grandeur of crime surrounds them like an atmosphere and adds a terrific vigor to their fiery desperation.

Certainly it must be acknowledged that tho' the Devils never break out in absolute impiety, yet upon the whole, one's moral feeling is weakened. Their enthusiasm seizes daring minds; you would rather dwell with such grand fellows than hymn with 'evertuned harps.' You ought not to feel so, but do you not?

From the *Diary* of Benjamin Robert Haydon, 30 August 1813

The Worst of Punishments

The Devil it is said, before his fall, as an angel of the highest rank and the most splendid accomplishments, placed his peculiar delight in doing good. But the inflexible grandeur of his spirit, mailed and nourished by the consciousness of the purest and loftiest designs, was so secure from the assault of any gross or common torments that God was considerably puzzled to invent what he considered an adequate punishment for his rebellion; he exhausted all the varieties of smothering and burning and freezing and cruelly lacerating his external frame, and the Devil laughed at the impotent revenge of his conqueror. At last the benevolent and amiable disposition which distinguished his adversary furnished God with the true method of executing an enduring and a terrible vengeance. He turned his good into evil, and, by virtue of his omnipotence, inspired him with such impulses as, in spite of his better nature, irresistibly determined him to act what he most abhorred and to be a minister of those designs and schemes of which he was the chief and the original victim. He is forever tortured with compassion and affection for those whom he betrays and ruins; he is racked by a vain abhorrence for the desolation of which he is the instrument; he is like a man compelled by a tyrant to set fire to

[346]

his own possession, and to appear as the witness against and the accuser of his dearest friends and most intimate connections, and then to be their executioner and to inflict the most subtle protracted torments upon them. As a man, were he deprived of all other refuge, he might hold his breath and die – but God is represented as omnipotent and the Devil as eternal.

Percy Bysshe Shelley, 'Essay on the Devil and Devils, c.1819–20

Remorse

The monster continued to utter wild and incoherent self-reproaches. At length I gathered resolution to address him in a pause of the tempest of his passion. 'Your repentance,' I said, 'is now superfluous. If you had listened to the voice of conscience, and heeded the stings of remorse, before you had urged your diabolical vengeance to this extremity, Frankenstein would yet have lived.'

'And do you dream?' said the dæmon; 'do you think that I was then dead to agony and remorse? – He,' he continued, pointing to the corpse, 'he suffered not in the consummation of the deed – oh! not the ten-thousandth portion of the anguish that was mine during the lingering detail of its execution. A frightful selfishness hurried me on, while my heart was poisoned with remorse. Think you that the groans of Clerval were music to my ears? My heart was fashioned to be susceptible of love and sympathy; and, when wrenched by misery to vice and hatred, it did not endure the violence of the change, without torture such as you cannot even imagine.

'After the murder of Clerval, I returned to Switzerland, heart-broken and overcome. I pitied Frankenstein; my pity amounted to horror: I abhorred myself. But when I discovered that he, the author at once of my existence and of its unspeakable torments, dared to hope for happiness; that while he accumulated wretchedness and despair upon me, he sought his own enjoyment in feelings and passions from the indulgence of which I was for ever barred, then impotent envy and bitter indignation filled me with an insatiable thirst for vengeance. I recollected my threat, and resolved that it should be accomplished. I knew that I was preparing for myself a deadly torture; but I was the slave, not the master, of an impulse, which I detested, yet could not disobey. Yet when she died! – nay, then I was not miserable. I had cast off all feeling, subdued all anguish, to riot in the excess of my despair. Evil thenceforth became my good. Urged thus far, I had no choice but to adapt my nature to an element which I had willingly chosen. The completion of my demoniacal design became an insatiable passion. And now it is ended; there is my last victim!'

I was at first touched by the expressions of his misery; yet, when I called to mind what Frankenstein had said of his powers of eloquence and persuasion, and when I again cast my eyes on the lifeless form of my friend, indignation was rekindled within me. 'Wretch!' I said, 'it is well that you come here to whine over the desolation that you have made. You throw a torch into a pile of buildings; and, when they are consumed, you sit among the ruins, and lament the fall. Hypocritical fiend! if he whom you mourn still lived, still would he be the object, again would he become the prey, of your accursed vengeance. It is not pity that you feel; you lament only because the victim of your malignity is withdrawn from your power.'

'Oh, it is not thus – not thus,' interrupted the being; 'yet such must be the impression conveyed to you by what appears to be the purport of my actions. Yet I seek not a fellow-feeling in my misery. No sympathy may I ever find. When I first sought it, it was the love of virtue, the feelings of happiness and affection with which my whole being overflowed, that I wished to be participated. But now, that virtue has become to me a shadow, and that happiness and affection are turned into bitter and loathing despair, in what should I seek for sympathy? I am content to suffer alone, while my sufferings shall endure: when I die, I am well satisfied that abhorrence and opprobrium should load my memory. Once my fancy was soothed with dreams of virtue, of fame, and of enjoyment. Once I falsely hoped to meet with beings, who, pardoning my outward form, would love me for the excellent qualities which I was capable of unfolding. I was nourished with high thoughts of honour and devotion. But now crime has degraded me beneath the meanest animal. No guilt, no mischief, no malignity, no misery, can be found comparable to mine. When I run over the frightful catalogue of my sins, I cannot believe that I am the same creature whose thoughts were once filled with sublime and transcendent visions of the beauty and the majesty of goodness. But it is even so; the fallen angel becomes a malignant devil. Yet even that enemy of God and man had friends and associates in his desolation; I am alone.'

Mary Shelley, Frankenstein, 1818

It Is Not So With Me

'I am made to sow the thistle for wheat, the nettle for a nourishing dainty.

'I have planted a false oath in the earth; it has brought forth a poison tree.

'I have chosen the serpent for a councellor, & the dog
'For a schoolmaster to my children.
'I have blotted out from light & living the dove & nightingale,
'And I have caused the earth worm to beg from door to door.

'I have taught the thief a secret path into the house of the just.
'I have taught pale artifice to spread his nets upon the morning.
'My heavens are brass, my earth is iron, my moon a clod of clay,
'My sun a pestilence burning at noon & a vapour of death in night.

'What is the price of Experience? do men buy it for a song?
'Or wisdom for a dance in the street? No, it is bought with the
   price
'Of all that a man hath, his house, his wife, his children.
'Wisdom is sold in the desolate market where none come to buy,
'And in the wither'd field where the farmer plows for bread in vain.

'It is an easy thing to triumph in the summer's sun
'And in the vintage & to sing on the waggon loaded with corn.
'It is an easy thing to talk of patience to the afflicted,
'To speak the laws of prudence to the houseless wanderer,
'To listen to the hungry raven's cry in wintry season
'When the red blood is fill'd with wine & with the marrow of lambs.

'It is an easy thing to laugh at wrathful elements,
'To hear the dog howl at the wintry door, the ox in the slaughter
   house moan;
'To see a god on every wind & a blessing on every blast;
'To hear sounds of love in the thunder storm that destroys our
   enemies' house;
'To rejoice in the blight that covers his field, & the sickness that cuts
   off his children,
'While our olive & vine sing & laugh round our door, & our children
   bring fruits & flowers.

'Then the groan & the dolor are quite forgotten, & the slave grinding
   at the mill,
'And the captive in chains, & the poor in the prison, & the soldier
   in the field
'When the shatter'd bone hath laid him groaning among the happier
   dead.

'It is an easy thing to rejoice in the tents of prosperity:

> 'Thus could I sing & thus rejoice: but it is not so with me.'

William Blake, The Four Zoas, 1795–1804

Looking God in the Face

CAIN: Are ye happy?

LUCIFER: We are mighty.

CAIN: Are ye happy?

LUCIFER: No: art thou?

CAIN: How should I be so? Look on me!

LUCIFER: Poor clay!
  And thou pretendest to be wretched! Thou!

CAIN: I am: – and thou, with all thy might, what art thou?

LUCIFER: One who aspired to be what made thee, and
  Would not have made thee what thou art.

CAIN: Ah!
  Thou look'st almost a god; and –

LUCIFER: I am none:
  And having fail'd to be one, would be nought
  Save what I am. He conquer'd; let him reign!

CAIN: Who?

LUCIFER: Thy Sire's maker, and the earth's.

CAIN: And heaven's,
  And all that in them is. So I have heard
  His seraphs sing; and so my father saith.

LUCIFER: They say – what they must sing and say, on pain
  Of being that which I am, – and thou art –
  Of spirits and of men.

CAIN: And what is that?

LUCIFER: Souls who dare use their immortality –
  Souls who dare look the Omnipotent tyrant in
  His everlasting face, and tell him that
  His evil is not good! If he has made,
  As he saith – which I know not, nor believe –
  But, if he made us – he cannot unmake:
  We are immortal! – nay, he'd have us so,
  That he may torture: – let him! He is great –
  But, in his greatness, is no happier than
  We in our conflict! Goodness would not make
  Evil; and what else hath he made? But let him

[350]

Sit on his vast and solitary throne –
Creating worlds, to make eternity
Less burthensome to his immense existence
And unparticipated solitude;
Let him crowd orb on orb: he is alone
Indefinite, indissoluble tyrant;
Could he but crush himself, 'twere the best boon
He ever granted: but let him reign on!
And multiply himself in misery!
Spirits and men, at least we sympathize –
And, suffering in concert, make our pangs
Innumerable, more endurable,
By the unbounded sympathy of all
With all! But *He*! so wretched in his height,
So restless in his wretchedness, must still
Create, and re-create – perhaps he'll make
One day a Son unto himself – as he
Gave you a father – and if he so doth
Mark me! – that Son will be a Sacrifice.

Lord Byron, *Cain*, 1822

Even If I Were Wrong

'Oh, Alyosha, I am not blaspheming! I understand, of course, what an upheaval of the universe it will be when everything in heaven and earth blends in one hymn of praise and everything that lives and has lived cries aloud: "Thou art just, O Lord, for Thy ways are revealed." When the mother embraces the fiend who threw her child to the dogs, and all three cry aloud with tears, "Thou art just, O Lord!" then, of course, the crown of knowledge will be reached and all will be made clear. But what pulls me up here is that I can't accept that harmony. And while I am on earth, I make haste to take my own measures. You see, Alyosha, perhaps it really may happen that if I live to that moment, or rise again to see it, I, too, perhaps, may cry aloud with the rest, looking at the mother embracing the child's torturer, "Thou art just, O Lord!" but I don't want to cry aloud then. While there is still time, I hasten to protect myself, and so I renounce the higher harmony altogether. It's not worth the tears of that one tortured child who beat itself on the breast with its little fist and prayed in its stinking outhouse, with its unexpiated tears to "dear, kind God"! It's not worth it, because those tears are unatoned for. They must be atoned for, or there can be no harmony. But how? How are you going to atone for them? Is it possible? By their being avenged? But what do I care for avenging them? What do I care for a hell for oppressors? What good can hell do, since those children have already been tortured? And what becomes of harmony, if there is hell? I want to forgive. I want to embrace. I don't want more suffering. And if the sufferings of children go to swell the sum of sufferings which was necessary to pay for truth, then I protest that the truth is not worth such a price. I don't want the mother to embrace the oppressor who threw her son to the dogs! She dare not forgive him! Let her forgive him for herself, if she will, let her forgive the torturer for the immeasurable suffering of her mother's heart. But the sufferings of her tortured child she has no right to forgive; she dare not forgive the torturer, even if the child were to forgive him! And if that is so, if they dare not forgive, what becomes of harmony? Is there in the whole world a being who would have the right to forgive and could forgive? I don't want harmony. From love for humanity I don't want it. I would rather be left with the unavenged suffering. I would rather remain with my unavenged suffering and unsatisfied indignation, *even if I were wrong*. Besides, too high a price is asked for harmony; it's beyond our means to pay so much to enter on it. And so I hasten to give back my entrance ticket, and if I am an honest man I am bound to give it back as soon as possible. And that I am doing. It's not God that I don't accept, Alyosha, only I most respectfully return Him the ticket.'

'That's rebellion,' murmured Alyosha, looking down.

Fyodor Dostoevsky, *The Brothers Karamazov*, 1880; trans. Constance Garnett, 1912

The Chained Liberator

PROMETHEUS: Monarch of Gods and Dæmons, and all Spirits
But One, who throng those bright and rolling worlds
Which Thou and I alone of living things
Behold with sleepless eyes! regard this Earth
Made multitudinous with thy slaves, whom thou
Requitest for knee-worship, prayer, and praise,
And toil, and hecatombs of broken hearts,
With fear and self-contempt and barren hope.
Whilst me, who am thy foe, eyeless in hate,
Hast thou made reign and triumph, to thy scorn,
O'er mine own misery and thy vain revenge.

Three thousand years of sleep-unsheltered hours,
And moments aye divided by keen pangs
Till they seemed years, torture and solitude,
Scorn and despair, – these are mine empire: –
More glorious far than that which thou surveyest
From thine unenvied throne, O Mighty God!
Almighty, had I deigned to share the shame
Of thine ill tyranny, and hung not here
Nailed to this wall of eagle-baffling mountain,
Black, wintry, dead, unmeasured; without herb,
Insect, or beast, or shape or sound of life.
Ah me! alas, pain, pain ever, for ever!

No change, no pause, no hope! Yet I endure.
I ask the Earth, have not the mountains felt?
I ask yon Heaven, the all-beholding Sun,
Has it not seen? The Sea, in storm or calm,
Heaven's ever-changing Shadow, spread below,
Have its deaf waves not heard my agony?
Ah me! alas, pain, pain ever, for ever!

The crawling glaciers pierce me with the spears
Of their moon-freezing crystals, the bright chains
Eat with their burning cold into my bones.
Heaven's wingèd hound, polluting from thy lips
His beak in poison not his own tears up
My heart; and shapeless sights come wandering by,
The ghastly people of the realm of dream,
Mocking me: and the Earthquake-fiends are charged
To wrench the rivets from my quivering wounds
When the rocks split and close again behind:
While from their loud abysses howling throng
The genii of the storm, urging the rage
Of whirlwind, and afflict me with keen hail.
And yet to me welcome is day and night,
Whether one breaks the hoar frost of the morn,
Or starry, dim, and slow, the other climbs
The leaden-coloured east; for then they lead
The wingless, crawling hours, one among whom
– As some dark Priest hales the reluctant victim
Shall drag thee, cruel King, to kiss the blood
From these pale feet, which then might trample thee

If they disdained not such a prostrate slave.
Disdain! Ah no! I pity thee. What ruin
Will hunt thee undefended through wide Heaven!
How will thy soul, cloven to its depth with terror,
Gape like a hell within! I speak in grief,
Not exultation, for I hate no more,
As then ere misery made me wise.

Percy Bysshe Shelley, *Prometheus Unbound*, 1820

'A Memorable Fancy'

Once I saw a Devil in a flame of fire, who arose before an Angel that sat on a cloud, and the Devil utter'd these words: 'The worship of God is: Honouring his gifts in other men, each according to his genius, and loving the greatest men best: those who envy or calumniate great men hate God; for there is no other God.'

The Angel hearing this became almost blue; but mastering himself he grew yellow, & at last white, pink, & smiling, and then replied:

'Thou Idolater! is not God One? & is not he visible in Jesus Christ? and has not Jesus Christ given his sanction to the law of ten commandments? and are not all other men fools, sinners, & nothings?'

The Devil answer'd: 'bray a fool in a morter with wheat, yet shall not his folly be beaten out of him; if Jesus Christ is the greatest man, you ought to love him in the greatest degree; now hear how he has given his sanction to the law of ten commandments: did he not mock at the sabbath, and so mock the sabbath's God? murder those who were murder'd because of him? turn away the law from the woman taken in adultery? steal the labor of others to support him? bear false witness when he omitted making a defence before Pilate? covet when he pray'd for his disciples, and when he bid them shake off the dust of their feet against such as refused to lodge them? I tell you, no virtue can exist without breaking these ten commandments. Jesus was all virtue, and acted from impulse, not from rules.'

William Blake, *The Marriage of Heaven and Hell*, 1790–93

Proverbs of Hell

The tygers of wrath are wiser than the horses of instruction.

Expect poison from the standing water.

You never know what is enough unless you know what is more than enough.

Listen to the fool's reproach! it is a kingly title!

The eyes of fire, the nostrils of air, the mouth of water, the beard of earth.

The weak in courage is strong in cunning.

The apple tree never asks the beech how he shall grow; nor the lion, the horse, how he shall take his prey.

The thankful reciever bears a plentiful harvest.

If others had not been foolish, we should be so.

The soul of sweet delight can never be defil'd.

When thou seest an Eagle, thou seest a portion of Genius; lift up thy head!

As the catterpiller chooses the fairest leaves to lay her eggs on, so the priest lays his curse on the fairest joys.

To create a little flower is the labour of ages.

Damn braces: Bless relaxes.

The best wine is the oldest, the best water the newest.

Prayers plow not! Praises reap not!

Joys laugh not! Sorrows weep not!

The head Sublime, the heart Pathos, the genitals Beauty, the hands & feet Proportion.

As the air to a bird or the sea to a fish, so is contempt to the contemptible.

The crow wish'd every thing was black, the owl that every thing was white.

Exuberance is Beauty.

If the lion was advised by the fox, he would be cunning.

Improve[me]nt makes strait roads; but the crooked roads without Improvement are roads of Genius.

Sooner murder an infant in its cradle than nurse unacted desires.

Where man is not, nature is barren.

Truth can never be told so as to be understood, and not be believ

Enough! or Too much.

William Blake, *The Marriage of Heaven and Hell*, 17

Another Pride

– 'But I feel another pride,' answered Melmoth, and in a proud tone he spoke it, – 'a pride, which, like that of the storm that visited the ancient cities, whose destruction you may have read of, while it blasts, withers, and encrusts paintings, gems, music, and festivity, grasping them in its talons of annihilation, exclaims, Perish to all the world, perhaps beyond the period of its existence, but live to me in darkness and in corruption! Preserve all the exquisite modulation of your forms! all the indestructible brilliancy of your colouring! – but preserve it for me alone! – me, the single, pulseless, eyeless, heartless embracer of an unfertile bride, – the brooder over the dark and unproductive nest of eternal sterility, – the mountain whose lava of internal fire has stifled, and indurated, and inclosed for ever, all that was the joy of earth, the felicity of life, and the hope of futurity!'

Charles Robert Maturin, *Melmoth the Wanderer*, 1820

The Outcast Rejoices in the Curse

LUCIFER (*after a pause*): Dost thou remember, Adam, when the curse
  Took us in Eden? On a mountain-peak
  Half-sheathed in primal woods and glittering
  In spasms of awful sunshine at that hour,
  A lion couched, part raised upon his paws,
  With his calm, massive face turned full on thine,
  And his mane listening. When the ended curse
  Left silence in the world, right suddenly
  He sprang up rampant and stood straight and stiff,
  As if the new reality of death
  Were dashed against his eyes, and roared so fierce
  (Such thick carnivorous passion in his throat
  Tearing a passage through the wrath and fear)
  And roared so wild, and smote from all the hills
  Such fast keen echoes crumbling down the vales
  Precipitately, – that the forest beasts,
  One after one, did mutter a response
  Of savage and of sorrowful complaint
  Which trailed along the gorges. Then, at once,

He fell back, and rolled crashing from the height
Into the dusk of pines.

ADAM: It might have been.
I heard the curse alone.

EARTH SPIRITS: I wail, I wail!

LUCIFER: That lion is the type of what I am.
And as he fixed thee with his full-faced hate,
And roared, O Adam, comprehending doom,
So, gazing on the face of the Unseen,
I cry out here between the Heavens and Earth
My conscience of this sin, this woe, this wrath,
Which damn me to this depth.

EARTH SPIRITS: I wail, I wail!

EVE: I wail – O God!

LUCIFER: I scorn you that ye wail,
Who use your petty griefs for pedestals
To stand on, beckoning pity from without,
And deal in pathos of antithesis
Of what ye *were* forsooth, and what ye are; –
I scorn you like an angel! Yet, one cry
I, too, would drive up like a column erect,
Marble to marble, from my heart to heaven,
A monument of anguish to transpierce
And overtop your vapoury complaints
Expressed from feeble woes.

EARTH SPIRITS: I wail, I wail!

LUCIFER: For, O ye Heavens, ye are my witnesses,
That *I*, struck out from nature in a blot,
The outcast and the mildew of things good,
The leper of angels, the excepted dust
Under the common rain of daily gifts, –
I the snake, I the tempter, I the cursed, –
To whom the highest and the lowest alike
Say, Go from us – we have no need of thee, –
Was made by God like others. Good and fair.
He did create me! – ask Him, if not fair!
Ask, if I caught not fair and silverly
His blessing for chief angels on my head
Until it grew there, a crown crystallized!
Ask, if he never called me by my name,
Lucifer – kindly said as 'Gabriel' –
Lucifer – soft as 'Michael!' while serene

I, standing in the glory of the lamps,
Answered 'my Father,' innocent of shame
And of the sense of thunder. Ha! ye think,
White angels in your niches, – I repent,
And would tread down my own offences back
To service at the footstool? *that*'s read wrong!
I cry as the beast did, that I may cry –
Expansive, not appealing! Fallen so deep,
Against the sides of this prodigious pit
I cry – cry – dashing out the hands of wail
On each side, to meet anguish everywhere,
And to attest it in the ecstasy
And exaltation of a woe sustained
Because provoked and chosen.
                                        Pass along
Your wilderness, vain mortals! Puny griefs
In transitory shapes, be henceforth dwarfed
To your own conscience, by the dread extremes
Of what I am and have been. If ye have fallen,
It is but a step's fall, – the whole ground beneath
Strewn woolly soft with promise! if ye have sinned,
Your prayers tread high as angels! if ye have grieved,
Ye are too mortal to be pitiable,
The power to die disproves the right to grieve.
Go to! ye call this ruin? I half-scorn
The ill I did you! Were ye wronged by me,
Hated and tempted and undone of me, –
Still, what's your hurt to mine of doing hurt,
Of hating, tempting, and so ruining?
This sword's *hilt* is the sharpest, and cuts through
The hand that wields it.
                                        Go! I curse you all.
Hate one another – feebly – as ye can!
I would not certes cut you short in hate,
Far be it from me! hate on as ye can!
I breathe into your faces, spirits of earth,
As wintry blast may breathe on wintry leaves
And lifting up their brownness show beneath
The branches bare. Beseech you, spirits, give
To Eve who beggarly entreats your love
For her and Adam when they shall be dead,
An answer rather fitting to the sin

Than to the sorrow – as the heavens, I trow,
For justice' sake gave theirs.
                              I curse you both,
Adam and Eve. Say grace as after meat,
After my curses! May your tears fall hot
On all the hissing scorns o' the creatures here, –
And yet rejoice! Increase and multiply,
Ye in your generations, in all plagues,
Corruptions, melancholies, poverties,
And hideous forms of life and fears of death, –
The thought of death being alway imminent,
Immovable and dreadful in your life,
And deafly and dumbly insignificant
Of any hope beyond, – as death itself,
Whichever of you lieth dead the first,
Shall seem to the survivor – yet rejoice!
My curse catch at you strongly, body and soul,
And HE find no redemption – nor the wing
Of seraph move your way; and yet rejoice!
Rejoice, – because ye have not, set in you,
This hate which shall pursue you – this fire-hate
Which glares without, because it burns within –
Which kills from ashes – this potential hate,
Wherein I, angel, in antagonism
To God and his reflex beatitudes,
Moan ever, in the central universe,
With the great woe of striving against Love –
And gasp for space amid the Infinite,
And toss for rest amid the Desertness,
Self-orphaned by my will, and self-elect
To kingship of resistant agony
Toward the Good round me – hating good and love,
And willing to hate good and to hate love,
And willing to will on so evermore,
Scorning the past and damning the to-come –
Go and rejoice! I curse you.
                    [LUCIFER vanishes.]

Elizabeth Barrett Browning, 'A Drama of Exile' in *Poems*, 1844

A Protest Against Innocence

The demoniac despair is the most potentiated form of the despair which despairingly wills to be itself. This despair does not will to be itself with Stoic doting upon itself, nor with self-deification, willing in this way, doubtless mendaciously, yet in a certain sense in terms of its perfection; no, with hatred for existence it wills to be itself, to be itself in terms of its misery; it does not even in defiance or defiantly will to be itself, but to be itself in spite; it does not even will in defiance to tear itself free from the Power which posited it, it wills to obtrude upon this Power in spite, to hold on to it out of malice. And that is natural, a malignant objection must above all take care to hold on to that against which it is an objection. Revolting against the whole of existence, it thinks it has hold of a proof against it, against its goodness. This proof the despairer thinks he himself is, and that is what he wills to be, therefore he wills to be himself, himself with his torment, in order with this torment to protest against the whole of existence. Whereas the weak despairer will not hear about what comfort eternity has for him, so neither will such a despairer hear about it, but for a different reason, namely, because this comfort would be the destruction of him as an objection against the whole of existence. It is (to describe it figuratively) as if an author were to make a slip of the pen, and that this clerical error became conscious of being such – perhaps it was no error – but in a far higher sense was an essential constituent in the whole exposition – it is then as if this clerical error would revolt against the author, out of hatred for him were to forbid him to correct it, and were to say, 'No, I will not be erased, I will stand as a witness against thee, that thou art a very poor writer.'

Søren Kierkegaard, *The Sickness unto Death*, 1849;
trans. Walter Lowrie, 1944

'La Tristesse du Diable'

Silencieux, les poings aux dents, le dos ployé,
Enveloppé du noir manteau de ses deux ailes,
Sur un pic hérissé de neiges éternelles,
Une nuit, s'arrêta l'antique Foudroyé.

La terre prolongeait en bas, immense et sombre,
Les continents battus par la houle des mers;

Au-dessus flamboyait le ciel plein d'univers;
Mais Lui ne regardait que l'abîme de l'ombre.

Il était là, dardant ses yeux ensanglantés
Dans ce gouffre où la vie amasse ses tempêtes,
Où le fourmillement des hommes et des bêtes
Pullule sous le vol des siècles irrités.

Il entendait monter les hosannas serviles,
Le cri des égorgeurs, les *Te Deum* des rois,
L'appel désespéré des nations en croix
Et des justes râlant sur le fumier des villes.

Ce lugubre concert du mal universel,
Aussi vieux que le monde et que la race humaine,
Plus fort, plus acharné, plus ardent que sa haine,
Tourbillonnait autour du sinistre Immortel.

Il remonta d'un bond vers les temps insondables
Où sa gloire allumait le céleste matin,
Et, devant la stupide horreur de son destin,
Un grand frisson courut dans ses reins formidables.

Et se tordant les bras, et crispant ses orteils,
Lui, le premier rêveur, la plus vieille victime,
Il cria par delà l'immensité sublime
Où déferle en brûlant l'écume des soleils:

– Les monotones jours, comme une horrible pluie,
S'amassent, sans l'emplir, dans mon éternité;
Force, orgueil, désespoir, tout n'est que vanité;
Et la fureur me pèse, et le combat m'ennuie.

Presque autant que l'amour la haine m'a menti:
J'ai bu toute la mer des larmes infécondes.
Tombez, écrasez-moi, foudres, monceaux des mondes!
Dans le sommeil sacré que je sois englouti!

Et les lâches heureux, et les races damnées,
Par l'espace éclatant qui n'a ni fond ni bord,
Entendront une Voix disant: Satan est mort!
Et ce sera ta fin, œuvre des six Journées!

Leconte de Lisle, 1864, in *Poèmes Barbares*, 1872

'Lucifer in Starlight'

On a starred night Prince Lucifer uprose.
Tired of his dark dominion swung the fiend
Above the rolling ball in cloud part screened,
Where sinners hugged their spectre of repose.
Poor prey to his hot fit of pride were those.
And now upon his western wing he leaned,
Now his huge bulk o'er Afric's sands careened,
Now the black planet shadowed Arctic snows.
Soaring through wider zones that pricked his scars
With memory of the old revolt from Awe,
He reached a middle height, and at the stars,
Which are the brain of heaven, he looked, and sank.
Around the ancient track marched, rank on rank,
The army of unalterable law.

George Meredith, from *Poems and Lyrics of the Joy of the Earth*, 1883

Satan's Daughter Liberty Asks Permission to Sack the Bastille

Mon père, écoute-moi. Pour baume et pour calmant,
Pour mêler quelque joi à ton accablement,
Tu n'as jusqu'à cette heure, en ton âpre géhenne,
Essayé que la nuit, la vengeance et la haine;
Essaie enfin la vie, essaie enfin le jour!
Laisse planer le cygne à ta place, ô vautour!
Laisse un ange sorti de tes ailes répandre
Sur les fléaux un souffle irrésistible et tendre.
Faisons lever Caïn accroupi sur Abel.
Assez d'ombre et de crime! Empêchons que Babel
Elève encor plus haut ses hideuses spirales.
Oh! laisse-moi rouvrir les portes sépulcrales
Que, du fond de l'enfer, sur l'âme tu fermais!
Laisse-moi mettre l'homme en liberté. Permets
Que je tende la main à l'univers qui sombre.
Laisse-moi renverser la montagne de l'ombre;
Laisse-moi jeter bas l'infâme tour du mal!

[362]

Permets que, grâce à moi, dans l'azur baptismal
Le monde rentre, afin que l'éden reparaisse!
Hélas! sens-tu mon cœur tremblant qui te caresse?
M'entends-tu sangloter dans ton cachot? Consens
Que je sauve les bons, les purs, les innocents;
Laisse s'envoler l'âme et finir la souffrance.
Dieu me fit Liberté; toi, fais-moi Délivrance!
Oh! ne me défends pas de jeter, dans les cieux
Et les enfers, le cri de l'amour factieux;
Laisse-moi prodiguer à la terrestre sphère
L'air vaste, le ciel bleu, l'espoir sans borne, et faire
Sortir du front de l'homme un rayon d'infini.
Laisse-moi sauver tout, moi ton côté béni!
Consens! Oh! moi qui viens de toi, permets que j'aille
Chez ces vivants, afin d'achever la bataille
Entre leur ignorance, hélas! et leur raison,
Pour mettre une rougeur sacrée à l'horizon,
Pour que l'affreux passé dans les ténèbres roule,
Pour que la terre tremble et que la prison croule,
Pour que l'éruption se fasse, et pour qu'enfin
L'homme voie, au-dessus des douleurs, de la faim,
De la guerre, des rois, des dieux, de la démence,
Le volcan de la joie enfler sa lave immense!

Tandis que cette vierge adorable parlait,
Pareille au sein versant goutte à goutte le lait
A l'enfant nouveau-né qui dort, la bouche ouverte,
Satan, toujours flottant comme une herbe en l'eau verte,
Remuait dans le gouffre, et semblait par moment
A travers son sommeil frémir éperdûment;
Ainsi qu'en un brouillard l'aube éclôt, puis s'efface,
Le démon s'éclairait, puis pâlissait; sa face
Etait comme le champ d'un combat ténébreux;
Le bien, le mal, luttaient sur son visage entre eux
Avec tous les reflux de deux sombres armées;
Ses lèvres se crispaient, sinistrement fermées;
Ses poings s'entre-heurtaient, monstrueux et noircis;
Il n'ouvrait pas les yeux, mais sous ses lourds sourcils
On voyait les lueurs de cette âme inconnue;
Tel le tonnerre fait des pourpres sous la nue.
L'ange le regardait, les mains jointes; enfin
Une clarté, qu'eût pu jeter un séraphin,

Sortit de ce grand front tout brûlé par les fièvres.
Ainsi que deux rochers qui se fendent, ses lèvres
S'écartèrent, un souffle orageux souleva
Son flanc terrible, et l'ange entendit ce mot:
≪Va!≫

Victor Hugo, *La Fin de Satan*, 1886

Théophile's Wings

'It's a little place, but it's comfortable,' said Théophile.

And gazing out of the window which looked out on the russet-coloured night, with its myriad lights, he added, 'One can see the *Sacré Cœur*.' His hand on Arcade's shoulder he repeated several times, 'I am glad to see you.'

Then dragging his former companion in glory into the kitchen passage he put down his candlestick, drew a key from his pocket, opened a cupboard, and raising a linen covering disclosed two large white wings.

'You see,' he said, 'I have preserved them. From time to time, when I am alone, I go and look at them; it does me good.'

And he dabbed his reddened eyes. He stood awhile overcome by silent emotion. Then holding the candle near the long pinions which were moulting their down in places, he murmured, 'They are eaten away.'

'You must put some pepper on them,' said Arcade.

'I have done so,' replied the angelic musician sighing. 'I have put pepper, camphor and powder on them. But nothing does any good.'

Anatole France, *La Révolte des Anges*, 1914;
trans. Emilie Jackson, 1914

Jane Lampton Clemens

Her interest in people and the other animals was warm, personal, friendly. She always found something to excuse, and as a rule to love, in the toughest of them – even if she had to put it there herself. She was the natural ally and friend of the friendless. It was believed that, Presbyterian as she was, she could be beguiled into saying a soft word for the devil himself; and so the experiment was tried. The abuse of Satan began; one conspirator after another added his bitter word, his malign reproach, his pitiless censure, till at last, sure enough, the unsuspecting subject of the trick walked into the trap. She admitted that the indictment was sound; that Satan was utterly wicked and abandoned, just as these people had said; *but*, would any claim that he had been treated fairly? A sinner was but a sinner; Satan was just that, like the rest. What saves the rest? – their own efforts alone? No – or none might ever be saved. To their feeble efforts is added the mighty help of pathetic, appealing, imploring prayers that go up daily out of all the churches in Christendom and out of myriads upon myriads of pitying hearts. But who prays for Satan? Who, in eighteen centuries, has had the common humanity to pray for the one sinner that needed it most, our one fellow and brother who most needed a friend yet had not a single one, the one sinner among us all who had the highest and clearest *right* to every Christian's daily and nightly prayers for the plain and unassailable reason that his was the first and greatest need, he being among sinners the supremest?

Mark Twain, 'Jane Lampton Clemens', in *Autobiography*,
ed. Albert Bigelow Paine, 1924

Satan Dreams of Victory at Last

Michael went to announce to his God that the Holy Mountain would fall into the hands of the demon in twenty-four hours, and that nothing remained for the Master of the Heavens but to seek safety in flight. The Seraphim placed the jewels of the celestial crown in coffers. Michael offered his arm to the Queen of Heaven, and the Holy Family escaped from the palace by a subterranean passage of porphyry. A deluge of fire was falling on the citadel. Regaining his post once more, the glorious archangel declared that he would never capitulate, and straightway advanced the standards of the living God. That same evening the rebel host made its entry into the thrice-sacred city. On a fiery steed Satan led his demons. Behind him marched Arcade, Istar, and Zita. As in the ancient revels of Dionysus, old Nectaire bestrode his ass. Thereafter, floating out far behind, followed the black standards.

The garrison laid down their arms before Satan. Michael placed his flaming sword at the feet of the conquering archangel.

'Take back your sword, Michael,' said Satan. 'It is Lucifer who yields it to you. Bear it in defence of peace and law.' Then letting his gaze fall on the leaders of the celestial cohorts, he cried in a ringing voice:

'Archangel Michael, and you, Powers, Thrones, and Dominations, swear all of you to be faithful to your God.'

'We swear it,' they replied with one voice.

And Satan said:

'Powers, Thrones, and Dominations, of all past wars, I wish but to remember the invincible courage that you displayed and the loyalty which you rendered to authority, for these assure me of the steadfastness of the fealty you have just sworn to me.'

The following day, on the ethereal plain, Satan commanded the black standards to be distributed to the troops, and the winged soldiers covered them with kisses and bedewed them with tears.

And Satan had himself crowned God. Thronging round the glittering walls of Heavenly Jerusalem, apostles, pontiffs, virgins, martyrs, confessors, the whole company of the elect, who during the fierce battle had enjoyed delightful tranquillity, tasted infinite joy in the spectacle of the coronation.

The elect saw with ravishment the Most High precipitated into Hell, and Satan seated on the throne of the Lord. In conformity with the will of God which had cut them off from sorrow they sang in the ancient fashion the praises of their new Master.

And Satan, piercing space with his keen glance, contemplated the little globe of earth and water where of old he had planted the vine and formed the first tragic chorus. And he fixed his gaze on that Rome where the fallen God had founded his empire on fraud and lie. Nevertheless, at that moment a saint ruled over the Church. Satan saw him praying and weeping. And he said to him:

'To thee I entrust my Spouse. Watch over her faithfully. In thee I confirm the right and power to decide matters of doctrine, to regulate the use of the sacraments, to make laws and to uphold purity of morals. And the faithful shall be under obligation to conform thereto. My Church is eternal, and the gates of hell shall not prevail against it. Thou art infallible. Nothing is changed.'

And the successor of the apostles felt flooded with rapture. He prostrated himself, and with his forehead touching the floor, replied:

'O Lord, my God, I recognise Thy voice! Thy breath has been wafted like balm to my heart. Blessed be Thy name. Thy will be done on Earth, as it is in Heaven. Lead us not into temptation, but deliver us from evil.'

And Satan found pleasure in praise and in the exercise of his grace; he loved to hear his wisdom and his power belauded. He listened with joy to the canticles of the cherubim who celebrated his good deeds, and he took no pleasure in listening to Nectaire's flute, because it celebrated nature's self, yielded to the insect and to the blade of grass their share of power and love, and counselled happiness and freedom. Satan, whose flesh had crept, in days gone by, at the idea that suffering prevailed in the world, now felt himself inaccessible to pity. He regarded suffering and death as the happy results of omnipotence and sovereign kindness. And the savour of the blood of victims rose upward towards him like sweet incense. He fell to condemning intelligence and to hating curiosity. He himself refused to learn anything more, for fear that in acquiring fresh knowledge he might let it be seen that he had not known everything at the very outset. He took pleasure in mystery, and believing that he would seem less great by being understood, he affected to be unintelligible. Dense fumes of Theology filled his brain. One day, following the example of his predecessor, he conceived the notion of proclaiming himself one god in three persons. Seeing Arcade smile as this proclamation was made, he drove him from his presence. Istar and Zita had long since returned to earth. Thus centuries passed like seconds. Now, one day, from the altitude of his throne, he plunged his gaze into the depths of the pit and saw Ialdabaoth in the Gehenna where he himself had long lain enchained. Amid the everlasting gloom Ialdabaoth still retained his lofty mien. Blackened, and shattered, terrible and sublime, he glanced upwards at the palace of the King of Heaven with a look of proud disdain; then turned away his head. And the new god, as he looked upon his foe, beheld the light of intelligence and love pass across his sorrow-stricken countenance. And lo! Ialdabaoth was now contemplating the Earth and, seeing it sunk in wickedness and suffering, he began to foster thoughts of kindliness in his heart. On a sudden he rose up, and beating the ether with his mighty arms, as though with oars, he hastened thither to instruct and to console mankind. Already his vast shadow shed upon the unhappy planet a shade soft as a night of love.

And Satan awoke bathed in an icy sweat.

Anatole France, *La Révolte des Anges*, 1914; trans. Emilie Jackson, 1914

A Critic of Man

THE DEVIL: Have you walked up and down upon the earth lately? I have; and I have examined Man's wonderful inventions. And I tell you that in the arts of life man invents nothing; but in the arts of death he outdoes Nature herself, and produces by chemistry and machinery all the slaughter of plague, pestilence, and famine. The peasant I tempt today eats and drinks what was eaten and drunk by the peasants of ten thousand years ago; and the house he lives in has not altered as much in a thousand centuries as the fashion of a lady's bonnet in a score of weeks. But when he goes out to slay, he carries a marvel of mechanism that lets loose at the touch of his finger all the hidden molecular energies, and leaves the javelin, the arrow, the blowpipe of his fathers far behind. In the arts of peace Man is a bungler. I have seen his cotton factories and the like, with machinery that a greedy dog could have invented if it had wanted money instead of food. I know his clumsy typewriters and bungling locomotives and tedious bicycles: they are toys compared to the Maxim gun, the submarine torpedo boat. There is nothing in Man's industrial machinery but his greed and sloth: his heart is in his weapons. This marvellous force of Life of which you boast is a force of Death: Man measures his strength by his destructiveness. What is his religion? An excuse for hating me. What is his law? An excuse for hanging you. What is his morality? Gentility! An excuse for consuming without producing. What is his art? An excuse for gloating over pictures of slaughter. What are his politics? Either the worship of a despot because a despot can kill, or parliamentary cock-fighting. I spent an evening lately in a certain celebrated legislature, and heard the pot lecturing the kettle for its blackness, and ministers answering questions. When I left I chalked up on the door the old nursery saying 'Ask no questions and you will be told no lies.' I bought a sixpenny family magazine, and found it full of pictures of young men shooting and stabbing one another. I saw a man die: he was a London bricklayer's laborer with seven children. He left seventeen pounds club money; and his wife spent it all on his funeral and went into the workhouse with the children next day. She would not have spent sevenpence on her children's schooling: the law had to force her to let them be taught gratuitously; but on death she spent all she had. Their imagination glows, their energies rise up at the idea of death, these people: they love it; and the more horrible it is the more they enjoy it. Hell is a place far above their comprehension: they derive their notion of it from two of the greatest fools that ever lived, an Italian and an Englishman. The Italian described it as a place of mud, frost, filth, fire, and venomous serpents: all torture. This ass, when he was not lying about me, was maundering about some woman whom he saw once in the street. The Englishman described me as being expelled from Heaven by cannons and gunpowder; and to this day every Briton believes that the whole of his silly story is in the Bible. What else he says I do not know; for it is all in a long poem which neither I nor anyone else ever succeeded in wading through. It is the same in everything. The highest form of literature is the tragedy, a play in which everybody is murdered at the end. In the old chronicles you read of earthquakes and pestilences, and are told that these shewed the power and majesty of God and the littleness of Man. Nowadays the chronicles describe battles. In a battle two bodies of men shoot at one another with bullets and explosive shells until one body runs away, when the others chase the fugitives on horseback and cut them to pieces as they fly. And this, the chronicle concludes, shews the greatness and majesty of empires, and the littleness of the vanquished. Over such battles the people run about the streets yelling with delight, and egg their Governments on to spend hundreds of millions of money in the slaughter, whilst the strongest Ministers dare not spend an extra penny in the pound against the poverty and pestilence through which they themselves daily walk. I could give you a thousand instances; but they all come to the same thing: the power that governs the earth is not the power of Life but of Death; and the inner need that has nerved Life to the effort of organising itself into the human being is not the need for higher life but for a more efficient engine of destruction. The plague, the famine, the earthquake, the tempest were too spasmodic in their action; the tiger and crocodile were too easily satiated and not cruel enough: something more constantly, more ruthlessly, more ingeniously destructive was needed; and that something was Man, the inventor of the rack, the stake, the gallows, the electric chair; of sword and gun and poison gas: above all, of justice, duty, patriotism, and all the other isms by which even those who are clever enough to be humanely disposed are persuaded to become the most destructive of all the destroyers.

George Bernard Shaw, *Man and Superman*, 1903

My Best Feelings

'My dear friend, above all things I want to behave like a gentleman and to be recognised as such,' the visitor began in an access of deprecating and simple-hearted pride, typical of a poor relation. 'I am poor, but . . . I won't say very honest, but . . . it's an axiom generally accepted in society that I am a fallen angel. I certainly can't conceive how I can ever have been an angel. If I ever was, it must have been so long ago that there's no harm in forgetting it. Now I only prize the reputation of being a gentlemanly person and live as I can, trying to make myself agreeable. I love men genuinely, I've been greatly calumniated! Here when I stay with you from time to time, my life gains a kind of reality and that's what I like most of all. You see, like you, I suffer from the fantastic and so I love the realism of earth. Here, with you, everything is circumscribed, here all is formulated and geometrical, while we have nothing but indeterminate equations! I wander about here dreaming. I like dreaming. Besides, on earth I become superstitious. Please don't laugh, that's just what I like, to become superstitious. I adopt all your habits here: I've grown fond of going to the public baths, would you believe it? and I go and steam myself with merchants and priests. What I dream of is becoming incarnate once for all and irrevocably in the form of some merchant's wife weighing eighteen stone, and of believing all she believes. My ideal is to go to church and offer a candle in simple-hearted faith, upon my word it is. Then there would be an end to my sufferings. I like being doctored too; in the spring there was an outbreak of smallpox and I went and was vaccinated in a foundling hospital – if only you knew how I enjoyed myself that day. I subscribed ten roubles in the cause of the Slavs! . . . But you are not listening. Do you know, you are not at all well this evening? I know you went yesterday to that doctor . . . well, what about your health? What did the doctor say?'

'Fool!' Ivan snapped out.

'But you are clever, anyway. You are scolding again? I didn't ask out of sympathy. You needn't answer. Now rheumatism has come in again –'

'Fool!' repeated Ivan.

'You keep saying the same thing; but I had such an attack of rheumatism last year that I remember it to this day.'

'The devil have rheumatism!'

'Why not, if I sometimes put on fleshly form? I put on fleshly form and I take the consequences. Satan *sum et nihil humanum a me alienum puto.*'

'What, what, Satan *sum et nihil humanum* . . . that's not bad for the devil!'

'I am glad I've pleased you at last.'

'But you didn't get that from me.' Ivan stopped suddenly, seeming struck. 'That never entered my head, that's strange.'

'*C'est du nouveau, n'est-ce pas?* This time I'll act honestly and explain to you. Listen, in dreams and especially in nightmares, from indigestion or anything, a man sees sometimes such artistic visions, such complex and real actuality, such events, even a whole world of events, woven into such a plot, with such unexpected details from the most exalted matters to the last button on a cuff, as I swear Leo Tolstoy has never invented. Yet such dreams are sometimes seen not by writers, but by the most ordinary people, officials, journalists, priests. . . . The subject is a complete enigma. A statesman confessed to me, indeed, that all his best ideas came to him when he was asleep. Well, that's how it is now, though I am your hallucination, yet just as in a nightmare, I say original things which had not entered your head before. So I don't repeat your ideas, yet I am only your nightmare, nothing more.'

'You are lying, your aim is to convince me you exist apart and are not my nightmare, and now you are asserting you are a dream.'

'My dear fellow, I've adopted a special method to-day, I'll explain it to you afterwards. Stay, where did I break off? Oh, yes! I caught cold then, only not here but yonder.'

'Where is yonder? Tell me, will you be here long. Can't you go away?' Ivan exclaimed almost in despair. He ceased walking to and fro, sat down on the sofa, leaned his elbows on the table again and held his head tight in both hands. He pulled the wet towel off and flung it away in vexation. It was evidently of no use.

'Your nerves are out of order,' observed the gentleman, with a carelessly easy, though perfectly polite, air. 'You are angry with me even for being able to catch cold, though it happened in a most natural way. I was hurrying then to a diplomatic *soirée* at the house of a lady of high rank in Petersburg, who was aiming at influence in the Ministry. Well, an evening suit, white tie, gloves, though I was God knows where and had to fly through space to reach your earth. . . . Of course, it took only an instant, but you know a ray of light from the sun takes full eight minutes, and fancy in an evening suit and open waistcoat. Spirits don't freeze, but when one's in fleshly form, well . . . in brief, I didn't think, and set off, and you know in those ethereal spaces, in the water that is above the firmament, there's such a frost . . . at least one can't call it frost, you can fancy, 150 degrees below zero! You know the game the village girls play – they invite the unwary to lick an axe in thirty degrees of frost, the tongue instantly freezes to it and the dupe tears the skin off, so it bleeds. But that's only in 30 degrees, in 150 degrees I imagine it would be enough to put your finger on the axe and it would be the end of it . . . if only there could be an axe there.'

'And can there be an axe there?' Ivan interrupted, carelessly and disdainfully. He was exerting himself to the utmost not to believe in the delusion and not to sink into complete insanity.

'An axe?' the guest interrupted in surprise.

'Yes, what would become of an axe there?' Ivan cried suddenly, with a sort of savage and insistent obstinacy.

'What would become of an axe in space? *Quelle idée!* If it were to fall to any distance, it would begin, I think, flying round the earth without knowing why, like a satellite. The astronomers would calculate the rising and the setting of the axe; *Gatzuk* would put it in his calendar, that's all.'

'You are stupid, awfully stupid,' said Ivan peevishly. 'Fib more cleverly or I won't listen. You want to get the better of me by realism, to convince me that you exist, but I don't want to believe you exist! I won't believe it!'

'But I am not fibbing, it's all the truth; the truth is unhappily hardly ever amusing. I see you persist in expecting something big of me, and perhaps something fine. That's a great pity, for I only give what I can –'

'Don't talk philosophy, you ass!'

'Philosophy, indeed, when all my right side is numb and I am moaning and groaning. I've tried all the medical faculty: they can diagnose beautifully, they have the whole of your disease at their finger-tips, but they've no idea how to cure you. There was an enthusiastic little student here. "You may die," said he, "but you'll know perfectly what disease you are dying of!" And then what a way they have of sending people to specialists! "We only diagnose," they say, "but go to such-and-such a specialist, he'll cure you." The old doctor who used to cure all sorts of disease has completely disappeared, I assure you, now there are only specialists and they all advertise in the newspapers. If anything is wrong with your nose, they send you to Paris: there, they say, is a European specialist who cures noses. If you go to Paris, he'll look at your nose; I can only cure your right nostril, he'll tell you, for I don't cure the left nostril, that's not my speciality, but go to Vienna, there there's a specialist who will cure your left nostril. What are you to do? I fell back on popular remedies, a German doctor advised me to rub myself with honey and salt in the bath-house. Solely to get an extra bath I went, smeared myself all over and it did me no good at all. In despair I wrote to Count Mattei in Milan. He sent me a book and some drops, bless him, and, only fancy, Hoff's malt extract cured me! I bought it by accident, drank a bottle and a half of it, and I was ready to dance, it took it away completely. I made up my mind to write to the papers to thank him, I was prompted by a feeling of gratitude, and only fancy, it led to no end of a bother: not a single paper would take my letter. "It would be very reactionary," they said, "no one will believe it. *Le diable n'existe point.* You'd better remain anonymous," they advised me. What use is a letter of thanks if it's anonymous? I laughed with the men at the newspaper office; "It's reactionary to believe in God in our days," I said, "but I am the devil, so I may be believed in." "We quite understand that," they said. "Who doesn't believe in the devil? Yet it won't do, it might injure our reputation. As a joke, if you like." But I thought as a joke it wouldn't be very witty. So it wasn't printed. And do you know, I have felt sore about it to this day. My best feelings, gratitude, for instance, are literally denied me simply from my social position.'

Fyodor Dostoevsky, *The Brothers Karamazov*, 1880;
trans. Constance Garnett, 1912

Eleven

MISERY

A Young Man from Lombardy

There was (after a sermon made, wherein this storie of *S. Margaret* was recited, for in such stuffe consisted not onelie their service, but also their sermons in the blind time of poperie:) there was (I saie) a certeine yoong man, being a *Lombard*, whose simplicitie was such, as he had no respect unto the commoditie of worldlie things, but did altogither affect the salvation of his soule, who hearing how great *S. Margarets* triumph was, began to consider with himself, how full of slights the divell was. And among other things thus he said; Oh that God would suffer, that the divell might fight with me hand to hand in visible forme! I would then surelie in like maner overthrow him, and would fight with him till I had the victorie. And therefore about the twelfe houre he went out of the towne, and finding a convenient place where to praie, secretlie kneeling on his knees, he praied among other things, that God would suffer the divell to appeare unto him in visible forme, that according to the example of *S. Margaret*, he might overcome him in battell. And as he was in the middest of his praiers, there came into that place a woman with a hooke in hir hand, to gather certeine hearbs which grew there, who was dumme borne. And when she came into the place, and saw the yoong man among the hearbs on his knees, she was afraid, and waxed pale, and going backe, she rored in such sort, as hir voice could not be understood and with hir head and fists made threatening signes unto him. The yoong man seeing such an ilfavoured fowle queane, that was for age decrepit and full of wrinkles, with a long bodie, leane of face, pale of colour, with ragged cloathes, crieng verie lowd, and having a voice not understandable, threatning him with the hooke which she carried in hir hand, he thought surelie she had beene no woman, but a divell appearing unto him in the shape of a woman, and thought God had heard his praiers. For the which causes he fell upon hir lustilie, and at length threw hir downe to the ground, saieng; Art thou come thou curssed divell, art thou come? No no, thou shalt not overthrow me in visible fight, whome thou hast often overcome in invisible temptation.

And as he spake these words, he caught hir by the haire, and drew hir about, beating hir sometimes with his hands, sometimes with his heeles, and sometimes with the hooke so long, and wounded hir so sore, that he left hir a dieng.

Reginald Scot, *The Discoverie of Witchcraft*, 1584

Geillis Duncan

Within the towne of *Trenent* in the Kingdome of *Scotland*, there dwelleth one *Dauid Seaton*, who being deputie Bailiffe in the saide Towne, had a maide seruant called *Geillis Duncane*, who vsed secretly to be absent and to lye foorth of her Maisters house euery other night: this *Geillis Duncane* took in hand to help all such as were troubled or greeued with any kinde of sicknes or infirmitie: and in short space did perfourme manye matters most miraculous, which thinges forasmuch as she began to doe them vpon a sodaine, hauing neuer doon the like before, made her Maister and others to be in great admiracion, and wondred thereat: by means wherof the saide *Dauid Seaton* had his maide in some great suspition, that she did not those things by naturall and lawfull wayes, but rather supposed it to be doone by some extraordinary and vnlawfull meanes.

Whervpon, her Maister began to growe very inquisitiue, and examined her which way and by what meanes she were able to perfourme matters of so great importance: whereat she gaue him no answere, neuerthelesse, her Maister to the intent that he might the better trye and finde out the trueth of the same, did with the helpe of others, torment her with the torture of the Pilliwinckes vpon her fingers, which is a greeuous torture, and binding or wrinching her head with a corde or roape, which is a most cruell torment also, yet would she not confesse any thing, whereupon they suspecting that she had beene marked by the Diuell (as commonly witches are) made dilligent search about her, and found the enemies marke to be in her fore crag or foreparte of her throate: which being found, she confessed that all her dooings was doone by the wicked allurements and inticements of the Diuell, and that she did them by witchcraft.

Newes from Scotland, 1591

Dr Fian

Thus all the daie this Doctor *Fian* continued verie solitarie, and seemed to haue care of his owne soule, and would call vppon God, shewing himselfe penitent for his wicked life, neuerthelesse the same night hee founde such meanes, that hee stole the key of the prison doore and chamber in the which he was, which in the night hee opened and fled awaie to the Salt pans, where hee was alwayes resident, and first apprehended. Of whose sodaine departure when the Kings maiestie had intelligence, hee presently commanded diligent inquirie to bee made for his apprehension, and for the better effecting thereof, hee sent publike proclamations into all partes of his lande to the same effect. By meanes of whose hot and harde pursuite, he was agayn taken and brought to prison, and then being called before the kings highnes, hee was reexamined as well touching his departure, as also touching all that had before happened.

But this Doctor, notwithstanding that his owne confession appeareth remaining in recorde vnder his owne hande writing, and the same therevnto fixed in the presence of the Kings maiestie and sundrie of his Councell, yet did hee vtterly denie the same.

Wherevpon the kinges maiestie perceiuing his stubbourne wilfulnesse, conceiued and imagined that in the time of his absence hee had entered into newe conference and league with the deuill his master, and that hee had beene agayne newly marked, for the which hee was narrowly searched, but it coulde not in anie wise bee founde, yet for more tryall of him to make him confesse, hee was commaunded to haue a most straunge torment which was done in this manner following.

His nailes vpon all his fingers were riuen and pulled off with an instrument called in Scottish a *Turkas*, which in England wee call a payre of pincers, and vnder euerie nayle there was thrust in two needels ouer euen up to the heads. At all which tormentes notwithstanding the Doctor neuer shronke anie whit, neither woulde he then confesse it the sooner for all the tortures inflicted vpon him.

Then was hee with all conuenient speed, by commandement, conuaied againe to the torment of the bootes, wherein hee continued a long time, and did abide so many blowes in them, that his legges were crushte and beaten togeather as small as might bee, and the bones and flesh so brused, that the bloud and marrowe spouted forth in great abundance, whereby they were made unseruiceable for euer. And notwithstanding all these grieuous paines and cruell torments hee would not confesse anie thing, so deepely had the deuill entered into his heart, that hee vtterly denied all that which he had before auouched, and woulde saie nothing therevnto but this, that what hee had done and sayde before, was onely done and sayde for feare of paynes which he had endured.

Newes from Scotland, 1591

Major Weir and his Sister

This man Thomas Weir *was born in* Clydsdaile, *near to* Lanerk, *who had been a* Lieutenent *in* Ireland *long since. What way he came to get some public command in the City of* Edinburgh, *in the year* 49. *and* 50. *I know not; but it seems he has been alwayes called* Major Weir, *since that time. Many things might be narrated of him, which for brevities sake I cannot meddle with; since I intend to speak only of his* Sorceries, *and other things relateing thereunto. It seems, he had, before he was burnt, some charge over the* Waiters *at the Ports of the City, being as it were a* Check *to them. Coming one day as his custome was, he found some of them in a Cellar, taking a cup of Aile, neglecting their Charge. After a gentle reproof, one of them replyed, that some of their number being upon duty, the rest had retired to drink with their old Friend and Acquaintance Mr. Burn. At which word, he started back, and casting an eye upon him, repeated the word* Burn *four or five times. And going home, he never any more came abroad, till a few weeks after, he had discovered, his impieties. It was observed by some, that going to* Liberton *sometimes, he shunned to step over that* Water-brook, *which is ordinarly called* Liberton-burn, *but went about to shun it. Some have conjectured, that he had adviseth beware of a* Burn, *or some other thing, which this equivocal word might signify,* as burn in a fire. *If so, he has foreseen his day approaching. A year before he discovered himself, he took a sore sickness, during which time he spake to all, who visited him like an Angel, and came frequently abroad again.*

This man taking some dreadful tortures of Conscience, and the Terrours of the Almighty being upon his Spirit, confessed to several Neighbours in his own house, and that most willingly, his particular sins which he was guilty of, which bred amazement to all persons, they coming from a man of so high a repute of Religion and Piety. He ended with this remarkable expression, Before GOD *(says he)* I have not told you the hundred part of that I can say more, and am guilty of. *These same very abominations he confessed before the Judges likewise. But after this, he would never till his dying hour confess any more, which might have been for the glorifying of* GOD, *and the Edification of others, but remained stupid, having no confidence to look any Man in the face, or to open his eyes* . . .

During the time of his imprisonment, he was never willing to be spoken to, and when the Ministers *of the City offered to pray for him, he would cry out in fury,* Torment me no more, for I am tormented already. *One* Minister *(now asleep) asking him, if he should pray for him? was answered,* not at all. *The other replyed in a kind of holy anger.* Sir I will pray for you in spite of your teeth, & the Devil your master too: *Who did pray, making him at least to hear him: but the other stairing wildly, was senseless as a Brute. Another, who is likewise at rest, demanded,* if he thought there was a God. *Said the Man,* I know not. *That other smartly replyed.* O man the Argument that moveth me to think, there is a God, is thy self, for what els moved thee to inform the world of thy wicked life. *But* Weir *answered* let me alone. *When he peremptorly forebad one of his own Parish* Ministers (*yet alive*) *to pray. One demanded, if he would have any of the* Presbyterian perswasion to *pray. He answered,* Sir, you are now all alike to me. *Then said the* Minister *to him,* I will pray with you. Do it not said the other upon your Peril, looking up to the beams of the house. *But* Prayer *was offered up, so much the more heartily, because the company about expected some vision. It is observable, that in things common, he was pertinent enough; but when any thing about* Almighty God, *and* his souls *condition came about, he would* Shrugg, *and* Rub *his* Coat *and* Breast, *saying to them,* torment me not before the time. *When he was at the* stake *to be burnt, the* City Ministers *called to a* Church-man *there, looking on, being one of that perswasion, whereof* Weir *was formerlie deemed to be, to speak to him; but no sooner he opened his mouth, than he made a sign with his hand and his head to be silent. When the* Roap *was about his neck to prepare him for the fire, he was bid say,* Lord be merciful to me, But *he answered* let me alone, I will not, I have lived as a beast, and I must die as a Beast. *The* fire *being kindled, both* He *and his* Staff, *a little after fell into the flames. Whatever* Incantation *was in his* Staff, *is not for me to discuse. He could not officiat in any holy duty without this* Rod *in his hand, and leaning upon it, which made those who heard him pray, admire his fluency in* Prayer . . .

There was one Minister *in the* city, *that could never be perswaded to speak with him in Prison, but no soonner was he dead, but he went to the* Tolbooth, *and called for his* Sister, *who had some remorse, of whom I shall now speak. He told her, that her Brother was burnt, and how he died (though he saw him not execute, as I heard from himself) She believed nothing of it, but after many attestations, she asked* Where his staff Was? *for it seems, she knew that his strength and life lay therein. He told her, it was burnt with him. Whereupon, notwithstanding of her age, she nimbly, and in a furious rage fell on her knees, uttering words horrible to be remembred. And in rising up, as she was desired, her rageing agony closed with these words.* O Sir, I know he is with the Devils, for with them he lived. *She intreated that* Minister *to assist her, and attend her to her death, which at her violent importunity he yeelded unto, though it was not his course to wait upon condemned Persons. What she said in private to himself, he says must die with him. She avouched,* that from her being sixteen years of age, to her fiftieth, her Brother had the incestuous use of her body, and then loathed her for her age. *She was pretty old at this time, and he when he died was about* seventy. *He asked her,* if ever she was with Child to him? *She declared with great confidence,* he hindred that by means abominable, *which she beginning*

[378]

to relate, the Preacher stopped her. Some bystanders were desirous to hear the rest, but saies he (Gentlemen) the speculation of this iniquity is in it self to be punished.

In often and returned visits, she was interrogat if she had any hand in her Brothers Devilry? She declared, but in a passive way, and gave this for an instance. A fiery Chariot, or Coach, as she called it, coming to his door, at broad day, a stranger invited him and her to goe visit a friend at Dalkeith a small town some four miles from Edinburgh. They both entered, and went foreward in their visit, at which time (says she) one came and whispered something in his ear, which affected him. They both returned after the same manner, that they had gone out. And Weir going after, to make some visits, told them he had strong apprehensions, that, that day, the Kings Forces were routed at Worcester, which within two or three days was confirmed by the Post. She affirmed that none saw the Coatch, but themselves. *The Devil hath wrought far greater Farelies in his time than this.*

She knew much of the inchanted Staff, *for by it he was enabled to pray, to commit* filthiness, *not to be* named, *yea even to reconcile* Neighbours, *Man and Wife, when at varience. She oft hid it from him, and because without it, he could do nothing, he would threaten and vow to discover her incest, fearing which, she would deliver it again.*

Being asked the cause of her much spinning, which she was famous for? She denyed any assistance from the Devil, but found she had an extraordinary faculty therein, far above ordinary Spinsters: Yet owned, that when she came home, after her being abroad, she found, there was more yarn on her wheel than she left. And that her Weaver could not make cloath thereof, the yearn breaking or falling from the Loom.

Once there came a stranger to her, while she was at her Wheel, and proposed a way to her to make her rich, for they both lived almost upon Alms. The way was this, Stand up and say, all Crosses and Cares go out of this house. *She answered,* GOD forbid I say that, but let them be welcome when GOD sends them. *After two or three visits more, she asked this stranger,* where she dwelt? *She replyed,* in the Potter-raw, *a street in the Suburbs of that* City, *but finding neither such a house, nor such a woman, I judged, said she, it was the Devil, one of my brothers acquaintance; for I know, he had familiarity with the Devil . . .*

She was asked anent her Parents? She was perswaded her mother was a Witch; for the secretest thing that either I my self, or any of the family could do, when once a mark appeared on her brow, she could tell it them, though done at a distance. Being demanded what sort of mark it was? She answered, I have some such like mark my self, when I please, on my forehead. *Whereupon she offered to* uncover her head for visible satisfaction. The Minister refusing to behold it, and forbidding any discovery, was earnestly requiested by some Spectators to allow the freedom. He yeelding, she put back her head-dress, and seeming to frown, there was seen an exact Horse-shoe shaped for nails in her wrinckles. Terrible though I assure you to the stoutest beholder.

In the morning before her execution, she told the Minister, she resolved to die with all the shame she could, to expiate (under Mercy) her shameful-life. This he understood to be an ingenuous confession of her sins, in opposition to her brothers despair, and desperate silence, to which he did encourage her. At her parting with him, she gave him hearty thanks for his pains; and shaking his hands, (offering to kiss them) she repeated the same words, which he bade her perform. Ascending up the ladder, she spake somewhat confusedly of her sins, of her brother, and his inchanting-staff; and with a ghaistly countenance, beholding a multitude of Spectators, all wondering, and some weeping, he spake aloud. There are many here this day, wondering and greeting for me, but alace, few mourns for a broken Covenant. At which words, many seemed angry. Some called to her to mind higher Concerns. And I have heard it said, that the Preacher declared, he had much ado to keep a composed countenance. The Executioner falling about his duty, she prepares to die stark naked: then and not before, were her words relating to shame understood. The Hangman strugled with her, to keep on her cloaths, and she strugled with him to have them off. At last he was forced to throw her over open-fac'd, which afterwards he covered with a cloath.

George Sinclair, *Satans Invisible World Discovered*, 1685

Three Hundred Swedish Children

Being asked how they could go with their Bodies *through* Chimneys, *and* broken pans *of* Glass, *they said, that the* Devil *did first remove all that might hinder them in their flight, and so they had* Room *enough to go.*

Others were asked, how they were able to carry so many Children with them, They answered, that when the Children *were asleep they came into the Chamber, and laid hold of the Children, which straightway did awake, and asked them, whether they would go to a* Feast *with them? To which some answered, yes. Others no, Yet they were all forced to go. They only give the* Children *a Shirt, a Coat, and a* Doublet, *which was either* Red *or* Blew, *and so they did set them upon a* Beast *of the* Devils *providing, and then they rid away.*

The Children confessed the same thing: and some added, that because, they had very fine Cloaths *put upon them, they were very willing to go.*

Some of the Children concealed it from their Parents, *but others discovered it to them presently.*

The Witches *declared moreover, that till of late, they had never power to carry away Children, but only this year and the last, and that the* Devil *did at this time force them to it: that heretofore it was sufficient to carry but one of their Children, or a Strangers Child with them, which happened seldom, but now he did plague them, and whip them, if they did not* procure *him many* Children, insomuch that they had no Peace, nor Quiet for him: And whereas that *formerly one journey a week would serve turn, from their own Town to the place aforesaid, now they were forced to run to other towns and places for* Children, *and that they brought with them, some* fifteen *some* sixteen Children *every night.*

For their journey, they said they made use of all sorts of Instruments, *of* Beasts, *of* Men, *of* Spits *and* Posts, *according as they had opportunity: if they do ride upon* Goats, *and have many* Children *with them, that all may have room, they stick a* Spit *into the* Back-side *of the* Goat, *and then are anointed with the aforesaid* Ointment. *What the manner of their journey is,* GOD *alone knows. This much was made out, that if the* Children *did at any time name the names of those, either* Men *or* Women *that had been with them, that had carried them away, they were again carried by force either to* Blockula, *or to the* Cross-way, *and thereby beaten, in so much that some of them died of it. And this some of the* Witches *confessed, and added, That now they were exceedingly troubled and tortured in their minds for it.*

The Children *thus used lookt mighty* Bleak Wan *and* Beaten. *The* Marks *of the* Whips *the* Judges *could not perceive in them, except in one* Boy, *who had some* wounds *and* holes *in his* Back, *that were given him with* Thorns. *But the* Witches *said, they would quickly vanish.*

After this usage, the Children *are exceeding weak. And if any be carried over-Night, they cannot recover themselves the next* Day: *and they often fall into* Fits, *the coming of which they knew by an extraordinary paleness, that seizes on the Children. And when a* Fit *comes upon them, they lean on their Mothers Arms, who sits up with them, sometimes all night. And when they observe the paleness coming, shake the* Children, *but to no purpose.*

They observe further, that their Childrens Breasts *grow cold at such times; and they take sometimes a burning candle, and stick it in their hair, which yet is not burned by it. They* Swoun *upon this paleness, which* Swoun *lasteth sometimes half an* hour, *sometimes an hour, sometimes two hours, and when the* Children *come to themselves again, they mourn and lament and groan most miserablie, and beg exceedinglie to be eased. This the* old men *declared upon Oath before the* Judges, *and called all the inhabitants in the Town to witness, as Persons that had most of them experience of the strange* Symptome *of their* Children.

George Sinclair, *Satans Invisible World Discovered,* 1685

The Tradesman's Dream

I knew another, who being a tradesman, and in great distress for money in his business, dreamed that he was walking alone in a great wood, and that he met a little child with a bag of gold in its hand, and a fine necklace of diamonds on its neck; upon the sight, his wants presently dictated to him to rob the child; the little innocent creature, (just so he dreamed) not being able to resist, or to tell who it was; accordingly he consented to take the money from the child, and then to take the diamond necklace from it too, and did so.

But the Devil, (a full testimony, as I told him, that it was the Devil) not contented with that, hinted to him, that perhaps the child might some time or other know him, and single him out, by crying or pointing, or some such thing, especially if he was suspected and shewed to it, and therefore it would be better for him to kill the child, prompting him to kill it for his own safety, and that he need do no more but twist the neck of it a little, or crush it with his knee; he told me he stood debating with himself, whether he should do so or not; but that in that instant his heart struck him with the word murder, and he entertained a horror of it, refused to do it, and immediately waked.

He told me, that when he waked, he found himself in so violent a sweat as he never had known the like; that his pulse beat with that heat and rage, that it was like a palpitation of the heart to him, and that the agitation of his spirits was such, that he was not fully composed in some hours: Though the satisfaction and joy that attended him when he found it was but a dream, assisted much to return his spirits to their due temperament.

Daniel Defoe, *The History of the Devil*, 1726

'Me and the Devil Blues'

Early in the morning
When you knocked upon my door
Early in the morning
When you knocked upon my door
And I said, Hello Satan,
I believe it's time to go

Me and the Devil
Was walking side by side
Me and the Devil
Was walking side by side
I'm going to beat my woman
Until I get satisfied

She said she don't see why
That I always be dog her 'round
She said she don't see why
That I be dog her 'round
It must be that old evil spirit
So deep down in the ground

You may bury my body
Down by the highway side
You may bury my body
Down by the highway side
So my old evil spirit
Can get a greyhound bus and ride

Robert Johnson, reputed to have sold his soul to the devil at a
Mississippi crossroads, in exchange for the blues, 1936–7

'Beasts'

The corner video club has got in *Babes of Satan*
and Sandra's made black candles. Frank from Tidy Tots
has promised to run up some cloaks in shiny satin
since Babs' and mine got spoiled last time – blood got on my tits
with spunk and other stuff that won't wash off. It was great
when Mr Lumley from the chemists used the cross
on Sandra and she squealed so much you really had to grit
your teeth until it sort of poured out – like the curse
only, you know, you could see a bit more what it was.
Sandra fainted, so she missed the part with the oven.
Keith and Babs and me did it all different ways
while Mr Lumley said the words. I've got to help the coven
by getting knocked up too, Keith says. It's more fun than 'Sting's'
on a Friday night. Keith's seen a picture of Frank's niece –
eight or nine, looks great in hot pants and a halter

top. We're round at Franks this time. She's called Denise.
I seed they give me sumthing and I was sreched on a allter.
I sore reel men in hoods. There big red things.

'A Divine Image'

Cruelty has a Human Heart,
And Jealousy a Human Face;
Terror the Human Form Divine,
And Secrecy the Human Dress.

The Human Dress is forged Iron,
The Human Form a fiery Forge,
The Human Face a Furnace seal'd,
The Human Heart its hungry Gorge.

William Blake, *Songs of Innocence and Experience*, 1789–94

Acknowledgments

The editor and publishers gratefully acknowledge permission to reprint copyright material as follows:

David Campbell Publishers Ltd for 'Genesis', from *Anglo-Saxon Poetry*, translated by S. A. J. Bradley, copyright © 1926; HarperCollins Publishers for excerpts from Anselm de Canterbury, *Truth, Freedom and Evil*, translated by Jasper Hopkins and Herbert Richardson, copyright © 1966, 1967; The Estate of Max Beerbohm for an excerpt from Max Beerbohm, 'Enoch Soames', from *The Works of Max Beerbohm*, copyright © 1922–28; Routledge Ltd for extracts from K. M. Briggs, *Dictionary of British Folk Tales*, copyright © 1971; HarperCollins Publishers for extracts from M. Bulgakov, *The Master and Margarita*, translated by Michael Glenny, copyright © 1967; William Heinemann for extracts from Fyodor Dostoevsky, *The Brothers Karamazov*, translated by Constance Garnett, copyright © 1912; The Council of the Early English Text Society for extracts from *Ludus Coventriae*, ed. K. S. Block, *The Chester Mystery Cycle* ed. Lumiansky and Mills, 1974, and *The Macro Plays*, ed. M. Eccles 1969; Oxford University Press, Watson Little Ltd and the author for two poems from D. J. Enright, *A Faust Book*, copyright © 1979; The Hogarth Press and the Institute of Psycho-analysis, and Basic Books Inc for an excerpt from Sigmund Freud, 'A Seventeenth Century Demonological Neurosis' ('The Motive for the Pact with the Devil' and 'The Devil as a Father Substitute') in *The Standard Edition of the Complete Psychological Works of Sigmund Freud*, vol xix, translated by James Strachey, copyright © 1961; Harvard University Press for extracts from *The Diary of Benjamin Robert Haydon*, edited by Willard Bissell Pope, copyright © 1960, 1963 by the President and Fellows of Harvard College, reprinted by permission of the publishers; *New Statesman and Society* for the poem 'Beasts' by Alan Jenkins, copyright © 1991; The Hogarth Press and the Institute of Psychoanalysis for an excerpt from *On The Nightmare*, by Ernest Jones, copyright © 1931; Princeton University Press for an extract from Søren Kierkegaard, *The Sickness Unto Death*, translated by Walter Lowrie, copyright © 1941, 1969; HarperCollins Publishers for extracts from C. S. Lewis, *The Screwtape Letters*, copyright © C. S. Lewis PTE Ltd 1942, and *Perelandra*, copyright © C. S. Lewis PTE Ltd, 1943; Oxford University Press for an extract from C. S. Lewis *A Preface to Paradise Lost*, copyright © C. S. Lewis PTE

1942; Martin Secker and Warburg Ltd for extracts from Thomas Mann, *Dr Faustus*, translated by H. T. Lowe-Porter; Elaine Greene Ltd for an extract from Arthur Calder Marshall, *The Fair to Middling*, copyright © Estate of Arthur Calder Marshall, 1959; The Athlone Press for an extract from 'Epistola Luciferi' in *Medieval Literature and Civilisation*, ed. D. A. Pearsall and R. A. Waldron, copyright © 1969; Yale University Press for an excerpt from *The Complete Works of Sir Thomas More*, ed. Louis Mavitz and Frank Manley, copyright © 1976; Cambridge University Press for an extract from *Origen Contra Celsum*, translated by Henry Chadwick, copyright © 1953; The Society of Authors on behalf of the Bernard Shaw Estate for extracts from *Man and Superman*, copyright © 1901 and *The Devil's Disciple*, copyright © 1903; David Higham Associates for an extract from Charles Williams, *War in Heaven*, copyright © 1930.

Index